Understanding ISIS and the New Global War on Terror

A Primer

by Phyllis Bennis

OLIVE
BRANCH
PRESS

An imprint of Interlink Publishing Group, Inc.
www.interlinkbooks.com

First published in 2015 by

OLIVE BRANCH PRESS
An imprint of Interlink Pulishing Group, Inc.
46 Crosby Street, Northampton, MA 01060
www.interlinkbooks.com

Library of Congress Cataloging-in-Publication Data available
ISBN 978-1-56656-094-8

Cover image, Helicopters in attack © Serban Enache | Dreamstime

Printed and bound in the United States of America

To request our free 48-page, full-color catalog, write to us at
Interlink Publishing, 46 Crosby Street, Northampton, Massachusetts 01060,
call us toll-free at 1-800-238-LINK, or visit our website at www.interlinkbooks.com

Contents

Introduction

The rise of the Islamic State in Iraq and Syria, or ISIS, and the US war against ISIS, have exploded into a regional and global conflagration. Once again, civilians are paying the price for both extremist attacks and US wars.

When ISIS swept across northern Syria and northwestern Iraq in June 2014, occupying cities and towns and imposing its draconian version of Islam on terrified populations, to many around the world it looked like something that had popped up out of nowhere. This was not the case, but the complicated interweaving of players, places, and alliances make understanding ISIS seem almost impossible. But ISIS has a traceable past, a history and a political trajectory grounded in movements, organizations, governments, and political moments that form a long story in the Middle East: from Saudi Arabia to al-Qaeda, from the US invasion and occupation of Iraq to the Arab Spring, to regime change in Libya and the chaos of Syria's civil war.

The US war against ISIS, President Obama's iteration of George Bush's much-heralded and long-failed "global war on terror," presents us with an equally complex set of paradoxes and contradictions: The US is fighting against ISIS alongside Iran and the Iranian-backed Baghdad government in Iraq, and fighting in Syria against ISIS alongside (sort of) the Iranian-backed and US-opposed government in Damascus. And all the while, the US and its Arab Gulf allies are arming and paying a host of largely unaccountable, predominantly Sunni militias that are fighting against the Syrian government and fighting—sort of—against ISIS. Meanwhile, in Iraq, the Iranian government is arming and training a host of largely unaccountable, predominantly Shi'a militias that are fighting against ISIS and—sort of—alongside the US-backed Iraqi government.

It's a mess.

That's why this book came to be written. It's designed to help readers sort out the history and the players, identify who's doing what to whom, who's on what side, and most of all, figure out what we can do to help stop the killing. That's why the last questions in the book are perhaps the most important—what would an alternative US policy toward ISIS, toward the region, toward war and peace, actually look like? What can we all do to bring those alternative approaches into the light of day?

For more than a century, US policy in the Middle East has been rooted largely in maintaining access to and control of oil. For roughly three-quarters of a century, US policy has been grounded in oil plus the Cold War-driven strategic interest in stability and US bases to challenge competitors and project power. And for almost a half-century, US policy has been built on a triple play of oil plus stability plus Israel.

While each component of this triplet played the dominant role at different times, overall US interests in the region remained constant. But some changes are under way. Oil is still important to the global economy, but as the threat posed by oil's role in global warming becomes better understood and sustainable alternatives continue to emerge, it is less of a factor than it once was. And where it comes from is changing too. The United States is producing and exporting more oil than ever, and while the Middle East is still a huge exporter of oil, Africa surpassed the Middle East as a source of US oil imports in 2010.

The US continues to pay more than $3.1 billion every year of taxpayer money to the Israeli military, and continues to provide absolute protection to Israel in the United Nations and elsewhere, assuring that no Israeli officials are held accountable for potential war crimes or human rights violations. But with rising tensions between Washington and Tel Aviv over settlement expansion and especially over Israel's efforts to undermine Washington's negotiations with Iran, President Obama in 2015 for the first time hinted at a shift, indicating that the US might reconsider its grant of absolute impunity to Israel. With public opinion shifting dramatically away from the assumption that Israel can do no wrong, and influential, increasingly mainstream campaigns pushing policymakers in that direction, a real shift in US policy may be on its way. We're not there yet, but change is coming.

That leaves the strategic stability, military bases, and ability to "project power"—read: send troops and bombers—in and from the Middle East as the most important "national interest" driving US policy. This means that the war on terror, the seemingly permanent US response to instability in the region, is strategically more important—and far more dangerous—than ever.

That war is rooted in the aftermath of the September 11, 2001 attacks—the US invasion of Afghanistan, and especially the 2003 invasion and occupation of Iraq. Twelve years after the invasion of Iraq, several groups of physicians attempted to accomplish what the "we don't do body counts" Pentagon had long refused to do: calculate the human costs of the US war on terror. In "Body Count: Casualty Figures After Ten Years of the War on Terror," the Nobel Peace Prize-winning International Physicians for the Prevention of Nuclear War, Physicians for Social Responsibility, and Physicians for Global Survival together reached the staggering conclusion that the war was responsible for the loss of at least 1.3 million lives in Iraq, Afghanistan, and Pakistan from the September 11, 2001 attacks until 2013.

And that total didn't take into account the more than 500,000 Iraqi children killed by US-imposed economic sanctions in the 1990s in the run-up to the war. It didn't take into account the expansion of the wars to Libya and Syria, or include President Obama's expanding drone war in Somalia and Yemen. It didn't take into account the rapidly escalating casualty figures in 2014 and 2015 throughout the theaters of the war on terror. But the breathtaking realty of 1.5 *million* dead is still a vital reality check on those who would assert that somehow the war on terror is "worth the price," as former Secretary of State Madeleine Albright famously described the death of half a million Iraqi children under sanctions.

This book aims to help probe behind the propaganda, help sort out the facts from the mythology, help figure out what we need to know to build a path away from war as the default option. There may be some duplication between some of the questions, and some sections provide different levels of detail than others. The questions are organized by subject, designed for readers to pick and choose, find a subject of interest and delve into the questions most relevant to that subject, then come back later to other issues.

Inevitably, writing a book like this presents enormous challenges, not least the rapid pace of events. Just when you think you've got most of the region covered, Yemen explodes. Just when you think you've clarified the possibilities and dangers for the Iran nuclear talks, the interim agreement is announced and anti-diplomacy hard-liners in Tehran and especially in Washington start their campaigns to undermine it. This is not a full, definitive account of ISIS, its theology, or its strategy. This is an overview, designed to provide a basic understanding so we can move toward identifying and implementing new alternative strategies, instead of war.

Ultimately, that is the reason for this book: to help activists, policymakers, journalists, students—and all the people in their orbit—with the hard task of changing the discourse and turning United States policy around. The basic assumption underlying this book is that you can't bomb extremism—you can only bomb people. And even if some of the people you bomb are extremists, those bombing campaigns cause more extremism, not less. We need to move away from war as an answer to extremism, and instead build a new approach grounded in diplomacy and negotiation, arms embargos and international law, the United Nations, humanitarian assistance, and human rights.

Phyllis Bennis
Washington D.C.
May 2015

—PART I—

THE GLOBAL WAR ON TERROR

What is the "global war on terror"?

One day after the September 11 attacks on New York's World Trade Center and the Pentagon in 2001, then-President George W. Bush announced that the US response to this crime would be to lead a global war on terror.

The first target was Afghanistan, despite the fact that none of the 19 hijackers responsible for the attack were Afghans (they were Saudis and Egyptians), none of them lived in Afghanistan (they lived in Hamburg), none went to flight school in Afghanistan (they went to flight school in Florida), none trained in Afghanistan (they trained in Minnesota). But the leaders of al-Qaeda, the organization the hijackers were linked to, had found refuge in Afghanistan, which was then under the rule of the extreme Islamist Taliban government. Using the language of "bringing those responsible to justice," the Bush administration launched a war of aggression that soon stretched far beyond Afghanistan, in countries with no connection to al-Qaeda, targeting nonexistent organizations and individuals who were still children when the Twin Towers were attacked.

That war continues today—some call it Permanent War.

Since 9/11, the US has gone to war in Afghanistan and Iraq, in the Philippines and Libya, Somalia, Yemen, Djibouti, Saudi Arabia, Syria, and beyond. For much of the world the war was defined by CIA-run "rendition," in which people were snatched off the streets, smuggled to so-called black sites around the world, or to the Pentagon-run prison at Guantánamo Bay, and subjected to years of detention without trial, and interrogation using a limitless range of torture techniques. International law and US law were routinely violated. The US partnered with Israel's Mossad intelligence service to assassinate Hezbollah leader Imad Mughniyah in Damascus in 2008, using a car bomb as he took an evening walk down a quiet street. Car bombing, according to Mary Ellen O'Connell, a leading professor of international law at the University of Notre Dame, is "a killing method used by terrorists and gangsters. It violates one of the oldest battlefield rules." But neither the international law prohibition against "murder by treachery of individuals belonging to the hostile nation or army" nor the longstanding US law prohibit-ing assassination was of any concern to US officials, who regularly authorize the use of such a method. Indeed, one US official justified the killing by referencing Hezbollah operations in US-occupied Iraq: "Remember, they were carrying out suicide bombings and IED at-tacks," the official told the *Washington Post*. Apparently, so long as the terrorists were doing it, it was fine for the US to do it too.

Among Americans, initial support for the Afghanistan "war on terror" was based on cries for vengeance. Bush told a stunned and frightened nation that the choice the US faced was to either go to war or let them get away with it. And since letting the perpetra-tors "get away with it" was an unacceptable option, the vast majority of Americans chose war. On October 7, weeks after the attacks, the US launched a massive air and ground war against Afghanistan, overthrowing the Taliban government and bombing cities, villages, and vast stretches of the impoverished country. Tens of thousands of Afghans were killed. At the height of troop deployments, 100,000 US forces and tens of thousands more NATO troops occupied Afghanistan. More than fourteen years later, thousands of US troops were still in Afghanistan, in what had long ago become the longest war the United States ever fought.

What is terrorism?

Terrorism has no single definition. The word is politically charged and its meaning is rarely agreed upon. Well over 100 definitions of the word exist in different countries, among different organizations, and under varying sets of laws.

US law requires the State Department to report to Congress every year on terrorist attacks around the world. It defines terrorism as "premeditated, politically motivated violence perpetrated against noncombatant targets by sub-national groups or clandestine agents." That definition might sound objective and neutral, but it leaves lots of questions unanswered. Who are "noncombatant" targets? Not the same as civilians, apparently, since the attacks on the armed warship

USS Cole, the US Marine Corps barracks in Beirut, the Pentagon, and other military installations are routinely referred to as "terrorist" attacks. Does it mean soldiers are noncombatants if they're sleeping, or just not on patrol at that moment? Then there's the confusion over the "sub-national groups or clandestine agents" part. Does that mean "state terrorism" is not a recognized reality, or might "clandestine agents" include agents of a state, to explain the common US references to "Iranian terrorist attack"? If noncombatant—real noncombatants, like civilians—are deliberately attacked by national, not sub-national groups, like the Israeli Air Force in Gaza for instance, in a "premeditated, politically motivated" campaign, is that exempt from the term "terrorism"?

What are the implications of the world's inability to agree on a definition of terrorism?

What happens in the real world of US and western leaders, US policy, US media, and too many people is that "terrorism" is used almost exclusively to describe political violence committed by extremist Muslims. It's a term used to create fear and to justify repressive actions, whether in the United States or in the context of the "global war on terror."

Often in the United States an act of "premeditated, politically motivated violence" is assumed to be an act of terror, rather than the result of mental illness or some other possible cause, when the perpetrator is Arab or Muslim. For example, following the 2009 deadly attack on soldiers at Fort Hood, Texas by US Maj. Nidal Malik Hasan, the question of Hasan's mental state was never addressed. In incidents when the perpetrator is white, the term is carefully avoided, and mental illness is often asserted as the most likely cause, as was the case in the 2011 attack on Rep. Gabrielle Giffords in Tucson, Arizona. Similarly, "an argument over a parking space" was claimed as the reason a white neighbor killed three young Muslim Americans in North Carolina in 2015, despite the killer having expressed hatred of Islam and other religions and having threatened the victims earlier by displaying his guns.

Similarly, whether an act perpetrated by Muslims abroad is deemed terrorism by the United States also depends on *which* Muslims are held responsible. In official US circles, for example, the beheadings routinely carried out by the Saudi government as part of a judicial system designed to terrify political opponents are never referred to as terrorist acts, but ISIS beheadings are routinely identified as proving the terrorist nature of the organization.

In early 2015, Saudi Arabia passed a new law that defined any form of political opposition as terrorism. Saudi King Abdullah, who died in February 2015, had already declared that political dissidents were terrorists no different from violent organizations, and that atheism equaled terrorism. Just days after Abdullah's death, the Saudi government announced a new anti-terrorism law, of which Article One defined terrorism as "calling for atheist thought in any form, or calling into question the fundamentals of the Islamic religion on which this country is based."

The foregoing examples demonstrate how the use of the terms "terrorism" and "terrorist" depends on who is using the term, supporting the common notion that "one person's terrorist is another person's freedom fighter." Nelson Mandela was placed on the US "anti-terrorist" list in 1988 by then-President Ronald Reagan, who excoriated the revered South African leader as a communist during the height of the Cold War. Long after his 1990 release from prison, and even when he was elected president of South Africa in 1994, President Mandela remained on that list. It took until 2008 for his name to finally be removed.

In US federal criminal law, "international terrorism" is defined as violence or acts dangerous to human life that appear to be intended "to intimidate or coerce a civilian population; to influence the policy of a government by intimidation or coercion; or to affect the conduct of a government by mass destruction, assassination, or kidnapping." This definition doesn't limit terrorism to attacks by non-state actors.

Ambassador Edward Peck, a retired US diplomat with experience throughout the Arab world, described on *Democracy Now!* his work as deputy director of the White House Task Force on Terrorism under then-President Ronald Reagan. The task force, he said, was asked

> to come up with a definition of terrorism that could be used throughout the government. We produced about six, and each and every case, they were rejected, because careful reading would indicate that our own country had been involved in some of those activities. ...After the task force concluded its work, Congress [passed] US Code Title 18, Section 2331...the US definition of terrorism. ...[O]ne of the terms, "international terrorism," means activities that, I quote, "appear to be intended to affect the conduct of a government by mass destruction, assassination or kidnapping." ...Yes, well, certainly, you can think of a number of countries that have been involved in such activities. Ours is one of them. ...And so, the terrorist, of course, is in the eye of the beholder.

How did the fight against al-Qaeda in Afghanistan shift to Iraq?

Afghanistan was never the main target. Vice President Dick Cheney, Defense Secretary Donald Rumsfeld, and others leading the Bush administration's war drive, particularly the heavily represented neoconservative ideologues staffing the vice president's office and the Pentagon, had Iraq in their sights from the moment the planes hit the Twin Towers. Pretexts for going to war against Iraq abounded: phony assertions regarding self-defense, made-up allegations that Iraqi leader Saddam Hussein had ties to al-Qaeda, forged documents about Iraq purchasing yellow-cake uranium from Niger, fictitious reports of aluminum tubes from China that could "only" be used to build nuclear weapons, sham warnings of Iraq's supposed stockpiling of weapons of mass destruction.

All were false, and an unprecedented global anti-war movement arose, climaxing on February 15, 2003, when record-breaking crowds of between 12 and 14 million people filled streets across the globe, united around the slogan "The World Says No to War." Protests were launched in more than 665 cities, with the largest reserved for Italy, Spain, and Britain, whose leaders had agreed to join Bush's imminent war despite overwhelming popular opposition. The breadth and depth of the protests moved the *New York Times* to acknowledge on its front page that "there may still be two superpowers on the planet: the United States and world public opinion." Unwilling to give in to US pressure, a wide range of governments backed the street protests. So did the United Nations Security Council, which stood firm for eight months against US and British pressure to endorse the coming war.

But plans to attack Iraq were already under way, and not even a worldwide outcry could prevent it. The Pentagon, backed by British forces, launched the invasion and occupation of Iraq on March 19, 2003. Within a month, US troops overthrew the Iraqi regime.

What were the consequences of the overthrow of Saddam Hussein?

The US forces disbanded Iraq's military and dismantled Iraq's government, seizing power in occupied Iraq in the name of the Coalition Provisional Authority. The CPA was made up of thousands of US bureaucrats, most of them chosen more for loyalty to the Bush administration than for any experience in the vast and disparate areas of governance they controlled. The CPA was itself backed by billions of dollars and hundreds of thousands of US occupation troops, as well as thousands of "coalition" troops and Pentagon-paid military mercenaries. Hundreds of thousands of Iraqi troops, including most of the generals, were unceremoniously dismissed. Hundreds of thousands of Iraq's government officials and civil servants, most of whom had been required to sign on to the ruling Baath Party to get their job, were sent packing in the name of "de-Baathification."

Anger and opposition to the occupation rose immediately, with supporters of the old regime, nationalists of various stripes, and many ordinary Iraqis mobilizing political as well as military resistance.

A year later the CPA was replaced by an interim Iraqi government, which provided Iraqi faces in government posts but was still appointed by and dependent on the US occupation. Washington created new political parties, all based on sectarian identities. Ostensibly they were designed to reflect the relative size and power of Iraq's various religious communities. Under Saddam Hussein's Baath Party, many Sunni Iraqis had found access to elite positions in the military, business, and elsewhere, while majority Shi'a in many cases were discriminated against, or at least were denied privileged financial and social status. With the overthrow of the government, that position was reversed, and the majority Shi'a emerged as the most powerful political force. They were strengthened by the many Iraqi exiles who had spent years as refugees in Shi'a Iran or in the West, and were now returning with strong US backing. But as Iraqi national identity was forcibly abandoned in favor of the smaller and narrower categories of Sunni, Shi'a, Christian, Kurd, Turkoman, Yazidi, etc., sectarian conflict began to rise.

The US occupation of Iraq remained the centerpiece of Bush's "global war on terror." As a result, an entire population, already suffering from decades of war and 12 years of crippling economic sanctions that had shredded much of the country's social fabric, now faced the devastation of full-scale war. Under the new Shi'a-dominated Iraqi government that the US backed, parties based on religion recruited their own militia forces, and the war took on an increasingly sectarian cast. The US occupation forces created and perpetuated the new system, although Shi'a-led militias were among a range of forces fighting against the US.

What was the response in Iraq to the US occupation?

As is the case in any foreign military occupation, resistance was both broad and deep, including militias and resistance forces from across Iraq's crazy-quilt population. There were armed supporters of Sunni tribal leaders, Shi'a militias with close ties to Iran, former Baathist-led secular forces, and widely diverse and popular resistance organizations. As the occupation extended over years, an increasingly extremist sectarian resistance grew, and a civil war erupted alongside the anti-US resistance, pitting Sunni against Shi'a.

In 2004, Abu Mussab al-Zarqawi, a Sunni militant, created what was first known as al-Qaeda in Iraq; soon after, Zarqawi pledged fealty to Osama bin Laden and the main al-Qaeda organization. Al-Zarqawi was killed two years later, and in October 2006 a new leader, Abu Bakr al-Baghdadi, who had been released from the US-run Bucca prison in Iraq at the end of 2004, announced the organization had been renamed the Islamic State of Iraq, or ISI. The organization would resurface later as ISIS, or the Islamic State.

What was the Sunni Awakening?

In 2006–2007, as the Iraqi opposition became more sectarian, the US made a strategic calculation that it was better off co-opting the Sunni resistance sector instead of continuing the failed attempt to defeat them militarily. That plan became the "Sunni Awakening" movement, in which the US paid Sunni tribal leaders massive sums to fight alongside, instead of against, US occupation forces and the US-backed Iraqi government army.

The Sunni Awakening was the key component of what was known as Bush's "surge," which included an increase of 30,000 US troops. With many of the Sunni-based opposition groups bought off by US funds, the occupation troops shifted their focus to the newly ascendant Shi'a resistance forces, especially those led by the Shi'a cleric Moqtada al-Sadr, along with the most extreme of the Sunni organizations, including ISI. The "surge" was deemed a success when sectarian violence waned somewhat in 2007–08. But this result was not only, or even primarily, due to the presence of the additional US troops. It stemmed from other elements, including the buy-off of most Sunni opposition forces, a unilateral ceasefire declared by al-Sadr's forces, and perhaps most important, the horrifying reality that the years of sectarian warfare had already largely succeeded. Mixed towns were now "ethnically pure"; historically diverse cities, including Baghdad itself, were now divided into ethnically defined neighborhoods separated by cement walls. Sectarian fighting largely ended because it had accomplished its goals.

Fighting resumed around 2009–10, largely in response to the sectarian practices of the US-backed prime minister, Nuri al-Maliki. The Shi'a-dominated government refused to continue paying off the Sunni tribal leaders and their militias, and escalated sectarian attacks against Sunni communities. A kind of Sunni uprising against the Iraqi government began in response, even as US troops were being pulled out.

—PART II—

ISIS

What are the origins of ISIS?

Political Islam in its modern form, as Mahmoud Mamdani states in *Good Muslims, Bad Muslims*, is "more a domestic product than a foreign import." It was not, he reminds us, "bred in isolation...Political Islam was born in the colonial period. But it did not give rise to a terrorist movement until the Cold War." The Muslim Brotherhood in Egypt was born almost a century ago. Its followers in neighboring countries contested for power (rarely winning any) with governments across the region. The mobilization against the US-backed shah in Iran in the 1970s resulted in the establishment of the Islamic Republic of Iran under the leadership of Ayatollah Ruhollah Khomeini in perhaps the most powerful, self-defined Islamic government of the twentieth century. But today's movement known as political Islam, with its military mobilizations holding the pride of place ahead of its political formations, emerged in its first coherent identity with the US-armed, US-paid, Pakistani-trained mujahideen warriors who fought the Soviet troops in Afghanistan starting in 1979. Continuing in the post-Vietnam Cold War 1980s, the Afghanistan War ended with the defeat and ultimate collapse of the Soviet Union.

The specific origins of ISIS, also known as ISIL or the Islamic State, lie in the 2003 US invasion and occupation of Iraq. The country was already in terrible shape, following decades of war (the Iran–Iraq War from 1980–89, then the first US Gulf War in 1991) and a dozen years of crippling economic sanctions imposed in 1990. Even after the first wars, and despite brutal repression of any potential opposition and the long-standing political and economic privileging of the large (20 percent or so) Sunni minority, the majority of Iraqis lived middle-class lives, including government-provided free health care and education, with some of the best medical and scientific institutions in the Arab world. The sanctions, imposed in the name of the United Nations but created and enforced by the United States, had shredded much of the social fabric of the once-prosperous, secular, cosmopolitan country. The Pentagon's "shock and awe" bombing campaign that opened the US invasion destroyed much of Iraq's physical infrastructure, as well as the lives of over 7,000 Iraqi civilians.

How did the US invasion of Iraq affect the growth of ISIS?

Among the first acts of the US occupation were the dissolution of the Iraqi military, the dismantling of the civil service, and the overthrow of Saddam Hussein's ruling Baath Party. All three institutions represented core concentrations of secular nationalist interests in Iraq, and their collapse was part of the reason for the turn toward religious and sectarian identity that began to replace national identity for many Iraqis. At the same time, in all three institutions, particularly at the highest echelons, Sunni Iraqis were more likely to suffer from the loss of income and prestige—since Sunnis held a disproportionate share of top jobs and top positions in the military and the Baath Party. So right from the beginning, a sectarian strand emerged at the very center of the rising opposition to the US occupation.

Despite the Bush administration dismissals of the opposition as nothing but Baathist leftovers and foreign fighters, the Iraqi resistance was far broader. Within months after the March 2003 invasion, militias and informal groups of fighters were challenging the US-UK occupation across the country. One of the earliest was al-Qaeda in Iraq or AQI, sometimes known as al-Qaeda in Mesopotamia, a Sunni militia created in 2004 by Abu Mussab al-Zarqawi. He was Jordanian, although it appears most of the early members of AQI were Iraqis. Al-Zarqawi announced publicly that AQI had pledged loyalty to the leadership of al-Qaeda and specifically to Osama bin Laden. The militia's tactics included bombings and improvised explosive devices (IEDs), as well as reported kidnappings and beheadings. While AQI began with a focus on the US and other coalition forces, aiming to rid Iraq of foreign occupiers, it soon expanded to a more explicitly sectarian agenda, in which the Shi'a-dominated Iraqi government, military, and police forces as well as Shi'a civilians were also targeted.

Over the next several years, the forces fighting against the US occupation in Iraq became more sectarian, moving toward what would become a bloody civil war fought alongside the resistance to occupation. Beginning in 2006, the US shifted its Iraq strategy, deciding to move away from direct fighting against Sunni anti-occupation fighters and instead to try to co-opt them. The essence of the Sunni Awakening plan was that the US would bankroll Sunni tribal leaders, those who had earlier led the anti-US resistance, paying them off to fight *with* the occupation and US-backed government instead of against them. They would also fight against the Sunni outliers, those who rejected the Awakening movement, which included al-Qaeda in Iraq. And just about the time that the Sunni Awakening was taking hold, al-Qaeda in Iraq changed its name—this time to Islamic State of Iraq, or ISI.

In August 2014, when Iraq's Anbar province had been largely overrun by ISIS, its governor, Ahmed al-Dulaimi, described for the *New York Times* the trajectory of an ISIS leader whom al-Dulaimi had taught in military school. "'It was never clear that he would turn out like that,' Mr. Dulaimi said. 'He was from a simple family, with high morals, but all his brothers went in that direction,' becoming jihadists. After the United States invaded Iraq in 2003, Mr. Nijim joined al-Qaeda in Iraq and was detained by American forces in 2005, Mr. Dulaimi said. 'We continue to live with the consequences of the decision to disband Saddam's army...All of these guys got religious after 2003...Surely, ISIS benefits from their experience.'"

Who is Abu Bakr al-Baghdadi and what was his role in the rise of ISIS?

In June 2006 al-Zarqawi was killed by US bombs. According to some sources, four months later Abu Bakr al-Baghdadi was announced as the new leader of AQI, having been released from ten months or so in the US-run Bucca prison in Iraq. Other sources claim that al-Baghdadi spent as much as five years in the US prison, and that after the death of al-Zarqawi, AQI was taken over by a different person with a similar name—Abu Omar al-Baghdadi—who may have led the organization until 2010.

However long Abu Bakr al-Baghdadi spent at Bucca under the control of US troops, there is little doubt he would have seen, heard of, and perhaps experienced at least some of the brutality that characterized US treatment of prisoners in Iraq. Only a few months before al-Baghdadi was imprisoned at Bucca prison, the torture photos from Abu Ghraib prison had been made public. It is unclear whether any prisoners who experienced that brutality at Abu Ghraib or elsewhere were present at Bucca with al-Baghdadi, but it is certain that reports of the torture were extensive throughout the US prison system in Iraq.

The time in prison was also an opportunity for strategy planning and recruiting for AQI's expanding anti-occupation and anti-Shi'a resistance. Other former prisoners, in Bucca in 2004 and later, recall al-Baghdadi's arrival and the role he and others played in education, organizing and planning for future military actions. There is little doubt that al-Baghdadi's time in US custody was instrumental in his rise as leader of what would become one of the most powerful extremist militias in the Middle East.

Before and during al-Baghdadi's incarceration in the US military prison, the anti-occupation resistance was rapidly expanding. As *The Guardian* described it, "When Baghdadi, aged 33, arrived at Bucca, the Sunni-led anti-US insurgency was gathering steam across central and western Iraq. An invasion that had been sold as a war of liberation had become a grinding occupation. Iraq's Sunnis, disenfranchised by the overthrow of their patron, Saddam Hussein, were taking the fight to US forces—and starting to turn their guns towards the beneficiaries of Hussein's overthrow, the country's majority Shi'a population."

Did the US troop surge in 2008 diminish sectarian fighting?

Although the Bush administration claimed that its troop "surge" of 30,000 additional US military forces was the reason for the relative decline in sectarian fighting by 2008, the reality was far more complicated. It included the buying off of most of the leaders of Sunni tribal militias, the impact of a unilateral ceasefire declared in August 2007 by Shi'a militia leader Moqtada al-Sadr, and the horrific reality that the sectarian battles had largely achieved their goal. That is, by 2008 most mixed villages and towns had been ethnically cleansed to become virtually entirely Sunni or Shi'a. Baghdad, historically a cosmopolitan mashup of every religion and ethnicity, had become a city of districts defined by sect. Whether Sunni, Shi'a, Christian, or other, neighborhoods were largely separated by giant cement blast walls.

In 2008, the US turned its commitment to paying the Sunni Awakening militias over to the Shi'a-dominated Iraqi government. Almost immediately, payments stopped, and the US-backed government under Prime Minister Nuri al-Maliki escalated its sectarian practices. More and more Sunni generals and other military leaders, as well as ordinary Sunni Iraqis, turned against the government even as US troops were slowly being withdrawn, and by 2009 and into 2010, a serious Sunni uprising was under way.

The Islamic State in Iraq, or ISI, had never joined the Sunni Awakening. It maintained its focus on fighting against the US occupation and the Iraqi government, although its military activities had diminished somewhat as the overall sectarian warfare had waned. But as the sectarian fighting escalated again in 2010, ISI reemerged as a leading Sunni force, attacking the government, the official Iraqi military, and the expanding Shi'a militias allied to the government, as well as targeting Shi'a civilians. Abu Bakr al-Baghdadi was by that point (whether newly in power or not) the clear chief of ISI, and he began to strengthen the military capacity of the organization, including by several attacks on prisons aimed at freeing key military leaders of the group.

How did ISIS begin to expand beyond Iraq?

By 2011, ISI emerged for the first time across the border in Syria. The uprising there was just beginning to morph into a multifaceted civil war, and already the sectarian Sunni–Shi'a split was becoming a major component. That started with the proxy war between regional powers—Sunni Saudi Arabia and Shi'a Iran—but soon spilled over to include an internal divide between Syria's majority Sunni population and the minority but privileged Alawites, an offshoot of Shi'a Islam. ISI took up arms against the Alawite/Shi'a regime of Bashar al-Assad in Syria. ISI was fighting alongside the wide range of secular and Sunni militias—including the al-Qaeda-linked Jabhat an-Nusra, or Nusra Front—that were already confronting the regime. Soon, ISI turned to fight against those same anti-Assad forces, challenging those who rejected ISI's power grabs, its violence, or its extremist definitions of Islam.

ISI changed its name again, this time to ISIS—for the Islamic State in Iraq and Syria. By some accounts the acronym actually referred to the Islamic State in Iraq and al-Sham, Arabic for "greater Syria." (See p. 34 for further discussion of the name.)

Still led by al-Baghdadi and loyal to al-Qaeda, ISIS was rapidly gaining strength, not least from its recruiting of experienced fighters and acquisition of heavier arms in Iraq. It fought on both sides of the Iraq-Syria frontier, against governments and civilians in both countries, capturing crossing posts and essentially erasing the border altogether. In Anbar province and other Sunni-majority parts of northern and central Iraq, ISIS was able to establish a large military presence, supported by many Sunnis as a useful protector against the Shi'a-dominated government's sectarian practices.

A major difference between ISIS and other militias, and particularly between ISIS and al-Qaeda, was that ISIS moved to seize territory. In doing so, it was not only asserting the theoretical goal of creating a future "caliphate," it was actually doing so by occupying, holding, and governing an expanding land base across the Iraq-Syria border. In 2012 and into 2013, ISIS expanded its reach, establishing territorial control over large areas of northern Syria, including in and around the Syrian commercial center of Aleppo. ISIS based its core governing functions in the city of Raqqa, which by mid-2014 was named its official capital.

Soon, however, relations deteriorated between ISIS and al-Qaeda, and between ISIS leader al-Baghdadi and al-Qaeda leader Ayman al-Zawahiri. From 2013 on, al-Baghdadi tried to bring the "official" al-Qaeda Syrian franchise, the Nusra Front, under the control of ISIS. At one point ISIS announced that Nusra had "merged" with ISIS, although Nusra denied the claim. Al-Qaeda leader al-Zawahiri, watching the rising power of ISIS and its ambitious leader, restated his official endorsement for the Nusra Front as al-Qaeda's official Syrian counterpart. There were other disagreements as well, including the divergence between al-Qaeda's religiously defined goal of establishing a global caliphate at some indeterminate point in the future and ISIS's tactic of seizing land, imposing its version of Sharia law, and declaring it part of a present-day ISIS-run caliphate. The disagreements and power struggles continued, and in February 2014 al-Zawahiri officially renounced ISIS, criticizing, among other things, its violence against other Muslims.

Five months later, ISIS declared itself a global caliphate. Al-Baghdadi was named caliph, and once again the organization's name changed—this time to the "Islamic State." Since that time, small groups of Islamist militants in Sinai, Pakistan, Afghanistan, and elsewhere have declared their loyalty to al-Baghdadi and the Islamic State, although it remains doubtful those links are operational. Throughout the summer of 2014, as the Iraqi military largely collapsed, ISIS moved aggressively to seize and consolidate its hold on large chunks of both Syria and Iraq, including Mosul, Iraq's second-largest city.

In August 2014 Patrick Cockburn wrote in the *London Review of Books* that

The frontiers of the new Caliphate declared by Isis on 29 June are expanding by the day and now cover an area larger than Great Britain and inhabited by at least six million people, a population larger than that of Denmark, Finland or Ireland. In a few weeks of fighting in Syria Isis has established itself as the dominant force in the Syrian opposition, routing the official al-Qaida affiliate, Jabhat an-Nusra, in the oil-rich province of Deir Ezzor and executing its local commander as he tried to flee. In northern Syria some five thousand Isis fighters are using tanks and artillery captured from the Iraqi army in Mosul to besiege half a million Kurds in their enclave at Kobani on the Turkish border. In central Syria, near Palmyra, Isis fought the Syrian army as it overran the al-Shaer gasfield, one of the largest in the country, in a surprise assault that left an estimated three hundred soldiers and civilians dead. Repeated government counter-attacks finally retook the gasfield but Isis still controls most of Syria's oil and gas production. The Caliphate may be poor and isolated but its oil wells and control of crucial roads provide a steady income in addition to the plunder of war.

The birth of the new state is the most radical change to the political geography of the Middle East since the Sykes-Picot Agreement was implemented in the aftermath of the First World War.

As the militants continued to enlarge their territory and consolidate their control of an ever-expanding population across the two countries, the Obama administration renewed consideration of direct US military intervention against ISIS. By late summer 2014 at least 3,000 US troops were heading back into Iraq. And with the very real humanitarian crisis of Yazidi Syrians trapped on Mount Sinjar as a pretext, the US launched airstrikes against Syria.

America was officially at war with ISIS. As Peter Baker of the *New York Times* described it, "In sending warplanes back into the skies over Iraq, President Obama...found himself exactly where he did not want to be. Hoping to end the war in Iraq, Mr. Obama became the fourth president in a row to order military action in that graveyard of American ambition."

Is there any precedent for the barbaric violence perpetrated by ISIS?

Much of what ISIS does is clear from massive international media coverage: Kidnapping for ransom, whipping and other physical punishments, large-scale killing of civilians, and seizure of women and girls for rape and forced "marriage" to fighters have all been well documented. Reports of ISIS destruction of irreplaceable, centuries-old works of art have devastated historians and archaeologists around the world. Some of the most shocking reported actions are used against those ISIS deems non-believers, including crucifixion and stoning to death. Some of those actions hark back to punishments used in ancient times. As is true of the eras in which the holy texts of other influential religions were written, the years of Muhammed's life were also years of wars and constant battles for survival; that harsh wartime reality, including its punishments and its brutality, is reflected in the Quran as much as it is in the Torah, the Bible, and other texts.

And yet some of these acts are also all too modern. Beheadings, for example, are currently used by governments, including the government of Saudi Arabia, as part of contemporary penal systems. Other actions, such as burning to death, also have contemporary forebears in the vigilante justice of mob actions, including the torture and burning to death of Christians in Pakistan or the "necklacing" with burning tires during the most difficult period of the South African liberation struggles. Perhaps no image is as powerful as these highly publicized killings—beheadings, particularly of western journalists and aid workers, and most recently the torture-death of Muath al-Kaseasbeh, a captured Jordanian bomber pilot, who was burned alive in a cage.

Those gruesome killings have come to symbolize the cruelty and violence at the core of ISIS, although it should be noted that these actions are hardly particular to the extremist organization. ISIS didn't invent the modern version of burning someone alive for revenge: Israeli extremists kidnapped a young Palestinian boy and burned him to death in June 2014, following the unrelated killing of three Israeli teenagers. Not too long ago, hundreds of mainly African-American men were burned to death—often after other horrifying tortures—in lynchings across the American South. That's aside from the even more common and more recent realities of burning people to death—civilians, children—with weapons of war designed to do just that, such as the napalm and white phosphorous used by the US in Vietnam and Iraq and by Israel in Gaza. There is also a long history of beheadings in world history; during the French revolution the Jacobins are thought to have beheaded 17,000 people. Much more recently, in September 2014, the US-backed Free Syrian Army beheaded six ISIS captives, just days after ISIS beheaded two US journalists. And there is a longstanding legacy much closer to home, and much closer to ISIS: Saudi Arabia itself. In the first two weeks of 2015 alone, the government of Saudi Arabia beheaded ten people for "crimes" including apostasy, sorcery, and witchcraft.

There are differences, of course. The Saudis arrested the journalist who leaked video of a recent beheading to the world; ISIS posts its carefully constructed videos on YouTube and other social media platforms to trumpet its crimes. The reason has much to do with ISIS's assumption that showing that level of violence, up close and personal, will also somehow demonstrate strength and commitment—and crucially, that it will show ISIS as winning. For some, there is also the attraction of violence itself. There are reports that some ISIS fighters and wannabe fighters, particular international supporters, do not hold strong Islamic beliefs at all, but are actually attracted to the organization by the violence itself. Understanding that frightening reality is crucial to understanding how an organization so identified with violence can still gain support.

What are the motives and root causes underlying the ISIS tactic of public execution?

Each time ISIS kills a western journalist or a Jordanian bomber pilot, the United States, or Jordan, Japan, or others, escalate their own direct military engagement. It was only after ISIS beheaded American journalists James Foley and Steven Sotloff in summer 2014 that the Obama administration finally announced it would send troops back to Iraq. It then returned to bombing Iraq and launched the first attacks in Syria. Japanese Prime Minister Shinzo Abe responded to the killing of Japanese journalist Kenji Goto with efforts to undermine Japan's longstanding pacifist constitution and promises to increase its engagement with the anti-ISIS war. Following the horrific killing of pilot Muath al-Kaseasbeh, the king of Jordan announced plans to increase its direct bombing raids against Syria and Iraq within the US "coalition."

As Stephen Kinzer wrote in the *Boston Globe* even before the killing of al-Kaseasbeh, "By cleverly using grotesque theatrics, the Islamic State seems to be achieving its goal of luring the United States back into war. It knows that the presence of American soldiers in the Middle East will attract more radicals and misguided idealists to its cause. For many of these young men and women, fighting Kurds or Shiite militias may not seem especially glorious. To face the mighty United States on Middle Eastern soil, and if possible to kill an American or die at American hands, is their dream. We are giving them a chance to realize it. Through its impressive mastery of social media, the Islamic State is already using our escalation as a recruiting tool."

What does ISIS believe?

It is not possible to generalize with any accuracy what individual ISIS fighters, supporters, or allies—reluctant or otherwise—think or believe. Many of those who support or even join ISIS appear to be motivated as much by diverse combinations of political, personal, or economic reasons as they are by adherence to any specific theological framework. For some, the humiliation of foreign occupation, the indignity of repressive rulers, and the sense of disenfranchisement from one's own country play key motivating roles. We may never know exactly what each of those supporters believe. But the views of the leadership and the official positions of the organization are important for understanding who they are and why they act as they do—not to justify or apologize for its actions but precisely to figure out strategies that could actually work to stop its brutality, undermine its influence, and win its supporters away.

One way of defining what ISIS believes is to examine what distinguishes the group from its closest spiritual cousin and forebear, al-Qaeda, and the jihadi organizations still tied to al-Qaeda. Those distinctions include the nature of the "caliphate" that al-Qaeda supports and ISIS has declared, the role and legitimacy of government, and—crucial to understand given the horrific brutality that characterizes ISIS—the role and purpose of violence.

When ISIS leader Abu Bakr al-Baghdadi declared himself the caliph, or leader, of his just-announced Islamic state, or caliphate, in June 2014, he was claiming a direct linkage to a much older religious/political position of power. The last caliphate was dissolved by the newly secular Turkish Republic in 1924 following the defeat of the Ottoman Empire in World War I. Like earlier Islamist organizations, including al-Qaeda, ISIS had already been advocating the idea of rebuilding the original caliphate, a term for the territory ruled by an Islamic leader, which came into use following the death of the Prophet Muhammed. But unlike al-Qaeda, ISIS actually went ahead and acted to create a caliphate. The Islamic State declared by ISIS would be built in an undefined swath of the Arab world and perhaps beyond, beginning with the territory ISIS already controlled across Syria and Iraq. But its call for all Muslims and Islamist organizations to pledge fealty to al-Baghdadi as the new caliph was seen as a direct challenge, especially to al-Qaeda, which had already been feuding with ISIS over both political and religious differences.

A major point of divergence was precisely on the question of whether the caliphate could be declared now, today, as ISIS claimed, or whether it was a goal to be sought in the future, as al-Qaeda's leaders had long asserted. Part of that question has to do with whether the legitimacy of a caliphate requires its collective approval by Muslim scholars, or even the *umma*, or Muslim community as a whole, or whether an individual Muslim leader can simply proclaim a caliphate as his own.

As the *Times'* David Kirkpatrick described the two sides, "Al Qaeda's ideologues have been more vehement. All insist that the promised caliphate requires a broad consensus, on behalf of Muslim scholars if not all Muslims, and not merely one man's proclamation after a military victory. 'Will this caliphate be a sanctuary for all the oppressed and a refuge for every Muslim?' Abu Muhammad al-Maqdisi, a senior jihadist scholar, recently asked in a statement on the Internet. 'Or will this creation take a sword against all the Muslims who oppose it' and 'nullify all the groups that do jihad in the name of God?'"

Al-Baghdadi's Manichean approach in declaring his caliphate—demanding that every Muslim must pledge loyalty to him, and judging those who do not apostates or worse—echoes the all-or-nothing announcement of George W. Bush's global war on terror. "Either you're with us or you're with the terrorists," Bush declared on September 20, 2001. Governments who weren't "with us," even if they condemned the 9/11 attacks but disagreed with the US plan for war as a response, faced the possibility that their country would become a US target in an undefined, unlimited war. And any individual who wasn't "with us" faced the possibility of being treated like "them": as a terrorist. That meant the risk of being kidnapped, detained without trial, tortured, killed, injured, made homeless, forced into exile...

Another point of disagreement between al-Qaeda and ISIS has to do with government. When the original caliphate, which held both religious and governing power, was dismantled in 1924, the Muslim Brotherhood in Egypt was the first Islamist organization to emerge in that new period. Its goal was to contend for political power with the new secular forces rising in the Islamic world.

The Muslim Brotherhood became the model for generations of Islamist organizations that followed, engaging in political struggles—sometimes armed, often not—to win political power. But supporters of the most literal Wahhabi traditions refused to support any secular government; they recognized only the caliphate itself as holding legitimate power. All others, anyone who supported a secular or even religious government, would be considered a traitor, often sentenced to death. This shapes the antagonism of ISIS to organizations like today's Muslim Brotherhood in Egypt, the democratic Islamist Ennahda Party in Tunisia, Hamas in Palestine, and others, and it forms much of the basis of the split between ISIS and al-Qaeda itself.

Al-Qaeda, of course, never attempted to govern on its own. Its goals had to do with overthrowing governments, particularly the Saudi monarchy, which it deemed insufficiently pious and too corrupt to be worthy of support. But it didn't try to create a replacement government. When al-Qaeda took refuge in Afghanistan in the 1990s, it did nothing to challenge the Taliban government, nor to attempt any efforts to rule anywhere in the country.

But ISIS—having swept through and captured huge swaths of territory in both Iraq and Syria, including large cities with a population estimated at five to six million people—now has to figure out how to govern in the modern world. However medieval its ideology, this urgency explains the group's efforts to recruit doctors, engineers, teachers, and other professionals, and to bribe and threaten local experts into remaining on the job. ISIS officials need to find people able to keep the electricity on and the water clean and flowing, to keep hospitals open and medicine accessible. That means money, which means increasing efforts to sell oil, mostly though not entirely on the black market, from oil-producing areas under its control, and to raise other funds through taxes on businesses under its authority, along with extortion and kidnappings for ransom.

Al-Qaeda could concentrate on carrying out acts of violence aimed at destroying ungodly governments; ISIS needs to govern. And it may be that over time, the inability to provide ordinary people caught in ISIS-controlled territory with the ordinary requirements of life—jobs, electricity, schools, water, food, doctors—may lead to the collapse of its seemingly endlessly rising trajectory of power.

Finally there is a significant divide regarding the use of violence. It's not quite accurate to claim, as many in the media did, that al-Qaeda broke with ISIS because it was "too violent." The conflict is less over the amount or nature of the violence than it is about the purpose and the chosen victims. The essential al-Qaeda critique, in a sense, is not that ISIS was "too violent" but that it used violence for the wrong reasons against too many Muslims.

For al-Qaeda, violence was primarily understood as necessary to overthrow heretical, or insufficiently devout governments—starting with Saudi Arabia because the monarchy there has power over the holiest shrines of Islam—and those governments that keep them in power, most notably the United States. ISIS looked back to an earlier tradition. Princeton scholar Bernard Haykel describes ISIS as relying on "a kind of untamed Wahhabism" that saw violence as having a much more privileged position.

As the *New York Times* describes it, "al-Qaeda grew out of a radical tradition that viewed Muslim states and societies as having fallen into sinful unbelief, and embraced violence as a tool to redeem them. But the Wahhabi tradition embraced the killing of those deemed unbelievers as essential to purifying the community of the faithful." That is the ISIS approach. Haykel described how "violence is part of their ideology. For al-Qaeda, violence is a means to an end; for ISIS, it is an end in itself."

Another aspect of the ISIS belief system has to do with an apocalyptic vision of end times, which they believe is coming very soon. The ISIS countdown to Armageddon is shaped by a Manichean notion (based on some early Islamic theology) of a battle between Muslims and crusaders. In its particular version ISIS will lead the Muslims to victory in or near the small Syrian town of Dabiq, near the Turkish border, which ISIS occupied in the summer of 2014.

As Graeme Wood described in his widely read *Atlantic* article examining the group's theology and beliefs, "ISIS has attached great importance to the Syrian city of Dabiq, near Aleppo. It named its propaganda magazine after the town, and celebrated madly when (at great cost) it conquered Dabiq's strategically unimportant plains.

It is here, the Prophet reportedly said, that the armies of Rome will set up their camp. The armies of Islam will meet them, and Dabiq will be Rome's Waterloo or its Antietam....The [ISIS] magazine quotes Zarqawi as saying, 'The spark has been lit here in Iraq, and its heat will continue to intensify...until it burns the crusader armies in Dabiq.'"

There is historical significance to Dabiq. In 1516 the town was the site of a major defeat of the Mamluk Sultan by the early Ottomans. But for ISIS, what is most important is the belief that Islam—in this case ISIS itself—will defeat the armies of Rome, or the crusaders, in Dabiq. For the ISIS leadership, the importance of conquering this militarily insignificant town seems to have been based on the idea that ISIS can wait there for the arrival of an enemy army which it will then conquer.

The willingness of ISIS to wait for the crusader army to show up explains a great deal about the goal of its most gruesome atrocities. ISIS wants to provoke an attack by its enemies—the US, the west, the crusaders—on its own turf, just as the Quran predicts. The ISIS propaganda strategy is based on the understanding that the odds of western armies coming across the world to attack ISIS in its own territory rise dramatically if ISIS can outrage western publics. And the strategy has worked. The US and its allies decided to attack ISIS directly, rather than through proxies, only after public outrage at the horrors of ISIS treatment of prisoners and captured civilians.

In sending US planes to bomb ISIS in Syria and US troops and special forces to fight against ISIS in Iraq, in supporting US allies like Saudi Arabia, Turkey, Jordan, and the UAE to attack ISIS throughout the region, the United States and its allies are giving ISIS exactly what it wants.

What is Wahhabism? Why is it relevant to understanding ISIS?

For the leaders of ISIS, and despite the intensity of official Saudi opposition to it, the group's roots lie directly in the Wahhabi branch of Sunni Islam, which officially governs Saudi Arabia.

At its core and in its practice, ISIS is a thoroughly modern organization, but understanding it means going back to the eighteenth century, when the Muslim caliphate within the Ottoman Empire was losing territory and power. As the renowned scholar of religion Karen Armstrong noted in the *New Statesman*, this occurred in the same period when Europe was just beginning to separate church and state—a new phenomenon tied to modernism and the Enlightenment. The Muslim leadership of the caliphate did not believe in such a divide, and instead a variety of reformist movements emerged, whose followers believed that "if Muslims were to regain lost power and prestige, they must return to the fundamentals of their faith, ensuring that God—rather than materialism or worldly ambition—dominated the political order. There was nothing militant about this 'fundamentalism'; rather, it was a grassroots attempt to reorient society and did not involve jihad."

One of those movements was led by a scholar from central Arabia named Muhammad Ibn Abd al-Wahhab. Many local leaders rejected his approach, but he found a patron in a powerful local tribal leader, Muhammad Ibn Saud. In the local wars rising among the largely nomadic desert tribes for goods and land, Saud used Wahhabism to justify its opposite: his military campaigns were clearly fought for political and economic power. As Armstrong describes it, "two forms of Wahhabism were emerging: where Ibn Saud was happy to enforce Wahhabi Islam with the sword to enhance his political position, Ibn Abd al-Wahhab insisted that education, study, and debate were the only legitimate means of spreading the one true faith."

When Wahhab died, Saud and later his sons continued to claim that Wahhabism was the only legitimate version of Islam and that it could be "enforced with the sword." Enforcing the Wahhabi version of Islam along with the practice of *takfir*, meaning identifying other Muslims as unbelievers and therefore deserving of death, became common ways of justifying mass killings that actually were committed for political or economic goals. Armstrong describes how, after Wahhab's death, "Wahhabism became more violent, an instrument of state terror. ...Saud's son and successor used *takfir* to justify the wholesale slaughter of resistant populations. In 1801, his army sacked the holy Shia city of Karbala in what is now Iraq, plundered the tomb of Imam Husain, and slaughtered thousands of Shias, including women and children; in 1803, in fear and panic, the holy city of Mecca surrendered to the Saudi leader."

That was the origin of what would later—following World War I and British and French colonial machinations—become the state of Saudi Arabia. During the decades that followed, competing violent strands of Wahhabism vied for power and influence, including a rebel movement known as the Ikhwan, or brotherhood. With the quashing of the Ikhwan rebellion in 1930, the replacement of its rejection of modernity, and its extreme violence against civilians who disagreed with it, the official Saudi state presented a changed version of Wahhabism. Saudi Arabia abandoned the majority of the most violent practices, including the territorial expansion efforts that lay at the heart of early Wahhabism.

Not surprisingly, not everyone agreed with that shift. There were struggles over the definitions, goals, and traditions of Wahhabi Islam, and in many ways ISIS now shows its roots in some of those earlier practices. As Karen Armstrong describes the trajectory, "the Ikhwan spirit and its dream of territorial expansion did not die, but gained new ground in the 1970s, when the kingdom became central to western foreign policy in the region. Washington welcomed the Saudis' opposition to Nasserism (the pan-Arab socialist ideology of Egypt's second president, Gamal Abdel Nasser) and to Soviet influence. After the Iranian Revolution, it [Washington] gave tacit support to the Saudis' project of countering Shia radicalism by Wahhabizing the entire Muslim world. ...Like the Ikhwan, IS represents a rebellion against the official Wahhabism of modern Saudi

Arabia. Its swords, covered faces and cut-throat executions all recall the original Brotherhood."

Of course the immediate political trajectory of ISIS as an organization lies in the much more recent past, specifically the years of US occupation of Iraq and the rise of al-Qaeda. (See p. 16 for more on ISIS origins and history.) But its religious and ideological touchstones have much older roots, in Saudi Arabia, not Iraq.

How did the name ISIS evolve?

The organization known as ISIS, or the Islamic State in Iraq and Syria (or for some, the Islamic State in Iraq and al-Sham), traces its origins to the earlier ISI, or Islamic State in Iraq, which was itself an outgrowth of al-Qaeda in Iraq (AQI), sometimes known as al-Qaeda in Mesopotamia. Beginning in June 2014, ISIS changed its name again and began to refer to itself as the Islamic State, or IS. (See p. 16 for more on the history of ISIS.) Contemporaneously with ISIS, the organization has also been known as ISIL, or the Islamic State in Iraq and the Levant. In much of the Arab world, it is known as Daesh, the Arabic acronym for al-Dawla al-Islamiya fil-Iraq wash-Sham (more or less the same as ISIS).

The original name, al-Qaeda in Iraq, reflected the origins of the group, claiming the Iraqi franchise of the al-Qaeda brand. The name change from al-Qaeda in Iraq, or AQI, to Islamic State of Iraq, or ISI, took place during the US troop surge in 2006–07, when many Sunni militias were abandoning their opposition to the US occupation and instead joining the US-initiated Awakening movement, which paid them to fight with the US occupation forces instead of against them. The newly renamed ISI, which rejected the Awakening movement and continued its anti-occupation military attacks, was thus distinguishing itself from its former allies among other Sunni militias.

The next change, to ISIS or the Islamic State in Iraq and Syria, came when the organization, after the 2009–10 period of not-quite-defeat but certainly significant setbacks in Iraq, reemerged in Syria as a rising player on the anti-Assad side of the Syrian civil war.

This change also heralded the more ambitious self-definition of the group's intentions—beyond the geographic expansion from Iraq to Syria, it was also now looking toward the elimination of the Syrian-Iraqi border as part of its goal. ISIS, whether one defines the final "S" as Syria or al-Sham, refers to an older, pre-colonial definition of the territory: what was long known as "Greater Syria."

Al-Sham, Arabic for Greater Syria, referred to a wide and diverse territory that had been under control of the Ottoman Empire for 400 or so years. It included more or less today's Syria, Lebanon, Jordan, and historic Palestine, including what is now Israel. So "ISIS" generally refers both to the location of the group's fighters and supporters—contemporary Iraq and Syria—and the aspirations of the organization. ISIS has been public about its goal of erasing colonial borders, starting with the border between Iraq and Syria, but it is easy to see its goals extending to reversing the colonially imposed divide between Syria and Lebanon and beyond. ISIS has said little about the issue of Palestine, but it's difficult to imagine any discussion of colonial borders in the Middle East that did not quickly turn to Israel-Palestine.

The alternative contemporary version of the name, ISIL, or Islamic State in Iraq and the Levant, may have emerged as a consequence of translation, rather than as the organization's own choice. The group itself uses "al-Sham" in its names, thus ISIS in translation. But al-Sham, historically, was the same thing as the Levant, a European term both colonialist and orientalist in its origins and usage. So the Obama administration's conscious choice to use "ISIL" rather than "ISIS" reflects a deliberate intention to be doubling insulting.

As Public Radio International's "The World" program explains it, "The term Levant first appeared in medieval French. It literally means 'the rising,' referring to the land where the sun rises. If you're in France, in the western Mediterranean, that would make sense as a way to describe the eastern Mediterranean." Thus the colonialist legacy. PRI goes on, "Levant was also used in English from at least 1497. It's kind of archaic, but still used by scholars in English, though more widely in French. The Germans have a similar term for the same region: *Morgenland*, or 'the land of the morning.' It's even more archaic in German and kind of implies an imaginary, romantic, never-never land." Thus the orientalist part.

Even the *New York Times* identified "Levant" as "a once-common term that now has something of an antique whiff about it, like 'the Orient.' Because of the term's French colonial associations, many Arab nationalists and Islamist radicals disdain it, and it is unlikely that the militant group would choose 'Levant' to render its name." But for the White House, apparently colonialist language does not seem to present a problem. At least through the spring of 2015, ISIL has remained the Obama administration's chosen term. There has been significant media attention paid to the word choice, but no clarity from the White House itself.

Among Arabic speakers, the most common choice is the acronym Daesh, or Da'ish, essentially the Arabic version of ISIS, but with quite negative overtones. *The Guardian* notes that "in Arabic, the word lends itself to being snarled with aggression. As Simon Collis, the British ambassador to Iraq, told *The Guardian*'s Ian Black: 'Arabic speakers spit out the name Da'ish with different mixtures of contempt, ridicule and hostility. Da'ish is always negative.'"

Not surprisingly, some news outlets, governments, analysts, and others have been reluctant to use the term "Islamic State" to describe the militants seeking power across large parts of Iraq and Syria. They believe that using the term would give credibility to the violent extremist organization's claim that it is a real state, a caliphate or Islamic state, that somehow has authority over the world's Muslims or at least is deserving of recognition as a state. For those who do use the term, the reasoning seems to be grounded primarily in pragmatic considerations: If this is the title the organization has given itself, we'll use it for now, but using it doesn't imply any endorsement.

But the term "Islamic State," or IS, without the geographic specificity of the earlier ISI and ISIS versions, does have a propaganda purpose. The organization's name change was not arbitrary;

indeed it was announced in the context of the declaration of a caliphate—not as a religious vision for end times but in today's real world, in real territory, in which it is governing real cities populated by real people. NPR quoted a former Senate Foreign Relations Committee staff analyst who described the name change to Islamic State as "a very potent area of propaganda, because ISIS has attracted potentially thousands of foreign fighters, and none of these foreign fighters see themselves as terrorists. They see themselves as knights. They see themselves as mujahideen. They see themselves as freedom fighters. ...So they're very interested in fighting for the Islamic State."

Over time the brutality of ISIS rule and its inability to provide for the basic needs of the populations it controls will certainly undermine support it does have. But in the meantime, the claim of creating a whole new society, an Islamic State, however brutal it may be, has played a major role in encouraging the large-scale recruitment to ISIS-controlled territory not only of fighters but also of doctors, engineers, computer nerds, indeed whole families from around the world.

Did ISIS emerge because Obama pulled troops out of Iraq?

Many political opponents of the Obama administration, including (though not limited to) supporters of even more robust US military action in the Middle East, claim that the seemingly sudden emergence of ISIS was the direct result of the pullout of US troops from Iraq. This notion gained traction because of the timing of the two events. ISIS's powerful military sweep across northern Syria and then into Iraq began just over a year after the last US troops left Iraq in December 2011. But the troop withdrawal was not the reason for the rise of ISIS in either Iraq or Syria.

ISIS's re-emergence in Iraq after a period of relative quiescence in 2009–10 came in response to the escalating anti-Sunni sectarianism of the Shi'a-dominated government in Baghdad that was still armed, paid, and supported by the United States even while troop numbers were being reduced.

Before that, the origins and influence of ISIS in Iraq lie in the invasion and occupation of that country, which began in 2003 under George W. Bush, not in the 2011 withdrawal of US troops. ISIS emerged in Iraq in 2004, as one of numerous Sunni militias fighting against the US, British, and other coalition forces and later against the so-called Iraqi Interim Government.

As the anti-occupation war became increasingly sectarian, the Sunni AQI/ISIS continued to clash with the Shi'a-dominated, US-backed Iraqi government.

In 2006 and '07, the Bush administration sent thousands of additional troops during the so-called surge in Iraq and organized the Sunni Awakening movement. (See p. 13 for more on the surge and the Sunni Awakening.)

ISIS had not joined the Awakening movement, but it was significantly weakened in the 2007–08 period, when it lost support of Sunni communities and tribes, many of which were taking money from the Awakening movement and pulling back from the military struggle. When the US turned over responsibility for paying the Sunni tribes to the Shi'a-dominated—and increasingly sectarian—Iraqi government, the government of Prime Minister Nuri al-Maliki stopped payments and escalated attacks against Sunni communities. Inevitably, the sectarian tensions increased and set the stage for the emergence of what amounted to a Sunni revolt against the government and an increase in Sunni support for ISIS.

Large-scale fighting started again by early 2009, and ISIS re-emerged as a major force, this time within the renewed Sunni uprising. Its target was primarily the Shi'a government, which had already signed an agreement with the Bush administration requiring the withdrawal of all US troops and all Pentagon-paid military contractors from Iraq by the end of 2011.

The new Obama administration actually reopened the withdrawal plan, trying to convince Iraq to allow up to 20,000 US troops to remain, but the negotiations foundered over the question of impunity. Prime Minister al-Maliki was reportedly in favor of keeping US troops in Iraq beyond the deadlines. But Iraq refused to grant Washington's demand that US troops be assured of absolute immunity for any war crimes they might commit, and without that impunity, presumably knowing that US troops would certainly continue to commit war crimes, the US refused to keep any troops in Iraq.

The repression by the Shi'a-dominated Iraqi government increased, the Sunni uprising escalated, and full-scale sectarian war resumed, with US participation through the end of 2011 and without the US starting in 2012. War continued, and ISIS played a major role in the sectarian battle. Under US pressure in August 2014 al-Maliki was replaced by another politician from the same Shi'a party.

New Prime Minister Haider al-Abadi talked a more inclusive line, including announcing that his government would stop bombing Sunni communities, but he did little to change the sectarian practices of the military and police agencies, and thus the sectarian pressures continued. Sunni former generals, Sunni tribal leaders, and others continued to resist the repression. Many of them continued their alliance with ISIS, seeing it as the strongest opposition to the US-backed government. Using a combination of conventional military tactics and the brutality it had become known for, including kidnappings, beheadings, and sex slavery, ISIS fought against both Iraqi government forces and civilians: Shi'a, Christians, Yazidis, even Sunnis who did not accept its extremist interpretation of Islam. The Sunni revolt continued even as ISIS moved to consolidate its seizure of land and expansion into Syria, which would define the regional war for years to come.

Whatever the beliefs and intentions of ISIS leadership, its revival and renewed Sunni support—which made possible its rapid success within the Sunni revolt in Iraq—were directly linked to the continuing sectarian marginalization and repression against Sunnis by the US-backed and Shi'a-dominated government in Baghdad. So the origins and rise of ISIS stem from the US invasion and occupation of Iraq, not the belated withdrawal of US troops.

Where does ISIS get its money from?

Along with selling oil it produces from oilfields and refineries in territories it has seized (see p. 160 for more on oil), ISIS relies on several other sources of funding, including taxes levied on businesses within, and transporting of goods in and out of, cities, towns, and areas under its control. As ISIS consolidated its governance in northern Syria and western Iraq after declaring itself the Islamic State "caliphate" in 2014, it began to operate as if it were an actual government. While some of this was purely for appearances, ISIS did begin to issue commercial, building, and drivers' licenses to carry out at least the basics of running public utilities, the operation of schools and medical facilities, and to collect taxes.

Taxes took the form of official-sounding taxes that any government might assess for commercial or other actions, as well as straight-up extortion. That reportedly included ISIS skimming money off the top of salary funds the Iraqi government is still paying to civil service workers in ISIS-occupied Mosul. Since ISIS took control of the central bank in Mosul, the salaries of government workers were paid in cash picked up weekly by emissaries from the occupied city who meet directly with Iraqi government officials outside of Mosul.

ISIS has also gained hundreds of thousands, if not millions, as ransom from the families, businesses, or governments of its kidnapping victims. While the United States and Britain maintain staunch "no payment of ransom" positions and have seen numerous US and British nationals killed by ISIS (as well as by other extremist organizations), various European, Asian, and other countries—both governments and companies—have brought their people home after quietly paying ransoms generally far lower than those demanded for American or British citizens.

Then there is the massive funding, by some reports second only to oil income, accruing to ISIS from sales of plundered ancient artifacts, putting the historical legacy of Syria and to some degree Iraq at even greater risk. The human rights section of the American Association for the Advancement of Science took satellite images

in 2014 that, according to a scholar on the project, "show the destruction of ancient artifacts, architecture, and most importantly,
archaeological context that is the record of humanity's past. From
the origins of civilization to the first international empires, Syria's
cultural heritage and these sites in particular are vitally important
to our understanding of history." Some of those looted artifacts are
being sold to collectors and dealers in the United States. According
to a February 2015 *Wall Street Journal* investigation, "in the US alone,
government data show the value of declared antiques imported from
Syria jumped 134% in 2013 to $11 million. US officials estimate the
value of undeclared pieces is many multiples higher."

And ISIS is not the only force threatening Syria's cultural trea-
sure. The *Journal* article reports that "video published by a Syrian
opposition media network on YouTube shows soldiers fighting for
President Bashar al-Assad 's regime at Palmyra with delicate grave
reliefs loaded onto a truck. And senior Free Syrian Army fighters,
the secular opposition that has received aid from the US, have long
conceded to Western media that looting antiquities is an important
source of funding."

In early 2015, the United Nations Security Council passed a
series of resolutions aimed at choking off sources of funding for ISIS
as well as other extremist organizations including the al-Nusra Front.
The Council condemned the purchase of oil from those organizations. But although it passed the resolution under Chapter VII of the
UN Charter, which can authorize the use of force, it did little to bring
real pressure on the global oil market to stop the trade, threatening
only to send any violators to the UN Sanctions Committee for possible listing as a violator of UN sanctions. It called on all UN member
states to freeze the assets of people who commit terrorist acts, and to
"take appropriate steps to prevent the trade in Iraqi and Syrian cultural
property and other items of...historical, cultural, rare scientific and
religious importance illegally removed from Iraq since 6 August 1990
[when the first resolution aimed at protecting Iraqi cultural heritage
was passed] and from Syria since 15 March 2011." The resolution also
reaffirmed that payment of ransom to any organization on the UN's

al-Qaeda sanctions list, regardless of who pays, would be considered a violation of international legal obligations.

Then there is the politically embarrassing (for the US, at least) source of some of the most crucial funding for ISIS—important because it provides political and military as well as direct financial support. That source is the US-backed, US-armed petro-monarchies of the Arab Gulf: Saudi Arabia, Kuwait, the UAE, Qatar, and beyond.

Writing in *CounterPunch* in February 2015, Patrick Cockburn reported that ISIS

> is still receiving significant financial support from Arab sympathizers outside Iraq and Syria, enabling it to expand its war effort, says a senior Kurdish official. The US has being trying to stop such private donors in the Gulf oil states sending to Islamic State (ISIS) funds that help pay the salaries of fighters who may number well over 100,000. Fuad Hussein, the chief of staff of the Kurdish President, Massoud Barzani, told *The Independent* on Sunday: "There is sympathy for Da'esh [ISIS] in many Arab countries and this has translated into money—and that is a disaster."
> ...Dr Mahmoud Othman, a veteran member of the Iraqi Kurdish leadership who recently retired from the Iraqi parliament, said there was a misunderstanding as to why Gulf countries paid off IS. It is not only that donors are supporters of IS, but that the movement "gets money from the Arab countries because they are afraid of it," he says. "Gulf countries give money to Da'esh so that it promises not to carry out operations on their territory."

Some of the most extensive reports are of direct funding to ISIS (as well as to the plethora of extreme Islamist organizations that preceded ISIS) from Saudi Arabia, though the exact combination of government funds, state-linked institutional funds, donations from individual princes within the vast royal family, and contributions from wealthy individuals and businesses in the kingdom remains murky. This isn't a new, or an ISIS-specific phenomenon. As Patrick Cockburn notes in his book *The Jihadis Return*, "in 2009, eight years after 9/11, a cable from the US Secretary of State, Hillary Clinton, revealed by WikiLeaks, complained that donors in Saudi

Arabia constituted the most significant source of funding to Sunni terrorist groups worldwide. But despite this private admission, the US and Western Europeans continued to remain indifferent to Saudi preachers whose message, spread to millions by satellite TV, YouTube and Twitter, called for the killing of the Shi'a as heretics. These calls came as al-Qaeda bombs were slaughtering people in Shi'a neighborhoods in Iraq. A sub-headline in another State Department cable in the same year reads: 'Saudi Arabia: Anti-Shi'ism As Foreign Policy?' Now, five years later, Saudi-supported groups have a record of extreme sectarianism against non-Sunni Muslims." The US knew, but despite it all, the Saudi monarchy—known for its tight control over its own population—remained a key Washington ally.

There was of course a long history of Saudi funding of Islamic extremists in official and unacknowledged partnerships with the United States. During the 1980s it was Saudi money that paid for the Afghan mujahideen warriors, trained and backed by the CIA and Pakistan's ISI intelligence services, who battled Soviet-backed forces at Washington's behest at the height of Reagan's Cold War. There are countless reports of Saudi involvement in the 9/11 attacks themselves, in which 15 of the 19 hijackers were Saudi citizens; the storied 28-page section of the official 9/11 report, which remains fully redacted and unavailable to the public, allegedly details some of that involvement. The focus on that potential scandal had waned in recent years. But it gained new prominence with the sudden announcement in February 2015 that al-Qaeda operative and so-called 20th hijacker Zacarias Moussaoui, serving a life sentence in a US prison, had testified in a related trial about the powerful Saudi princes who had funded bin Laden's and others' terrorist actions. He named names, including Prince Turki al-Faisal, the former Saudi intelligence chief; Prince Bandar Bin Sultan, Saudi ambassador to the US; influential billionaire Prince al-Waleed bin Talal; and many of Saudi Arabia's most powerful clerics. All the princes (though probably not the imams) had long experience in and with the US, some in close relationships at the highest levels of US government.

Other regional leaders have been even more direct in holding the Gulf monarchies responsible for the rise in extremism. US-backed Iraqi President Nuri al-Maliki, in March 2014, blamed Saudi Arabia and Qatar. As quoted by Patrick Cockburn in *The Jihadis Return*, Maliki told an interviewer that "these two countries are primarily responsible for the sectarian, terrorist and security crisis in Iraq." While part of his goal was to deflect his government's own responsibility for its sectarian, anti-Sunni repression, Maliki went on to say that the two governments were also "buying weapons for the benefit of these terrorist organizations." According to Cockburn, "there was considerable truth in Maliki's charges."

Such allegations are consistent with longstanding and now public US government unease over funding of terrorists coming from the Gulf states allied to the US. When *The Guardian* and other outlets were releasing the huge trove of WikiLeaks cables in 2009-10, one set dealt directly with US concerns about Saudi and other Gulf states' funding of Islamist extremists, in the years when ISIS was still functioning as al-Qaeda in Iraq and as the Islamic State of Iraq.

According to *The Guardian*,

> Saudi Arabia is the world's largest source of funds for Islamist militant groups such as the Afghan Taliban and Lashkar-e-Taiba— but the Saudi government is reluctant to stem the flow of money, according to Hillary Clinton. "More needs to be done since Saudi Arabia remains a critical financial support base for al-Qaeda, the Taliban, LeT [the Pakistani terrorist group Lashkar-e-Taiba, responsible for the deadly Mumbai attack of 2008] and other terrorist groups," says a secret December 2009 paper signed by the US secretary of state.
>
> "Donors in Saudi Arabia constitute the most significant source of funding to Sunni terrorist groups worldwide," she said. Three other Arab countries are listed as sources of militant money: Qatar, Kuwait and the United Arab Emirates. ...Saudi officials are often painted as reluctant partners. Clinton complained of the "ongoing challenge to persuade Saudi officials to treat terrorist funds emanating from Saudi Arabia as a strategic priority"...

In common with its neighbours Kuwait is described as a "source of funds and a key transit point" for al-Qaeda and other militant groups. While the government has acted against attacks on its own soil, it is "less inclined to take action against Kuwait-based financiers and facilitators plotting attacks outside of Kuwait."

Saudi funding, whether from individuals, government-backed institutions, or Saudi princes themselves, would certainly fit with the religious/political support for Sunni Islamist extremism that has characterized Saudi domestic and foreign policy for decades. That policy has included a powerful anti-Shi'a component that fits easily with lethal treatment by ISIS of Shi'a in the areas it controls. Storied Middle East correspondent Robert Fisk, in July 2014, wrote that,

> Some time before 9/11, Prince Bandar bin Sultan, once the powerful Saudi ambassador in Washington and head of Saudi intelligence until a few months ago, had a revealing and ominous conversation with the head of the British Secret Intelligence Service, MI6, Sir Richard Dearlove. Prince Bandar told him: 'The time is not far off in the Middle East, Richard, when it will be literally "God help the Shi'a." More than a billion Sunnis have simply had enough of them.'
>
> The fatal moment predicted by Prince Bandar may now have come for many Shi'a, with Saudi Arabia playing an important role in bringing it about by supporting the anti-Shi'a jihad in Iraq and Syria.
>
> Since the capture of Mosul by the Islamic State of Iraq and the Levant (ISIS) on 10 June, Shi'a women and children have been killed in villages south of Kirkuk, and Shi'a air force cadets machine-gunned and buried in mass graves near Tikrit. In Mosul, Shi'a shrines and mosques have been blown up, and in the nearby Shi'a Turkoman city of Tal Afar 4,000 houses have been taken over by Isis fighters as "spoils of war.".. .
>
> Dearlove, who headed MI6 from 1999 to 2004, emphasized the significance of Prince Bandar's words, saying that they constituted "a chilling comment that I remember very well indeed." He does not doubt that substantial and sustained funding from private donors in Saudi Arabia and Qatar, to which the authorities

may have turned a blind eye, has played a central role in the Isis surge into Sunni areas of Iraq.

He said: "Such things simply do not happen spontaneously." This sounds realistic since the tribal and communal leadership in Sunni majority provinces is much beholden to Saudi and Gulf paymasters, and would be unlikely to cooperate with ISIS without their consent.

Dearlove's explosive revelation about the prediction of a day of reckoning for the Shi'a by Prince Bandar, and the former head of MI6's view that Saudi Arabia is involved in the ISIS-led Sunni rebellion, has attracted surprisingly little attention.

Perhaps that refusal to pay attention is not so surprising, particularly in Washington. For much of that time, the US not only relied on Saudi Arabia as one of its most important Middle East strategic partners, but also sold tens of billions of dollars worth of the most sophisticated US weapons. In return, of course, the Saudis guaranteed the US access to and significant levels of influence on their enormous oil production process.

How does ISIS treat women and what is the role of women within the organization?

Islamic fundamentalists, as is the case with most of their counterparts in other religions, do not believe women are equal to men. From ISIS to al-Qaeda, from the Taliban to the government of Saudi Arabia, women are deemed not only different from men but lesser. Although some parts of Islamic law provide (at least aspirationally) some level of social protections for women, including economic security, in the real world women have little access to basic human rights. Women are excluded from much of public life, with severe restrictions on whether and in what jobs they can work. Many basic aspects of women's lives, including decisions regarding their children, access to health care and education, legal status, and passports, remain under the control of their husbands, fathers, sons, or other male relatives.

In areas under ISIS control, women live under an extreme version of these restrictions. Aside from the limits on carrying out daily life, the reports of what ISIS does to women in areas it captures are truly horrifying. Women kidnapped, raped, murdered, sold as slaves to fighters, the list goes on. Women are often taken and held as sex slaves or other roles when the men in a captured village or town are killed on the spot. The women targeted for such crimes are often non-Sunnis—Shi'a or Yazidi or Christian perhaps—but in some cases they may also include Sunnis who do not accept the extremist definitions of religion demanded by ISIS. In November 2014 CBS News reported an assault on a Sunni tribe in Iraq, in Ras al-Maa, a village near Ramadi, the capital of Anbar Province, now largely controlled by ISIS. In that attack, a senior member of the local Sunni al-Bu Nimr tribe described how at least 50 people were lined up and shot, one by one, of whom four were children and six were women.

So the punishments unique to women—including rape and forced "marriage" to ISIS fighters—are carried out even as women suffer the non-gender-specific attacks alongside men. Women, indeed whole families, become victims of kidnappings, are forced from their homes, and face the risks inherent in US and coalition air strikes and other attacks aimed at ISIS.

Unfortunately many of the atrocities committed specifically against women are more quantitatively than qualitatively different from misogynistic traditions still in practice in some areas where ISIS has established a base and elsewhere. Forced marriage, for example, including the marriage of young girls, is a widespread phenomenon in poor rural areas of several countries, Arab, African, and Asian. The period of Taliban rule in Afghanistan, and its overthrow in the US invasion and occupation that began in October 2001, provides a useful model. Treatment of women under Taliban rule was abysmal; many schools shut down, girls forced to leave school, urban women forced out of many professions, violently enforced restrictions on women's actions, autonomy, dress, and more. Many women were forced into marriages against their will; young girls were forced into marriage. The US justified much of its anti-Taliban military engagement in

Afghanistan with the language of protecting Afghan women. But it turned out that many of the warlords who had fought and lost to the Taliban, and later came back to fight with the US against the Taliban, held medieval-era views of women's role in society that were strikingly similar to those of the Taliban.

When the US imposed a modern, more or less gender-equality-based constitution and laws, life improved for a small sector of Afghan women—those in Kabul and the few other large cities. But for the majority of women in the country, things did not get better. Forced marriages were a longstanding custom in many regions of rural Afghanistan (where the vast majority of the population lived), and they did not disappear when the US and its chosen proxies overthrew the Taliban.

After the US and its allies overthrew the Taliban in 2001, the US-armed and US-financed Northern Alliance became the main local power in Afghanistan. The US appointed the powerful Uzbek warlord from the Northern Alliance, Gen. Ahmad Rashid Dostum, who was commander of the Junbish-e-Millie militia, to be the chief of staff of the new US-backed Afghan army. Dostum and his militia were responsible for a variety of atrocities including the notorious Dasht-e-Leili massacre of up to 3,000 Taliban prisoners in December 2001. By early 2002, Western media were also reporting on the group's involvement in a particularly savage campaign of rape of Pashtun women, including very young girls. But such public knowledge was not enough to discredit Dostum in contemporary Afghanistan. In 2014, when the US-backed, Western-oriented, former World Bank official Ashraf Ghani was elected president of Afghanistan, the same warlord was at his side, sworn in as the new vice-president. The US cheered the election as evidence of Afghanistan's new democracy. Yet creating a new government didn't transform reactionary traditions regarding women.

(For the record, the Soviet Union had also imposed a modern, gender-equality-based constitution and laws in the 1970s, turning Kabul into a Western-appearing capital for a decade or more, but it also failed to change the conditions for women outside of the city.)

Aside from the direct attacks on women, ISIS restrictions on women in public life are severe, including limits on schooling, separation of the sexes, prohibitions on many areas of work. There is no question the actions of ISIS are brutal and misogynistic. But it is also true that with the announcement of the Islamic State as a "caliphate," ISIS asserted the goal of building a fully Islamic society, requiring the involvement of whole families, including women and children.

That state-building project is one of the key distinctions between ISIS and other extremist Islamist organizations. *Time* magazine's Vivienne Walt described how

> in al-Qaeda's wars in Afghanistan and Iraq, young armed men holed up on the battlefield far from their families. But in Syria ISIS aims to install a purist Islamic state—an entire new country—as its name denotes. And so ISIS fighters are looking to build lives that are far broader than fighting the war, ones in which they can come home after a day's battle to a loving wife and children, and home-cooked meals. As such, recruiting women into ISIS is not simply about expanding the organization. It is the essential building block of a future society. ISIS members have said their women do not fight, but are there to help build the new society.

In fact there are reports of significant numbers of women fighting for ISIS, including in an entire separate battalion of women fighters. Writing in *Foreign Affairs*, UN gender and conflict analyst Nimmi Gowrinathan described women fighters in ISIS within the historical context of women fighters in other violent movements:

> Living in deeply conservative social spaces, they faced constant threats to their ethnic, religious, or political identities -- and it was typically those threats, rather than any grievances rooted in gender, that persuaded them to take up arms. ISIS' particularly inhumane violence can obscure the fact that the conflict in Iraq is also rooted in identity: at its base, the fight is a sectarian struggle between Sunni and Shiite Muslims, with several smaller minorities caught in between. It makes sense, therefore, that the all-female al-Khansaa Brigade of ISIS relies heavily on identity politics for recruitment, targeting young women who feel oppressed

as Sunni Muslims. Indeed, anonymous fatwas calling for single women to join the fight for an Islamic caliphate have been attractive enough to draw women to ISIS from beyond the region.

Certainly the majority of people living in the so-called caliphate are local Iraqis or Syrians, held against their will by a violent movement controlling their villages or towns. But among those responding to ISIS recruiting efforts, the creation of the "caliphate" as a physical place has drawn not only fighters but whole families to the territory under ISIS domination.

The *Washington Post* reported on how ISIS recruits families to its territory.

> "The more they are successful at creating a whole new society, the more they are able to attract entire families," said Mia Bloom, a professor of security studies at the University of Massachusetts at Lowell who has written extensively about women and terrorism. "It's almost like the American dream, but the Islamic State's version of it."
>
> In the Syrian city of Raqqa, the group's main stronghold, the extremists have established a clinic for pregnant women run by a female gynecologist trained in Britain. Boys attend school, studying almost exclusively religion, until they are 14, when they are expected to start fighting, [British analyst Melanie] Smith said. Girls stay in school until they are 18; their instruction is about the Koran and sharia law, as well as learning how to dress, keep house, cook, clean and care for men, all according to a strict Islamic code.
>
> Bloom said the Islamic State also appeals to women by providing electricity, food and a salary of up to $1,100 per month—a huge sum in Syria—for each fighter's family. The largesse is funded with money looted from banks, oil smuggling, kidnappings for ransom, and the extortion of truckers and others who cross Islamic State territory....
>
> The United Nations has documented extreme brutality toward women by Islamic State radicals, including reports of women, particularly from minority groups, being stoned to death or sold into prostitution or sex slavery for its fighters.

But the Islamic State uses family imagery in its aggressive and highly polished online recruiting on social media, including videos showing fighters pushing children on swings and passing out toys, and children playing on bouncy castles and bumper cars, riding ponies, and eating pink cotton candy.

Certainly ISIS will not be able to maintain the reality of those illusory descriptions. But understanding the various reasons why some women might choose to support ISIS—the search for identity, wanting a sectarian or religious life, a sense of political or economic dispossession—remains as important in challenging ISIS influence as is the need to grasp the depth of the organization's attacks on women.

How did ISIS suddenly become so powerful? Why didn't anyone see it coming?

In 2014 ISIS was not new. It had been around at least since 2004, and had claimed its current name in 2011. But few outside of the region were paying much attention when this relatively small, relatively un-known organization suddenly swept across much of northern Syria, ignoring the border with Iraq and moving to occupy a huge swath of territory of western and central Iraq including Mosul, the second largest city in Iraq.

The ISIS announcement that it was establishing a caliphate, with the now-occupied Syrian city of Raqqa as its capital, was shockingly sudden and unexpected. That announcement was one reason new recruits from outside of Iraq and Syria, even outside the Middle East, began joining ISIS in much larger numbers. But the US response was most concerned with developments in Iraq, where ISIS trampled the huge Washington-funded and Pentagon-trained military, whose soldiers and commanders mostly ran away, leaving their US weapons behind for ISIS to capture.

The immediate question was how ISIS was able to win what looked like such a lopsided battle. As Patrick Cockburn recounts in the preface to *The Jihadis Return*,

"ISIS captured Iraq's northern capital, Mosul, after three days of fighting. The Iraqi government had an army with 350,000 soldiers on which $41.6 billion had been spent in the three years since 2011, but this force melted away without significant resistance. Discarded uniforms and equipment were found strewn along the roads leading to Kurdistan and safety. The flight was led by commanding officers, some of whom changed into civilian clothes as they abandoned their men. Given that ISIS may have had as few as 1,300 fighters in its assault on Mosul, this was one of the great military debacles in history."

So how could ISIS win, even temporarily, against powerful militaries in Iraq and Syria? There are two answers. In Syria, it was the chaos of an exploding civil war, with the regime's military stretched thin in some areas, and the anti-Assad opposition fighters—divided, poorly armed, and badly led—that allowed a better-armed, wealthier militia such as ISIS move to a far more powerful position. There was simply too little opposition, and it was able to take over whole cities, such as its erstwhile capital, Raqqa, as well as sections of Aleppo and elsewhere, without serious opposition.

In Iraq, ISIS triumphed because it did not fight alone. It was able to take advantage of crucial support from three components of Iraq's Sunni community, support shaped by the increasingly repressive actions of the Shi'a-dominated sectarian government in Baghdad. They included Sunni tribal leaders, Sunni former military officers including Saddam Hussein-era Baathist generals, and ordinary Sunni communities who bore the brunt of the US-backed Baghdad government's often brutal tactics.

Why did Sunnis support ISIS?

The reason for the Sunni support for ISIS had less to do with what ISIS stands for—many Iraqi (and Syrian) Sunnis are profoundly secular, and most remained very much opposed to the brutality of ISIS—and far more to do with the disenfranchisement of Sunni communities under the rule of Shi'a-controlled governments in

Baghdad. For many, the ongoing repression at the hands of their own government made an alliance with ISIS an acceptable, even preferable option—despite, rather than because of, its extremism.

From the beginning of the US invasion and occupation of Iraq, the large Sunni minority had been at the forefront of opposition. Sunnis had been privileged under the Baathist rule of Saddam Hussein and held positions of power inside the government, especially in the military. All those positions were lost as the US occupation dismantled the civil service and destroyed the Iraqi army. Both before and after the creation of ISIS and its forebears, Sunni militias, some linked to tribal organizations and often led by former generals, played a huge role in fighting the US and the new US-created government and security forces being established in Baghdad.

The US-created Sunni Awakening, paying off Sunni militias to fight for the US and its allies rather than against them, worked for a while—the intensity of the civil war diminished. But the repression aimed at Sunni communities across Iraq never really ended during the Awakening movement's heyday, and when the US and Maliki stopped paying off the tribes, the repression escalated and Sunni opposition rose again.

Maliki's government had become a major part of the problem of sectarianism in the country. As a consequence, Sunnis were far more likely to join with ISIS, seeing them as an armed force that would defend Sunni interests, or at least challenge some of the worst abuses of the Shi'a-led government. Despite the US having created the Iraqi government, and armed and funded it for more than a decade, by 2013 or so the Obama administration recognized that Maliki's sectarianism had become a major strategic threat to US interests.

As the pan-Arab *Al Arabiya* newspaper noted in August 2014, "While Iraqi Sunni tribes were crucial in defeating al-Qaeda in 2005, they have not shown the same determination in battling the Islamic State of Iraq and Syria (ISIS) despite reports of them fighting the militant group. Political observers say this is due to the disfranchisement of the Sunni population by outgoing Shiite Prime Minister Nouri al-Maliki....Michael Pregent, an adjunct lecturer at the National Defense University in Washington, said the central government broke its promise to integrate 90,000 Sunnis who fought al-Qaeda into the security apparatus, and provide them with jobs. 'They helped get rid of al-Qaeda, but the government fired all of them and put a lot of their leaders in jail,' Pregent, a former US Army officer who was embedded with Iraqi Kurdish forces, told *Al Arabiya*."

Washington campaigned hard to get Maliki replaced in the 2014 elections, and that finally happened—but the result was disappointing. The new prime minister, Haider al-Abadi, was from Maliki's same Shi'a political party, and while his rhetoric tended to favor a more unitary and less sectarian approach, the ministries responsible for most of the repression (intelligence and defense) remained essentially unchanged.

And so did the Sunni resistance. The various components of Sunni support enabled ISIS to increase its strength and capacity. Some of the tribal leaders provided militia fighters to fight alongside, if not actually with, ISIS. In February 2015, National Public Radio noted that while the Sunni tribes are mainly in western Iraq,

> you can also find them in neighboring Jordan. Sheik Ahmed Dabbash, speaking from his house on a sleepy street in the capital Amman, says his tribe fought side-by-side with al-Qaeda against the Americans a decade ago....Now Dabbash's group is in a de facto alliance with ISIS. His views are typical of a broad spectrum of Sunnis in Iraq—Islamists, tribesmen, one-time supporters of Saddam Hussein. They feel victimized by Iraq's Shi'a-led government and many fight against the Shi'a-dominated army—either by joining ISIS or allying with them, even if they find the group extreme.

Those "one-time supporters of Saddam Hussein" include military leaders, who may or may not have actually supported the former Baathist leader but who played key roles in the powerful Iraqi military. Those officers are widely believed to be providing both training and crucial strategic planning for ISIS military campaigns. According to the *New York Times*, ISIS leader Abu Bakr al-Baghdadi's "leadership team includes many officers from Saddam Hussein's long-disbanded army. They include former Iraqi officers like Fadel al-Hayali, the top deputy for Iraq, who once served Mr. Hussein as a lieutenant colonel, and Adnan al-Sweidawi, a former lieutenant colonel who now heads the group's military council. The pedigree of its leadership, outlined by an Iraqi who has seen documents seized by the Iraqi military, as well as by American intelligence officials, helps explain its battlefield successes: Its leaders augmented traditional military skill with terrorist techniques refined through years of fighting American troops, while also having deep local knowledge and contacts. ISIS is in effect a hybrid of terrorists and an army."

Even recognizing the *Times*' sloppy use of the term "terrorist"— whose multiple definitions all start with attacking civilians or noncombatants, not an occupying army—it is clear that the unexpected military capacity of ISIS is bound up with the military training of former army officials of the Saddam Hussein era.

It is equally clear that changing the balance of power on the ground and reducing ISIS's power means severing the still-strong alliance between ISIS and Sunni communities and institutions. That will be difficult, perhaps impossible, as long as the US and its coalition continue large-scale bombing of ISIS targets in the midst of heavily populated Sunni cities, towns, and regions, and as long as the Shi'a-led government in Baghdad continues its sectarian attacks on the Sunni community. The goal of winning Sunnis away from ISIS is undermined every time a US or Jordanian or British bomber or fighter-jet attacks Raqqa, for instance, or "in ISIS-controlled Fallujah." Both of those cities, in Syria and in Iraq, are heavily populated, and the likelihood of civilian casualties is almost inevitable. When US bombs are dropped and US policymakers cheer, Sunni Iraqis see it as another betrayal.

Because of the US military campaign, the claimed US goal of making new deals with Sunni tribes and winning over broader Sunni community support for the anti-ISIS struggle remains impossible to achieve. As NPR reported in February 2015, the "US view on how to defeat ISIS involves making a deal with Sunnis like [tribal leader] Dabbash, and even incorporating their men into a sort of Iraqi National Guard. 'The guard is a breakthrough idea, because it will ensure that Iraqis are protected by people with whom they are familiar and in whom they have trust. It'll break down some of the sectarian divide,' said US Secretary of State John Kerry. But that trust is sorely lacking among Dabbash and other Sunni leaders who have yet to show signs that they are ready to make a truce with the government in Baghdad."

As long as they can count on support—or even the lack of op-position—from Iraq's Sunni tribes, and as long as the multi-party civil war continues to rage across Syria, ISIS is likely to maintain its power at a level vastly disproportionate to its size.

Why are people from foreign—including Western—countries joining ISIS and other extremist Islamist organizations in the Middle East?

There is a long history of foreign militants or wannabe militants traveling to the greater Middle East region to join Islamist campaigns. Perhaps the best known in recent years is the massive influx of foreign fighters who traveled to Afghanistan throughout the 1980s to join the indigenous mujahideen, or holy warriors, fighting against the Soviet Union at the height of the Cold War. One of their most famous was Osama Bin Laden. The mujahideen were armed by the CIA, paid by Saudi Arabia, trained by CIA allies in Pakistan's ISI intelligence service, and welcomed at the White House by President Ronald Reagan, who called them "freedom fighters."

More recently, foreign fighters traveled to Iraq to join various militias—including extremist Islamist groups, some of them linked to al-Qaeda—to fight against the United States occupation. But the numbers were never enough to have a determinative impact on the military balance of power.

From the first months of the Syrian civil war, foreign activists arrived to support the anti-Assad opposition. As the initial non-violent political campaign morphed into the devastating civil war, many more arrived as humanitarian aid workers, driving ambulances, helping distribute international assistance. As the Islamist forces among the anti-Assad opposition rose in power and began to take over the major military roles from the secular democratic opposition, more Muslims from around the world arrived to join them. In some of the Islamist organizations, foreign fighters soon outnumbered Syrians.

In early 2015, the *New York Times* chronicled the wide range of reasons for the surge of potential fighters flocking to Syria to join the most extremist organizations. "Young men in Bosnia and Kosovo are traveling to Syria for financial gain, including recruiting bonuses some groups offer, counterterrorism specialists say. Others from the Middle East and North Africa are attracted more by the ideology and the Islamic State's self-declared status as a caliphate. Counterterrorism specialists have seen criminal gang members from as far as Sweden seeking adventure and violence in the fight."

There is no question that the process of embracing extremist Islamism very often begins in response to long histories of dispossession, disenfranchisement, exclusion, and denial of rights among immigrant, Muslim or particular Islamic sects, and other minority communities in countries around the world. In the United States, federal and state government policies are in place that continue to marginalize Muslim, Arab, and other immigrant communities. Members of those communities, particularly young people, often are targeted during wars in the Middle East. President Obama acknowledged that "engagement with communities can't be a cover for surveillance. It can't securitize our relationship with Muslim Americans, dealing with them solely through the prism of law enforcement." But he didn't do or even propose anything to actually change the US and local state and municipal policies that do just that. Further, he made the statement at a conference designed to counter recruiting by ISIS and similar organizations, which was held a full seven months after he ordered the bombing of Syria to begin.

In many European, American, and other western Muslim communities, support for ISIS, al-Qaeda, and other Islamist organizations exists despite, rather than because of, the violence of these groups. In 2013 and 2014, reports surfaced of European Muslims traveling to Syria to join ISIS with their entire families, babies and children included, to establish new lives in the so-called caliphate. At the end of 2014, the *Washington Post* profiled a British father, arriving in Syria to join ISIS with his family—his "first four children had been born in London, his native city, but his new baby, wrapped in a fuzzy brown onesie, was born in territory controlled by the Islamic state."

For many supporters from Western countries, the embrace of ISIS or other extremist organizations is often rooted in longstanding grievances at home. Those include permanent unemployment, discrimination, poverty, political dispossession, anger at rising Islamophobia, and the sense of not belonging to their country despite being born and raised there. Laws in Europe that prohibit hate speech are widely seen as perpetuating double standards, since they prohibit anti-Semitism but allow racist and Islamophobic slurs under the guise of free expression. Paris Imam Mehdi Bouzid spoke of Cherif Kouachi, one of the *Charlie Hebdo* attackers, saying, "We had lost him. Their message—the message [of radical Islam]—is tempting to those like Cherif. It promises them a place, acceptance, respect. They do not have that here."

For some young people growing up in the squalid immigrant slums that surround many European cities, desperation and the lack of opportunity set the stage for often-petty criminal activity and sequential jail terms in violent prisons, which sometimes leads to indoctrination into some of the most radical versions of political Islam. Shortly after the *Charlie Hebdo* attack in Paris, the international press started paying attention to studies indicating that, as Reuters described it, "prison radicalization is a problem in countries ranging from Britain and the United States to Afghanistan. However, France stands out because over half its inmates are estimated to be Muslim, many from communities blighted by poverty and unemployment." The disproportion of French prisoners who are Muslims, at 50 percent compared to their estimated 5–10 percent share of the population, reflects the same harsh reality that civil rights attorney and author Michelle Alexander, in her seminal book *The New Jim Crow*, highlighted regarding African-Americans in US prisons: that the criminal justice system perpetuates racial inequality.

In one of the distinctions between ISIS and other jihadi organizations, including al-Qaeda, the declaration of a "caliphate" has led ISIS to focus on recruiting professionals—e.g., doctors and engineers—and families to come to live in this new quasi-state. Images of family life in the "caliphate" are part of the very slick, Web-based recruiting campaigns. In Raqqa, the ISIS "capital" in Syria, thousands of local residents have been forced out, their homes distributed to ISIS fighters, supporters, and their families, who also receive money, electricity, and health care. Reportedly, education for children—boys and girls—is available, shaped by the ISIS version of Islam and Shariah, or Islamic, law. At the same time, extreme brutality—toward local civilians, particularly women, non-Muslims, anyone who opposes ISIS rule, anyone who differs from the ISIS leadership's fanatical interpretations of Islam—remains the norm.

Is the typical ISIS fighter a Muslim of Middle Eastern descent?

Not all foreign supporters are coming from Western countries. As an imprisoned Saudi human rights activist told the *Washington Post*, "So many Saudis are engaged with the Islamic State because of the lack of political freedoms in our country. They are frustrated because they cannot express themselves." Describing young prisoners being recruited to join the Islamic State, he said, "It's like committing suicide for them to join the Islamic State, but they feel that their lives don't matter because of the injustice in this country. That's what happens when people are deprived of their rights."

But throughout 2014, reports also began to surface regarding young people, mainly Europeans, who were either almost secular, non-practicing Muslims or not Muslim at all, choosing to join ISIS or other violent organizations because of alienation or other reasons unrelated to religious extremism. As the author of *Inside British Islam*, Innes Bowen, told *Business Insider* magazine, "There was no single type of person who becomes a radical in the UK, and no single pathway to their ideology. 'There must be a range of motivations—a sense of adventure, a misplaced sense of duty or idealism—some of those recruited are well versed in ideology and the politics of their radical cause, others are surprisingly ignorant.'" Numerous press outlets reported the story of young recruits in Europe who purchased *Islam for Dummies* and *The Koran for Dummies* on Amazon before leaving for the Middle East.

The assumption that most would-be terrorist recruits are likely to be practicing Muslims, most likely from an Arab or other immigrant background, and somehow identifiable through racial and religious profiling, needs to remain suspect. A classified 2008 report from Britain's MI5 that was leaked to *The Guardian* acknowledged that,

> Far from being religious zealots, a large number of those involved in terrorism do not practice their faith regularly. Many lack religious literacy and could...be regarded as religious novices. ...The MI5 analysts concluded that "a well-established religious identity actually protects against violent radicalization...." British-based terrorists are as ethnically diverse as the UK Muslim population, with individuals from Pakistani, Middle Eastern, and Caucasian backgrounds. MI5 says assumptions cannot be made about suspects based on skin colour, ethnic heritage or nationality. ...The researchers conclude that the results of their work "challenge many of the stereotypes that are held about who becomes a terrorist and why." Crucially, the research has revealed that those who become terrorists "are a diverse collection of individuals, fitting no single demographic profile, nor do they all follow a typical pathway to violent extremism."

While circumstances—particularly the rise of social media— have certainly changed since 2008, the notion that terrorists are most likely to come from particular communities that can be identified by law enforcement needs to be continually challenged.

—PART III—

THE NEW GLOBAL WAR ON TERROR

What are the origins of the "new" global war on terror?

In 2011, ISI reemerged in Iraq and, for the first time, in Syria, in the context of the devastating civil war then beginning to rage across that country. The group changed its name again, this time to ISIS—the Islamic State in Iraq and Syria, or, by some accounts, Islamic State in Iraq and al-Sham (Arabic for "Greater Syria"). In Syria, though, relations between ISIS and the al-Qaeda leadership deteriorated even as ISIS gained strength and began to seize and hold territory in both Syria and Iraq, effectively erasing the long border between the two countries. ISIS leader al-Baghdadi tried to assert control of Jabhat an-Nusra, or the Nusra Front, the "official" al-Qaeda affiliate in Syria, which had been there much longer than ISIS. In response to that as well as other theological and political power struggles, al-Qaeda leader Ayman al-Zawahiri reiterated his support for the Nusra Front as its Syrian representative, and in February 2014 issued a statement renouncing ISIS.

Just a few months later, ISIS began an escalated military campaign, including its seizure of major cities both in Syria (Raqqa), and in Iraq (Mosul, the second largest city in the country). In response, the United States sent thousands of troops back into Iraq and began airstrikes over Syria. The second edition of Washington's global war on terror was under way.

And as that war ground on and expanded, US military producers were among the only beneficiaries. On April 18, 2015, the *New York Times* reported that "to wage war in Yemen, Saudi Arabia is using F-15 fighter jets bought from Boeing. Pilots from the United Arab Emirates are flying Lockheed-Martin's F-16 to bomb both Yemen and Syria. Soon, the Emirates are expected to complete a deal with General Atomics for a fleet of Predator drones to run spying missions in their neighborhood. As the Middle East descends into proxy wars, sectarian conflicts, and battles against terrorist networks, countries in the region that have stockpiled American military hardware are now actually using it and wanting more. The result is a boom for American defense contractors looking for foreign business in an era of shrinking Pentagon budgets—but also the prospect of a dangerous new arms race in a region where the map of alliances has been sharply redrawn."

How does Obama's war on terror differ from Bush's war on terror?

George W. Bush's original global war on terror never really ended. President Obama came into office pledging to end what he called the "dumb" war in Iraq, but also promising to pay more attention to—read "escalate"—the supposedly "good" war in Afghanistan. He did both. (It should be noted that the final troop withdrawal from Iraq was not in fact the president's choice. Obama tried and failed to persuade the Iraqi parliament to grant impunity to US occupying troops after 2011; if he had succeeded, thousands of them would not have been withdrawn at all.)

In his first months in office in 2009, President Obama immediately escalated the US presence in Afghanistan, sending first 17,000 and then 33,000 additional troops there. By February 2015 about 11,000 of those troops remained, with plans for them to continue combat, training, and special operations until at least the end of 2016. Obama joined the European-initiated NATO air assault on Libya in 2011, and throughout his presidency he has escalated drone strikes in Yemen and Somalia and continued strikes in Pakistan and Afghanistan. In September 2014 thousands of US troops were back in Iraq for training and special operations, and US warplanes were bombing ISIS, Nusra Front and other targets in Iraq and Syria. In February 2015 the *New York Times* editorial board called it "Washington's new war in the Middle East," and two months later, in May 2015, the US announced publicly that its special forces were indeed on the ground in Syria killing and capturing alleged ISIS militants.

In fact, the earlier edition of the war never really ended. Some of the same reasons for the war remain—issues of oil, stability, military bases, strategic reach across the broader Middle East are still important. Military response is still the default position when the public or policymakers pressure the powers that be to "do something."

But the global war on terror was always about shaping public opinion in the United States as well as carrying out the war itself. And by the time of the temporary withdrawal of all US troops from Iraq at the end of 2011 and the significant reduction of US troop numbers in Afghanistan under way from that same period, and the reduced public awareness of the escalating drone attacks, the power of the "global war on terror" paradigm to shape America's overall role in the world had already begun to diminish.

President Obama quickly rejected Bush's phraseology, but he continued the global war on terror in practice. He eventually settled on a more dispassionate-sounding handle to describe the wars raging in Iraq and Afghanistan, as well as his less publicized drone and assassination wars. The Pentagon's office of security review made it official in a May 2009 email to Defense Department staff, which stated, "[T]his administration prefers to avoid using the term 'Long War' or 'Global War on Terror.' Please use 'Overseas Contingency Operation.'"

There were other differences too. Under Obama, the White House and the Pentagon were not led by neo-conservative extremists with an ideological commitment to using war to expand US influence around the world. There are numerous strategic differences between the administrations as well, including on questions of where the war is fought, who and what are the targets, who is defined as the "enemy," the relative reliance on drones and reluctance to use large-scale ground forces. But ultimately, Obama's version of the global war on terror has largely continued in the same vein as his predecessor. Regardless of who was in the White House, the war has clearly never succeeded in any of its ostensible goals, whether ending the threat of terrorism or bringing pro-American stability, development, and maybe even democracy to conflict-ridden and human rights-denying (but resource-rich) countries.

Obama continued the use of military force as a supposed answer to terrorism, but he had campaigned against the Iraq war, and was widely seen as reluctant to embrace the full-scale use of force. His agreement to go to war in Libya came only in response to pressure from supporters of "humanitarian intervention" in the State Department, including then-Secretary of State Hillary Clinton, National Security Adviser Susan Rice, and UN Ambassador Samantha Power. He came close to attacking Syria directly in 2013, but pulled back in the face of the loss of British support and of massive antiwar mobilization at home. This was not a Bush-style administration in which ideologues eager for war held every powerful seat in the departments of state and defense as well as the White House.

Bush's first request for an authorization for the use of force (AUMF), just two days after 9/11, allowed the president to use "all necessary and appropriate force against those nations, organizations, or persons he determines planned, authorized, committed, or aided the terrorist attacks that occurred on September 11, 2001, or harbored such organizations or persons, in order to prevent any future acts of international terrorism against the United States by such nations, organizations or persons."

It contained no restrictions as to place, kind of weapons, concern for civilians, or length of time. The authorization was for global, endless war. Only one member of Congress, Representative Barbara Lee of California, voted against the resolution. (Other members have since said that their biggest regret in Congress was having voted for the use of force.) A separate AUMF was passed approving war in Iraq in 2002; again it contained no limits as to time, place, or anything else. Even though the White House eventually requested a new authorization specific to ISIS, the Obama administration maintained the claim that at least the 2001 and maybe the 2002 AUMFs provided sufficient authorization for its use of force in Syria and Iraq in 2014.

In 2010 and 2011, as US troops were being pulled out of Iraq and the war in Afghanistan stalled, President Obama seemed to shift toward greater engagement with some Islamist governments and political forces. While the wars, particularly the drone war, continued at the same pace, a closer US alliance with Turkey's Islamist-leaning government emerged. Then, when the Arab Spring erupted at the end of 2010, the Obama administration began a cautious shift away from some longstanding pro-US dictatorships. It moved to recognize, if not embrace, some of the Islamist parties and leaders who came to power through popular uprisings in which they were allied with broad secular coalitions, including leftist and labor, women's rights and human rights organizations, as well as pro-western political forces and ultimately parts of the military.

In Tunisia, the White House leaned toward new openness to, if not actual support of, the Islamist (often described as "moderate Islamist") Ennahda Party, which won early elections after the overthrow of the country's US-backed Zine el Abidine Ben Ali, who had ruled with an iron fist for almost a quarter-century. As protests spread across Egypt in January 2011, then-Secretary of State Hillary Clinton reaffirmed US support for longstanding US-armed and -funded dictator Hosni Mubarak, saying, "Our assessment is that the Egyptian government is stable and is looking for ways to respond to the legitimate needs and interests of the Egyptian people." As the uprising of Tahrir Square broke out, with millions of Egyptians filling the streets, the administration relented. After some days of refusing to relinquish support for Mubarak, the White House, however reluctantly, called for Mubarak to step down. It later recognized, though never supported, the democratically elected President Mohamed Morsi, who came to power with the backing of the Muslim Brotherhood, the largest component of the broad secular-religious movement that had swept away Mubarak's legitimacy and pushed the military to depose him.

It's unclear whether that tentative shift toward recognition of Islamist social forces might have slowed the US drive to war. But the shift never reflected an all-sided split from traditional US strategic goals—even the recognition of Islamist-oriented governments was still based on Washington's search for regional pro-US stability rather than any commitment to democracy or representation of all sectors of Arab society. In any event, the shift was not to last.

Even as the US recognized President Morsi, the $1.8 billion of US aid to Egypt continued to flow from the Pentagon directly to the

Egyptian military, bypassing the government. When Egypt's military carried out its brutal anti-Morsi coup in the summer of 2012, the US continued its military-to-military relationship as if nothing had changed. The tentative feints toward a closer relationship with the democratically elected, Islamist-oriented government in Turkey soon faded, and the traditional relationship—"NATO ally but not a close one"—reemerged.

As Islamist forces rose to the most influential and powerful positions in the anti-Qaddafi uprising in Libya and the once-democratic and secular anti-Assad rebellion in Syria, the US found itself fighting on the same side as some of the most brutal Islamist forces in the region. Yet it still claimed, against an increasingly visible reality, to be allied only with the secular and "moderate" forces, not the Islamists.

Obama continued to resist acknowledging that he was commanding a widening war in the Middle East. It was the renewed pressure for just such a full-scale war against ISIS in 2014 that brought the "global war on terror" back to public attention. So it's not really a new war that Obama no longer denies, but a re-energized and escalated one, with renewed airstrikes against targets in Iraq and Syria, a new commitment to send thousands of US troops back to Iraq, long delays in withdrawing troops from Afghanistan, and an Obama administration effort to gain congressional authorization for the use of force against ISIS. (If the White House has its way, that authorization will have no limits on geographic scope, breadth of targets, or years of validity.)

How did the overthrow of Qaddafi in Libya lead to ongoing conflict there?

In 2011, what began as a non-violent political challenge to the erratic dictatorship of Muammar al-Qaddafi in Libya quickly morphed into an armed effort to overthrow the regime. With the regime's brutal response to the protests as a pretext, NATO quickly agreed to requests by Europe and then the US to intervene militarily. The US/NATO air assault, authorized by the United Nations Security

Council for humanitarian protection only, immediately (as predicted) turned into another military campaign of regime change in the Middle East. Qaddafi was overthrown, captured, and murdered, and the country descended into a maelstrom of competing militias. Extremist Islamist forces emerged among the most powerful, and the regime's vast arsenal of weapons disappeared from warehouses only to reappear throughout the country and across Libya's borders to fuel new—mainly Islamist—insurgencies across Africa and the Middle East. The Libyan weapons continue to fuel Washington's opponents in the global war on terror.

What was the significance of the fall of Mosul?

As Patrick Cockburn, perhaps the best Western journalist working in the broader Middle East, described it in his seminal book *The Jihadis Return: ISIS and the New Sunni Uprising*, "the 'war on terror,' the waging of which has shaped the political landscape for so much of the world since 2001, has demonstrably failed. Until the fall of Mosul, nobody paid much attention."

When Mosul, Iraq's second-largest city, was overrun by ISIS in June 2014, the US-trained, US-armed, and US-paid Iraqi military largely fled the advance of a few thousand ISIS fighters, leaving behind most of their weapons. ISIS then imposed its extreme version of Islam, and devastating hardships, upon the people of Mosul. After Mosul, President Obama's version of the global war on terror was reborn and re-energized, with US troops back to Iraq, renewed US bombing in Iraq, and the expansion of bombing and on-the-ground special forces raids in Syria. Weapons from post-Qaddafi Libya, brought about by the US-NATO air war authorized by Obama in 2011, flooded the region, many of them turning up in the hands of ISIS fighters. Many more civilians were killed—many by ISIS and still more under US bombs. It was after "the fall of Mosul," in Cockburn's words, but while a lot more people were paying attention, the new global war still wasn't helping the people forced to live under ISIS rule.

How effective have the Obama administration's strategies played out in this new war?

President Obama stated his official goal in the new global war on terror plainly: "Our objective is clear: We will degrade, and ultimately destroy [ISIS] through a comprehensive and sustained counterterrorism strategy." But there is a huge disconnect between that goal and the action the administration is taking.

Obama began using that language in early September 2014, just as he was launching the US bombing of Syria and returning US troops to Iraq. At just about the same time, according to a classified document quoted later in the *New York Times*, Maj. Gen. Michael K. Nagata, commander of US special forces in the Middle East, confessed, "We do not understand the movement [ISIS], and until we do, we are not going to defeat it. We have not defeated the idea. We do not even understand the idea."

That was quite an admission. Understanding one's perceived enemy must always be the first step in deciding what to do about it. The close proximity of "we don't understand" and "we're sending the troops and the bombs" provides a good indication of why the goals of "degrade and destroy" have not been achieved. Rather, the US military involvement has left ISIS intact and to some degree even stronger than before.

By the time the *Times* wrote about Nagata's efforts to understand the terrorist organization, months into Obama's military campaign, ISIS was expanding, not collapsing, under the bombs. When the bombing of Syria and Iraq began in the fall of 2014, the White House had said its stated goal was to destroy the headquarters of the violent and extremist ISIS. But you can't bomb extremism out of existence. The US had tried that with al-Qaeda in Afghanistan and it didn't work there either. By 2010 the CIA admitted that only somewhere between 50 and 100 Afghan fighters were left in all of Afghanistan, though nearly 100,000 US troops remained in the country. The bombing campaigns had killed some fighters and forced many more to flee across Afghanistan's borders, but the organization's offshoots had already started taking root in a host of neighboring countries.

The same thing is happening with ISIS. On September 30, 2014, Vice News reported, "Coalition warplanes launched a fresh wave of airstrikes against Islamic State targets across Syria on Saturday, despite demonstrations in the town of al-Atareb condemning the US-led assault, which residents have blamed for the deaths of at least 27 people, including civilians, in the area. The protests in al-Atareb on Friday brought together dozens of people who marched and chanted through the streets, some holding placards. One sign written in English read: 'Don't kill our children by your aircrafts.' The outcry from residents comes three days after coalition forces conducted joint drone and plane strikes against a militant base. The bodies of at least 27 locals were pulled out of the rubble, including an unspecified number of civilians, according to a report from a group called the al-Atareb Civil Defense."

The bombs the US dropped on the ISIS capital did not land on "extremism," they fell on al-Atareb, or on Raqqa, a 2,000 year-old Syrian city with a population of more than a quarter-million people: men, women and children who had no say in the ISIS takeover of their city. The Pentagon reported the bombing of targets like a post office and the governor's compound, so the likelihood of large number of casualties among civilians unable to flee was almost certain, although with Raqqa remaining under ISIS control at least through April 2015, it is not possible to confirm casualty numbers.

US airstrikes and bombing have not brought about any strategic defeats of ISIS. The Syria bombing began in Kobane, for example, in September 2014, following graphic media coverage of the ISIS assault on the city, just over the Turkish border. The US launched its bombing campaign in response to the humanitarian disaster, which appeared nightly on high-def video streamed directly from cameras on the Turkish side of the border, available to every television and social media platform in the world. Yet just a couple of weeks into the bombing campaign, Secretary of State John Kerry announced in a public speech that Kobane was not even a "strategic objective" for the US.

In its January 2015 issue, *Mother Jones* magazine, noting Kobane's lack of strategic significance, asked and answered the question, "So why all those bombs?"

> Since September 23, when air strikes in Syria began, US and coalition forces have pummeled both Syria and Iraq with nearly 2,000 air strikes. As of early this week, 870 of those strikes were in Syria; almost 70 percent of these Syrian strikes have focused on Kobane and its surroundings. The total area, about the same size as Rhode Island, covers less than two percent of Syria and the majority of the population are ethnic Kurds.

> There's a reason that Kobane became so symbolically important: Stories of the brave Kurdish fighters defending the small border city against ISIS swept international headlines last September, and the public demanded that the US step in to prevent a humanitarian disaster. The Kurds, unable to defeat ISIS on their own, turned the tide once they had coalition air support. "Seventy-five percent of all US strikes in Syria were on Kobane," Thomas Pierret, a Syria specialist at the University of Edinburgh told *Ekurd Daily*, a Kurdish news site last week. "You give any force on the ground that kind of aerial support and they will get the upper hand." It has cost taxpayers $8.2 million a day, on average, to conduct the entire airstrike campaign.

By January 2015, ISIS was mostly pushed out of Kobane. Victory was declared. It was another example of what used to be called "the CNN factor" (but might today be known as the Twitter factor): A media-driven public demands that the government "do something," usually defined as something military, and the government accedes to that demand. But, as *Mother Jones* noted at the time, "ISIS now occupies one-third of Syria, or twice what it did when the campaign began, and around 400,000 people have fled Kobane alone. US military officials have conceded that Kobane isn't strategically important."

By the time the US was ready to make that admission, the damage had been done. As *Al Jazeera* reported, "tens of thousands of Syrian Kurds who fled their homes due to fighting in Kobane have returned to find at least half of the town destroyed, Kobane officials said.... Rafaat al-Rifai, reporting from Kobane, said destruction was visible everywhere, especially in places where ISIL fighters were based and later targeted by US-led air strikes." The twisted logic of Vietnam could be applied once again to Kobane: "It became necessary to destroy the town to save it."

What was behind the US decision to escalate its direct military involvement in Middle East conflicts in 2014?

The question remains as to why the United States chose—and it was a choice, not a necessity—to resume direct engagement in the global war on terror after several years of winding down US troops and airstrikes in favor of an expanded drone war fought from afar. The horrific up-close-and-personal violence of ISIS, its imposition of draconian punishments and a legal system rooted in the seventh century, even its capture of swaths of territory, all made the terrorist organization dangerous to people living under its control. But that didn't make it a threat to the US.

In early September 2014, just as the US bombing resumption and troop return was being prepared, the outgoing head of the National Counterterrorism Center, Matthew Olsen, said "there is no credible information that [ISIS] is planning to attack the United States," and there is "no indication at this point of a cell of foreign fighters operating in the United States—full stop."

So why were some influential Washington voices so eager to go to war in Syria and to return to Iraq? For some, regime change against all of the Middle Eastern states that rejected Washington's domination—Iraq, Syria, Iran (Libya was perhaps a bonus)—remained a continuing commitment. They and others recognized that Iran was the most important Middle East power remaining hostile to US and Israeli interests, and Tehran was the key regional supporter of the Assad regime in Damascus. So in the early part of the Syrian civil war, US actions against Syria were aimed less at going after the Syrian regime for its own sake than at weakening Iran by undermining its most important Arab ally. Few voices urged greater US military engagement primarily to protect Syrian or Iraqi civilians—if that happened, it would be a side effect, useful for mobilizing public support.

Until about May 2013, Obama was leading the faction of his administration that was very reluctant to participate directly in the Syria civil war. Despite incremental US military involvement—sending 500 CIA agents to train rebel fighters in Jordan, helping Turkey "facilitate" weapons transfers to make sure they went to the "right" rebel forces, and allowing (perhaps encouraging) Saudi Arabia and Qatar to send US weapons directly to rebel forces—Obama himself seemed unwilling to go further. There was no rising majority in Washington for a no-fly zone, for arming the rebels directly, or for airstrikes against Syrian missile defenses.

But the pressure continued from political forces who had long wanted the US to support regime change in Damascus and from the anti-Iran contingent. The shift for the administration came in August 2013, with the (still unproved) claim that Bashar al-Assad was responsible for a chemical weapons attack in the outskirts of Damascus. The media coverage showing graphic evidence of the attack helped push a previously war-averse public toward a renewed demand that the US "do something." The pro-war officials and their counterparts among the right-wing think tanks, the punditry, and the media escalated the pressure as well, and the Obama administration relented, threatening to go to war directly in Syria.

Still, a majority in the US opposed or at least were hesitant about entering a new war in the Middle East, and the Obama administration faced the risk of significant opposition from the president's political base. A decision by the British parliament to reject joining the US in a Syrian war allowed Obama to pivot toward Congress to decide. In response, a massive anti-war mobilization immediately took shape, pressuring Congress and ultimately forcing the administration to accept a face-saving arrangement initiated by Russia. (See p. 101 for more on the US decision.) A new escalation to a US war in Syria was averted—temporarily.

How did the US justify its return of troops to Syria and Iraq?

A year later, officially in response to the crisis facing the Syrian Yazidis besieged by ISIS on Mount Sinjar, the new war was officially launched. That war, to "degrade and destroy ISIS," has largely failed. ISIS continues to control huge swaths of territory and millions of people, despite the US and allied airstrikes killing what the Pentagon estimates may be up to 6,000 ISIS fighters, despite the local success of Syrian PYG Kurdish forces in Mount Sinjar in September 2014 and PYG plus Iraqi Kurdish peshmerga troops in Kobane in January 2015. Even the successful expulsion of ISIS from Tikrit in April 2015—accomplished by Iraqi Shi'a militias backed by some of the Iraqi military along with first Iranian and then US airstrikes—does not mean ISIS is finished.

In his January 2015 State of the Union address, President Obama said his goal was to diminish the primacy of the military overseas. "When we make rash decisions," he said, "reacting to the headlines instead of using our heads; when the first response to a challenge is to send in our military—then we risk getting drawn into unnecessary conflicts, and neglect the broader strategy we need for a safer, more prosperous world. That's what our enemies want us to do."

He was absolutely right. The problem was that his policy responding to the ISIS crisis, beginning in August 2014, was precisely what he warned against: It was a rash decision, it was driven by headlines, it privileged immediate military action while only mentioning non-military options in passing. It drew the United States into an unnecessary conflict and was exactly what ISIS wanted. And it not only neglected the broader strategy, it rendered much of it impossible—closing the Guantánamo Bay prison becomes much less of a priority while US troops are on the ground and US bomber pilots are above the skies over Iraq and Syria.

Later in his speech Obama bragged that "in Iraq and Syria, American leadership—including our military power—is stopping

ISIL's advance. Instead of getting dragged into another ground war in the Middle East, we are leading a broad coalition, including Arab nations, to degrade and ultimately destroy this terrorist group. We're also supporting a moderate opposition in Syria that can help us in this effort, and assisting people everywhere who stand up to the bankrupt ideology of violent extremism."

But the reality was starkly different. Neither American leadership nor anything else was stopping the advance of ISIS, as demonstrated by ISIS gains in Ramadi and Palmyra in 2015. Far from avoiding "another ground war in the Middle East," the US was already in another ground war, with thousands of troops back in Iraq. In February 2015 Secretary of State John Kerry made clear his view that the door should be left open for ground troops in Syria as well. And a month later, the chairman of the Joint Chiefs of Staff, Gen. Martin Dempsey, said he would not rule out sending US ground troops into Syria.

The "moderate opposition" in Syria used to mean what the US described as secular and generally pro-Western armed anti-Assad rebels, but most of them have either collapsed or joined ISIS or one of the other not-so-moderate opposition forces. And as for "people everywhere who stand up to the bankrupt ideology of violent extremism," in Obama's words, in Iraq that would mean primarily Iran along with the Shi'a militias it supports, which by early 2015 were playing the largest military role in fighting ISIS in Tikrit.

How did the Obama administration gain authorization for the US return to Syria and Iraq?

In 2013 Obama tossed decision-making to Congress as a way of deflecting the pressure for war in Syria over chemical weapons, but in 2014 the Obama administration left Congress completely out of the equation in the decision to launch its war in Syria and return troops to Iraq. Instead, the White House claimed its war was legal by relying on the Authorizations for the Use of Military Force passed in 2001 (against al-Qaeda) and 2002 (against Iraq). Neither of those authorizations, of course, actually legitimized new wars in Iraq or Syria.

The 2001 authority, passed just three days after the 9/11 attacks, allowed war against countries, organizations, or people who "planned, authorized, committed, or aided the terrorist attacks that occurred on September 11" or who "harbored such organizations or persons." ISIS did not even exist in 2001—its original organizational predecessor only emerged in 2004 in response to the US invasion of Iraq.

The 2002 AUMF was drafted to give the president authority to "defend the national security of the United States against the continuing threat posed by Iraq; and (2) enforce all relevant United Nations Security Council resolutions regarding Iraq." With the Iraqi government at least officially on board with the US-led anti-ISIS "coalition" a decade later, it would be hard for the administration to justify relying on that earlier authority.

But rely it did. And Congress was, for some months, only too willing to allow the administration to carry out the new war without its permission. Many Republicans supported the war and had little interest in curbing presidential power (even a president they despised) to wage it. And while many Democrats opposed the war, loyalty to the Democratic president slowed their efforts to mobilize against it. Some in Congress chose a middle ground as a way to avoid taking a clear position, claiming that the White House must first propose language for a new AUMF and standing back until it did.

Seven months into the new war on terror, in mid-February 2015, the administration finally submitted language to Congress for a new authorization. It would finally repeal the Iraq authorization, but the 2001 al-Qaeda authority would stay in place. Conveniently, that authorization had no sunset clause, no end point, so the White House could continue to rely on it for anything too restrictive in a new AUMF.

The White House language was broadly drafted, calling for at least three more years of military force without geographic restrictions. It would allow deployment of unlimited troops with the only prohibition on "enduring offensive ground combat operations," a description so vague as to be meaningless, particularly since new deployments of ground troops had already been sent back to Iraq by the time the AUMF was proposed. Like the 2001 authorization, it defined the "enemy" in extremely broad terms, calling for war against any person "fighting for, on behalf of, or alongside [ISIS] or any closely-related successor entity in hostilities against the United States or its coalition partners."

Both Congress and the administration estimated it would take months to agree on the final terms of a new authorization. In the meantime the war would continue.

Have US airstrikes stemmed the growth of ISIS and al-Qaeda?

Every bomb the US drops recruits more supporters. As the Pentagon-linked RAND Corporation noted in March 2013, the 2003 American invasion of Iraq "provided al-Qaeda with a new front, a new recruiting poster, and a new destination for global jihadists." The Chatham House research organization in London reported that the war "gave a boost to the al-Qaeda network's propaganda, recruitment and fundraising." Today's ISIS fighters will likely see the same boost in morale and enrollment from US planes dropping bombs and from US troops coming back on the ground, even if some military targets are destroyed or some ISIS supporters (or their families) killed.

The US military is not stopping ISIS. In fact the influence of ISIS, if not its actual organization, is growing as US airstrikes continue. In February 2015 the *New York Times* reported that ISIS was "expanding beyond its base in Syria and Iraq to establish militant affiliates in Afghanistan, Algeria, Egypt and Libya, American intelligence officials assert, raising the prospect of a new global war on terror. Intelligence officials estimate that the group's fighters number 20,000 to 31,500 in Syria and Iraq. There are less formal pledges of support from 'probably at least a couple hundred extremists' in countries such as Jordan, Lebanon, Saudi Arabia, Tunisia and Yemen, according to an American counterterrorism official."

Such reports are likely severely exaggerated—"a couple hundred extremists" does not make a global terrorist organization. Even the *Times* article itself acknowledged that it was unclear "to what extent this is an opportunistic rebranding by some jihadist upstarts hoping to draft new members by playing off the notoriety of the Islamic State."

It is far from certain that pledges of loyalty to ISIS from small groups of jihadis, or even from larger organized groups that may indeed pose a local threat, such as Boko Haram in Nigeria, represent anything close to a real increase in ISIS's threat. But claims of ISIS expansion—many of them becoming front-page stories in major US newspapers—do ratchet up the fear factor among the US public. A similar phenomenon occurred during George W. Bush's global war on terror. Abu Sayyaf, a violent but quite tiny gang of criminal thugs in the southern island of Mindanao in the Philippines explained their violence in an Islamist framework. In a claim accepted unequivocally by the mainstream US press, the Bush administration upgraded the status of the gang to that of the just-discovered Southeast Asian branch of al-Qaeda, leading to a vast escalation in US military involvement in the Philippines. That was, of course, before extremist organizations had come to use the Internet and social media to issue their own declarations. But the relative truth of the claims of ISIS connections remains equally suspect.

US intelligence analysts told the *New York Times* in March 2015 that "it remained unclear what specific fighting capabilities, if any, the relationship [with ISIS] would add to Boko Haram, or how soon." But by that time the US had already significantly increased its military presence in Africa. The *Times* reported more than 200 US special operations troops training local forces just in West Africa, plus Air Force Reaper surveillance drones supporting on-the-ground French military actions in Niger and Mali. Significantly, the US military escalation also included Navy SEALS training Nigerian commandos—not to go after Boko Haram, but "for action in the oil-rich delta" where the Nigerian government has historically collaborated with western oil companies in a savage military campaign against the indigenous population and environment of the Niger Delta.

Whether or not any of the US actions under way in Africa have anything to do with ISIS remains uncertain. What is in fact clear is that seven months of airstrikes that have killed thousands of ISIS fighters, along with unknown numbers of civilians, have not stopped ISIS from advancing in Iraq and Syria. That should not be surprising. Fourteen years of airstrikes and ground war in Afghanistan didn't conquer extremism, or even eliminate al-Qaeda or the Taliban. Twelve years of fighting (in the most recent US war) in Iraq didn't overcome extremists or bring about inclusive or democratic governance. There's no reason to think years of more US fighting in Syria and Iraq or in Egypt and Libya—or Yemen, Somalia, Pakistan, or the other far-flung battlefields of the global war on terror—will lead to any better results. The danger is that US reliance on military action first—and most of the time, military action only—will be expanded far beyond the current war theater to any country where militants of any sort, threats to the United States or not, decide to claim, for reasons of pride or propaganda, some version of the name ISIS for their own.

Are drones playing a different role in this war than they did during the Bush years?

George W. Bush used drones in both Afghanistan and Iraq from the beginning of the wars. He also ordered a relatively small number of drone attacks in Pakistan and Yemen. But under Obama, the use of drones in the US war on terror has vastly expanded, both in intensity and geography, with the drone war conducted far beyond the "official" war zones of Iraq and Afghanistan.

Bush's first drone strike outside of Afghanistan was in Yemen in November 2002. Then there was a break of 18 months, until June 2004 when the first CIA-run drone attack hit Pakistan.

According to the Bureau of Investigative Journalism (BIJ) in London, by the time Obama took office in January 2009, Bush had carried out 51 drone strikes outside of Iraq and Afghanistan, killing between 410 and 595 people, of whom 167 to 332 were civilians, including 102 to 129 children.

Obama left that record in the dust. The BIJ determined that by early 2015, "there have now been nearly nine times more strikes under Obama in Pakistan, Yemen and Somalia than there were under his predecessor, George W. Bush." Obama ordered his first drone strike only three days into his presidency. Since then, US drones have killed more than 3,000 people outside the declared war zones—meaning at least Pakistan, Yemen, and Somalia—of whom nearly 500 were civilians.

While drone strikes continue to kill in Afghanistan—terrorists, "militants," civilians, and children among the victims—the massive expansion of the drone war in countries far from those official war zones, combined with the explicit use of drones for specific assassinations, is perhaps Obama's signature war strategy. The Pentagon conducts drone strikes in Afghanistan (even if based on CIA-compiled intelligence and planning), so these are not kept quite as secret as the CIA drone campaigns elsewhere.

Obama's early choice of the drone war strategy reflected his recognition that along with growing outrage regarding the war in Iraq, long-standing public support for the war in Afghanistan was quickly eroding as well. A weapon that could guarantee that no US casualties would occur—only people "over there" would be killed—would fit easily into that reality. Drones were the perfect weapon for a war based on American exceptionalism.

What are the pros and cons of using drones versus troops on the ground?

Even putting that moral collapse aside, the military value of drone strikes remains suspect. Five months into Obama's first term, noted counterinsurgency expert David Kilcullen and Andrew Exum of the Center for New American Security wrote an op-ed in the *New York Times* describing the use of drones, particularly in Pakistan. They also described other examples: "This is similar to what happened in Somalia in 2005 and 2006, when similar strikes were employed against the forces of the Union of Islamic Courts. While the strikes did kill individual militants who were the targets, public anger over the American show of force solidified the power of extremists. The Islamists' popularity rose and the group became more extreme."

Then, as if anticipating those who later chose, however reluctantly, to support ISIS, they wrote, "While violent extremists may be unpopular, for a frightened population they seem less ominous than a faceless enemy that wages war from afar and often kills more civilians than militants."

In the United States, as more information emerged regarding the Obama administration's reliance on drones, including in the assassination of American citizens and the existence of Tuesday-morning White House meetings devoted to updating the "kill or capture" list, the drone war became a focus of growing anti-war pressure. Debate arose over why Obama, a legal scholar who seemed light years from the Bush administration's disdain for the rule of law, chose to rely so heavily on a tactic so clearly in violation of international law.

Writing in a February 2011 *Newsweek* article titled "Inside the Killing Machine," Tara McKelvey described how "[s]ome counter-terrorism experts say that President Obama and his advisers favor a more aggressive approach because it seems more practical—that administration officials prefer to eliminate terrorism suspects rather than detain them. 'Since the US political and legal situation has made aggressive interrogation a questionable activity anyway, there is less reason to seek to capture rather than kill,' wrote American University's Kenneth Anderson, author of an essay on the subject that was read widely by Obama White House officials."

So apparently Obama administration pragmatism, combined with the combination of public outrage over torture and Obama's inability to close the prison at Guantánamo Bay, meant that killing suspects instead of capturing them was simply deemed easier for all concerned. And drone strikes were by far the quickest, cheapest, and easiest method for such assassinations, even if they were not nearly as accurate, let alone moral, as was claimed.

How has Obama expanded the drone war?

Later in 2011, documents released by WikiLeaks indicated that the US was launching drone attacks against both Yemen and Somalia from a base in Djibouti on the northwest African coast, and the US was planning another drone base in Ethiopia.

Obama's expansion of the drone war was not only geographic. It also included expansion of potential targets. Originally aiming drones at specific, identified individuals—extra-judicial assassination, already way outside the bounds of international law—the administration soon created a particularly frightening version known as "signature" strikes. This meant that any person or group of people acting in a certain way, or present in a particular area, would be considered appropriate targets for drone strike because of their "signature" actions.

While the White House has claimed it no longer relies on such tactics, it has done nothing to repeal the self-granted permission to use them. The *New York Times* reported in 2012 that when Obama "applies his lawyering skills to counterterrorism, it is usually to enable, not constrain, his ferocious campaign against al-Qaeda—even when it comes to killing an American cleric in Yemen, a decision that Mr. Obama told colleagues was 'an easy one.'"

The assassination of American citizens also pulled the drone war into public view. A February 2013 document leaked to NBC News created new outrage, although perhaps not as much as might have been anticipated. It was a memo from Obama's Department of Justice, outlining the

> legal framework for considering the circumstances in which the US government could use lethal force in a foreign country outside the area of active hostilities against a US citizen who is a senior operational leader of al-Qaeda or an associated force of al-Qaeda....Here the Justice Department concludes only that

where the following three conditions are met, a US operation using lethal force in a foreign country against a US citizen who is a senior operational leader of al-Qaeda or an associated force would be lawful: (1) an informed, high-level official of the US government has determined that the targeted individual poses an imminent threat of violent attack against the United States; (2) capture is infeasible and the United States continues to monitor whether capture becomes feasible; and (3) the operation would be conducted in a manner consistent with applicable law of war principles.

Constitutional protection, due process, the right to a trial would be abandoned. International legal prohibitions against targeted assassination would be ignored. And the drone war would be the framework for carrying out this newly "legal" authority—all rooted, we were told, in the 2001 Authorization for the Use of Military Force, which Bush had brought to Congress three days after the 9/11 attacks.

What are the immediate effects of the drone war?

Even putting aside considerations of morality and law, the effect of the drone strikes is devastating. The *Times* reported that "Mr. Obama's ambassador to Pakistan, Cameron P. Munter, has complained to colleagues that the CIA's strikes drive American policy there, saying 'he didn't realize his main job was to kill people,' a colleague said." It went on to note that "drones have replaced Guantánamo as the recruiting tool of choice for militants; in his 2010 guilty plea, Faisal Shahzad, who had tried to set off a car bomb in Times Square, justified targeting civilians by telling the judge, 'When the drones hit, they don't see children.'"

In his 2015 State of the Union address, President Obama said he wanted to impose "prudent limitations" on the drone war. But the only limit that would be remotely "prudent" would have to involve ending the drone war. It violates US and international law, kills civilians, foments more terrorism, and doesn't make anyone safer either in the US or in the countries where the strikes are aimed. The president admitted "we will not be safer if people abroad believe we strike within their countries without regard for the consequence." The problem, of course, is that the hallmark of Obama's drone war is precisely that the US *does* exactly what "people abroad believe"— striking in their countries without regard for the human, legal, or moral consequences. The only way to solve problem is to *stop* the drone war altogether—not just to strike more prudently.

Instead, a month after his speech, the Obama administration announced it would for the first time allow the almost unlimited export of armed drones. The administration crafted a set of principles for recipient countries, many of which have some of the worst human rights records in the world, but those principles are unlikely to have much impact on the longstanding practice of governments like those in Saudi Arabia, Bahrain, or others. The new policy, as the *Times* described it, would be "a delicate balancing act for the Obama White House, which has sought to elevate human rights in its foreign policy but also has employed drone strikes like no other government in history."

That balancing act became even more precarious in late April 2015, when a CIA drone attack targeting alleged al-Qaeda operatives in Pakistan killed two Western hostages, American development expert Warren Weinstein and Italian aid worker Giovanni Lo Porto. President Obama apologized to the families, but maintained, according to the *Wall Street Journal*, that "the initial US assessment of the strike shows it was fully consistent with the guidelines under which his administration conducts such counterterrorism operations."

—PART IV—

THE SYRIAN WAR
IN THE GLOBAL WAR ON TERROR

What is the war in Syria all about?

The Syrian uprising that began in early 2011 was part of the broader regional rising that became known as the Arab Spring. The particular origins and later trajectory of Syria's uprising were also rooted in a terrible drought that was a direct result of climate change, lack of irrigation, and human-caused desertification. It affected about 60 percent of Syrian land and had hit Syria's agricultural production from at least 2007. According to the United Nations, in the first two years alone about 1.3 million people were affected and over 800,000 lost their entire livelihood. As more and more farmers were driven off their land, unable to survive, they flooded the cities looking for work. But as in so many places, job scarcity meant that the few jobs available were likely to go to those who knew someone in power. In Syria it was the Alawites, the long privileged minority group that included the Assad family, who held sway.

The result was that non-Alawites, most of them majority Sunnis, were the least likely to find work, causing a rise in sectarian tensions. Modern Syria had not been a particularly religious country; the Alawite-dominated government had always been ruthlessly secular. But secular or not, it had created a system of economic and political privilege for Alawites. The identity-based politics and privilege were very real, so the new pressures caused by the economic consequence of the climate crisis led to an upsurge in sectarian divides and antagonisms.

At the beginning of the uprising, Syria's non-violent protesters poured into the streets with political/democratic demands that broke open a generations-long culture of fear and paralysis. They did not initially call for the overthrow of the regime of President Bashar al-Assad, but for massive reforms and an end to the terrible repression.

It is important to recognize the crucial divergence between the role the Assad regime has played domestically and its perceived regional position. As *Jadaliyya* co-editor Bassam Haddad wrote, "most people in the region are opposed to the Syrian regime's domestic behavior during the past decades, but they are not opposed to its regional role. The problem is the Syrian regime's internal repression, not its external policies." That could describe the view of many Syrians as well.

Assad was not, like the leaders in Egypt and Tunisia, a U.S.-backed dictator. His domestic policies were brutal, though he remained popular among some sectors of the Syrian population. In the region, Assad served as the self-proclaimed leader of the region's supposed anti-western arc of resistance. That contradiction led some global activists to support the Syrian government as a bastion of anti-imperialism and therefore to condemn all opposition forces as lackeys of Washington.

Such a position of course denied Syrians political agency in their own country, including the right to rise up against a repressive government. But Syria's assumed regional resistance role was far from a complete reality as well. Based on its alliance with Iran (and somewhat for its support of Hezbollah in Lebanon) the United States clearly viewed Syria as an irritant. But Damascus has never been a consistent opponent of US interests. In 1991 the first President Assad, Bashar's father Hafez, sent warplanes to join the US coalition attack against Iraq in Operation Desert Storm. After 9/11 the US collaborated with Bashar al-Assad to send innocent detainees to be interrogated and tortured in Syria.

As to Syria's supposed anti-Israel role in the region, despite the rhetorical and diplomatic antagonism between the two, Syria had been a generally reliable, predictable, and often useful neighbor for Tel Aviv. For example, in 1976 Damascus backed a murderous attack by right-wing Falangists and other Christian militias against the Palestinian refugee camp at Tel al-Zaatar during Lebanon's civil war. Overall, the occasional border clash or small-scale eruption of violence aside, Assad had kept the border, and thus the strategic and water-rich Golan Heights, illegally occupied by Israel since 1967, largely quiescent.

The uprising that began in early 2012 had everything to do with the Syrian government's domestic repression, not its regional or international role. It started with a group of teenage boys in Dera'a, who wrote slogans against the regime on public walls. They were caught, viciously beaten, and tortured in prison. A mass protest movement was the response. At first the protesters did not call for the overthrow of the regime, nor were they calling for the militarization of their struggle or for international military intervention. The Assad government responded with brutal force, and then promised a set of reforms. But it never delivered.

It was defectors from the Syrian military who first took up arms in response to the regime's brutal suppression of the initially non-violent protests. In July 2012, a year into the increasingly militarized struggle, one of the early political opposition leaders, Michel Kilo, said, "If this destruction goes on and the ruling regime wins, it will rule over ruin and thus suffer a strategic defeat. If the opposition wins, it will inherit the country in an unmanageable condition. In any case, it is necessary to stop this violence, stop this bloodshed."

The US and its allies, like some but not all of the Syrian opposition, rejected any negotiations that were not based on Assad stepping down as a precondition to any talks. The military battles escalated, and the defensive use of arms quickly morphed into a network of militias and fighters, largely unaccountable to anyone and uncoordinated among themselves, who began carrying out attacks on security forces and calling for international military assistance. It would soon transform the Syrian uprising into a full-scale civil war, as well as what UN Secretary General Ban Ki-moon in August 2012 described as a "proxy war" in which the "acts of brutality that are being reported may constitute crimes against humanity or war crimes."

Some of the secular opposition militias formed a coalition known as the Free Syrian Army, or FSA, with a political wing, the National Coalition for Syrian Revolution and Opposition Forces, based originally in the tiny Gulf state of Qatar. The US and some of its allies agreed to provide money and arms if the disparate militias united under a single organization. But unity among the various fighting groups, and between the FSA and the coalition, was never achieved, and tensions were exacerbated as competing outside forces, primarily in the region but global as well, began to champion various factions as proxies for their own interests. The US provided some training by CIA teams in Jordan and "non-lethal" military aid, but the Obama administration initially balked at large-scale military support. US allies in the region, particularly Saudi Arabia, Turkey, Qatar, and the UAE, moved much more quickly to provide funds, weapons, and access to illicit border crossings to arm and supply the various militias. In September 2014 Washington officially agreed to provide more and bigger weapons, more training, and more money to the opposition. Soon after, the US initiated direct airstrikes—against ISIS and the Nusra Front, not against the regime—inside Syrian territory.

How successful was US involvement in the Syrian war by 2015?

Far more serious than the issue of the language used to authorize a war that was already under way was the fact that the war itself was failing. A *Wall Street Journal* report in late January 2015 analyzed one of the signature strategies of the US war: the campaign to arm and train so-called moderate forces in Syria. Although the US priority had shifted in Syria from regime change to getting rid of ISIS, the role of the anti-Assad rebels vetted and approved (in some cases first mobilized) by the US remained key. It was not an optimistic view.

> All sides now agree that the U.S.'s effort to aid moderate fighters battling the Assad regime has gone badly. The CIA program was the riskiest foray into Syria since civil war erupted in 2011. Syrian President Bashar al-Assad is clinging to power after more than 200,000 deaths blamed on the war. Moderate fighters control only a fraction of northern Syria, while Islamic State and al-Qaeda's official affiliate, the Nusra Front, have gained ground. Last fall, Nusra overran one trusted commander and seized another's equipment.
>
> Entire CIA-backed rebel units, including fighters numbering in the "low hundreds" who went through the training program,

have changed sides by joining forces with Islamist brigades, quit the fight or gone missing....

Some Obama administration officials say the covert effort accomplished about as much as it could considering the chaotic circumstances in northern Syria and policy disagreements in Washington and elsewhere.

So little was accomplished, not only because of chaos in Syria and policy fights in Washington, the failures resulted also from the reliance of military actions in situations where no military solution was possible. The administration was guaranteed to fail.

So much of what was—and still is—needed to respond to the catastrophe of the Syrian civil war and the rise of ISIS across the region has been ignored, sidelined, or simply done badly.

- There was no serious (meaning equivalent to that invested in the military campaign) effort by the administration to create new diplomatic initiatives with Iran and Russia through the investment of money, presidential attention, the assignment of top diplomats, or other measures.

- There was insufficient continuing work to recognize the centrality of the United Nations in establishing a new forum for regional and global diplomacy aimed at ending the Syrian war.

- The administration did not sufficiently support the UN's effort, begun in 2014, to create local ceasefires in Syria designed to provide immediate humanitarian assistance to besieged communities and potentially achieving broader ceasefire goals in the future.

- The US never showed enough initiative or support for initiatives by other countries or civil-society initiatives to bring opposing sides together for negotiating processes.

- The US provided insufficient financial support for humanitarian assistance for the massive expansion of refugees and internally displaced people, while spending billions on military escalation.

- The US has not acknowledged that its foreign policy not only antagonizes people across the region but in many cases leads to support for even the most extreme terrorist organizations—particularly the invasion and occupation of Iraq; the war on terror's rendition, detention, interrogation, and torture policies; and the uncritical economic, political, and diplomatic backing and protection of Israel's occupation and apartheid policies.

- The administration has achieved nothing beyond a limited understanding of how the war on terror relied on anti-Arab racism and Islamophobia to shape a militarized, surveillance-based law enforcement approach to respond to terrorism that not only violated the US Constitution and international human rights laws and imposed collective punishments on entire targeted communities, but was also guaranteed to fail. And the recognition of the problem never led to alternative policies even being proposed, let alone imposed.

- The US claimed that diplomatic, humanitarian, and other strategies were necessary as well as military action, but the Obama administration never seriously tried to carry out those other goals, and in fact the military attacks made the other work far more difficult.

- The consequences of the US military responses to the Syrian civil war and to the rise of ISIS have made the situation worse, not better. Whatever else the US has learned from more than ten years of US intervention in Iraq, it should be eminently clear that it is not possible to defeat Islamist extremists with airstrikes.

The civil war in Syria seems so complicated —is it really just one war?

Initially a political, largely non-violent popular uprising against a repressive regime, the Syrian civil war became a military conflict that morphed into at least seven separate wars, mainly proxy battles for outside players. They all involved governments within and outside the region that provided money and arms, with some also involving outside fighters, and direct military participation. Whatever the level of outside involvement, these wars were being fought to the last Syrian.

The first was the original civil war that pitted large sectors of the Syrian population—first non-violent political opposition movements and later armed militias of various sorts—against the regime of Bashar al-Assad. During the first years, many, though certainly not all, of Syria's businesspeople as well as numerous minority communities, including the Alawites, other Shi'a, Christians, Druze, some Kurds, and others, tended to side with the government. The Assad regimes, from 1970 through at least 2015, had long protected those minority groups, especially privileging the Alawites. With the erupting civil war, many of those Syrians feared the possibility of a takeover by the majority Sunnis and saw the government as a safer bet despite its brutal treatment of political opponents. The Assad government was armed and backed by Russia and Iran. As the war dragged out for years, and especially with the destruction of much of Aleppo, Syria's business center, by both government and opposition attacks (including by ISIS), business support for the regime diminished. The escalating war also destroyed many of the original non-violent political activists and organizations that had first challenged the regime, with many imprisoned, dead, or injured, or forced into exile; by mid-2013 or so, their voices had been largely suppressed by the violence of the war.

Second was the regional war for hegemonic power, largely between Saudi Arabia and Iran. The other wealthy pro-US oil states of the Gulf, Qatar, Bahrain, and the UAE, along with Jordan, Turkey, and Egypt after the overthrow of elected President Mohamed Morsi, sided with Saudi Arabia (although Qatar and Saudi Arabia competed for influence in Syria as well, backing separate Islamist factions). Iran was backed by the Shi'a Hezbollah party and militia in Lebanon, as well as the Syrian regime itself.

Third was the sectarian war for regional influence, involving the same forces as those above, but shaped around the Sunni-Shi'a divide in the Middle East. Saudi Arabia, backed by the tiny Gulf petro-states, was joined by Egypt, Jordan, and Turkey in a Sunni arc backing the Syrian rebels—"moderate" and Islamist alike. Their Shi'a opponents, led by Iran with the support of Iraq and the power-ful Shi'a militia Hezbollah in Lebanon, are standing by the Syrian government. This does not mean that all these governments are at-tempting to create theocratic states based on their own dominant sects. The government in Syria, for instance, was always ruthlessly secular. But the al-Assad family, which has dominated Syria since 1970, is Alawite (an offshoot of Shi'a Islam). So, when the jobs and perks that come with state power were available for distribution, the Alawite community often received first pick, and then began trying to protect their privileges by allying themselves with other minori-ties—Christians, Druze, and others—against the Sunni majority. It was this war that attracted most of the foreign and primarily Sunni jihadist fighters to Syria. They had little interest in supporting Saudi Arabia's government (and in fact most jihadi organizations from the 1970s and '80s initially emerged to challenge the Saudi monarchy as insufficiently devout), but participating in a war in which Sunni jihadists were winning some victories against the Shi'a/Alawite "in-fidels" proved to be a powerful draw.

Fourth was Syria as another venue for the war between the US and Israel versus Iran. Until the rise of ISIS in Syria and its dissolu-tion of the border between Syria and Iraq, Iran's role as arms sup-plier and strategic backer of the government in Damascus was the primary reason for US interest in Syria. Iran is the most important Middle East power that remains hostile to US and Israeli interests, including opposition to Tel Aviv's nuclear weapons monopoly in the

Middle East. With the rise of ISIS, Syria has become more important as a US target in its own right. But with Tehran still relying on its strategic alliance with Assad, the US maintained its goal of weakening Iran by undermining its most important Arab ally. By late 2014 that effort had been further complicated by Iran's new role against ISIS, with Tehran backing the Iraqi government and providing the most important military and economic support to the Syrian government. Its opposition to ISIS was consistent with its earlier opposition to the pre-ISIS Syrian rebels. The difference now was that Iran's opposition to ISIS put it into a significant, if unspoken, partnership with the United States, even as the US continued efforts to isolate and weaken Iran.

The fifth war positioned Syria as the key Middle East arena of global competition between the US and Russia for regional military/strategic power and influence. Moscow's hold on its naval base at Tartus, on Syria's southern Mediterranean coast, is a key reason for its support for the Syrian government, just as Washington remains committed to the port in Bahrain that hosts the Pentagon's Fifth Fleet. Russia will fight for its Tartus base to the last Syrian, just as the US will do anything, including arming and supporting the 2011 Saudi–UAE military intervention against peaceful Bahraini protesters, to keep its Fifth Fleet in place. US-Russian competition for the region's resources—especially control of oil and natural gas pipelines that could either bypass Syria (aiding US allies) or go through Syria (helping Russia and its allies)—also fuels the conflict. The US-Russia tension played a particularly damaging role in the failed 2012 effort to convene multilateral negotiations to end the Syrian crisis.

The sixth war emerged slightly later, as a battle between the secular and Islamist forces within the anti-Assad opposition. This became increasingly brutal in 2013 and 2014, as powerful Islamist militias either sidelined or, in many cases, attacked secular anti-Assad forces in order to seize territory the secular forces controlled and more often, to seize weapons. The Free Syrian Army (FSA) and other secular forces, some of whom were vetted and deemed "moderate" by the United States, were provided with significant arms. They promised to maintain control of those weapons, including promising to "record the serial number" of every weapon, but it quickly became clear that they had no military capacity to prevent the weapons from falling into the hands of the better-armed, and often better disciplined and better trained, ISIS and other Islamist forces. In fact many secular Syrian fighters themselves defected and joined the Nusra Front and other Islamist militias, including ISIS, desperate to join what looked like a winning (and more reliably salary-paying) side against the Assad government.

By late 2013, the seventh war emerged, this time as a battle within the Islamist forces themselves. It pitted a variety of Islamist groups, most notably the al-Qaeda-linked Nusra Front, against the more powerful, brutal ISIS militia, and was fought over weapons and the control of territory wrested away from the regime.

What was the story behind the chemical weapons attack that led President Obama to threaten to bomb Syria in 2013?

By June of 2013 the civil war in Syria had expanded, with civilians being killed, injured, and dispossessed in huge numbers. Discussions were under way about an international peace conference, but they weren't getting very far. Even as the United States and Russia continued talking about such a meeting, arms shipments from and to all sides continued to threaten even greater escalation.

Arms, mainly US arms, were flowing to Syrian rebel forces from Qatar, the UAE, and Saudi Arabia via Turkey and Jordan as well as directly from the United States. Britain and France forced the European Union to end its prohibition on sending arms to the opposition, and the US cheered the EU decision. Russia announced it was sending Damascus advanced anti-aircraft missiles, and Israel threatened to bomb those missiles if they arrived in Syria.

The war in Syria was more than two years old and had already claimed almost 100,000 deaths. Although US government and media reports often claimed that almost all the dead were civilians and that the Assad regime was responsible for virtually all the violence of the war, the reality was that most of the victims were actually military, and the largest number were supporters of the regime. By June 2013, according to the most widely quoted (and largely pro-opposition) source, the Syrian Observatory for Human Rights, 43 percent of the dead were government soldiers and pro-regime militia fighters. Seventeen percent were anti-Assad fighters, including armed civilians, Syrian army defectors, and foreign supporters of the armed opposition groups. Civilians, many of them in communities that had supported the regime, accounted for 37 percent of the casualties. (By January 2015, the 2014 total casualty figures indicated the percentage of civilians killed that year had dropped to 24 percent.)

Starting early in 2013, pressures began to mount on the Obama administration to engage even more directly in Syria, to establish a no-fly zone, create "safe corridors" for rebel forces, send heavy weapons to the US-identified "good guys" among the rebels, train additional rebels beyond those the 200 CIA agents in Jordan were then training, even to conduct direct airstrikes on Syrian targets. All were on the wish list of the "we want to attack Syria and we want to do it now" caucus in Congress, the punditry, and beyond, who raised numerous reasons why the US should go to war, including claims of chemical weapons being used by the Syrian regime, but without evidence to back up the claims.

President Obama resisted the pressure. But his defiance was weak and cautious. We don't have enough evidence yet, White House officials said on numerous occasions. It's not clear the red line has been crossed. The clear implication was that if there *was* more evidence, if some claimed red line *was* crossed, then all bets would be off. It wasn't clear that the enormous costs—in US taxpayers' money and in Syrian lives—would have been a sufficient deterrent. And the diplomatic rhetoric maintained the ominous "all options are on the table."

By the summer of 2013, the political pressure began to rise again. On August 21, reports surfaced of a poison gas attack against civilians in the suburbs of Damascus, the Syrian capital. What was clear was that it was a horrific attack, with hundreds of people, including many children, dead and injured. What remained unclear and unconfirmed was almost everything else, including how many had died and, crucially, who was responsible.

Initial reports from activists on the ground said about 300 people had been killed. The international aid organization Medicins San Frontieres (MSF, Doctors Without Borders) reported at least 3,600 patients with "neurotoxic" symptoms at hospitals it supported, of whom 355 died. The Syrian Observatory for Human Rights said it had confirmed 502 deaths. French intelligence sources said the figure was at least 281 deaths. And the United States claimed that 1,429 people had been killed. The huge disparity in casualty figures has never been fully explained. There were reports that the US number included all the people who had been killed in the area around Ghouta and nearby Baghdad suburbs within the same three-day period as the chemical attack, meaning many who were killed by other weapons by unknown forces would have been included in the numbers. But that was never confirmed.

The United Nations sent inspectors shortly after the attack to determine the nature of the chemical and the kind of weapons used to disseminate it. They were able to confirm that sarin gas had been used, but they were not mandated to, and did not, determine who was responsible. Even before the UN or any investigation had begun, US officials immediately asserted that the Syrian regime had launched the attack. Human Rights Watch carried out its own investigation and reached the same conclusion based on the trajectory of rockets involved in the attack.

But other sources soon raised serious questions about the validity of the assumption that the Syrian government was the only possible culprit. Fuller examinations, including an AP report of Washington officials punching holes in the administration's allegations, and a widely read investigation by the award-winning journalist Seymour Hersh demonstrated significant weaknesses in the White House claims that only the regime could have launched the attack. Hersh opened his mid-December analysis in the *London Review of Books* with the assessment that

Barack Obama did not tell the whole story this autumn when he tried to make the case that Bashar al-Assad was responsible for the chemical weapons attack near Damascus on 21 August. In some instances, he omitted important intelligence, and in others he presented assumptions as facts. Most significant, he failed to acknowledge something known to the US intelligence community: that the Syrian army is not the only party in the country's civil war with access to sarin, the nerve agent that a UN study concluded—without assessing responsibility—had been used in the rocket attack. In the months before the attack, the American intelligence agencies produced a series of highly classified reports, culminating in a formal Operations Order—a planning document that precedes a ground invasion—citing evidence that the Nusra Front, a jihadi group affiliated with al-Qaida, had mastered the mechanics of creating sarin and was capable of manufacturing it in quantity. When the attack occurred Nusra should have been a suspect, but the administration cherry-picked intelligence to justify a strike against Assad.

For many, the insistence that only the Assad regime could have been the perpetrator, that none of the other military forces in the country (including military defectors and Islamist extremists) could have stolen or produced sarin, echoed the Bush administration's insistence on claims of Baghdad's weapons of mass destruction to justify the invasion and occupation of Iraq ten years earlier. The claims in 2002–03 were demonstrably false, but the war went ahead. A decade later, the clear uncertainty over who might have carried out the chemical attack was almost never taken seriously in the mainstream press, which largely continued to base its coverage on the assumption that the Assad regime was responsible.

The issue shifted quickly from the attack itself to how the United States would/should/might respond. The Obama administration immediately began using the language of "red lines." The Syrian government's use of chemical weapons, we now heard, meant it had crossed a red line and now US military intervention would be on the agenda. The double assumption was that first, the Syrian regime was the known culprit, and second, that "red lines" mean only military options are available, that diplomacy has no role to play. By the end of August, just a week after the chemical attack, the US began moving troops and other military assets into position "just in case." The *Wall Street Journal* quoted an anonymous "senior defense official" who said the military strikes being considered "would be conducted from ships in the Eastern Mediterranean using long-range missiles, without using manned aircraft. 'You do not need basing. You do not need over-flight. You don't need to worry about defenses.'"

Domestic pressure from Congress, pundits, and much of the press continued to rise. Turkey, Britain, and Germany all indicated support for some kind of military action. By early September Israel joined the demand, although Tel Aviv had previously not called for a military assault on Syria. That was partly because the Syrian regime, despite its "resistance" rhetoric, had historically been very useful to Israel, keeping the occupied Golan Heights and the border with Israel quiet. But with the "red line" talk, Prime Minister Netanyahu and others appeared to fear that if there were no US military strike against Syria, Iran would draw the conclusion that Tehran's crossing of a supposed "red line" some time in the future might not result in a military strike either, and therefore Israel joined those calling for military assault on Syria.

Why didn't the US attack Syria over the chemical weapons issue in 2013?

There were numerous impediments to going to war. Neither side of the war debate in Washington seriously took into account that the escalating crisis in the Middle East was taking place simultaneously with a significant decline of US influence. With US economic and diplomatic power reduced, military force remained the one arena in which the US was the indisputable champ. But even 2013's $800 billion US military budget could no longer determine history by itself. For example, US participation in the 2011 NATO campaign in Libya was partly, though not entirely, an attempt to remilitarize the US role in the region and thus reassert US centrality. But whether or not US policymakers were prepared to acknowledge it, that military intervention, like its predecessors in Iraq and Afghanistan, had already failed.

And whether or not they were prepared to anticipate or acknowledge it, military intervention in Syria was certain to fail as well. War always hurts civilians, but US wars generally hurt and kill civilians far from the US, so, unfortunately, the direct human consequences remain far from US public consciousness where they might spark more consistent anti-war opposition.

The greater political problem for US policymakers was that an arms embargo, a necessary component of any serious diplomatic alternative, would also hurt some of their most important campaign contributors: the arms dealers. Despite the increasing recognition that military intervention has failed, the US remains the largest arms exporter in the world; sending US arms to one side of Syria's civil war (and thus extending the war) helped to justify things like Washington's then-pending $10 billion joint arms sale to Israel, Saudi Arabia, and the UAE. Instability in Syria, whatever its cause, would help reinforce calls for increasing the existing $30 billion ten-year commitment of US military aid to Israel. Calling for an arms embargo was never going to be easy.

While it is unclear whether or how much it mattered to Washington decision-makers, there was also the problem of the fundamental illegality of any US military escalation. There are only two conditions in which a military attack by one country against another (including establishment of a no-fly zone) can be legal: Either it is authorized by the UN Security Council, or it is a case of immediate self-defense. Neither condition existed. The Council had been burned in 2011 after approving the use of force in Libya. The US and its allies had promised that the assault would be limited to humanitarian protection, but instead, as many had predicted, it immediately turned into a war for regime change. Two years later, the Security Council, whose veto-wielding permanent members included some of Syria's allies, was certainly not going to repeat that mistake, so there would be no UN authorization. And there was no way even the most hawkish warmongers in the US could claim that Syria's civil war represented an immediate national threat to the United States. Any US attack—with or without a congressional mandate—would have been a clear violation of international law.

There was also the problem of cost. In July 2013, then-Chairman of the Joint Chiefs of Staff, Gen. Martin Dempsey, testified in the Senate that creating a no-fly zone in Syria would cost over a billion dollars per month. He said that a bombing campaign designed, officially, to hit "high-value" targets inside Syria would mean sending hundreds of warplanes, Navy ships, even submarines. Even the more limited military goal of trying to gain control of Syria's chemical weapons stockpile would, Dempsey said, require thousands of Special Forces and many other troops on the ground. Perhaps having learned at least a few of the lessons of the disastrous wars in Afghanistan, Iraq, and most recently Libya, Dempsey acknowledged that, "We have learned from the past 10 years, however, that it is not enough to simply alter the balance of military power without careful consideration of what is necessary in order to preserve a functioning state."

The US government was clearly divided. On the one hand, it allowed the false dichotomy to stand, claiming the only two options were either a military strike or "we let 'em get away with it." The White House did not present alternatives for other kinds of international accountability, such as investigation by the International Criminal Court. Rumors circulated that, knowing that UN authorization was impossible, the US might ask NATO for approval of a military strike against Syria, recalling the Kosovo precedent of 1999. (The problem was, in 1999 and again in 2013, the UN Charter was very clear on what constitutes a legal use of military force—and permission from NATO was not part of that very short list.)

On the other hand, even President Obama had acknowledged that attacking Syria would mean violating international law. Two days after the chemical attack he said, "If the US goes in and attacks another country without a UN mandate and without clear evidence that can be presented, then there are questions in terms of whether international law supports it...and those are considerations that we have to take into account." But international law considerations were not finding much support. CNN described how officials were probably assessing that "the 'strictly legal' should not be allowed to cancel out a legitimate and necessary course of action, even if international law provides no clear support for intervention on humanitarian grounds." What would make an illegal action somehow "legitimate and necessary" was never spelled out.

The next escalation came when UN Secretary General Ban Ki-moon announced that UN inspectors would be withdrawn on August 29, anticipating likely US airstrikes. As *The Guardian* described it, "The accelerated departure of the UN weapons inspectors was reminiscent of similar hasty exit from Iraq more than a decade ago, after receiving a tip-off from western intelligence agencies that US air strikes against Saddam Hussein's regime were imminent." The threat of military engagement was growing.

But the failure of earlier wars in the Middle East—Iraq, Afghanistan, Libya—continued to resonate. Sixty percent of Americans remained opposed to US military intervention in Syria even if chemical weapons were involved. And quickly, anti-war organizations mobilized to build opposition to the drive toward war. The target was Congress, as well as the White House. The goal was to raise the political cost of US military intervention.

The anti-war pressure grew, and more members of Congress began to express hesitation, then opposition to a new US military intervention. Then the international conditions began to change. On August 29, the British Parliament voted against Prime Minister David Cameron's request for authorization for a military strike on Syria. It was a stunning rejection of the government. Cameron immediately announced, "It is clear to me that the British Parliament, reflecting the views of the British people, does not want to see British military action. I get that, and the government will act accordingly." It represented a major blow to the Obama administration's effort to establish an international coalition.

In response, President Obama changed his position. On August 31, he appeared in the White House Rose Garden and announced, "I have decided that the United States should take military action against Syrian regime targets. . . . Our military has positioned assets in the region. The Chairman of the Joint Chiefs has informed me that we are prepared to strike whenever we choose. Moreover, the Chairman has indicated to me that our capacity to execute this mission is not time-sensitive; it will be effective tomorrow, or next week, or one month from now. And I'm prepared to give that order. But having made my decision as Commander-in-Chief based on what I am convinced is our national security interests, I'm also mindful that I'm the President of the world's oldest constitutional democracy. I've long believed that our power is rooted not just in our military might, but in our example as a government of the people, by the people, and for the people. And that's why I've made a second decision: I will seek authorization for the use of force from the American people's representatives in Congress." It was a huge stand-down for the White House.

But the results weren't yet certain. Congress had yet to weigh in, and it was far from certain that Congress would stand up to the pro-war pressure from the White House, in the media, and beyond. Anti-war campaigning escalated quickly. Thousands, eventually hundreds of thousands, of letters, calls, visits, emails, and petitions flooded the offices of members of the House and the Senate. Activists followed members in their home districts, seizing the microphones at town meetings to demand debate over the threat of war. It was an unprecedented mobilization aimed at preventing Congress from authorizing a seemingly imminent war. More and more members were signing on to letters and statements saying they would oppose military force, but it was difficult because alternatives were still not widely familiar enough to provide political safety for many members. It began to appear that there would not be 60 votes in the Senate supporting the use of force, and the possibility of a positive vote in the House of Representatives was looking less and less likely.

A week later, Russian President Vladimir Putin offered a solution. At a September 9th press conference a journalist asked US Secretary of State John Kerry whether there was anything that could prevent a US attack on Syria. He replied, seemingly off the cuff, that Syria could surrender its chemical weapons stockpile to the international community within a week. His Russian counterpart, Foreign Minister Sergei Lavrov, responded with the offer that, "If the establishment of international control over chemical weapons in that country would allow avoiding strikes, we will immediately start working with Damascus... We are calling on the Syrian leadership to not only agree on placing chemical weapons storage sites under international control, but also on its subsequent destruction and fully joining the treaty on prohibition of chemical weapons." The Syrian government quickly agreed.

In response, the Senate majority leader announced that the war vote scheduled for September 11 would now be postponed. The Russian initiative to destroy Syria's chemical weapons quickly morphed into an international coalition. With US-Russian collaboration at its core, that multilateral disarmament alliance succeeded in identifying, removing, and destroying Syria's entire known chemical arsenal by the middle of August 2014.

Neither the House of Representatives nor the US Senate ever voted on military strikes against Syria. The anti-war mobilization had triumphed. For the moment...

Did the US start bombing Syria in August 2014 to save the Yazidis stranded on Mount Sinjar?

By the summer of 2014 virtually all US troops had been out of Iraq for two and a half years. The Middle East was aflame, with the aftermath of the Libya assault, the collapsing of the Arab Spring, especially in Egypt, and most of all the escalating multi-party Syrian civil war all causing new and greater violence. ISIS was gaining ground, seizing territory in what would soon become a huge swath of Syria and Iraq. In early June ISIS captured Mosul, Iraq's second-largest city, as Iraqi army units collapsed and fled, leaving their weapons behind.

On June 19, President Obama reassured a war-weary public— sort of. "American forces will not be returning to combat in Iraq." Then he added, "but we will help Iraqis as they take the fight to terrorists who threaten the Iraqi people, the region, and American interests as well." That caveat made clear that moves toward a new US war, again in Iraq and perhaps beyond, were coming closer.

The White House said it was "only" sending 275 soldiers to protect the already heavily guarded US embassy in Baghdad. It was "only" sending 300 Special Forces, and they were "only" advisers. The Pentagon said there was "only" one aircraft carrier in the region, and a few other warships. Missile strikes were "only" being considered, and no ground troops would be sent. Given the US failure to bring security or stability, let alone democracy, to Iraq with 150,000 troops at a time cycling through multiple deployments in an eight-year war, it wasn't clear what a few hundred troops, warplanes, and warships were supposed to accomplish.

But within two months the pressure mounted for even greater military engagement. The immediate cause was a humanitarian crisis emerging on Mount Sinjar, a mountainous area west of Mosul in Iraq just over the Syrian border. As was the case in other scenarios, the US focused on a particular attack on a non-Muslim minority community to justify its intervention—similar to the more common US/Western focus on "persecuted Christians" across the Middle East as a rationale for its escalating military engagement. The timing of the quite-sudden shift in US policy, in favor of an immediate military response to the horrific massacres, beheadings, and such that had been under way for some time already, also served as a useful distraction from the growing momentum of global opposition to Israel's then-under way 50-day war on Gaza.

ISIS militants attacked the mostly Kurdish Yazidi town of Sinjar on August 3, killing men and kidnapping women. Thousands fled the attack, seeking refuge on Mount Sinjar. There they found relative safety from the attacks, but conditions were dire. There were thousands of families, with many children, trapped on the mountain, facing the midsummer heat with virtually no water or food.

On August 6, President Obama spoke from the White House Rose Garden. "The United States cannot and should not intervene every time there is a crisis in the world," he said. But in the case of the Yazidis, he added, "I believe the United States cannot turn a blind eye." Obama authorized the Pentagon to go, and US planes dropped food and water on August 8.

Obama's authorization, however, went far beyond a humanitarian response—he used the same speech to call for direct military intervention against ISIS, starting with airstrikes in Iraq. "I know that many of you are rightly concerned about any American military action in Iraq, even limited strikes like these," he said. "I understand that. I ran for this office in part to end our war in Iraq and welcome our troops home, and that's what we've done. As commander in chief, I will not allow the United States to be dragged into fighting another war in Iraq."

But the president seemed to be limiting the definition of "another war in Iraq" to a scenario of tens or hundreds of thousands of US ground troops being sent to fight. Other military engagement apparently did not meet his criteria for another war in Iraq. The mantra "no boots on the ground" would continue to be heard, as if officially designated combat ground troops were the only force that equals war. President Obama's actual authorization called for targeted airstrikes not only to help the Yazidis stranded on Mount Sinjar but also to be used against ISIS forces thought to be moving toward Erbil, the capital of Iraq's semi-autonomous Kurdish region.

The authorization was explained as a response to the humanitarian crisis facing the Yazidis and protection of US citizens—the latter factor useful as an excuse for the Obama administration ignoring the need for congressional authorization to return to war in Iraq. It wasn't clear whether and which US citizens might be at risk; there were a few dozen US diplomats and perhaps 200 US troops in and around Erbil, as well as some number of Americans who lived and worked there, but there were no indications any of them had been particularly targeted. Some reports indicated that the US citizen justification was based on the notion that ISIS might try to destroy the Mosul dam, which could create major damage downriver, perhaps even in Baghdad—and there were 5,000 US diplomats, troops, and military contractors staffing one of the largest US embassies in the world there. But again, there was no indication, not even any claim, that Americans had been singled out. (Of course the numbers were small enough that if any or all of the few hundred US citizens in Erbil had been threatened, a single commercial plane could have taken off from the still-open airport and flown them all to safety.)

President Obama's claim that the US was "uniquely capable" of providing humanitarian assistance to the stranded Yazidis also turned out not to be true. The United Nations, even before Obama's August 6 statement, had offered to provide technical help to the Iraqi government to establish a humanitarian airdrop program—something that would have avoided the militarization inevitable in any Pentagon-run program. The Iraqi government had rejected the UN offer, claiming that the global organization did not have the technical capacity to carry it out. But instead of pressuring the US-backed government in Baghdad to take up the UN offer, perhaps agreeing to provide whatever support might have helped further boost United Nations capacity, the US ignored the UN and announced its own plan.

The US military already had experienced the problems inherent in linking humanitarian airdrops with bombing raids. The last time this happened was in November of 2001 in Afghanistan, when the United States Air Force was dropping food packs wrapped in bright yellow plastic to make them easily spotted by Afghan refugees fleeing the US bombing of the cities. But at the same time the US was dropping cluster bombs also wrapped with the same bright yellow plastic. No one knows how many children were killed running to pick up what they thought were food packages that turned out to be cluster bombs.

As it turned out, very little US airpower was used on or around Mount Sinjar—only about four sets of US airstrikes were launched at ISIS positions surrounding the mountain. Far more airstrikes were launched to protect Erbil. On Mount Sinjar itself, the Yazidis were saved not by the US military but by a Syrian Kurdish militia, known as the YPG, or People's Protection Units, which is the Syrian affiliate of the better-known PKK, or Kurdish Workers Party of Turkey. The PKK has long been on Washington's list of "foreign terrorist organizations," so there was a great reluctance in the White House and the Pentagon to acknowledge the role the YPG played in opposing ISIS in Syria in general and in rescuing those stranded on Mount Sinjar in particular. The Yazidis trapped there were able to escape not primarily as a result of US airstrikes, but because the YPG was able to punch an opening through ISIS lines, establishing a protected corridor. They led thousands of Yazidi families down the mountain to safety over the border into Syria, and then along the border to a much safer area where they were able to cross back into Iraq.

The Mount Sinjar crisis provided the Obama administration with the political cover necessary to return to war in Iraq. Despite statements from White House officials that the US was not there to act as the air force of the Kurds or of the Shi'a-dominated Iraqi government, that was exactly what was under way. As the *New York Times* put it, "offensive strikes on militant targets around Erbil and Baghdad would take American involvement in the conflict to a new level—in effect, turning the American Air Force into the Iraqi Air Force."

Who are the "moderates" in Syria?

The term "moderate" has come to be used in Syria to describe political and military forces—people and groups—who oppose the government of Bashar al-Assad, who are more or less secular rather than Islamist, and crucially, who are more or less pro-Western. It is the basis of the US effort to vet or approve opposition forces who might receive US or allied assistance—military, financial, or political. It has little to do with local support or legitimacy.

In early 2015, the Pentagon announced some of the details of its long-delayed plan to train Syrian rebels, who would supposedly be prepared to fight against both ISIS and the Syrian regime of Bashar al-Assad. Involving 1,000 would-be fighters to be trained in Turkey, Qatar, and Saudi Arabia for a year or more, the plan amounted to an acknowledgement that the US-backed "moderate" Syrian rebels that Washington had been talking about supporting for three or four years still did not exist as a genuine fighting force. Instead the US would try to create a whole new force.

The US faces enormous challenges in trying to identify, vet, arm, and train a "moderate" rebel army. As of September 2014, according to Syria scholar Joshua Landis,

> The US is arming and funding 12 to 14 militias in northern Syria and 60 more groups in the south, according to the head of the Syrian Opposition Coalition. These militias have not, thus far, been particularly successful on the battlefield, and none has national reach. Most are based on one charismatic commander or a single region and have not articulated clear ideologies. All depend on foreign money.
>
> The vast majority of Syria's rebel groups have been deemed too Islamist, too sectarian and too anti-democratic by the US—and these are the groups ranged against the ISIL. They span the Salafist ideological gamut, from al-Qaeda's Nusra Front to the 40,000-strong conglomeration of rebel forces united under the banner of the Islamic Front. Despite US skepticism, some of the Sunni Arab regimes Obama has courted as key allies in the anti-ISIL effort have worked with these groups.
>
> Gulf countries reportedly poured money into the Islamic Front until the US convinced them to stop. Islamic Front leaders decried democracy as the "dictatorship of the strong" and called for building an Islamic state. Zahran Alloush, the military chief of the Islamic Front spooked Americans by insisting that Syria be "cleansed of Shi'a and Alawites." ...
>
> Turkey insists that the US arm these anti-ISIL Islamist rebel groups, including the Nusra Front. Disagreement over which rebels to back is one of the reasons Ankara has refused the US requests to use Turkish territory to train rebel forces and as a base from which to carry out attacks on ISIL. The United States'

principal allies simply do not agree on which rebel forces are sufficiently moderate to qualify for support.

Last year the US tried to unite Western-friendly militias under a supreme military command, but that effort proved a debacle. In December the Islamic Front overran the supreme military command of the Free Syrian Army and ransacked its numerous warehouses and depots, making off with large stashes of US and Saudi supplies. The US-backed fighters were hogtied and left in their underwear. When US Ambassador Robert Ford requested that the Islamic Front return the stolen items, he received no response.

Along with its Gulf allies—Saudi Arabia, Qatar, Jordan, Turkey, the UAE in particular—Washington began urging those disparate opposition forces deemed secular and pro-Western enough, although already divided into dozens of separate organizations and militias, to form a unified political movement for negotiations and a unified military command with whom the US and other governments could engage. The forms took shape—the National Coalition for Syrian Revolution and Opposition Forces, known as the Syrian National Coalition, was created in November 2012 and was quickly anointed with US legitimacy as the official political force, and the Free Syrian Army became the official recipient of money and weapons from the Gulf states and talk of training from the United States. But the lack of substance behind those forms remained a problem.

Who are the key forces within the Syrian conflict?

The Syrian National Coalition was made up primarily of exiles— many of them longtime, brave opponents of the Assad regime, representing a wide range of politics, ideas, and constituencies (and some represented no clear constituencies at all). Not surprisingly, they had a very difficult time agreeing on strategy, negotiating positions, what to call for from the United States and the rest of the international community, or anything else. They bickered over leadership positions and spokespeople. And most important, they had few connections to, and even less accountability to, the internal opposition movement inside Syria. That movement included the remnants of the original non-violent political opposition activists, those who had not been arrested, forced into exile, wounded, or killed, many of whom still opposed the militarization of the popular movement, as well as the widely disparate political/military organizations that had emerged later. They made clear to the world, as individual organizations and to some degree collectively, that the Syrian National Coalition did not speak for or represent them. A key point of contention was on the question of negotiating with the regime—many internal opposition forces were willing to consider negotiations even if they were not based on the pre-condition of Assad being removed from power; most of the external leaders were not.

Then there was the Free Syrian Army. Based in Turkey and with its origins in the cohort of former Syrian soldiers who defected to the opposition with their weapons in the first months of the uprising, it seemed like the logical core of a unified rebel military. But soon after its creation in 2011, it expanded to include the wide array of militias and fighters, Islamist and secular, who agreed on little beyond a shared opposition to the Assad regime. By the middle of 2012, infighting within and between the various FSA groups had increased.

The credibility of the military opposition was soon compromised. Syrian refugees who had been driven out by the fighting expressed bitterness about the many officers and generals who had defected from the Syrian military and left the country. The refugees were angry that so many former soldiers chose to stay in Turkey, and they demanded that the experienced military officers return to Syria to assist the opposition fighters. At the same time, reports surfaced of the FSA and other opposition forces committing serious human rights violations and war crimes. According to the *Wall Street Journal*, "aid groups told the State Department that [al-Qaeda-linked] Nusra didn't interfere with their humanitarian deliveries, while elements of the Free Syrian Army, which included trusted commanders, sometimes did."

The practices of the Free Syrian Army were sometimes indistinguishable from some of the most extreme elements of the Islamist opposition. In September 2014, the FSA beheaded six captured ISIS prisoners—just days after the ISIS beheadings of two white Americans, journalists James Foley and Robert Sotloff. The brutality of the ISIS beheadings dominated mainstream media for days and was perhaps the single most important factor in turning US public opinion toward support for direct military re-engagement in Iraq. There was far less discussion of the FSA executions—the "moderate" rebel group first killed an African-American apparently fighting with ISIS and then beheaded the six non-American ISIS fighters they had captured.

At the same time Islamist or jihadi organizations, some of them Syrian but many made up primarily of foreign fighters, began to appear in Syria, especially in the north—and they soon became far more powerful than the FSA organizations. The most influential was the Nusra Front, which imposed a harsh form of Islamic law on its fighters and on civilians even as it led key battles against the regime's army and made clear that its goals linked the overthrow of Assad's government with the establishment of Shariah law in areas under their control. The FSA continued to lose power and influence to their Islamist "allies"— and many FSA fighters abandoned their secular militias to join Nusra or later ISIS—seeing that the Islamist forces were better armed, paid better salaries, and were actually winning more victories.

That phenomenon expanded when ISIS appeared as a separate force in Syria in early 2013, following its split with Nusra (see p.21). During those first months ISIS fought its Islamist and secular opposition rivals far more than it fought the Syrian regime's military. And ISIS continued to expand. *Al-Monitor* reported in November 2013 that "ISIS opened the door for new members without checking the quality of the new members. ISIS started paying $200 a month for each fighter, and thousands of men in ISIS's area of control joined the group."

It may have been partly because of the rising power of the Islamists and relative weakening of the secular FSA-linked forces that led the US to announce its intention of providing $123 million in aid to the Free Syrian Army in April 2013. But that aid was officially limited to "non-lethal" assistance, usually consisting of uniforms, food, and medicine, sometimes military gear such as night-vision goggles, but explicitly not weapons. Given the divisions and tensions within and between the various components of the FSA, it is unclear whether more weapons at that time would have changed the military situation on the ground, but either way the FSA continued to deteriorate, and it continued to lose fighters to the Nusra Front and other Islamist groups. From some time in 2012 the CIA was already engaged in training "vetted" rebel fighters in Jordan, but it was a small-scale (and officially covert) operation, and three years later, there was little evidence of an impact on the battlefield.

While many secular fighters joined ISIS, in other areas the so-called moderates fought alongside ISIS, often openly recognizing that they shared the goal of overthrowing the Syrian government. By late 2014 the US priority had explicitly shifted to attacking ISIS, with the Syrian regime a secondary or even tertiary target, but for the vast majority of opposition fighters—including those deemed "moderate," secular, pro-Western—the target remained the Assad regime. And whatever the priorities of the US, most of those "moderates" were prepared to work with anyone to achieve that goal.

But in fact the US did not believe that success was ever possible. As far back as 2013, Patrick Cockburn described how "the US and its allies have responded to the rise of Isis by descending into fantasy. They pretend they are fostering a 'third force' of moderate Syrian rebels to fight both Assad and Isis, though in private Western diplomats admit this group doesn't really exist outside a few beleaguered pockets." That view was even shared by some military leaders of the Free Syrian Army itself. In September 2014 an FSA commander told the *Washington Post* that Washington's effort to link the various FSA units into a unified military force was "a cut and paste of previous FSA failures."

A year later, in an August 2014 interview with Thomas Friedman of the *New York Times*, President Obama said that the idea that arming the Syrian rebels would have made a difference has "always been a fantasy. This idea that we could provide some light arms or even more sophisticated arms to what was essentially an opposition made up of former doctors, farmers, pharmacists, and so forth, and that they were going to be able to battle not only a well-armed state but also a well-armed state backed by Russia, backed by Iran, a battle-hardened Hezbollah, that was never in the cards."

In the cards or not, in September 2014 a new coalition of "moderate" militia groups was announced in Turkey, linking the Supreme Military Council of Syria, which included the FSA, as well as the predominantly Christian Syriac Military Council. Created under the auspices of several members of the US Congress and the staff of the US House Foreign Affairs Committee, the coalition's goal was ostensibly to organize a unified military fight against both the Assad government and ISIS. But, as CNN reported after the meeting, "While the Supreme Military Council of Syria includes the Free Syrian Army, which is considered one of the leading moderate forces, there are questions about other members of the alliance. The Syrian Revolutionary Front reportedly signed a deal with ISIS in one suburb in Damascus, and another—the Hazzam group—put out a statement this week condemning US airstrikes."

Syria expert Joshua Landis assessed that a victory by the US-backed opposition would be very dangerous. "The FSA wouldn't bring unified rule in Syria, they would bring Somalia," he said.

Wasn't the original Syrian opposition a non-violent movement? What happened to that movement?

The original democratic opposition was initially non-violent, and elements of this movement remain intact, although seriously weakened by the violence engulfing the country. As long-time ABC News Middle East chief Charles Glass described it,

> the other opposition, the people who actually started this, people who had done time in prison over the years, who were prisoners of the Assad regime who wanted popular demonstrations, who wanted civil disobedience, who wanted negotiations

with the regime, to have a transition—a peaceful transition—in which they would ultimately be free elections by which the regime could, would lose, those people's voices are being drowned out in the cacophony of artillery and rifle fire all around Syria at this time. These people, I think they are disenchanted with the United States. ...[T]hose people in the peaceful opposition do not want to become pawns in a super power game.

There are strategic costs paid by those who advocate taking up arms against regimes. Some opposition activists may have held a moral or other kind of commitment to non-violence. But for many more, the rejection of armed struggle, even in circumstances of horrific civilian casualties, was based on the recognition that once a non-violent protest movement turns to arms, it loses not only its moral legitimacy in the eyes of many, but more importantly loses its mass character. And it is the continuation of the mass, popular involvement of huge proportions that creates an engaged, mobilized population willing and prepared to defend the democratic gains of these revolutionary processes whenever they may be won.

Opposition activist Haytham Manna, described how in Syria

the first negative result of the use of arms was to undermine the broad popular support necessary to transform the uprising into a democratic revolution. It made the integration of competing demands—rural v urban, secular v Islamist, old opposition v revolutionary youth—much more difficult. The resort to arms gave birth to fragmented groups that have no political program. Turkey trained army dissidents on its territory, and a group of them announced the birth of the Free Syrian Army under the supervision of Turkish military intelligence. Most militants inside Syria now carry a "Free Army" logo, but beyond a name there is no coordination or organized political harmony.

In any political struggle, when mass mobilization is replaced by small groups waging military battles, non-participants in the armed struggle become victims, often of the violence from their "own" side. This is most glaring in situations of full-scale civil war, as in Syria.

One of the most influential coalitions of indigenous Syrian political activists is the Local Coordination Committees—Syria (LCC), which came together in mid-2011 in the first months of the uprising. Uniting separate committees and organizations from a number of Syrian cities, by early 2015 their website listed 14 local and regional groups—from Dara and Homs to the Syrian Coast, Damascus and Damascus Suburbs, and even Raqqa, the self-declared "capital" of ISIS.

In August 2011, when the first calls for US and other foreign military intervention were coming from Syrians inside and outside the country, the LCC issued the following statement:

> In an unprecedented move over the past several days, Syrians in Syria and abroad have been calling for Syrians to take up arms, or for international military intervention. This call comes five and a half months of the Syrian regime's systematic abuse of the Syrian people, whereby tens of thousands of peaceful protesters have been detained and tortured, and more than 2,500 killed. The regime has given every indication that it will continue its brutal approach, while the majority of Syrians feel they are unprotected in their own homeland in the face of the regime's crimes.
>
> While we understand the motivation to take up arms or call for military intervention, we specifically reject this position as we find it unacceptable politically, nationally, and ethically. Militarizing the revolution would minimize popular support and participation in the revolution. Moreover, militarization would undermine the gravity of the humanitarian catastrophe involved in a confrontation with the regime.
>
> Militarization would put the Revolution in an arena where the regime has a distinct advantage, and would erode the moral superiority that has characterized the Revolution since its beginning.
>
> Our Palestinian brothers are experienced in leading by example. They gained the support of the entire Palestinian community, as well as world sympathy, during the first Intifada ("stones"). The second Intifada, which was militarized, lost public sympathy and participation. It is important to note that the Syrian regime and Israeli enemy used identical measures in the face of the two uprisings.

The objective of Syria's Revolution is not limited to overthrowing the regime. The Revolution also seeks to build a democratic system and national infrastructure that safeguards the freedom and dignity of the Syrian people. Moreover, the Revolution is intended to ensure independence and unity of Syria, its people, and its society.

We believe that the overthrow of the regime is the initial goal of the Revolution, but it is not an end in itself. The end goal is freedom for Syria and all Syrians. The method by which the regime is overthrown is an indication of what Syria will be like post-regime. If we maintain our peaceful demonstrations, which include our cities, towns, and villages; and our men, women, and children, the possibility of democracy in our country is much greater. If an armed confrontation or international military intervention becomes a reality, it will be virtually impossible to establish a legitimate foundation for a proud future Syria.

The LCCs maintained their commitment to non-violence but also participated in the broader Syrian National Council, which included both non-violent political activists and those supporting the Free Syrian Army. The SNC is made up of a relatively wide range of reformist intellectuals, the Muslim Brotherhood, and many individual activists representing youth, Assyrian, and Kurdish movements. The SNC has been willing to consider negotiations with the Syrian regime, but mainly insisted that such talks focus on power transitions.

That was distinct from the position of the National Coordinating Committee, a bloc of primarily left and Kurdish parties inside Syria. Created around the same time as the Syrian National Council, the NCC also maintained a commitment to non-violence but was willing to negotiate with the regime without preconditions.

Numerous other grassroots organizations and coalitions were created as well, including those focused on mobilizing non-violent protests, media activism, providing humanitarian assistance especially to besieged communities, and documenting human rights violations. US and international attention largely ignored their work, choosing to engage instead with those political opposition groups supporting US and Western military intervention, and tied to the Free Syrian Army.

The work of the grassroots continued while facing enormous challenges. Not surprisingly, even the commitment to non-violence came under question. Two years after its statement that if "international military intervention becomes a reality, it will be virtually impossible to establish a legitimate foundation for a proud future Syria," the LCC faced the US threat of bombing Syria in retaliation for the chemical weapon attack of August 2013 (see p. 119).

In a statement showing how complex the considerations were, the LCC responded with a nuanced statement that made clear the activists were not endorsing a US military strike, but were setting conditions that any such strike would have to follow if it was to achieve anything of value for Syrians.

> The Syrian people have never welcomed a foreign military intervention in any country, but as it faced the oppression, it was forced to revolt out of a belief in its righteous cause, while the dictator's regime responded with gunfire, torture, arbitrary detention and denied the people their daily bread and the safety of their homes. The regime has confronted civilian protestors with tanks and heavy weaponry from the beginning of the Syrian revolution, and, since then, it hasn't stopped developing its methods of killing and violence. Arbitrary detention by security forces gradually turned into field executions, and gunfire has become an ongoing use of warplanes, ballistic missiles and heavy artillery, up till the moment when chemical weapons were used. The regime has never stopped challenging the entire world, relying on the support of Russia, China and Iran, and on the world being a silent accomplice. Its ongoing mass murder of the Syrian people, and its systematic destruction of the Syrian state, were its proof of humanity's failure in protecting itself from tyranny.

> Today, the signs are indicating a serious possibility to an American strike against the regime, that would merely defend the Red Line of the use of chemical weapons, which Assad has repeatedly challenged. Apparently, the main concern of the West in this regard is based on international balance and interests, not on the serious attempt to rescue a people who are striving for freedom and dignity, and dying for that, everyday.

A limited strike to merely warn Assad will lead to nothing but increase in his violence, as well as to his complete confidence that no one would prevent him from killing. Such a transient strike will only become an international community approval of his use of non-chemical weaponry, if it really succeeds in preventing future use of chemical. In the end no one will pay the price but the Syrian people.

It is a difficult moment and a turning point in the history of Syrians, it requires a high sense of responsibility, from us, and from the entire world, as well as wisdom, not hesitation and egoism.

Any strike to the regime must aim to paralyze, with attention and precision, its Air Forces, artillery, and missiles arsenal, being used continuously against civilian areas, with an impact not far from that of Mass Destruction weapons. A strike must also prioritize civilians and their safety, rather than being at their cost. Moreover, it needs to be accompanied by close coordination with, and sufficient support to the Syrian opposition, both political and armed; in order to allow for better organization and progress. Such an empowerment is crucial, as it enables hope in the hearts of Syrians, whose despair and agony are the basis for extremism.

As opposers, revolutionaries, and activists, it is our responsibility to stand side by side today, in order to clarify our national interests and humanitarian necessities, to tell the entire world that abandoning a people equals abandoning humanity itself, and that an intervention in Syria must be in favor of the Syrians' needs and voices, respecting them as well as their future's sovereignty.

The weakening of the non-violent political opposition continued. In early 2013 the noted Syrian writer and human rights activist Haytham Manna described the contradiction. On the one hand he continued to assert that, "In modern history, no state exists where gnarled violence gave rise to a democratic system…and we do not have a single case of a military victory in a similar situation that did not carry viruses of the spectrum of extremism, eradication and revenge. We have warned and continue to warn of the repercussions of violence on social cohesion and civil peace, and the unity of Syria. It is clearly visible that the project of political violence does not represent an expression of class status, or national demands or democratic aspirations. Political violence in Syria is pushing a thoughtful and deliberate social mobility towards sectarianism and factionalism and extremism as a custodian of death, murder and revenge."

But at the same time he recognized that even within his own organization, non-violent political mobilization had "shifted from being seen as high principles to being an accusation, and the three no's that were adopted by the National Coordination Body (no to violence, no to sectarianism, no to foreign intervention) were marked out as complicity and weakness in the face of dictatorial power."

That may not have been entirely true—in June that year *The Economist* described a meeting with two members of the NCB, both of whom had spent a decade or more imprisoned by the Assad regime. They said they wanted to see the fall of the regime, "but that the arming of the revolution has taken it down 'the wrong path.' 'We are against all arms,' says Safwan Akash, a member from Hama, the country's fourth city in which thousands were massacred by the regime in 1982. 'That was the biggest mistake in the revolution. At the moment, the only future is more killing, more fighting and more damage. And the vision of the opposition outside only offers more of that.'" But it was clear that supporters of the non-violent political movement did not have an alternative strategy to move forward.

By early 2014 the Lebanese magazine *al Akhbar* was asking the headline question: "Where are Syria's non-violent revolutionaries today?" What is clear is that as the armed groups took over the initiative of the anti-Assad uprising, many of the non-violent protesters refused to join the military struggle. *Al Akhbar* notes that, "Some preferred to leave the country in order to escape the new reality where the non-violent protest movement was in decline. ...Those whose circumstances did not allow them to leave, are living today the worst days of their lives. Some of them have persisted in their activism in non-governmental civil society organizations, whose numbers have increased during the events in Syria, or in the Coordinating Committees on social networking sites."

But there is no question they face extraordinary challenges, including repression and the threat of arrest or worse from the Syrian security forces or various armed groups, as well as the problems facing all Syrian civilians caught up in the midst of a brutal civil war. *Al Akhbar* quotes one young activist who blames the regime's response to the original protests, and adds, "We were a group of patriotic men and women participating in the protests and spreading the values of national unity. After the revolution became militarized, we had no role to play. The fighting destroyed the civil movement."

As Patrick Cockburn reminds us in *The Jihadis Return*, "revolutions are notorious for devouring their earliest and most humane advocates, but few have done so with the speed and ferocity of Syria's."

The little bit of good news is that the original, democratic, largely non-violent Syrian movement that rose in early 2011 as part of the Arab Spring has not entirely disappeared. But as the multi-sided civil war continues to devastate Syria, reclaiming the movement's role as the center of the country's political motion remains for the future.

—PART V—

THE ARAB SPRING

What was the Arab Spring all about?

The democratic movements that spread from Tunisia in 2010 on to Egypt early in 2011, to Bahrain and Libya, Yemen and Syria, and beyond, quickly became known collectively as the Arab Spring. Each had its own national particularities, but there were enough parallels and enough shared influence between them to legitimize a regional description. The uprisings began, in each case, as non-violent civil society protests against government repression, human rights violations, economic injustice. The demands varied somewhat, for bread or jobs, for the right to speak or the end of dictatorship, but at their core these were demands for the rights of citizenship, for dignity.

It was a set of uprisings that showed a level of revolutionary fervor not visible in the Middle East in perhaps a generation—and that meant that the legacy of US-dominated governments across the region would never be the same. It did not, however, mean that all—indeed any—of these revolutionary processes were actually revolutions. They were—and remain—transformative social movements, to varying degrees crossing fault-lines of class, religion, sect, gender. But they were not one-off events, in which the ousting of a dictator or the resignation of a hated autocrat and the calling for new elections necessarily meant the immediate announcement of a whole new society.

Crucially, there was never going to be a direct, nonstop trajectory toward the victory of democracy, equality, dignity, demands that were on every protester's lips. There would always be backward motion—even major disasters seeming to grow out of the initial protests. It was in that second phase—the defeats and reversals following the first heady mobilizations—that the first popularly elected president in Egypt was deposed in a coup followed by a long period of repression, that Libya collapsed into militarized anarchy, that Syria's escalating civil war led to the death of over 220,000 people, that ISIS emerged in the chaos, and that the US returned its troops and planes to the region in a new iteration of the global war on terror.

But it is much too early to give up on the Arab Spring's promise—that civil engagement, the creation of broad social movements,
and massive protest can indeed lead to new popular understandings of the rights of citizens, of human rights, of dignity. And those
movements continue to influence public discourse and public action. The ability of mass mobilization in the street to cause friction
and eventually division within the state apparatus—even within the
military, police, and other agencies of repression—remains a newly
recognized reality in the Arab world.

In Egypt, perhaps the most astonishing example of the Arab
Spring's promise and its failures is the recognition that mobilized
people in the streets led to the overthrow of a powerful, US backed
dictator. This certainly empowered the Egyptian public. It also set
the stage for the military coup against the democratically elected
President Mohamed Morsi, who had made numerous mistakes during his chaotic one-year reign, and whom many activists thought
could be turned out and replaced by the people themselves now
empowered by their mobilization. Instead, it led to widespread
popular support for a military coup, quickly backed by the US and
US allies across the region, that imprisoned Morsi, killed more than
a thousand peaceful protesters and arrested tens of thousands more,
attacked journalists and human rights defenders, and installed a general as the new military president. But even after years of the new
military dictatorship and repression, Egyptians continue to recognize, to hold on to their right to have a say in their government—to
claim the rights of citizens. It may be still more years ahead, but the
Arab Spring is not a process that is over.

The challenges, however, remain formidable. Libya's collapse
into armed chaos and Syria's descent into civil war represent the
most dangerous iterations of this second phase of the Arab Spring.
Human rights activists in Bahrain remain in jeopardy, with many
imprisoned and facing torture as the regime continues to suppress
the democratic movement that rose in 2011. Yemen's uprising accomplished the negotiated standing down of a US-backed autocrat
in 2012. Yet three years later, the country collapsed into civil war

as Houthi rebels seized the capital and several other cities and forced the replacement president to flee the country, while Saudi Arabia led an anti-Houthi air assault that killed hundreds of civilians. Reclaiming popular mobilization and rebuilding social movements is going to be a very long-term project across the region.

It is also important to recognize the breadth of public support and involvement in the Arab Spring uprisings. In the United States, the television coverage—one must single out the then-newly influential *Al Jazeera English* here—of the Tahrir Square mobilizations in Egypt accomplished a great deal in the struggle against anti-Arab racism and Islamophobia. Here were Egyptians—Arabs—speaking in their own voice, articulating their own demands, their own narrative. And they spoke English! And wore blue jeans and were on Facebook and had cellphones clamped to their ears! They were "just like us."

Except the vast majority of Egyptians don't speak English, don't use Facebook because they can't afford computers or Internet access, and are not "just like us." Certainly the young, English-speaking tech-savvy activists who used social media to mobilize people and who soon became familiar to Western television watchers and social media fans played a huge role in Egypt's uprising. But the Tahrir Square protests that led to the ousting of the US-backed dictator Hosni Mubarak did not begin on Facebook in 2011.

The movement originated with the labor protests of 2004, which led to huge strikes by textile workers in 2006. The mobilization of Egypt's workers, much of it outside the state-controlled official unions, played a huge role. The broader anti-dictatorship, democratic demands also had roots much earlier than the Facebook rebels of 2011, although many of the individual activists were part of both. In February 2003, Egyptian activists mobilized as part of the global protests against the then-looming US war in Iraq. Amazed by the millions of people pouring into the streets around the world, and embarrassed that they were unable to bring out many people in Cairo, they decided to work to build a movement for democracy—"to do better," as one of them explains in *We Are Many*, a film about the global protests. "Better" came in 2011 and resulted in the overthrow of a dictator. And the Muslim Brotherhood, the oldest Islamist organization in today's Arab world, eventually moved out of the shadowy sort-of-legal, sort-of-not position it had long held, to take its place at the center of the protests.

The point is not to underestimate the importance of the mainly young, urban, secular activists who led important components of the Arab Spring uprising in Egypt and elsewhere. Rather it is to recognize that the mobilizations gained their power from their inclusion of workers, rural residents, and older people as well, and the leadership these individuals brought. Many were not secular, but were motivated at least partly by their faith. Most Egyptian workers who participated in the labor strikes would not define themselves as secular. During the Arab Spring, mosques became crucial centers of information sharing, particularly when the regime shut down social media sites and sometimes the entire Internet at various points. Religious services in Tahrir Square rotated between Muslim prayers guarded by Coptic Christian activists and Christian services where Muslims kept watch, which presented an inter-religious, but not secular, identity for the protesters.

The protests in Tunisia evolved in similar fashion. From the start, workers and middle-class professionals were involved, but the core of the demonstrators came from the disenchanted, disempowered unemployed youth. Unlike in Egypt, they were often educated. Coming to symbolize their plight was Mohammed Bouazizi, the young man in the impoverished town of Sidi Bouzid, who set himself ablaze to protest not only the unemployment and poverty, but also the humiliation and degradation he faced. His act sparked the actions that became the Arab Spring.

Unquestionably some of the challenges to the Arab Spring uprisings came from the protesters' decision in some countries to take up arms. There is a strategic cost paid for such a decision—even in circumstances of horrific civilian casualties, once a non-violent protest movement turns to arms, it loses not only its moral legitimacy in the eyes of some, but also its mass character. And it is that mass, popular involvement of huge proportions of the population that makes possible victories against repressive regimes (Egypt, Tunisia) as well creates the potential for an engaged, mobilized population willing and prepared to defend the democratic gains of these revolutionary processes.

Similarly, the call for outside military intervention, however understandable in the face of terrible regime violence, risks losing independence to foreign sponsors. Opposition to the calls for such intervention is often grounded less in abstract principles than in a pragmatic recognition that an independent, mass-based popular movement has the best chance of strategic victory, both in overthrowing a dictator and in reclaiming civil society for a once-dispossessed population. Unfortunately, in Syria the devastating effect of the regime's attacks over several years, along with the escalation of military attacks by the opposition beginning in the summer of 2011, created a kind of desperation. This meant more people were willing to support anything—including international military involvement—that they hoped might, just might, hold some possibility of improving conditions. But unfortunately conditions didn't improve, and the countries were suddenly flooded with arms and even fighters from outside, and the violence escalated.

As Seamus Milne wrote about the Syrian rebels in *The Guardian* in August 2012,

> the rapidly mushrooming dependence of their uprising on foreign support is a disaster—even more than was the case in Libya. After all, it is now officials of the dictatorial and sectarian Saudi regime who choose which armed groups get funding, not Syrians. And it is intelligence officials from the US, which sponsors the Israeli occupation of Syrian territory and dictatorships across the region, who decide which rebel units get weapons. Opposition activists insist they can maintain their autonomy, based on deep-rooted popular support. But the dynamic of external backing clearly risks turning groups dependent on it into instruments of their sponsors, rather than the people they seek to represent.

When the Arab Spring emerged as a regional phenomenon, the Obama administration seemed initially open to accepting the new reality of collapsing dictators and emerging more-or-less Islamist-oriented democracies in some parts of the Arab world the US had long dominated. Not everywhere, of course. The US would almost certainly not have even considered accepting such a new reality in Saudi Arabia, where oil influence and weapons sales were at stake. And by supporting the Saudi military intervention to quell the 2011 Pearl Roundabout protest movement in Bahrain, Washington served notice it had no intention of supporting democratization in a country whose absolute monarchs host the US Navy's Fifth Fleet—something that a democratic government in Bahrain just might have reconsidered. But even as the US hesitated on whether to urge Mubarak to step down in Egypt, how to engage with Morsi and thus with the Muslim Brotherhood, there was still some evidence of a shift away from the position that US influence could be maintained only by backing dictators across the region. The US was not about to abandon its commitment to regional hegemony in the Middle East, but the Arab Spring did seem to make possible a different relationship with popular Islamist forces—at least those deemed "moderate" in US counter-terrorism jargon.

It was never certain, and Washington's rhetoric waffled. Before Mubarak stepped down Obama expressed cautious support for "a government that is responsive to the aspirations of the Egyptian people." Then-Secretary of State Clinton called for "change that will respond to the legitimate grievances of the Egyptian people which the protests are all about." But both stressed the need for an "orderly" transition—something quite the opposite of popular uprisings like Tahrir Square. And Clinton pulled back from anything that might even hint of an opening to Islamist forces, explicitly rejecting, in a clear reference to the Muslim Brotherhood, "any transition to a new government where oppression...would take root." The crises of post-Arab Spring Egypt, Libya, Yemen, and especially Syria allowed the United States to pull back from its tentative gesture of openness toward popular democracy and Islamism.

The origin of ISIS, it should be noted, goes back significantly before the Arab Spring erupted, to the US occupation of Iraq. It is true that the Arab Spring's victories for dignity and democracy also set the stage for the current period of conflict and violence across the region. The chaos of Syria's civil war, the spread of weapons across Libya's borders into the rest of the region, an escalating civil war in Yemen, the return of military dictatorship to Egypt—are huge setbacks. But they do not mean the Arab Spring has been permanently defeated.

Why did the US and NATO launch an air war in Libya to overthrow Qaddafi?

Like other countries' versions of the Arab Spring, the Libyan uprising against the government of Muammar Qaddafi began in February 2011 as a popular uprising protesting government repression, discrimination, and lack of democracy. The protests began around the same time as those earlier ones in Tunisia and Egypt, and followed an initially similar trajectory. As with Tunis and Cairo, the roots of Libya's opposition extend further back.

What was different in Libya from those earlier iterations of the democratic revolutionary processes that swept the Arab world throughout that period was that in Libya, the opposition quickly ousted the regime from major cities. In much of eastern Libya, large sectors of the military was defecting to the opposition. Despite that, the Qaddafi regime continued to attack opposition strongholds in the key eastern city of Benghazi and beyond, and very quickly Libyan activists moved to take up arms, joining with the defecting military units. Unlike Egypt and Tunisia, the other Arab states in which democratic upheavals were already under way, Libya moved quickly toward a direct military confrontation, much closer to a civil war.

The UN Security Council passed its first resolution on the Libya crisis on February 26, freezing assets, restricting the travel of Qaddafi and his inner circle, and sending the issue to the International Criminal Court for investigation. The fighting continued, and on

March 17 the Security Council passed another resolution, 1973, which formed the legal basis for military intervention in the Libyan civil war. It demanded "an immediate ceasefire" and authorized establishment of a no-fly zone and the use of "all means necessary" short of foreign occupation to protect civilians. But when implemented, the resolution quickly resulted in a full-scale air war with the goal of overthrowing Qaddafi—full-blown regime change was under way. (See p. 170 for more on the UN decision-making on Libya.)

Many of Libya's armed protesters, though certainly not all, explicitly rejected international intervention, and were still able to consolidate significant levels of control of towns and cities, first in the east and quite quickly in the west. Reports from the western city of Misurata, not far from the capital of Tripoli, indicated that protesters backed by defecting army units were in control of the city from February 21 on. The *Financial Times* quoted a local worker in Misurata describing how "the people are now organizing themselves into committees. Some are managing traffic, others are cleaning up after the fighting and the fires of previous days. There are also people handing out water and milk to the population." It looked, for a brief time, very much like the self-organization of protesters in Tahrir Square in Egypt, in the short-lived Pearl Roundabout protests in Bahrain—and very much like the non-violent, society-wide mobilization of the first Palestinian intifada of 1987–1993.

The regime itself was quickly splintering, with high-ranking ministers and other officials resigning. The interior minister announced his support for what he called the "February 17 Revolution" and urged the military to support the Libyan people's "legitimate demands." Libyan diplomats around the world, including the ambassadors to the US, Indonesia, Australia, India, Bangladesh, and elsewhere, as well as virtually the entire staff of the Libyan mission to the United Nations, all resigned in protest of the regime's violence. The regime was collapsing.

But somehow, despite the fact that opposition forces were claiming real victories against the Libyan military, allegations took hold in capitals and in the press around the world that Qaddafi's undoubted brutality meant that genocide was both inevitable and imminent. On the eighth anniversary of the US "shock and awe" assault against Iraq, March 19, airstrikes against Libya began. The first were by French warplanes that attacked Libyan government tanks in the desert outside of Benghazi—tanks which had been driven out of the city by rebel forces. Despite that evidence that the opposition was not facing imminent genocide and was in fact able to drive the regime's army out of the city, the ostensibly limited no-fly-zone resolution was quickly interpreted to justify full-scale air war.

Months of war followed, with the rapid collapse of the always-fragile structures of the Libyan state. In early April the armed opposition offered a ceasefire; neither the UN nor NATO used that offer to reengage with the Libyan government with new negotiations. On June 27 the International Criminal Court issued arrest warrants for Qaddafi and other officials on charges of crimes against humanity, and in September the United Nations lifted sanctions on the country and accepted the opposition's Transitional National Council as the legitimate government of Libya. Fighting continued, sporadically, and Qaddafi was found and killed by opposition forces in October. Three days later, the opposition TNC declared victory and the end of the war.

What was the impact of the regime change in Libya?

The real consequences of the destruction of the Libyan state began to become apparent once the war officially ended, first with widespread instability inside the country, then with the massive flow of weapons out of Qaddafi's storage facilities and out across Libya's borders to fuel unrest in central and north Africa and across the already roiling Middle East.

Then the other major consequence—anticipated or not by those who so quickly embraced regime change—erupted across Libya: The rise of extremist forces, Islamist and otherwise, as the state institutions, weak as they may have been, collapsed. Soon there were two separate rival parliaments, sitting a thousand kilometers apart, each claiming to be ruling post-Qaddafi Libya. A UAE newspaper described the scene in October 2014:

> Trucks fitted with anti-aircraft cannon, troops and cement roadblocks protect the five-star hotel in Tobruk that is now the surreal last bastion of Libya's fugitive parliament.
>
> Holed up in the Dar Al Salam seaside resort and pretending that all is normal, elected legislators debate laws and plan the future from the eastern city where they fled last month after losing control of Tripoli and much of the country.
>
> A thousand kilometres away in the capital, a rival parliament sits, shunned by the international community and made up of members of an earlier assembly whose mandate has expired. It is making its own decisions, taking over ministries and staking a competing claim to rule the country.
>
> Three years after Nato missiles helped overthrow Muammar Qaddafi, Libya is effectively divided, with two governments and two parliaments, each backed by rival militias.

And the two parliaments are backed not only by rival militias but by rival sets of international actors as well. The newer Tobruk parliament represents more or less secular, mostly Western-oriented Libyans, many of whom had spent years in exile and only returned after the overthrow of Qaddafi. It has defined itself largely as being "anti-Islamist," and its backing includes the militia of a US-trained Libyan general, Khalifa Hafter, who commanded part of Qaddafi's army before being arrested for trying to overthrow the regime. He was released in a US-brokered deal, became a US citizen, and lived in the US for 20 years. The Tobruk parliament is backed by Saudi Arabia, Egypt, and the UAE in the region—as well as by the US and its European allies. The originally elected parliament, whose mandate has since expired, sits in the original capital of Tripoli and includes a number of Islamist forces grouped into a coalition known as Libya Dawn. It has some international backing from Qatar and Turkey.

Writing in *al-Araby*, analyst Vijay Prashad described how "The NATO bombing of 2011 destroyed the state—the painfully thin institutions that held together this archipelago of cities. Out of the ashes of the Gaddafi regime emerged a NATO-authorized government that had more interest in central banks and oil contracts than the creation of a new Libya. The West and its allies were not interested in the surrender of the old regime, no interest in creating a platform of reconciliation and patriotism. Various armed groups thrived as western-backed liberals found themselves with little popular support and no real institutions to do their bidding. It is what sent Libya into spiraling into chaos."

During that chaos some Libyans traveled to Syria and Iraq to fight, joining jihadi forces in the civil wars and chaos there. Inside Libya, the post-Qaddafi civil war pushed some of the Islamist forces toward far more extreme positions, some of them joining with Ansar al-Shariah, an earlier extremist group formed in Benghazi after the US-NATO bombing campaign. By 2014, some of the Libyans who had gone to fight in Syria or Iraq and who had seen, or even participated in the rise of ISIS, began returning to Libya. Some of them began calling themselves ISIS as well. In early 2015 the group took responsibility for rounding up and killing 21 Egyptian Coptic Christian laborers who had come to Libya to find work.

In mid-April 2015, foreign ministers of the United States and several of its European allies issued a statement welcoming a new United Nations effort to organize a political unification process. They called on "all participants to the dialogue to negotiate in good faith and use this opportunity to finalize agreements on the formation of a National Unity Government and make arrangements for an unconditional ceasefire." In a presumably unintentional bit of irony, the governments responsible for the air war that created the chaos in Libya noted that "in particular, we call for the immediate cessation of airstrikes and ground offensives. Such provocations undermine the UN talks and threaten chances for reconciliation."

But in the meantime, the weapons set loose from Libyan arsenals during the earlier anti-Qaddafi uprising and the US-NATO air strikes continue to fuel escalations as new crises erupt throughout an expanding region: in Mali and elsewhere in central Africa, in the Egyptian Sinai, in Iraq and Syria, and beyond.

Where are all the weapons in the region, especially in Iraq and Syria, coming from?

The broadly defined Middle East remains one of the most heavily armed regions in the world. Many countries are awash with weapons left over from the Cold War, when the region was a key venue for US-Soviet proxy battles for power and influence. Those included the decade-long Afghanistan war, in which US-backed mujahideen challenged the Soviet-backed government. There were also a series of wars internal to the region. The Iran-Iraq war, which raged from 1980–1988, resulted in over a million casualties and resulted in enormous social and economic costs as well as long-term political consequences.

The end of the Cold War did not lead to a diminution of arms flooding into the region. Most governments in the region—including absolute monarchies, military or military-backed dictatorships, and partial democracies—continued to rely on powerful militaries and continued to buy and amass large amounts of weapons from abroad. Israel has by far the most powerful military in the region, as well as the only nuclear weapons arsenal in the Middle East. Additionally, since the end of the Cold War the region has seen a series of both internal armed battles in several countries, and especially several large-scale international invasions and wars mostly initiated and led by the United States. Beginning with Operation Desert Storm in 1991, the first US war against Iraq, and moving through the US invasion of Afghanistan in 2001, then the invasion and long-term occupation of Iraq starting in 2003, the Israeli war against Hezbollah in Lebanon in 2006 followed by the 2011 US/ NATO attack and regime change in Libya, the region has seen a virtually unending flood of conventional and high-tech weapons. The US occupation of Iraq and the air war in Libya have been responsible for the majority of the weapons spreading across the Middle East, North Africa, parts of Central Africa, and beyond.

In Libya, when the government of long-time ruler Col. Muammar Qaddafi was overthrown, weapons storage facilities and military bases across the country were essentially thrown open, abandoned by their guards, many of whom joined the anti-Qaddafi mobilization. The United States remained concerned about maintaining control of the chaotic country, awash with weapons, after the killing of Qaddafi. In October 2011, then-Secretary of State Hillary Clinton made a telling Freudian slip, describing US "concern as to how we disarm" the country. Only afterward did she catch herself and correct her statement to "or how the Libyans disarm everybody who has weapons."

The problem was that virtually everyone in Libya *did* have weapons—and rather than being disarmed, many people joined or created militias that turned post-Qaddafi Libya into a violent, turbulent country. Two governments competed for power and legitimacy, and a host of militias continued fighting. Some of the most powerful militias were politically identified with al-Qaeda. But the weapons poured out of government warehouses into the hands of militias and out of the country—quickly showing up to fuel conflicts in Iraq and Syria, in Mali, in next-door Egypt and beyond. By early 2015 the situation inside Libya remained chaotic, and the flood of Libyan weapons continued to destabilize the region.

The Iraq war, which continued after the 2011 withdrawal of US troops, saw the rise of a plethora of militias as well as the huge (though largely ineffectual) US-trained Iraqi military and police forces, all armed with billions of dollars' worth of US-provided weapons. With the reprised sectarian civil war that reemerged around 2009–10 and escalated after the US troop withdrawal the following year, militias of all sorts all found US arms easy to obtain. When the Iraqi military essentially collapsed in response to attacks by ISIS in 2014, huge caches of its weapons were abandoned, lost, sold on the black market, or provided to ISIS by defecting soldiers. Many of those weapons ended up strengthening ISIS as well as the al-Qaeda-linked Nusra Front and some of the smaller opposition forces in both Syria and Iraq.

The spread of weapons was of course not the only consequence of the ISIS defeat of Iraqi forces in 2014. Despite US and British efforts to rebuild the Iraqi military, it was still largely incapable of serious fighting. In mid-February 2015 the *New York Times* featured a front-page assessment that

> Shiite militias backed by Iran are increasingly taking the lead in Iraq's fight against the Islamic State, threatening to undermine US strategies intended to bolster the central government, rebuild the Iraqi army and promote reconciliation with the country's embittered Sunni minority. With an estimated 100,000 to 120,000 armed men, the militias are rapidly eclipsing the depleted and demoralized Iraqi army, whose fighting strength has dwindled to about 48,000 troops since the government forces were routed in the northern city of Mosul last summer, according to US and Iraqi officials.

In Syria, the early militarization of the opposition that began in 2011 was made possible by defecting Syrian soldiers who joined the rebels with their weapons. By 2012 the opposition forces appeared to be growing stronger, with defecting soldiers' own weapons bolstered by access to some heavy arms captured from government bases. Later that year Syrian rebels were reporting a relaxation of the previously strict US rules on what kinds of weapons were allowed across the border, and that portable anti-aircraft missiles had been released from Turkish warehouses where they had been impounded.

In March 2013, Matt Schroeder, who tracks the spread of such weapons for the Federation of American Scientists, said the appearance of modern, sophisticated anti-aircraft missiles in the hands of such fragmented rebel groups was deeply troubling because of their capacity to bring down civilian airlines. "This is a step above anything we've seen before in the hands of non-state actors," he said. "This is a new and unfortunate chapter in recent manpad [man-portable air-defense] proliferation."

Until September of 2014 the United States remained officially reluctant to provide arms directly to the anti-Assad rebels. At that time, in the context of the decision to conduct US airstrikes in Syria and Iraq and send troops back to Iraq, the US approved some relatively small-scale arms provisions. But even before that, the opposition's weapons were mostly of US manufacture, provided to the rebels by Saudi Arabia and Qatar, Jordan and the UAE, sent into Syria through Turkey. Most of those weapons had been sold to Washington's Gulf allies over the years in multi-billion-dollar arms deals. (France has sold some weapons to Gulf states as well.)

And despite its official refusal to provide arms, there is no question that the US either approved or discreetly ignored the reality that some of its closest allies in the region were directly providing arms (and money to buy more arms) to the entire range of Syrian opposition forces—"moderate" and extremist, Islamist and secular, ISIS and Nusra, and beyond. And there is no question that the United States chose not to move to stop those sales.

All US weapons sold internationally, including those sold to close allies, contain end-use restrictions. They limit how, where, and against whom they can be used, and they restrict whether and to whom the weapons can be resold. There is little doubt that the US could, if it chose, bring an immediate halt to the Saudi, Qatari, and other arms shipments heading to the Syrian opposition forces, by enforcing those end-use restrictions on pain of losing all future access to US arms.

The Syrian government, of course, has a well-armed and well-trained military, but it has taken serious casualties through the years of the civil war, and many of its weapons have been lost or degraded. Beginning in 2013 it began relying more significantly on military support from Hezbollah fighters from Lebanon—many of whose arms originally came through Syria in the first place. Iran and Russia remain the key military backers of the Syrian military.

While there have been discussions and some UN-based efforts toward a ceasefire (or local ceasefires) in Syria, as of early 2015 those plans had never included the possibility of an arms embargo.

Given the centrality of the Syrian civil war to the broader regional and global "war on terror," there is a clear need for an end to the flood of weapons that continues to escalate the conflict.

Neither side is prepared to offer a unilateral ceasefire. In the context of new negotiations toward a full or partial ceasefire, one possibility would be for the United States to call for and support a comprehensive international arms embargo. Washington could announce immediate plans to stop sending or enabling the provision of any arms to any rebel forces and to prevent US allies from doing so, while simultaneously renewing pressure on Russia and Iran to stop sending any arms to the Syrian government side. Washington would have to be prepared to strengthen and enforce end-use agreements on arms exports to exert necessary pressure on its regional allies, including Saudi Arabia, Qatar, the UAE, Turkey, Jordan, and Israel. Despite inevitable opposition from US arms manufacturers, the US government would need to make clear to these recipients that if they continue using or providing arms to any side in Syria, the US will cancel all existing weapons contracts with them. The US should make clear in the UN Security Council that it is prepared to support a resolution imposing a complete and enforceable arms embargo on all sides of the Syrian conflict.

Although an arms embargo will not alone solve the problems of ISIS and its cruel power, or the Syrian regime and its repression, or the unaccountable militias destroying the lives of too many ordinary Syrian civilians, no ceasefire can hold while weapons continue to flow. The constant refrain that "there is no military solution" in Syria or in Iraq remains true—the brutality of ISIS does not change that reality. The use of US weapons—airstrikes, bombings, and more— too often leads to more support for ISIS, not less. (See p. 52.) More weapons will continue to make things worse, not better.

—PART VI—

IN THE REGION AND THE WORLD

Why do so many Middle Eastern governments and opposition movements use religion to justify violence?

In much of the world, for much of history, religion played a powerful, often defining role in political contests, power struggles, conflicts over resources, and wars. In many parts of the world that is still the case: the Buddhist government's oppression of Muslim Rohingyas in Burma, the rebellion of Hindu Tamils against the Buddhist-dominated government of Sri Lanka, attacks on Christians, animists, and others by the Muslim-dominated government in Sudan (which also reflected the divide between Arabs of the north and Black Africans further south). And of course Israeli occupation and apartheid policies are based on privileging Jewish rights over those of non-Jews, whether Muslim or Christian.

Today's wars and conflicts—including internal struggles over power and resources, as well as broad movements against colonialism and imperialism—often are defined in religious and/or sectarian terms. Sunni against Shi'a, "true" Muslims against apostates, Jews against Muslims, etc. Most of the military struggles and some, though certainly not all, of the social movements mobilized against repressive and anti-democratic governments, against foreign occupation in the region, against Western encroachment, today define themselves in religious/sectarian terms. But as is always the case, the context goes far beyond the claim of "Muslim" or "Sunni" or whatever identity.

Like every social movement, every Islamist movement in the Arab world today has its own particular history and political trajectory. Some have much older roots. Egypt's Muslim Brotherhood, arguably the first modern Islamist organization in the region, goes back to the 1930s. But in most of those years, the organization and its offshoots across the region were brutally suppressed, with many leaders jailed or driven into exile. In post-Nasser Egypt, there were periods when "independents" known to be affiliated with the Brotherhood were allowed to run for parliamentary seats, but their influence was never allowed to challenge the secular US-oriented military dictatorships.

Overall, contemporary Islamist movements have all emerged in the context of the failure of earlier efforts to shape the challenges presented by Western colonial and post-colonial intervention and interference, corrupt despotic regimes, chronic impoverishment and unemployment, repression and the denial of human rights. Those failures included the Arab monarchies, Arab nationalism, pan-Arabism, Arab socialism, pro-Western, globalized Arab neoliberalism. None succeeded at ending poverty, protecting human rights, or ensuring "bread, freedom, and dignity," as many of the protesters in Egypt's Tahrir Square demanded. None guaranteed the rights of citizenship for ordinary people.

It was largely in response to those failures that the narrative of religion—Islamism—took hold as the mobilizing force bringing people into the streets. Beginning with the Iranian revolution of 1979 that overthrew the US-backed Shah and brought a Shi'a Islamic force to power under the Ayatollah Khomeini, political Islam has played a major role in shaping political momentum across the Middle East. After the first Gulf war against Iraq in 1991, and in the midst of a major economic crisis spurred by the diminishing price of oil, the Islamic Salvation Front, or FIS, was elected, supplanting for the first time since independence the secular third-world socialist model of the anti-colonial National Liberation Front of Algeria.

In some countries, colonial powers imposed religious or sectarian governing structures on local populations. In Lebanon, for example, in 1926 during the Mandate period, France imposed what was known as a confessional system, in which numbers of seats in the parliament, as well as specific positions (president, prime minister, etc.) were assigned to each of the six separate Muslim and 12 separate Christian sects. When Lebanon won its independence in 1943, France withdrew, but the confessional system remained and it remains today, still based on the last census, taken in 1936.

There is no question that the relative size of Lebanon's populations of various sects has changed. Christians are no longer anywhere close to the number of Muslims; Shi'a significantly outnumber Sunni, but fear of demographic instability, especially after the 1975–1990 civil war, has resulted in a refusal to conduct a new census. Many Lebanese still identify with sect-based political and even military forces that continue to supersede national identity, although significant political shifts have occurred. The Shi'a-based Hezbollah movement rose in 1982, splitting from the traditional Shi'a Amal party to launch a more militant challenge to the Israeli occupation of Lebanon. Some Christians now support Hezbollah, and there are reports of other parties organizing outside their traditional sectarian base. The consequence of colonial occupation remains, and what exists today is less a direct religious conflict than a power struggle in which religion is used to mobilize support for power grabs and violence against other groups.

If one looks at Iraq, the defeat of the monarchy in the late 1950s set the stage for the nationalist and pan-Arab regime of Saddam Hussein. An Iraqi Shi'a majority, with large Sunni Arab and Kurdish minorities and smaller communities of Christians, Yazidis, Turkomans, and others lived in relatively cosmopolitan circumstances, although Sunnis held disproportionately privileged positions in the military and government. Until 1991 Iraq was a modern secular society, with a large urban middle class. Iraqis, at least in the cities, had access to most economic and social rights, including advanced education and health care and relative equality for women, but also confronted a government known for its denial of most political and civil rights. Political opponents, communists, supporters of Kurdish nationalism, Shi'a marsh dwellers, and others faced vicious repression, including arbitrary arrests, torture, and extra-judicial killing.

Like its Baath Party counterpart in Syria, the Iraqi Baathists were ruthlessly secular. In both countries, minority communities— Sunnis in Iraq, Alawites (a branch of Shi'a Islam) in Syria—were disproportionately privileged in state patronage systems. Neither the Alawite al-Assad family in Syria nor the Sunni Saddam Hussein in Iraq had any interest in building Alawite or Sunni religious governance in their countries; both were secular as could be. But both used religious identity to divide and control populations, and to apportion political and economic rights and privileges.

After its first war against Iraq in 1991, the United States imposed twelve years of crippling economic sanctions on the country. The impact was genocidal, including the death of over half a million children, the destruction of much of the physical and intellectual infrastructure of the country, the shredding of the social fabric, and the collapse of much of Iraqis' national identity. Many Iraqis responded by turning even further away from the national toward smaller, more local identities shaped by religion, sect, ethnicity, and tribe.

Immediately following its second invasion and occupation in 2003, the US ordered the dissolution of Iraq's military and its civil service, thus destroying the most secular and nationalist institutions in the country, and leaving several million Iraqis bereft of their long-standing national identity as well as their jobs. The US occupation authorities imposed a new political system in which power was apportioned to sectarian political parties ostensibly based on the size of various religious and ethnic communities in Iraq.

As the US war and occupation dragged on, ethnicity, tribe, and especially religion became newly important in the assertion of Iraqis' identity and in their search for protection. So sectarian identity became the basis not only for the newly empowered US-backed Shi'a-dominated government, but for conflicts over land and money, control of oil and other resources, and political power. By the mid-2000s, those conflicts looked increasingly like a sectarian civil war.

A final example: In the Gaza Strip, the history of the Islamist Hamas movement reflects a different trajectory still. Hamas emerged in 1988, in the first months of the first Palestinian intifada, or uprising. Its political and ideological origins go back much further, reflecting the influence of the Egyptian Muslim Brotherhood, but it was only in the context of the uprising that Hamas emerged as an organizational reality. Israel encouraged Hamas's rise to power, counting on the religious movement to somehow reduce the power of the intifada and the influence of the secular nationalist Palestine Liberation Organization, or PLO, that Israel then defined as its top enemy. Former Israeli official Avner Cohen, who was responsible for religious affairs in Gaza until 1994, told the *Wall Street Journal* that, "Hamas, to my great regret, is Israel's creation."The popular appeal of Hamas quickly grew. Like so many other Islamist organizations, it first gained support less for its ideology than by providing the impoverished population with desperately needed services unavailable under the Israeli occupation: clinics, schools, summer camps, social and economic assistance, and more. It was only later, by the mid- to late-1990s, as poverty and immiseration hit Gaza especially hard, that many more in the population turned more toward religion, and the Islamist approach to social life advocated by Hamas won new adherents.

Similar trajectories emerged in many other countries, some of them much earlier. On a broader regional level, other factors were at work too. In countries where governments define themselves and claim legitimacy in religious terms (Saudi Arabia being the clearest example), as well as some of the military dictatorships in the region (such as Egypt under Hosni Mubarak), human rights, such as the rights of free speech and association, are often denied. In those situations, the mosque was often the only place to meet, and opposition forces often adopted religious approaches. The same demand for "bread, freedom, and dignity" that mobilized so many in Egypt rang out, with an overlay—often a very thin overlay—of religion.

There are specific push-and-pull factors as well. In the context of the Syrian civil war, for instance, many secular anti-Assad fighters, faced with an intractable enemy in Damascus and simultaneously challenged by much more powerful Islamist forces, such as ISIS, chose to abandon the US-backed Free Syrian Army or other ostensibly "moderate" militias to join ISIS. This weakened the secular forces, of course, and the additional fighters accelerated the strength and popularity of ISIS. By 2013 or so, ISIS was wealthier (from illicit oil sales, kidnap ransoms, "taxes" imposed on people, and businesses in territory ISIS controlled, and other sources) and better armed than any of the secular anti-Assad forces. So it was not surprising that some of the formerly secular fighters switched loyalties and joined ISIS—not because of a sudden conversion to the ISIS extreme brand of Islam, but despite it, because ISIS offered higher salaries, better weapons, and occasional military victories.

In many cases fighters would follow local leaders, powerbrokers who shifted loyalties between various militias, and brought their followers with them.

Of course, in many of these scenarios jihadist organizations use the veneer of religious orthodoxy simply to claim legitimacy for violent, brutal actions. Like Judaism, Christianity, and pretty much every other religion, Islam's sacred texts include language that can be interpreted to allow or even encourage violence. The Torah calls for death by stoning for blasphemy; the New Testament legitimizes slavery. While many Islamic scholars have made clear that some claims of Quranic authority made by ISIS—for actions like condoning death as punishment for depicting a likeness of the Prophet—are completely false, there is no doubt that language approving extreme punishment exists in all the holy texts, reflecting the mores of ancient societies. But there is also no question that religion is being severely misused in today's Syria, Iraq, Saudi Arabia, and beyond.

What is the Sunni-Shi'a split in the region all about?

While the legacies of colonialism, wars, and struggles over resources continue to shape the broad conflicts in the Middle East, a significant part of the conflict is rooted in the sectarian schism between Sunni and Shi'a Muslims. One of the seven separate conflicts that make up the Syrian civil war is the regional struggle between Sunni and Shi'a powers, a struggle played out with Saudi Arabia and Iran as the primary combatants. Patrick Cockburn subtitled his 2014 book "ISIS and the New Sunni Uprising." Much of the mid-2000s civil war, as well as the revived post-2013 fighting in Iraq, reflects the sectarian divide set in place by the US in 2003 when it invaded and overthrew the Sunni-dominated Iraqi government, dismantled the military and civil service in which Sunnis had long been privileged, and supported a new government in which the once relatively marginalized but majority Shi'a took over and governed on a thoroughly sectarian basis.

There is of course a theological basis to the split, the original divide within Islam. It began with a struggle over succession—who should be the leader of the Muslim community after the death of the Prophet Muhammad. The two sides each supported a different candidate—Abu Bakr, who had been a close colleague of Muhammad and was thought by many to be the best qualified to lead the community (although he was also Muhammad's father-in-law, that was not considered important), versus Ali ibn Abi Talib, who was related to Muhammad by blood (he was a cousin) and by marriage (he was also his son-in-law) and was supported by those who believed that there was a divine order to the succession.

The Sunnis are identified as followers of the *sunna*, or the way, referring to the Quran's description of how leaders should be selected. The word Shi'a comes from *si'atu Ali*, or "partisans of Ali." Ali became caliph for five years, then was assassinated, and the caliphate which had been based in what is now Saudi Arabia shifted to the dynasties ruling in Damascus and Baghdad. The Shi'as, who had followed Ali, opposed those rulers, and in a later battle in the Iraqi city of Karbala, Ali's son Husayn and many of his followers were killed by the soldiers of those caliphates. Karbala became a kind of symbolic center of Shi'a Islam, and following the battle—really a massacre of Shi'as—the split became stronger. Sunnis became the large majority, and Shi'as continued to be marginalized and oppressed. Today, Sunnis remain the vast majority of the world's Muslims (most estimates indicate 80–85 percent Sunni and 15–20 percent Shi'a).

Is this conflict just an intractable war between two Islamic sects intent on imposing their beliefs on the populace?

Though it may seem unlikely, it's not primarily religion that has made these groups mortal enemies. The contemporary Shi'a-Sunni divide is about power. Theocratic governments in Iran and Saudi Arabia impose versions of Shi'a or Sunni orthodoxy, respectively, on their populations, but other Muslim governments identify with one or the other sect largely in the context of political power and identity privilege. That is, the Sunni governments of Jordan, Qatar, Bahrain, the UAE, Turkey, Oman, and other countries privilege Sunni communities, often discriminate against their Shi'a populations (even when, as in Sunni-governed Bahrain, the Shi'a are actually the majority of the population)—but not with the goal of imposing rigid Sunni orthodoxy on the country. In Shi'a-dominated Iraq and in Syria, where the ruling family is Alawite, a branch of Shi'ism, Sunnis are often discriminated against, sometimes brutally, but again, the governments have no interest in imposing Shi'a interpretations of Islamic law or traditions on largely secular populations. In Shi'a-majority Bahrain, the Sunni monarchy brutally suppressed the democratic protesters of the 2011 Arab Spring uprising, and it continues to jail human rights activists and other government critics, almost all of whom are Shi'a—but the goal is preservation of the US-backed monarchy's absolute power over the population, not the imposition of Sunni practices.

In the foregoing cases, the contemporary Sunni-Shi'a split has much more to do with identity politics within the countries and the struggles for power and hegemony in the region. Over the last fifty years or so in the Middle East, only two countries possessed all three of the requirements to be indigenous (as opposed to derivative, such as Israel) regional powers: oil for wealth, size of land and population, and sufficient water. Those were Iraq and Iran. With the essential destruction of Iraq's economic and military power following twelve years of sanctions and a decade of war and occupation, Iran emerged as an uncontested regional power. It was in this context that George W. Bush's administration transformed the long-hostile US position toward Iran dating from the overthrow of the US-backed shah into full-scale "axis of evil" efforts at undermining the Iranian economy and covertly supporting regime change in Tehran.

Where does Saudi Arabia fit in?

Saudi Arabia, the largest, wealthiest and most powerful of the Gulf petro-monarchies, used its oil wealth to influence regional developments, maintain its strategic ties to the US, and build unacknowledged but strong ties with Israel—all largely under the public radar. It also spent billions on building and staffing *madrassas*, or Islamic schools, across the region and around the world, part of a large-scale campaign to win political as well as religious support for its brand of extreme Wahhabi Islam (see p.26 and p. 32 for more on Saudi influence on Islamist movements). Riyadh long saw Iran as its strategic challenger for dominance in the Middle East (which explains much of its coziness with Israel). But again, until about 2011 it was all under the table.

Saudi Arabia did not come forward publicly to lead a regional Sunni coalition against the Iran-led Shi'a grouping of Syria, Iraq, and Hezbollah in Lebanon until the Syrian uprising against the Assad regime was morphing into a multifaceted civil war. And in the context of that civil war, the overt regional power struggle between Riyadh and Tehran—for control of oil markets and pipelines and beyond—paralleled a sectarian battle between those same forces for positioning as the most important global voice of Islam.

The current version of Washington's global war on terror, and the battle against ISIS, takes place in the context of the wider regional sectarian battle already under way. In Iraq, where it is perhaps most concentrated, the large Sunni minority, disenfranchised from their privileged position when the US invaded and demolished the Iraqi civil service and military, has faced more than a decade of Shi'a-dominated and increasingly sectarian US-backed governments in Baghdad. Nuri al-Maliki, of Iraq's Shi'a Dawa Party, became prime minister in 2006, just as the sectarian civil war was exploding across the country alongside the anti-occupation resistance. Instead of moving to reduce the tensions, Maliki immediately enforced his own sectarian policies. His ministries of defense and intelligence, especially, were infamous for widespread brutality against individual Sunnis and Sunni communities, including mass arrests, torture in prisons, extra-judicial executions, even bombing of Sunni areas.

Not surprisingly, anti-government mobilization among Sunnis grew, rooted in the existing resentments of a community that had been consciously sidelined and faced continued discrimination during the years of US occupation and US-backed governments. That was the context in 2013, when ISIS suddenly rose to power. There was a shockingly high level of tolerance, even support for the extremist organization, even among largely secular Sunni communities, who saw ISIS as the lesser evil, a potential ally with better arms to defend Sunni communities against the continuing ravages of their own Shi'a-sectarian government.

It was for that reason that so many ISIS military strategists, trainers, and commanders are reported to come from the embittered Sunni former generals of Iraq's Saddam Hussein-era Baathist military. And for the same reason, every US airstrike or drone attack against ISIS fighters holed up in a Sunni community somewhere (a strike that might be greeted in the US with a cheer of "Yay, we got the bad guys") is greeted with an angry "There go the Americans again, bombing Sunnis in the interest of the Shi'a and the Kurds." So even though the Obama administration might claim that the US military war against ISIS must be matched by a political campaign to win Sunnis away from ISIS, the military strikes are actually ensuring the failure of any such political effort.

An early March 2015 military campaign to oust ISIS from the overwhelmingly Sunni city of Tikrit, which it had occupied since June 2014, provides an example of the longer-term effect of the sectarian actions of war. Tikrit, the second-largest Iraqi city controlled by ISIS, is on the road from Baghdad to Mosul, the largest ISIS-occupied city. Along with its strategic significance, Tikrit was also important as a symbol: As the birthplace of Saddam Hussein, it held special significance for many Sunnis. The attack was launched against Tikrit primarily by pro-government Iraqi Shi'a militias mostly trained by Iran, backed by airstrikes from the Iraqi military.

A reporter from McClatchy News Service told the BBC on March 2, 2015 that much of the population of the city had already fled. Describing the effect of the bombing and artillery strikes, he sounded a warning very familiar from the days of the war in Vietnam—"I don't know if they're going to liberate the city so much as destroy it," he said. If and when Tikrit's Sunni residents return to their ravaged city, it remains very uncertain whether they will hold ISIS, or their own government and its allied sectarian militias, responsible for the destruction.

What are the consequences of the Syrian war across the region?

Understanding the consequences of Syria's multi-sided civil war is much easier than understanding the dynamics that shaped and perpetuate it. The war has not resulted in any one side—neither the Syrian regime, nor the diverse array of anti-Assad opposition factions, nor ISIS—winning clear influence. Rather, military initiative and political positions have shifted back and forth among the contending forces and their regional and global backers.

The regime's defeats at the hands of various opposition forces have meant it no longer has the power to govern large swaths of Syrian territory, including major cities and most of whole provinces. That has set in place a division of the country into a variety of constantly shifting fiefdoms and micro-states that threatens the very existence of Syria as a unified nation-state. The Syrian divisions—some of which are grounded in sectarian and/or ethnic rifts—parallel the collapse of the long-unified Iraqi state into a mosaic of ethnically and religiously divided cantons created at gunpoint during Iraq's sectarian civil war of the mid-2000s.

The years of the Syrian war have also seen the rise of violent extremists, both Islamist and secular, whose organizations have taken advantage of the power vacuum in local and regional areas. That has resulted from the overwhelming discrediting and/or defeat of the regime in many areas and thus the loss of its ability to rule, plus the internal fighting inside the anti-Assad opposition, whose disunity renders it largely incapable of governing as well. The emergence of these new extremists—including ISIS—has also risen and fallen along with the growing or diminishing power of the regime and the opposition.

What has remained constant is the downward spiral of humanitarian disaster that has characterized Syria since very early in the conflict: deaths and injuries of hundreds of thousands, the creation of millions of refugees and internally displaced, the massive destruction of whole cities, including millennia-old historic and cultural sites, and the shredding of Syria's once-advanced and relatively egalitarian social fabric.

As of January 2015, the United Nations estimated that 220,000 had died in the war. Many of these were of course civilians—horrifyingly killed in "barrel bomb" attacks (crude weapons made of barrels stuffed with explosives, dropped from helicopters or planes with deadly impact, mainly on civilians) by Syrian government forces, in the shelling of cities by both government and opposition sides, in US and allied airstrikes aimed at ISIS fighters. By the end of 2014 the Syrian Observatory for Human Rights, London-based and largely pro-opposition, reported that at least 10,664 children had been killed, along with 6,783 women.

But many of those killed in the war have also been combatants on all sides—a reality largely ignored by US government officials and the mainstream US media, which consistently references total casualty figures as something for which the Assad regime is solely responsible. In the middle of 2013, for example, the Syrian Observatory calculated that 60 percent of the war dead were fighters. According to its calculations, 43 percent of the deaths were of Syrian military and police forces along with pro-government militias. The next-largest contingent was that of civilian non-combatants, who made up 37 percent. Making up the smallest sector were opposition fighters, including civilians who had taken up arms as well as military defectors and foreign fighters, at 17 percent.

The lethal effects of the war grew progressively worse. In January 2015 the Syrian Observatory reported that more than 76,000 people had died in the civil war in 2014 alone, of whom more than 3,500 were children. Those figures made 2014 the deadliest year in the then-four-year-old war—though, again, less than one-quarter of the casualties were civilians—the rest, again, were government soldiers, police and allied militia fighters, opposition fighters, and fighters from various extremist organizations. As 2015 began, the UN's World Health Organization estimated the total number of wounded to exceed one million.

Most aid organizations inside Syria were increasingly unable to provide basic services because of the expansion of the war and the failure of all sides to abide by international legal requirements for humanitarian access to civilians on all sides. ISIS in particular, and other extremist organizations to a lesser degree, continued to target humanitarian workers without regard to international law. Numerous aid workers were kidnapped, some were killed.

The dead and wounded were almost entirely inside Syria. But the humanitarian disaster rooted in the Syrian civil war spread far beyond Syria's borders. In December 2014, the United Nations launched a new appeal for humanitarian relief—for almost 18 million victims of the conflict needing assistance in 2015 alone. The numbers were so high because, for the first time, the appeal included some amount of development aid, meaning education, jobs, and public health, for communities in countries bordering Syria that have been overwhelmed with refugees.

The numbers are staggering. More than half of Syria's 22 million people have been forced to flee their homes because of the war. The UN reports that more than three million Syrians have become refugees in Jordan, Turkey, Lebanon, Egypt, and Iraq. Another seven million are displaced within Syria. The population of the country itself is dropping—the UN anticipates that the three million refugees will increase to 4.3 million by the end of 2015.

In December 2014 the UN High Commissioner for Refugees said, "Syria's war is still escalating and the humanitarian situation is becoming protracted. Refugees and internally displaced people have exhausted their savings and resources, and host countries are at breaking point. We need a new aid architecture that links support to the refugees with what is being done to stabilize the communities who host them."

But the chance of reaching that goal of "a new aid architecture" seemed remote. The $8.4 billion assistance request included, for the first time, aid to "over a million vulnerable people in host countries," meaning that it aimed to provide direct support to at least the poorer of the countries hosting large numbers of Syrian refugees: Egypt, Lebanon, and Jordan. The history of earlier UN efforts to raise huge sums for humanitarian assistance indicates that it remains difficult even to get commitments—and even harder to get payments of the promised amounts—for immediate refugee aid, let alone adding development funds for host countries affected by the crisis.

The crisis in those neighboring countries has been dramatic. By 2015, the 1.1 million Syrian refugees in Lebanon made up one-fifth of the population, with consequences that went beyond job scarcity to potentially threaten the very fragile demographic balance between diverse and competing ethnic and religious groups. In the desert kingdom of Jordan, a longstanding crisis of water scarcity was seriously exacerbated by an influx of more than 600,000 Syrian refugees. Turkey, a relatively wealthy country, managed to absorb more than 1.6 million Syrian refugees, but its capacity by 2015 was almost at its limit.

"Conflict has devastated millions of Syrians' lives, trapping them in conflict areas and denying them access to basic provisions and health care," said Valerie Amos, the United Nations Under Secretary General for Humanitarian Affairs. "This plan, if fully funded, can help us provide food and medicine for children, shelter families from the cold, and support those who are desperate and traumatized."

But the humanitarian crisis escalated far beyond the capacity of the United Nations and other international organizations to adequately respond. The UN's calls for immediate pledges of large-scale financial assistance did not fall entirely on deaf ears in the capitals of wealthy nations, but pledges tended to be made with public fanfare but with little connection to real money being sent in real time. For example, by the end of 2014 Kuwait had provided the second-highest amount of funding in response to the UN's annual appeal: $303 million. But at the donor conference ten months earlier, Kuwait had pledged 500 million, so the UN faced a shortfall of almost $200 million that it had budgeted for. That was only one country's non-payment. Almost a year after the conference, a quarter of the pledged funds had yet to be paid.

While the United States had paid the largest amount of any individual country, $380 million, that amount was dwarfed by what would be appropriate if the US paid a share of the $8.4 billion goal commensurate with its share of the global economy.

The regional consequences went far beyond immediate humanitarian concerns. Instability rooted in economic and social dislocation of people—especially the poorest in neighboring countries, a result of huge refugee inflows—represents a serious threat. Shortages of housing, food, schools, jobs, and, most urgently, water, continued to threaten individual countries and the region as a whole.

With that kind of instability and growing potential for social unrest, conditions remained ripe for mobilization by some of the most violent extremist forces, preying on people's desperation.

What is Iran's role in the US global war on terror?

The 2003 overthrow of Saddam Hussein's government in Iraq by the United States was a great boon to Iran in its strategic competition for regional hegemony. For decades, Iran and Iraq were the only two countries in the Middle East with all three of the key requirements for indigenous power: oil for wealth, size of land and population, and water. The two had competed for years, and for almost a decade in the 1980s fought a bitter war. The US provided arms to both sides, but tilted towards Iraq (providing seed stock for bio-weapons and satellite targeting intelligence for chemical weapons, among other things) because it was the weaker of the two, and it served US interests to have the two potential regional challengers fighting each other.

The Iran-Iraq war left over a million people dead in the two countries. With the years of US wars, sanctions, and occupation, Iraq was largely destroyed, leaving Iran without its traditional challenger. That brought it even more directly into the longstanding

US crosshairs. Iran had been targeted since the overthrow of the US-installed and US-backed shah and the creation of the Islamic Republic in 1979.

(In the early 2000s Turkey emerged as a potential regional power, having managed to create the 17th largest economy in the world without oil. With its size and copious water, that newly created wealth brought Turkey into the regional power mix as well. But as a NATO member and longtime US ally, Turkey's rising power—even under the leadership of the Islamist-oriented Justice & Development Party of prime minister and then President Recep Tayyip Erdogan—did not shift the US strategic focus on challenging Iran.)

When the US overthrew the Iraqi government and political system in 2003, the replacement was not a popular egalitarian democracy, but rather a thoroughly sectarian system of political parties based on the various ethnic and religious communities in Iraq's multi-faceted population. The Shi'a majority, who had long faced discrimination at the hands of the Sunni-led (though ruthlessly secular) government of Saddam Hussein, took power with US support, as Washington's occupation authority forcibly disbanded the Iraqi military and civil service. The sectarian struggle that resulted escalated to full-scale civil war by the mid 2000s, waged alongside the continuing war against US occupation. From quite early in the US occupation, Iran emerged as a major supporter of the US-backed Shi'a-led government, leading many analysts to conclude that the US war in Iraq had benefited Iran more than any other country in the region.

Iran has had a nuclear power program since the 1950s, largely because the United States convinced the shah's government, which was reluctant to invest in nuclear energy when it had what appeared to be an endless supply of oil, that it needed to diversify its energy sources. Iran ratified the Nuclear Non-Proliferation Treaty (NPT) in 1970, resulting in longstanding ongoing inspections of its enrichment and other nuclear activities by the UN's nuclear watch-dog agency, the IAEA. Under the terms of Article IV of the NPT, Iran like all non-nuclear weapons states has "the inalienable right of all the Parties to the Treaty to develop research, production and use of nuclear energy for peaceful purposes without discrimination."

As far back as 2007 all of the sixteen US intelligence agencies issued a joint National Intelligence Estimate (NIE) stating that Iran did not have nuclear weapons, and crucially, had not made the political/strategic decision to build a nuclear weapon. The NIE also affirmed earlier reports that Iran had abandoned any past research aimed at militarization or weaponization of its nuclear material back in 2003. In 2012 the NIE's conclusions were reaffirmed by the intelligence community.

But at the political level, despite the intelligence consensus that Tehran was not trying to build a nuclear weapon, Iran remained a consistent and public enemy of the United States. Despite close Iranian collaboration with the US during the initial invasion and overthrow of the Taliban in Afghanistan in 2001 after the 9/11 attacks, especially in establishing the US-backed transitional government in Afghanistan in December 2001, the Bush administration identified Iran as a strategic enemy in the global war on terror. In his state of the union address of January 2002, Bush linked Iran with Iraq and North Korea in a so-called "axis of evil," ending the cooperation that had characterized US-Iran relations for months earlier.

Anti-Iran rhetoric as well as serious cyber-attacks against Iran jointly involving the US and Israel continued through the years of the global war on terror under both the Bush and Obama administrations. Once the Iraqi government was overthrown, and throughout the years of the Iraq war in all its iterations, Israel kept up efforts to target Iran as a major enemy. Claims that Iran's nuclear program ostensibly represented an "existential threat" to Israel became a key component of Israeli leaders' efforts to keep US-led international sanctions on Iran. Those efforts, and the constant drumbeat of "Iran is a threat to Israel" helped deter any pressure that might have been brought to bear on Israel regarding its violations of human rights and international law in its occupation and apartheid policies towards the Palestinians.

When ISIS, in its earlier iteration as al-Qaeda in Iraq (AQI) and then Islamic State in Iraq (ISI) first emerged in 2004, it was one of many Sunni militias fighting alongside Shi'a militias against the US occupation and US-backed Iraqi forces. Many of the Sunni militias shifted loyalties during the 2006 Sunni Awakening campaign (see p. 13), in which the US began paying them to fight on the side of the US and the Iraqi government rather than against them. But ISI never joined the Awakening movement, and continued its anti-US and anti-Baghdad attacks, alongside many Shi'a militias.

While Shi'a Iran continued to provide political and sometimes more concrete support to the US-backed Shi'a-dominated government in Baghdad, it also funded and supported numerous independent Shi'a militias. When the US troop pull-out from Iraq began in 2010 and 2011, ISI didn't disappear, but its influence was significantly diminished. By the time it re-emerged in its later form, as ISIS, first in Syria and then back in Iraq, the Sunni militias that had been part of the Awakening movement had been abandoned by the US-backed government in Baghdad, and were once again part of an insurgency rising across Iraq.

By this time, around 2011 and 2012, Iran was playing a major role in simultaneously supporting both the US-backed Shi'a government in Baghdad and the Shi'a militias that were now fighting alongside the government against what had become a Sunni rebellion. ISIS became more powerful in the chaos of the Syrian civil war, and especially during its dramatic land-grabs of 2014 in both Iraq and Syria. At that point Iran supported the Shi'a government and Shi'a militias against ISIS in Iraq, as well as supporting (as it had for many years) the Alawite (an off-shoot of Shi'a Islam) government of Bashar al-Assad in Syria against ISIS and the Sunni forces supporting it.

So by 2014 Iran was fighting on the same side as the United States—against ISIS in both Iraq and Syria—despite the longstanding US-Iran enmity. At the same time and into 2015, Washington and Tehran were engaged in the final year of a long diplomatic process between Iran and what was known as the P-5 + 1 (the five Permanent Members of the UN Security Council—Britain, China,

France, Russia, and the US—plus Germany) to resolve disputes over Iran's nuclear power program and end the sanctions imposed against it. But negotiations or not, public antagonism towards Iran and opposition to a potential nuclear accord remained rampant in key political and media circles in the US.

Escalating threats from Israel, based on false claims of Iran's supposed nuclear danger (while refusing to acknowledge Israel's own decades-old arsenal of 100 to 300 uninspected nuclear weapons) and thinly-veiled threats from Tel Aviv to launch a unilateral war or pressure the US to join a war against Iran, ratcheted up political pressure in the United States as well. A highly-partisan and electorally-driven speech in the US congress by then-Israeli Prime Minister Binyamin Netanyahu just weeks before the culmination of the Iran nuclear negotiations, accused the Obama administration of appeasement in the face of a supposed Iranian danger, and renewed threats of war.

But at the same time Iran was playing an ever-more influential role in the military struggle against ISIS. In March 2015, Iraq's military and the even stronger Shi'a militias launched an offensive to retake the Sunni-majority city of Tikrit, known as the birthplace of Saddam Hussein, from ISIS control. The militias were largely armed and trained by Iran, and the offensive against Tikrit was commanded directly by Iranian General Qasem Soleimani, who had once led the elite Quds Force of Iran's Revolutionary Guard.

In official Washington circles, the two conflict-driven processes—the tense US-Iran negotiations over Iran's nuclear program and sanctions on the one hand, and Iran's central role on the US side in the war against ISIS on the other hand—were rarely discussed together. In fact the Iranian role in the anti-ISIS war was rarely mentioned at all.

In mid-March 2015 dangers remained high. Hard-line elements in Iran's parliament continued to oppose any compromise on a nuclear deal. Even tougher opposition rose in the US Congress. On March 10, forty-seven US senators sent a letter directly to Iran's leaders warning them that any agreement reached with the US regarding lifting sanctions would be simply the position of one president, and that the US government would not be bound by it.

But despite the naysayers, in early April 2015 negotiators won an initial huge victory for diplomacy over war. Both sides made concessions, though Iran gave up far more. Tehran accepted an agreement in which US and European sanctions would remain until the UN's nuclear watchdog agency verified Iranian compliance with its new nuclear obligations—which could take years. It accepted severe cuts in nuclear infrastructure, including reduction of centrifuges for enriching uranium from 19,000 to just over 5,000, as well as reconfiguring its nuclear plants to prevent production of any plutonium and to drastically reduce enrichment capacity. Iran also agreed to unprecedentedly intrusive new inspections.

The United States agreed that any future UN sanctions would have to come before the Security Council for a new vote, meaning that other countries could veto. And while the agreement didn't explicitly reaffirm Iran's rights under the Non-Proliferation Treaty, which include the right to pursue "nuclear energy for peaceful purposes without discrimination," the agreement did acknowledge Iran's "peaceful nuclear program" and sought to limit, not to end, Iran's enrichment capacity. The agreement's final text, including the all-important technical annexes, was to be concluded by June 30, 2015.

Congress continued its efforts to undermine the initial agreement, approving resolutions to delay implementation of the agreement until the House and Senate approved, and threatening to override President Obama's anticipated veto. But negotiators and political leaders in both Iran and the United States, recognizing that both faced similar political opposition from hard-liners in their respective parliaments and elsewhere, appeared willing to continue serious negotiations despite such posturing.

If the final agreement is reached, the global potential will be far more important than the partisan posturing of right-wing militarists and neoconservative ideologues. If it holds, the end of US-Iran hostility could set the stage for an entirely new set of diplomatic relationships and alliances in the Middle East. That potential for a "grand bargain" between Iran and the US could lead to serious negotiations between the US and Iran over how to impose a serious ceasefire and eventually an arms embargo on their respective sides in the Syrian civil war. It could set the stage for a real partnership in Baghdad aimed at forcing an end to sectarianism and a move towards real inclusivity by the Iraqi government, which would encourage an end to Sunni communal support for ISIS as well as support for other extremist elements, both Sunni and Shi'a, across Iraq. In the future, such a US-Iran rapprochement could eventually lead to a real normalization of relations between the US, its allies, and Iran. And with the end of the conflict over Iran's nuclear power program, a deal could also enable the creation and enforcement of a nuclear weapons-free, indeed a weapons of mass destruction-free Middle East—with no exceptions, including Israel's undeclared nuclear arsenal.

What role does oil play in all this?

Oil is at the root of the ISIS crisis for several reasons. Start with the century-old reality that the strategic value of the entire Middle East region, the reason wealthy and powerful countries care much more about war or instability in Middle Eastern countries than a conflict in Cameroon or Sri Lanka is because of the Middle East's massive oil reserves. Oil keeps global capitalism afloat.

Since 1967, US foreign policy interests in the region have remained tripartite: oil, Israel, and strategic power-projection. These elements were all present in the early 1970s, when, as religious history scholar Karen Armstrong wrote, the "soaring oil price created by the 1973 embargo—when Arab petroleum producers cut off supplies to the US to protest against the Americans' military support for Israel—gave the kingdom all the petrodollars it needed to export its idiosyncratic form of Islam." And of course Saudi Wahhabism lies at the root of the ISIS brand of radical Islamist extremism. More recently, while it's clear that the US invasion and occupation of Iraq in 2003 had many causes, one of the most important involved oil.

And that US occupation of Iraq set the precise conditions for the emergence of ISIS. As ISIS continues its territorial expansion and the US remains at war against ISIS, oil serves to enrich the Islamist organization. It connects ISIS to its putative enemies in Iraq, Syria, and beyond, and provides a potential weapon of diplomatic pressure.

When the renamed ISIS reemerged in Syria in 2011 and moved to seize cities and territory across northern Syria and western Iraq, oil—producing it, refining it, and selling it—became a core component of its financial survival. Syria was never a major oil producer by Middle Eastern standards, but its relatively small fields still accounted for about a quarter of the Syrian economy. By September 2014, according to *Business Insider*, ISIS was "cutting deals with local traders and buyers, even businessmen who support Syrian President Bashar al-Assad, and some of its oil has made its way back to government buyers through a series of middlemen. 'Islamic State makes not less than $2 million daily that allows them to pay salaries and maintain their operations,' said a former Western oil executive who worked in a foreign oil firm operating in Syria before the crisis and who is familiar with the nascent oil market."

One of the ironies of the multifaceted Syrian civil war is the degree to which trade and economic relations between the various sides continues, even through the brutal fighting. In the case of ISIS-controlled oil, the traders seeking profits from Syrian crude, sometimes refined using small-scale equipment smuggled into the country, find themselves buying from the extremist Islamist organization fighting against the Syrian government, then turning around to sell to businesspeople close to the repressive Syrian regime of Bashar al-Assad. Government officials in Syria also engage directly with ISIS across areas it controls to jointly protect access to electricity, water, and sometimes transportation.

In Iraq, where oil reserves are among the highest in the world and the territory under its control includes some of Iraq's productive fields, ISIS quickly became one of the richest insurgent organizations in the world. By November 2014, according to *The Guardian*,

> ISIS had consolidated its grip on oil supplies in Iraq and now presides over a sophisticated smuggling empire with illegal exports going to Turkey, Jordan and Iran, according to smugglers and Iraqi officials. Six months after it grabbed vast swaths of territory,

the radical militant group is earning millions of dollars a week from its Iraqi oil operations, the US says. Coalition air strikes against tankers and refineries controlled by Isis have merely dented—rather than halted—these exports, it adds.

The militants control around half a dozen oil-producing oilfields. They were quickly able to make them operational and then tapped into established trading networks across northern Iraq, where smuggling has been a fact of life for years. From early July until late October, most of this oil went to Iraqi Kurdistan. The self-proclaimed Islamic caliphate sold oil to Kurdish traders at a major discount. From Kurdistan, the oil was resold to Turkish and Iranian traders.

The amount of oil being produced by ISIS is much lower than what was produced by the Iraqi government. But there is no question that oil production remains a key component of ISIS financial strength and its ability to pay fighters, recruit professionals including doctors, engineers, and computer technicians, and to pay for at least some basic services in the areas it controls.

And in Iraq as well as in Syria, the ISIS-controlled oil business involves lots of other parties, including those who are fighting ISIS. Kurdish traders are known to be buying and selling ISIS oil in an illegal but widely acknowledged trading system. According to *The Guardian*, "One Kurdish parliamentarian admitted it hadn't been shut down altogether. 'I would say the illegal trade has decreased by 50%. We have detained several people who were involved in buying oil from Da'esh [ISIS]. The same people provided ISIS with petrol and over 250 pick-up trucks,' Mahmoud Haji Omar said. He added that even Shi'a militias fighting the extremists had profited from the trade by taxing oil tankers passing through territory they control."

Oil could also emerge as a source of diplomatic pressure in the context of the regional and global powers' engagement in the Syrian civil war. But that depends on developments in the global oil business. Many of those powers supporting various sides in Syria—Russia, the US, Saudi Arabia, Iran, Iraq, and more—are major oil producers who were seriously affected by the collapse of world oil prices that began in 2014. Russia and Iran, in particular, each a major oil producer highly dependent on oil exports as a large segment of its economy, faced severe consequences as its oil brought in rapidly diminishing amounts of hard currency from the global market.

Despite its similar dependence on oil exports, Saudi Arabia, still the largest Middle East oil exporter, could weather the price crisis much better because of its billions of dollars of oil wealth invested around the world. The Saudis are the dominant force in OPEC, the powerful global oil cartel, which largely allowed the precipitous price drop to happen without cutting production. Such a cut in supply would have had the immediate impact of a price rise—but the Saudis resisted that decision. Many analysts see the Saudi decision rooted in the kingdom's efforts to maintain control of its large global market share—something that it could lose if the practice of hydraulic fracturing, known as fracking, for instance, continues to increase production in the US. With the price of oil remaining low, the thinking goes, fracking becomes less viable (because it's really expensive to produce oil that way—aside from environmental consequences, fracking only makes sense financially if oil prices stay high). So if the amount of fracking-produced oil is reduced, Saudi Arabia keeps a bigger share of the market. The Saudi economy may be hurt by the lower prices, but Saudi wealth means it can survive much better than Russia or Iran.

That gives the Saudi monarchy a great opportunity to pressure Russia. And beginning in early 2015 reports surfaced that exactly that kind of a campaign was under way. As the *New York Times* described it, "Saudi Arabia has been trying to pressure President Vladimir V. Putin of Russia to abandon his support for President Bashar al-Assad of Syria, using its dominance of the global oil markets at a time when the Russian government is reeling from the effects of plummeting oil prices....Any weakening of Russian support for Mr. Assad could be one of the first signs that the recent tumult in the oil market is having an impact on global statecraft. Saudi officials... believe that there could be ancillary diplomatic benefits to the country's current strategy of allowing oil prices to stay low—including a chance to negotiate an exit for Mr. Assad."

Given Russia's longstanding support for Syria, particularly its provision of weapons and other military assistance, such a move could prove powerful. United States support for such a Russian move, however, would be politically complicated. A rise in global oil prices would be good for the US oil industry and good for the companies involved in environment-destroying fracking. But the other consequence of a successful Saudi-Russian oil-for-Assad deal would be a significant rise in oil prices in the US, which would have a huge impact on US consumers and virtually all of the non-energy sectors of the economy. Outside the US, while a major reduction in Russian support for Assad would have serious consequences on the Syrian government, Iranian support would be unlikely to change—and Iran would also benefit from higher oil prices. For the US, fighting the "global war on terror" means once again fighting wars at least partly over oil.

What do the Kurds have to do with the current war in Iraq and Syria?

The mobilization against ISIS has pushed Kurdish military forces to the center of global attention. The Obama administration's return to direct military engagement in Iraq started in 2014 with airstrikes in and around Kobane, although the official peshmerga, or Kurdish, militia in the autonomous Kurdish region of Iraq, were the main players in reclaiming Kobane from ISIS. The US identifies the Kurds as its most reliable military ally and coordinates airstrikes with Kurdish forces. And the Kurds have taken advantage of their newly recognized centrality, including by seizing control of the long-contested oil-rich Iraqi city of Kirkuk outside the official borders of the Kurdish region, to launch new campaigns for recognition, greater autonomy, and perhaps independence.

The crisis created by ISIS's conquest of territory across Syria and Iraq has further destabilized already shaky national unity in both countries. Much attention has focused on the Sunni-Shi'a divide, with many Sunnis, especially in Iraq, backing ISIS (reluctantly or not) as protection against the ravages of a sectarian, Shi'a-dominated government in Baghdad.

And with both Iraq and Syria already seriously divided along sectarian and ethnic lines, that religious split continues to undermine the existence of the nations themselves. In both countries, however, the ISIS crisis has created new opportunities as well as new challenges for Kurdish populations and their longstanding efforts to win at least greater autonomy, if not full-scale independence.

At the beginning of the civil war in Syria, the Kurds were able to maneuver into a position in which they could consolidate a higher level of autonomy, and the regime in Damascus mostly did not target them. While many Kurds remained strong critics of the government's repression, they mostly played a minor role in the Syrian opposition movements. In the summer of 2012 the Syrian military largely pulled out of several large Kurdish towns. Tensions between the Syrian Kurdish forces and Syrian rebels rose, and in 2012 near Aleppo and later in other areas there were direct clashes between militias of the US and western-backed Free Syrian Army and the multi-party Kurdish People's Defense Units (YPG) militias.

As *Time* magazine described it, "Even if they oppose Assad, many Kurds, particularly those aligned with the PYD [one of the most influential Syrian Kurdish parties], see the rebels as Islamist thugs acting on behalf of neighboring Turkey to control a post-Assad Syria. Many insurgents, meanwhile, resent the PYD and its armed supporters for staying out of the war against Assad, accusing it of being a cat's paw for the regime." While that may be somewhat overstated, it does give a good flavor of the contradictions between the sides. For the United States, the tension is further complicated by the fact that the PYD is allied with the PKK, the Kurdish Workers Party, in Turkey, which has long been included on the US anti-terrorism list even while its leaders were negotiating with Ankara.

In Iraq, the divide between Kurds, who dominate the northern sector of the country including key oil fields, and both the Shi'a-dominated government and Sunni-led rebel forces escalated throughout the years of US-imposed economic sanctions (1990–2003) and the US invasion and occupation (2003–2011) and continued after US troops were withdrawn. One of the key points of dispute was the city of Kirkuk—outside the official border of the Kurdish regional government's authority. Control of this mixed Kurdish-Arab-Turkoman city was, and is, an oil prize. Both the government in Baghdad and the Kurdish regional government had claimed the city.

In 2014, the success of ISIS in capturing territory in Iraq, and the resulting collapse of the Iraqi military in those regions, led to an unexpected opportunity for the Kurds, who were able to seize and maintain control of Kirkuk while Baghdad, its fractured military, its US and regional backers, and the world's press was focused solely on land grabs by ISIS. The Kurdish seizure of Kirkuk, with all its oil facilities, remained under the radar.

Kurdish fighters reemerged as key players in the escalating ISIS crisis in August 2014, when ISIS forces overran the largely Kurdish community in Sinjar, in Iraq near the Syrian border. Tens of thousands of the mainly Yazidi residents fled their town to the seek refuge on nearby Mount Sinjar. It was the Kurdish PYG, supported at the end by soldiers of the peshmerga—the militia of the officially recognized Kurdish regional authority in Iraq—who played the major role in saving the Yazidis (mainly Kurdish themselves) from their desperate situation trapped on top of the mountain. (see p. 74 for analysis of the US role in Mount Sinjar.)

The fighting in Kobane, the largely Syrian Kurdish town on the Turkish border, erupted in October 2014 when ISIS threatened to occupy the city. Kobane was not strategically important, but because Kobane was so close to the Turkish border, where international journalists could see the fighting, it quickly became emblematic of Kurdish identity, as well as of the failure of the US strategy to protect the civilian population and the refusal of the Turkish military (including soldiers based just across the border within view of Kobane) to intervene.

Facing domestic and international "Twitter factor" pressure, the United States launched a few airstrikes against ISIS around Kobane and eventually persuaded Turkey to allow a few carefully vetted units of the peshmerga to cross the border from Iraq to help defend the city. But in the midst of the Kobane crisis Secretary of State John Kerry announced that, "Kobane does not define the strategy for the coalition in respect to Da'esh [ISIS]. Kobane is one community and it is a tragedy what is happening there. And we do not diminish that. But we have said from day one that it is going to take a period of time to bring the coalition thoroughly to the table to rebuild some of the morale and capacity of the Iraqi army. And to begin the focus of where we ought to be focusing first which is in Iraq. That is the current strategy." For the United States, ensuring that ISIS did not take over oil-rich and strategically important Iraq was the issue—not the plight of Kurdish civilians in Syria.

The increasingly visible role of Kurdish fighters, both in Syria and Iraq, forced long-simmering Kurdish demands for greater autonomy and perhaps independence to the top of US and regional strategic considerations. Even allowing the peshmerga—the official Kurdish militia from Iraqi Kurdistan—to participate in protecting the population of Kobane was fraught with complications. The United States urgently wanted more local involvement on the ground, while its NATO ally Turkey remained adamant that the Iraqi Kurdish forces not be allowed to play a leading role, for fear that it would encourage greater demands for autonomy for Turkey's Kurds.

After months of fighting, ISIS was routed from Kobane, but by then the population had mostly fled and the town had been virtually destroyed. In February 2015 a BBC correspondent able to enter Kobane reported that, "Kurdish fighters are now consolidating their hold over the town. But driving the IS [ISIS] from here came at tremendous cost. Hundreds of coalition airstrikes have flattened most of the town."

But it was not the airstrikes that had beaten back ISIS. The *Washington Post* headline in late January 2015 read, "Kurds Drive Islamic State Fighters from Strategic Town of Kobane." More important for Kobane residents, credit for liberating their town had gone to Kurdish fighters, not to the US and its coalition allies. Talking to a BBC reporter, the 12-year-old granddaughter of one of the small number of Kobane residents who remained throughout the fighting said, "Kurdish officials didn't abandon us. We are going to school now. And we are very happy because we will be able to go back to our villages. They liberated our lands," she added proudly.

What role is the United Nations playing, and what more is needed?

During the early years of the first global war on terror, the George Bush–Tony Blair axis worked very hard to exclude the United Nations from any significant role. Within 24 hours after the 9/11 attacks, the Bush administration proposed a UN Security Council resolution that passed unanimously with enormous fervor, expressing sympathy and condolences to Americans and "unequivocally condemning" the terrorist acts. The Council called on all countries to "work together" to bring those responsible to justice, and agreed on "increased cooperation and full implementation of the relevant international anti-terrorist conventions and Security Council resolutions."

What the Security Council did not do was to authorize war—the resolution was not passed under the terms of Chapter VII, the one part of the UN Charter through which the Council can authorize the use of military force. It was not a situation in which Washington feared that a stronger resolution might not pass—it was clear anything proposed on that day, while the twin towers still smoldered and many UN diplomats and their families still faced the trauma of having been in the vicinity of the attack, that anything the US wanted, the US would get. The limited text reflected a deliberate decision by the Bush administration not to allow the United Nations to be in any kind of decision-making position.

In the run-up to the 2003 invasion of Iraq, Bush and Blair tried desperately to win Security Council approval for the war. But by that time a massive global peace movement had mobilized, putting unprecedented pressure on countries around the world. Europe split, and smaller, weaker, poorer countries that would ordinarily have quickly succumbed to US pressure stood firm against the call to war. For eight months, the United Nations did what its charter requires, but what it is too rarely allowed to do: stop the scourge of war. The US-UK invasion and occupation were not only illegitimate, immoral, and based on lies, under international law, they were also absolutely illegal.

Technically that changed in May 2003 when the UN's resistance collapsed and the Security Council passed a resolution endorsing the occupation and agreeing to collaborate with it. That decision, despite the predominantly humanitarian nature of the UN's actual work at that time, set the stage directly for the horrific suicide truck-bomb attack on the UN's Baghdad headquarters in August 2003, killing at least 22 people, of whom 16 were United Nations staff.

While it remained in the war-torn region in following years, working primarily to provide humanitarian assistance to occupation-devastated populations and on occasion sending special envoys to crisis zones, the United Nations did not emerge as a major political player in the war on terror again until the Libya crisis broke.

In March 2011, permanent Security Council members Britain and France began a campaign for a military assault starting with a no-fly zone in Libya. The US initially rejected the initiative because influential forces within the Obama administration, the Pentagon, Congress, and other US elites believed a no-fly zone would not protect civilians and, more important, would pull the US into a quagmire with no clear exit strategy or basis to declare "victory." But after a few days of internal debate, the pro-intervention forces, largely based in Hillary Clinton's State Department, won the day. The US then told the British and the French that they could not support the existing no-fly zone plan, but that instead of simply vetoing the proposed resolution, they would redraft it to fit US requirements.

The result was a vastly expanded resolution that not only endorsed a no-fly zone but also authorized "all necessary measures" to be used in the name of protecting civilians. The language legalized unlimited military force, and because "to protect civilians" was not defined, it was left to the US-NATO coalition forces themselves to decide how far they wanted to go.

The Security Council reached a very unusual near-consensus on approving the assault on Libya. The debate focused on the need to protect civilians, and indeed the text of the resolution started with the call for "the immediate establishment of a ceasefire and... he need to intensify efforts to find a solution to the crisis which responds to the legitimate demands of the Libyan people." It took note of the goal of "facilitating dialogue to lead to the political reforms necessary to find a peaceful and sustainable solution." But it was widely believed, at least outside the Security Council itself, that US-NATO intervention would never be limited to humanitarian efforts, and that regime change was certainly on the table.

That turned out to be true. A no-fly zone, attacks on Qaddafi's military, and escalating civilian casualties ensued. The Security Council resolution's language of using "all necessary means" quickly shifted from protecting civilians to open calls for regime change. It was never fully clear why countries such as South Africa gave in to the West's pressure campaign, nor why Russian and Chinese veto power was never asserted. South Africa's vote supporting the resolution appears to be the reason for an African Union delegation being turned away at Libya's border, where the group hoped to enter to begin some kind of negotiations.

A ceasefire didn't seem to be at the top of anyone's agenda, and certainly not that of the UN's most powerful members. The UN, having provided legality (if not legitimacy—it took Arab League and African Union endorsement for that) to the NATO-US air war against Libya, had little further role to play. And three months later, the head of South Africa's Ministry of Foreign Affairs admitted his country now "regretted" having voted for the no-fly zone.

At the core of the debates over Libya was the United Nations' concept of "responsibility to protect," the idea that when people face repression or worse from their own government, the international community has the obligation to step in, relying first on non-military means and only turning to military solutions as the last resort. But for Libya, it would have been far easier to accept the necessity of US-UK-French-NATO military intervention in Libya as based on humanitarian motives if *non-military* but active intervention had already been under way in similar (if smaller) crises.

For example, if the US had immediately cut all military and economic aid to Bahrain at the first sign that its king was bringing foreign troops in to suppress the uprising. If the US had immediately ended all arms sales and stopped the current weapons pipeline to Saudi Arabia when its soldiers crossed Bahrain's causeway. If the US had announced a complete halt in all military aid to Yemen when then-President Abdullah Ali Saleh's forces first attacked the demonstrators. Not to mention the possibility of a decision to cut military aid to Israel and end the decades of US-guaranteed impunity for war crimes. All of those actions were possible, appropriate, non-military, and would have had huge humanitarian impacts. When none of them was even attempted, it was difficult to accept the claim that military intervention in Libya was really grounded in humanitarian motives.

The United Nations was next called upon to respond to the rapidly escalating civil war in Syria. One of the first moves was by the UN's Human Rights Council, which voted to send a fact-finding mission in April 2011, soon after the crisis erupted. Later efforts to send investigation teams were mainly met by the refusal of the Syrian government to allow them access. In the first months of the crisis, as the Assad regime's military response to the unarmed political opposition morphed into a widening civil war, the Security Council took up the issue. Unable to reach agreement on a resolution, the Council's first move was to issue a statement urging the Syrian regime to comply with human rights norms, calling on all sides to stop the violence, and supporting a Syrian political process to end the crisis. Statements of concern, condemnation of the violence, and demands for ending the political repression and allowing humanitarian assistance continued to be issued by the UN Secretary-General, the Human Rights Council, and other agencies of the organization.

The Security Council continued to debate the Syria question, but the wide gap between the two groups of permanent members—the US, UK, and France versus Russia and China—made agreement on a resolution very difficult. The first to come to a vote, on February 4, 2012, resulted in vetoes by Russia and China, based on the resolution's support for an earlier Arab League plan requiring Assad to step down. It included broader language condemning violence on all sides, but Moscow and Beijing were not prepared to accept the call for Assad to resign and hand power to a deputy. The following day, US Secretary of State Hillary Clinton called for the formation of a "Friends of Democratic Syria" coalition outside the United Nations.

Soon after the Security Council resolution was vetoed, the General Assembly passed a similar resolution based on the Arab League plan, rather than using the opportunity to craft a different approach to demand an end to violence and a new diplomatic initiative.

Two later Security Council efforts also resulted in vetoes, but in both cases the draft resolutions were rooted in Chapter VII of the UN Charter, which permits sanctions but can also be used to authorize military action. In July 2012, when the second veto of a Chapter VII resolution took place, *The Guardian* quoted the British ambassador claiming that Security Council members had "offered flexibility on Russia and China's concerns," and that therefore it was "irrational" that those two countries "argued that a Chapter VII resolution is somehow designed to seek conflict through the backdoor." According to *The Guardian*, US Ambassador Susan Rice said that "the suggestion that the resolution would give the green light for foreign forces to enter Syria was 'paranoid if not disingenuous,'" and that the resolution "would in no way authorise or even pave the way for foreign military intervention." The following day, not long after that resolution was vetoed, the foreign military intervention began on all sides—leading, most recently, to the direct military engagement of US warplanes and missiles in Syria, as well as US, British, and their regional allies' arming, training, and funding of Syrian as well as foreign fighters.

The next United Nations move was the appointment in late February, jointly with the Arab League, of former Secretary-General Kofi Annan as the special envoy to Syria—tasked with engaging with all sides inside and outside Syria to end the violence and promote a peaceful resolution. In mid-March Annan submitted his six-point peace plan to the Security Council.

The plan called for the following:

- a Syrian-led political process to address the legitimate aspirations and concerns of the Syrian people

- a commitment to stop the fighting and respect a UN-supervised ceasefire by both the government and the opposition

- timely humanitarian assistance, including the implementation of a daily two-hour humanitarian pause

- release of arbitrarily detained persons, especially the most vulnerable, and political prisoners

- access and freedom of movement for journalists

- respect for the freedom of association and the right to peacefully demonstrate

The Syrian government accepted the plan on March 27, and a ceasefire as called for in the plan was announced on April 12, 2012, to be verified by a Security Council-mandated observer team. But the ceasefire was never implemented.

In March 2012 the UN's High Commissioner for Human Rights Navi Pillay cautioned against arming the Syrian opposition, stating that it threatened to escalate the violence. She was right—the additional arms flooding into both secular and most especially rising extremist forces in Syria, smuggled over the border from Iraq, accessed from newly accessible stockpiles in Libya, and especially provided directly by US allies in the region, all served to escalate the government's repression to full-scale civil war.

By August, Kofi Annan had resigned. It was clear that the special envoy was not even close to achieving a ceasefire, the starting point of his six-point peace plan, and prospects were looking dimmer than ever. But his resignation reflected two other stark realities. First, outside players—most especially the United States, Saudi Arabia, Qatar, Turkey, Jordan, the UAE, Russia, and Iran—were operating solely for their own narrow strategic interests, not on behalf of the Syrian people. Second, the UN Security Council and its member states provided no real support for any potential political solution that might actually work. Instead, they acted to strengthen the military forces on both sides.

It was significant that Annan directly criticized the Council and its members, especially the five permanent members—Britain, China, France, Russia, UK, US—known as the Perm Five. While the Council had endorsed the Annan plan early on, there was never any real support for it or for the work of the UN observer team in Syria. The three US-British-French resolutions on Syria called for harsh UN sanctions and a range of other economic and diplomatic pressures on the regime of Bashar al-Assad. They were all vetoed by Russia and China. The US and its allies had maintained (perhaps even truthfully at that pre-ISIS moment) that direct engagement in the military battle against the Syrian government was not their intention. But two of the three vetoed resolutions would have been taken under Chapter VII of the UN Charter—the same precondition required for the use of force.

The resolutions might well have set the political stage to legalize what would later occur anyway: direct US/European/NATO participation in the fighting. Looking at the precedent of the Security Council vote on Libya the year before, when the Council-authorized no-fly zone was immediately transformed into an all-out US/NATO air war, that kind of escalation was certainly a reasonable assumption. Further negotiations might well have rendered Security Council agreement on a resolution possible. Perhaps Russia and China might have accepted resolutions calling for pressure, even an arms embargo (prohibiting sales, assistance, repairs, or anything else) to both sides—if the resolution was not based on Chapter VII. But that proposal was not forthcoming, and instead the Council remained paralyzed.

When Special Envoy Kofi Annan resigned in early August 2012, it was clear that outside forces were not willing to impose enough pressure on their Syrian allies to make a ceasefire, an arms embargo, a new diplomatic initiative, or other necessary components of a peace process possible. He stated that "increasing militarization on the ground and the clear lack of unity in the Security Council have fundamentally changed the circumstances for the effective exercise of my role." He went on to add, "The bloodshed continues, most of all because of the Syrian government's intransigence and continuing refusal to implement the six-point plan, and also because of the escalating military campaign of the opposition, all of which is compounded by the disunity of the international community. At a time when we need—when the Syrian people desperately need action, there continues to be finger-pointing and name-calling in the Security Council."

A few weeks later the Council appointed veteran Algerian diplomat and international civil servant Lakhdar Brahimi to replace Annan as the joint special envoy. But as the war in Syria continued to escalate, he would have no more success than his predecessor. One of his first efforts, a ceasefire in October in honor of the Muslim holiday of Eid al-Adha, failed to achieve its goal.

In August 2013 the United Nations Security Council became the main venue where the debate on how to respond to the chemical weapons attack outside of Damascus went forward. (See p. 96 for more on the chemical weapons attack and responses.) But the role of the global institution was sidelined relative to the debate in the United States, Britain, and NATO regarding possible military responses.

Following the chemical weapons crisis, Brahimi turned to convening a major conference on Syria as the cornerstone of his work as special envoy. The UN acted as convener for the January 2014 "Geneva II" conference, an attempt to bring together key Syrian parties from both the government and the opposition. But the conference never succeeded, chiefly due to Washington's refusal to allow Iran to be invited, despite, or perhaps because of the fact that, Iran was a major player in the Syrian war. Recognizing that diplomacy that leaves out major players can never succeed, UN Secretary General Ban Ki-moon invited Tehran to participate. But after 24 hours of intense US pressure, he "disinvited" Iran's representatives. Negotiations went on for two weeks but failed to reach any agreement on ending the war or even temporary ceasefires or humanitarian corridors.

In May 2014 Brahimi resigned, expressing his "apologies once more that we haven't been able to help [the Syrian people] as much as they deserve, as much as we should have, and also to tell them that the tragedy in their country shall be solved…they have shown incredible resilience and dignity."

As political efforts floundered, the United Nations' greatest concern was the escalating humanitarian crisis. The UN children's agency, UNICEF, the refugee, food, and health agencies all moved into crisis mode to respond, but lack of sufficient financial support from UN member states meant that their work, while vitally important for the very survival of millions of Syrian refugees and displaced, was rarely sufficient.

Ironically, the great divide between the two groups of permanent members of the Security Council—the US, Britain, and France versus Russia and China—may have actually enabled the Council to abide by its UN Charter obligation to prevent the "scourge of war" from spreading even further. While a resolution focusing on a mutual ceasefire, arms embargo, and renewed political negotiations would have been important, it was clear that the US and its allies would never have allowed that without Chapter VII authorization and some reference to Assad stepping down. It remains unclear whether Russia and China might have supported such a resolution without those two deal-breakers. But certainly, if the two sides *had* agreed on a Chapter VII resolution, there would have been an even greater level of escalation and violence, and even less of a chance of bringing a quick end to the war.

There is a kind of revisionist history of the United Nations popularized by some in the United States and elsewhere, which claims that the UN fails when it refuses to endorse US, NATO, "Western" wars. During the "humanitarian interventions" of the 1990s and the Iraq War of 2003, the UN was excoriated as a failure when it *rejected* participation in military action, rather than being recognized as a failure when it *joined* the war train. But the reality is quite the opposite. In fact one of the greatest achievements of the United Nations was the refusal of the Security Council to endorse George W. Bush's war on Iraq. The eight months of UN resistance in 2002–03 brought the global institution into partnership with many governments, and more important, with the extraordinary global peace movement of that period—the moment when "the world said no to war." That should be a moment to reclaim, not to reject.

US involvement in the war in Afghanistan continued after its planned end and the US troop withdrawal slowed—was that part of Obama's global war on terror?

When Barack Obama was elected he promised to end what he called the "dumb war" in Iraq, but also to escalate the war in Afghanistan, which he promptly did. He sent an additional 47,000 US troops to Afghanistan in his first year in office, but made clear that his intention was to withdraw almost all US troops by the end of 2014. In mid-2010, Obama's second year in office, the total number of al-Qaeda fighters left in Afghanistan, according to then-CIA Director Leon Panetta, was "50 to 100, maybe less." But there were still almost 100,000 US troops occupying the country.

As al-Qaeda shifted its fighters to Pakistan, al-Qaeda affiliates sprang up in new venues across the region. Once again, US ground troops, air force pilots, and armed drones proved the limits of military force in defeating terrorism. Public support in the US was dropping rapidly, but support from the Pentagon stayed firm. Writing in *Foreign Policy in Focus* in December 2012, John Feffer described how, "[i]n this wait-and-see scenario, the Pentagon will be the lead player, just as it was during the period before the 'surge.' The US military is determined that if they can't call the Afghanistan operation a clear-cut 'win,' at least it won't go down in history as a 'loss.' What happens after 2014, when most US troops are gone, the Pentagon can then effectively blame on the Afghans themselves."

Many al-Qaeda and other fighters whom the US identified as "terrorists" were in fact killed in the US war. It was never clear exactly how many, because the Pentagon early on said, "We don't do body counts," and had no decent means of determining identities of the casualties of airstrikes. It was later revealed that all males of military age killed by US bombs or drones were automatically classified as militants. Whether "militant" also equaled "terrorist" was never spelled out. (See p. 7 for more on how "terrorists" are identified.)

What was certain was that many civilians were killed as well. In 2006 other agencies did begin some effort at counting civilian casualties—through 2013 that seven-year casualty estimate was about 18,700 Afghan civilians dead. An early 2014 United Nations report documented that a brief reduction in civilians killed in 2012 had already been reversed, with 2013's figures almost matching the civilian toll of 2011, the worst year for civilians since the counting began.

Those casualty counts, it should be noted, only began long after the massive bombing campaigns that opened the US war against Afghanistan in 2001—*The Guardian* estimated that up to 20,000 Afghans were killed just in the first months, from October 7, 2001, until February 2002.

The US explained the escalation of fighting in Afghanistan in rather convoluted terms as a way of speeding up an end to the US role in the war. In his January 2014 State of the Union address, Obama did mention one substantive change—that "while our relationship with Afghanistan will change, one thing will not: our resolve that terrorists do not launch attacks against our country." So that was the real shift. Now it was official that the US would continue occupying Afghanistan solely to defending US interests. It no longer had anything to do with protecting Afghans.

In May 2014 Obama announced a plan to withdraw most US troops and end their combat role in Afghanistan by the end of that year, leaving behind almost 10,000 troops until the end of 2016.

The US gradually reduced troop numbers, but by early December 2014 the White House announced another change, adding 1,000 more troops to remain in Afghanistan, for a total of almost 11,000, and an anticipated new US-NATO mission to begin some time in 2015. That new deployment would include 12,000 more US and NATO troops primarily focused on training the Afghan military, while some unknown thousands of US counter-terrorism troops would continue operating in Afghanistan, still ostensibly against al-Qaeda. (No one at the press conferences asked President Obama or then-Secretary of Defense Chuck Hagel if the number of al-Qaeda operatives in Afghanistan was still "50 to 100, maybe less" as Panetta had stated.)

In late November 2014 Hagel resigned. The White House claimed his departure did not indicate any change in strategy. But he had been brought in to oversee the withdrawal of troops and the ending of the Iraq and Afghanistan wars, and those wars were now escalating instead—more troops were being kept on a longer mission in Afghanistan, and US troops had returned to fight in Iraq. Hagel had essentially already ceded leadership of the Pentagon to Gen. Martin Dempsey, then-Chairman of the Joint Chiefs of Staff, who had been urging a much more aggressive military posture both in Afghanistan and Iraq.

Ashton Carter, the Pentagon insider who replaced Hagel as secretary of defense, traveled to Afghanistan just days after being confirmed. When he returned, new evidence of mission creep emerged. On February 22, 2015 an NPR host introduced Carter with the words, "When it comes to Afghanistan, the line out of the White House has been clear and consistent. US combat operations are over. US troops are coming home. And the Afghans are in charge. But this weekend, the new US secretary of defense flew to Kabul and said that might not be the case."

Some of the mission creep was rooted in delays that had plagued the contentious Afghan presidential elections of 2014. (See p. 48 for more on how the election returned one of the most notorious Afghan warlords to power as the new vice president in 2014.) The US and Britain promised they would not abandon Afghanistan after Western combat troops were withdrawn. No new money was pledged, and it remained unclear just what that "support" would look like other than keeping US and NATO troops in the country longer than planned.

The most important consideration for that decision was the continuation of the Afghanistan war, which was escalating despite the reductions in US and NATO troops and despite the fact that the vast majority of al-Qaeda operatives were gone.

The Taliban, another extremist Islamist organization, had won Afghanistan's civil war in 1996, then ruled the country until it was overthrown by the US invasion of October 2001. It was continuing to fight even as the US gradually withdrew troops. The original US invasion of Afghanistan had replaced the Taliban with a government made up of their longtime opponents, known as the Northern Alliance (many of whose leaders were just as extremist, misogynistic, and violent as the Taliban). This set the stage for a continuation of Afghanistan's longstanding civil war, fought by the Taliban and other insurgent forces against the US-backed Afghan government plus a host of pro-government but largely unaccountable militias. The revived conflict continued to create escalating numbers of civilian casualties.

It also provided the pretext for continuing US military engagement in the country, despite the acknowledgement that al-Qaeda, the original ostensible target of the US "global war on terror" in Afghanistan, was long gone. Early in 2014, when it was still unclear whether the government in Kabul would sign a security agreement with the US, top Pentagon officials made clear that they wanted to keep troops and continue fighting in Afghanistan. While some referred to threats of a serious attack against Kabul and the potential collapse of the US-backed government, the main point of reference was the possibility that Afghanistan could again be used as a base for international terrorism—the expressed concern was for US interests, not for the people of Afghanistan.

Obama's former defense policy chief, second in command at the Pentagon Michele Flournoy, focused in February 2014 on her belief that the insurgency could "gain momentum and territory, take over eastern Afghanistan, re-creating a safe haven for terrorist elements that still harbor an anti-US agenda. After all of this effort and all of this sacrifice and all of this progress [sic], you're back to a new safe haven for terrorists? It's like, it just makes no sense."

Less than a year later, Ashton Carter, the new secretary of defense, dismissed reports that some elements in Afghanistan were linking themselves to ISIS, saying they appeared to be just extremists "rebranding" themselves. "The reports I've seen still have them in small numbers," he told reporters on his way home from Afghanistan.

Yet those small numbers, whether of al-Qaeda or ISIS in Afghanistan, seemingly kept the US-backed Afghan military from defeating them. During 2014 more than 5,000 members of the Afghan security forces were killed, the highest yearly toll yet. In December of that year the *New York Times* cited outgoing commander of the US forces in Afghanistan, Lt. Gen. Joseph Anderson, who spoke to them after the ceremonies marking the end of the US combat mission. "The record casualties of Afghan forces are not sustainable, and neither are their astounding desertion rates, he said. Political meddling, not intelligence, drives Afghan military missions....It was a reflection on the mission that was in stark contrast to the unbridled renditions of success offered during the ceremony by commanders, including General Anderson."

It was also in stark contrast to the idea that somehow more years of US/NATO "training" of Afghan security forces with little or no loyalty to the US/NATO-created central government in Kabul, and more years of US-backed war, was going to do anything to end the attacks or help build better lives for the Afghan people—let alone win the global war on terror.

The US had yet to win that war—and more military engagement was unlikely to change that reality. A November 2014 poll indicated that despite many Afghans saying they would like to see a greater US commitment to Afghanistan, support for the Taliban doubled from 2010, to 20 percent of Afghans. Thirty-one percent support the presence of foreign jihadist fighters—also higher than 2010. Once again, military force fails to change people's hearts and minds.

On the same December 2014 day that the Obama administration announced its intention to keep an additional thousand US troops in Afghanistan after the supposed deadline, the results of a US military investigation were announced. As reported in the *Washington Post*, the investigation determined that the killing of a two-star US Army general, Harold J. Greene, and wounding of 18 other Afghan, US, German, and British military personnel at Afghanistan's National Defense University a few months earlier had been carried out by "a lone Afghan soldier who had no apparent ties to the Taliban."

What does all of this have to do with Palestine and Israel?

The new war on terror—meaning the war against ISIS, the civil war in Syria, the return of US troops to war in Iraq, the escalating drone war, and more—is not being directly fought in or by Palestine or Israel, Palestinians or Israelis. But that does not mean there is no connection. To the contrary, there are on-the-ground, political, regional/strategic, and ideological links.

While Palestinians inside Israel and the occupied territories are not directly affected, Palestinian refugees in and around Syria are facing serious war-related problems. The greatest crisis confronts the Palestinians who lived in refugee camps in Syria, most of them in and around Damascus. Those families included Palestinians who fled to Syria during the *nakba*, or catastrophe, the massive forced expulsion and dispossession of Palestinians from their land during the 1947–48 war of Israeli independence. Others were living in Syria after having been made refugees for the second, third, or even more times—some who escaped the *nakba* into the West Bank, perhaps, and then were forced out in 1967, ending up in Jordan. Maybe they were living in a refugee camp in Jordan and were expelled in 1970 during Jordan's anti-Palestinian campaigns. Maybe they ended up in one of the numerous Palestinian refugee camps in Lebanon and were expelled from there during the Israeli invasion and occupation of 1982.

With the outbreak of Syria's civil war, hundreds of thousands of Palestinian refugees still living in camps in Syria faced dire threats. Early in the Syrian crisis most Palestinians tried to avoid taking sides, fearing the consequences. But as the popular uprising shifted to a lethal, multi-faceted civil war, the situation became much worse. In July 2012 the United Nations agency responsible for providing basic survival services to Palestinian refugees, UNRWA, issued a statement of direct concern, particularly for the more than 100,000 refugees living in Yarmuk camp in Damascus.

"UNRWA views with increasingly grave concern the situation in Syria, particularly as regards the implications for the stability and protection of 500,000 Palestine refugees across the country," the agency said. "The current situation in the Damascus neighborhood of Yarmuk and in rural Damascus, home to both Syrian and Palestinian communities, is especially worrying."

UNRWA pushed all sides of the conflict to work "to preserve human life, to avoid forced displacement and to exercise the utmost restraint" and to demonstrate "respect for the neutrality and integrity of UN installations" and places where refugees and other civilians live. "UNRWA has appealed to the Syrian authorities to safeguard the security of Palestine refugees wherever they reside in Syria."

But safeguarding the security of refugees was not on the agenda of the Syrian military, nor was it a priority for any of the myriad of opposition forces. Many thousands of Palestinian refugees in Yarmouk and elsewhere in Syria were forced to flee their homes once again. Israel continued its post-1948 denial of the refugees' international-law-granted right of return to their homes, forcing many to seek refuge in already overcrowded refugee camps in Lebanon and Jordan, neither of whom were particularly welcoming of the newest refugee population.

In December 2012 Syrian military jets bombed areas of Damascus including Yarmouk, hitting a mosque and a school inside the camp. The already-severe humanitarian crisis in the camp turned dire. A photograph, which unexpectedly went viral around the world and was the basis for a #SaveYarmouk Twitter campaign, showed the desperation of the 18,000 Palestinians left in the camp, many of them children and elderly people, unable to flee.

It was perhaps the bitterest of ironies that many of the Palestinians fleeing Yarmouk who managed to get to Lebanon found refuge, of a sort, in the decrepit Beirut-area refugee camps known as Sabra and Shatila—the site of a brutal 1982 massacre by Lebanese Christian extremists armed and backed by the Israeli military.

The situation in Syria did not improve. By July 2013 the 18,000 Palestinians left in Yarmouk were fully under siege by the Syrian regime, and water was cut off in September 2014, meaning residents had to rely on untreated ground water or open wells, carrying cans of water since there was no electricity to fill tanks.

On February 25, 2015, UNRWA spokesman Chris Gunness issued the following statement:

> UNRWA was unable to distribute assistance in Yarmouk today, 25 February.
>
> UNRWA assesses the security situation in Yarmouk daily and requests relevant authorities to facilitate the distribution of humanitarian assistance to the civilian population. Over the previous two months, Yarmouk and its surrounding areas have seen a serious escalation in armed conflict, including frequent exchanges of fire and the use of heavy weapons, which have persistently disrupted the distribution of life-saving humanitarian aid to the 18,000 civilians trapped in the area. UNRWA remains deeply concerned that no successful distribution has been completed since 6 December 2014.
>
> Approximately 400 food parcels are required each day to meet the minimum food needs of this extremely vulnerable population. In 2014, on days when all concerned actors cooperated fully to give priority to meeting the humanitarian needs of civilians in Yarmouk, UNRWA proved capable of distributing up to 1,000 food parcels per day. To stop the suffering of Yarmouk's civilians, UNRWA calls for this level of cooperation to resume, for the immediate cessation of armed hostilities in and around

Yarmouk, and for all concerned parties to act in ways that promote the protection of Yarmouk's civilians and give the utmost
priority to their humanitarian needs.

UNRWA had issued the same statement, word for word, every
day for almost three months.

Writing in *Electronic Intifada*, Nael Bitarie described his own
flight from Yarmouk, where people had once tried to remain neutral in the uprising. "Our neutrality did not protect us from either
Assad's forces or from rebels, however. Not long ago, Yarmouk was
the capital of the Palestinian diaspora in Syria. Today, the camp has
been destroyed."

By April 2015 Yarmouk's destruction was virtually complete.
While the 18,000 people still inside (3,500 of them children) had
already suffered through months of the Syrian government's siege,
they now faced ISIS forces who invaded the camp. Fighting escalated,
with government and ISIS troops, as well as other militias, turning
the camp into a battlefield. According to Gunness, the refugees'
"lives are threatened. They are holed up in their battered homes too
terrified to move, which is why we are saying that there must be a
pause [in fighting], there must be humanitarian access for groups
like UNRWA."

When a reporter asked why the starving and dying residents of
Yarmouk didn't receive global attention until ISIS overran the camp,
Gunness replied, "The question is can this world attention be translated into political action. Because we have long said that the time
for humanitarian action alone has long passed, and what we need is
the world powers—the big players—to bring the necessary pressures to bear on the parties on the ground." As of the end of April
2015, no such initiative by the world powers was in sight.

Within the broader context of the Syrian civil war, one of the
seven separate wars making up the fighting in Syria was the fight between the US and Israel versus Iran. That made Israel a player in the
Syrian civil war, although one that was not directly supporting any
of the forces fighting on the ground. Israel did intervene directly,

bombing Syrian targets, particularly in the non-occupied side of the Golan Heights.

The unevenness of Israel's role reflects the counterintuitive reality that for decades the Syrian regime—led by Bashar al-Assad since 2000 and by his father, Hafez al-Assad since 1970—had served as an unacknowledged useful neighbor for Israel. Despite Syrian rhetoric about resistance and defending the Palestinians, both Assads were ultimately quite helpful to Israel, most especially by keeping the Israeli-occupied Golan Heights quiet, its population kept under tight control to prevent serious uprisings or resistance.

On the global political side, the renewed US involvement in the Iraq war and the relentless casualties of the Syrian civil war—though covered far less in the media than the up-close-and-personal violence of ISIS—both served as a diversion from the violence of occupation and apartheid that continue to shape Israeli policy and action toward the Palestinians. With the civil war raging inside Syria, Israel was able to attack Syrian positions with little fear of consequences.

Israel had long relied on Syria's backing of Hamas, the Islamist party elected in the Gaza Strip, as the basis for claiming Syria was supporting terrorism. It was a blow to that Israeli propaganda campaign when Hamas openly split from Syria, based on Damascus' repression against the popular uprising. And while some commentators attempted to equate the militancy and past use of armed resistance (some of which, in targeting civilians inside Israel, had indeed violated international law) to Israel's occupation with the brutal extremism of ISIS, the claimed linkage could not hold. The popularly elected Palestinian party that governs the still-occupied Gaza Strip continues to maintain ties with the now-outlawed Muslim Brotherhood in Egypt and the government of Qatar, not the extremists of ISIS or al-Qaeda.

Across the region as the 2010–11 Arab Spring erupted, many in the US and elsewhere in the West claimed that the core demands' focus on jobs and dignity somehow meant that the people of the Arab world no longer cared about Palestine and about Israeli occupation. But they were wrong. While the uprisings—and each had its own national particularities—shared a priority commitment to democracy, the rights of citizenship, and the basics of economic, social, and political rights, there is no question that just barely beneath the surface, support for Palestinian rights and outrage at Israeli treatment of Palestinians remained intense.

For many, in the Arab world and beyond, the issue of double standards also erupted powerfully in the connection between the Syrian civil war, the war on terror, and Israel's oppression of the Palestinians, particularly in Gaza. In the summer of 2014, when President Obama talked about the urgent need to protect the Yazidi Kurds on Mount Sinjar, he described them as "innocent people facing violence on a massive scale." That was certainly true. And across the region many people also recognized the people of Gaza—where Israel had just carried out a 50-day military onslaught that left almost 2,200 people dead, according to the UN more than 70 percent of them civilians and including many children—as "1.8 million innocent people facing violence on a massive scale." Many wondered why the US wasn't sending an airlift to overcome Israel's siege of Gaza, to force open Gaza's sealed border crossings and allow the people to escape their crowded, desperate enclave?

—PART VII—

LOOKING FORWARD

Isn't military force necessary against such a violent force as ISIS? What are the alternatives to war with ISIS?

President Obama was right when he said there is no military solution to the ISIS crisis. His decision to bomb Syria, and to return US troops to fight in Iraq, contradicts that recognition. It also violates Obama's own commitment, stated in his State of the Union address of 2014, to reverse Washington's "perpetual war footing." Instead, his renewal of a direct US military role in the region in the context of the rise of ISIS only makes that crisis worse. It gives ISIS and its allies a new basis for recruitment, it encourages extremists in other countries to link to and emulate ISIS, it strengthens the repressive Syrian government, it undermines Syria's struggling non-violent opposition movement, and it further consolidates the links between ISIS supporters in Syria and in Iraq.

There are limits to what any government—including the United States, the most powerful country in the world—is actually capable of doing. When the actions taken on the ground are in fact doing more harm than good, the response to those actions must be based on reclaiming the Hippocratic Oath: first, do no harm. That means rejecting actions—bombing, drone strikes, arming opposition forces, renewed US troop deployments—that are making the crisis worse.

And around the world, including in the US, Britain, France, and elsewhere, there is the need to create responses to ISIS (and other terrorist) recruiting that does not make that situation worse as well. President Obama himself acknowledged that "engagement with communities can't be a cover for surveillance. It can't securitize our relationship with Muslim Americans, dealing with them solely through the prism of law enforcement." But he didn't do or even propose anything to actually change the US and local state and municipal policies that do just that. He made the statement at a White House conference designed to figure out how to counter recruiting by ISIS and similar organizations. But it wasn't held until mid-February 2015, a full seven months after Obama ordered the bombing to begin. In the meantime, a policy that depended precisely on using "engagement with communities" as a "cover for surveillance" and a law enforcement-based "securitized relationship with Muslim Americans" remained in effect. Prioritizing the law enforcement response at home remained the parallel to prioritizing the military response in Syria, Iraq, Afghanistan, and beyond.

A month earlier, meeting with British Prime Minister David Cameron at the White House, President Obama described the "phenomenon of violent extremism," saying, "I do not consider it an existential threat." Unlike the British leader, Obama did not use the term "Islamic extremism." He noted it was "important for Europe not to simply respond with a hammer and law enforcement and military approaches to these problems," but he did not indicate then, or at the conference later, anything he would actually do to stop the reliance on precisely those approaches in his own country.

At the end of January 2015 the *New York Times* editorial board wrote, "American officials see an emerging international consensus on the need for a long-term diplomatic solution between Mr. Assad and diverse rebel groups. There is also interest in United Nations-led ceasefires in local communities like Aleppo that might serve as a basis for a broader peace....But it's unclear how plausible any of the ideas are, and no one seems to have figured out how to tie these disparate pieces into a coherent game plan." In fact it remained unclear just who in Washington, let alone in the rest of the world, actually believed there was an emerging consensus on anything regarding Syria diplomacy—and as long as that was the case, US reliance on military instead of diplomatic solutions would continue to carry the day.

When it comes to dealing with US policy toward ISIS, there are two critical understandings. One requires rejecting George W. Bush's post-9/11 claim that the only choice was "we either go to war, or we let 'em get away with it." That was not the only choice for dealing with al-Qaeda then; it is not the only choice for dealing with ISIS now. War or nothing is never the only choice.

The other understanding means recognizing that there is often no strategy, no tactic that will successfully end an immediate attack, •

or resolve another kind of crisis, without causing much greater harm in the medium and long term. Whether or not military action is appropriate or legitimate is not dependent solely on how violent the potential target is. There are critical questions of law—international as well as domestic. There are questions of efficacy—will it work, will it make the threat go away or actually enable the threat to grow? There are challenging questions of consequence—what will happen, and who will come to power the day after? And there are the crucial questions of morality—when we know so many more people will die as a result of anticipated actions, how can we justify carrying them out? And of hypocrisy—when one country's actions have already been so culpable in creating a crisis, how dare that same government claim legitimacy in choosing to kill again, to destroy again, in the name of solving the crisis?

No US military action will result in ISIS immediately disappearing. And even if US or allied airstrikes manage to get the right target sometimes, and take out a rocket launcher or kill a truckload of ISIS fighters or destroy a house where an ISIS commander lives, the inevitability remains of family members being killed, of local anger being stoked, of homes and villages and whole cities being wiped out, of more people beginning to sympathize with violent extremists. All of this undermines any potential immediate military value.

Arming the so-called moderate opposition in Syria doesn't mean the US is supporting the good guys. It means sending arms to the Free Syrian Army—and thus risking the almost inevitable result that the weapons will be expropriated by far more powerful violent extremists. It also means supporting FSA fighters who themselves, according to the *New York Times*, "went on to behead six ISIS fighters…and then posted the photographs on Facebook" shortly after ISIS beheaded the US journalist James Foley.

In Syria, the CIA and Pentagon-run program to vet and train thousands of new anti-ISIS fighters (the same ones who were going to be trained to fight against Assad) means creating an entirely new US proxy army, almost certainly with little or no indigenous legitimacy. In Iraq, arming the Iraqi government and its allied militias doesn't solve the problem there. It means supporting a sectarian, Shi'a-dominated government in Baghdad, backed by even more sectarian militias, both responsible for terrible violence against Sunni communities.

The US went to war in Afghanistan seeking revenge for the September 11 attacks. Jordan sent waves of airstrikes over Syria to avenge the killing of its bomber pilot. Japan's premier vowed revenge for ISIS killing two Japanese citizens in Syria. But while a military strike might bring some immediate public satisfaction, revenge is a dangerous basis for foreign policy.

Military attacks are wrong in a host of ways. Most are illegal under international law, immoral because of civilian casualties, and a distraction from vitally needed diplomacy. They also make real solutions impossible.

So what do serious alternatives to military solutions look like? To start, we must recall why ISIS is so powerful in the first place.

ISIS has good weapons. Since 2011, the post-Qaddafi chaos in Libya has brought a new flood of arms to a region already awash in weapons—mostly US-supplied and acquired directly or through Saudi Arabia and other Gulf states—for more than 15 years. So there needs to be a strategy of how to achieve a real arms embargo on all sides.

ISIS also has good military leadership. In Iraq, Sunni generals who were kicked out of their positions in the military when the US invaded are now providing training, strategy, and military leadership to ISIS-allied militias and ISIS itself. Many of them reject religious extremism, and would be unlikely to continue support for ISIS if they believed a new, truly inclusive government in Iraq would give them some chance of recovering their lost jobs, prestige, and dignity. It was not enough to elect a new prime minister in 2014 who speaks in more inclusive language, but announces a new government made up of too many of the same old sectarian faces. There needs to be a real strategy to convince those former military leaders that there is a place for them in a new and different Iraq.

ISIS draws additional strength from the support it receives from Sunni tribal leaders in Iraq—the very people President Obama says he wants to "persuade" to break with ISIS. But these people are loyal to ISIS because, first during the US invasion and especially in the years of the US-backed Shi'a-controlled sectarian government of Nuri al-Maliki, they have suffered grievously. They were demonized, attacked, and dispossessed by the government in Baghdad, and many of them see ISIS as the only possible ally and protector, with the potential to challenge that government. These are often the same people who control large and powerful militias willing to fight alongside ISIS against the government in Baghdad. Clearly what's needed is an entirely new, inclusive political culture to replace Iraq's toxic sectarian divides.

ISIS also has the support of many ordinary Iraqi Sunnis. This largely secular constituency may hate what ISIS stands for, its religious extremism and violence, but having faced arrest, torture, and extra-judicial execution under successive sectarian Shi'a-controlled governments in Baghdad, many often choose to stand with ISIS. Some also are willing to ally at least temporarily with ISIS against Baghdad. The Iraqi populace, especially Sunnis, must be convinced that the new government in Iraq really represents a break with the anti-Sunni sectarianism of the past to reverse the escalation of violence.

Ending the support that ISIS relies on from tribal leaders, military figures, and ordinary Sunnis requires local mobilization, not US intervention. Washington needs to be pressed to acknowledge the limitations imposed by its damaged legitimacy and credibility. There are, however, many things that the US—some that *only* the US—can and must do to help end the brutal violence spreading across the Middle East.

Step 1: Remembering that doing no harm must be the top priority, the first step is to stop the airstrikes. Because while people in the US may respond with "Hooray, we got the bad guys," to many in Iraq (especially the very Sunnis President Obama wants to persuade to break with ISIS) the bombings and drone strikes are the result of the US acting as the air force of the Kurds and the Shi'a against the Sunnis. Rather than undermining popular support for ISIS, the airstrikes actually serve to strengthen the extremist organization.

Step 2: Make real the commitment to "no boots on the ground" and withdraw the troops. After withdrawing all the US forces in 2011, the White House has authorized two deployments in 2014, sending a total of more than 3,100 troops back to Iraq, officially for training and counterterrorism. No one knows how many unacknowledged pairs of CIA and JSOC (special operations forces) sneakers may also already be on the ground in Iraq or indeed in Syria. The presence of US troops provides exactly what ISIS and other extremist organizations want: US troops on their territory, providing potential recruits with renewed evidence of US meddling in Muslim countries, as well as providing thousands of new targets. This is identical to al-Qaeda's goal of 15 years ago, which was to provoke US troops into returning to their territory and fight them there.

Step 3: The US must stop flooding the region with arms. The weapons always seem to wind up in extremists' hands. The US-supplied Syrian "moderates," too often are overrun by (or their fighters defect to) ISIS or other not-so-moderate militias. And when Iraqi army generals abandon their troops, their troops in turn abandon their weapons and flee when faced with even small numbers of ISIS fighters. Whether these weapons are deployed by extremists or by the US-backed supposedly "moderate" governments or militias, the result is more and more violence against civilians. Washington must end its policy of ignoring the violations of human rights and international law committed with its weapons and by its allies. Consistent enforcement of the Leahy Law prohibiting assistance to any foreign military units known to violate human rights must be an urgent demand. Only when the US stops providing weapons to its regional allies, who are arming the whole range of opposition forces from the Free Syrian Army to the most extreme Islamists, will Washington have any credibility to urge Iran and Russia to end their arming of the Syrian regime.

Step 4: The US should change its laws to reverse *Holder v. Humanitarian Law Project*, the Supreme Court decision that criminalizes as "material support for terrorism" the teaching of non-violence training, conflict resolution, or how to access the United Nations human rights system to any organization on Washington's list of "foreign terrorist organizations." That prohibition undermines any effort to win people in those organizations away from violence by providing information about non-violent alternatives. The US should end its prohibitions on virtually any kind of contact with those listed as "foreign terrorist organizations," including many in Syria and elsewhere in the region. The politicization of the list is a huge problem. This was evident in 2014 when the US resisted talking with or even acknowledging that the central players in saving the Yazidis besieged on Mount Sinjar were from a Kurdish militia in Syria allied with the PKK (Turkish Workers Party). The PKK had remained on the US anti-terrorism list so no US contact was allowed, even while the Turkish government was negotiating directly with them.

Step 5: There must be a real diplomatic partnership to respond to the ISIS crisis. The US is carrying out airstrikes and deploying new troops in Iraq even while top US officials and much of the rest of the world agree there is no military solution. Diplomacy must be returned to center stage. That means serious engagement with Iran, among other players. Tehran has more influence in Baghdad than Washington does. Any serious effort to encourage Iraqi government acceptance of a truly inclusive approach to power will require joint pressure from the US and Iran. Even though Iran is predominantly Shi'a itself and its government claims global leadership of Shi'a Islam, the country's leaders are very worried about the instability in their next-door neighbor resulting from the years of Shi'a sectarianism in Baghdad. So there is every reason to anticipate Iranian support for tamping down the sectarian-based violence in Iraq. The US-Iran nuclear agreement, when finalized, should be the basis for broadened talks toward a real "grand bargain" between the US and Iran to include all the related crises, including normalization of Iran's role in the region. The US should open direct talks with Iran and Russia, based initially on shared opposition to ISIS—with Iran to jointly push for ending anti-Sunni sectarianism in the Iraqi government, and with Russia to jointly work toward ending the multi-party civil war in Syria.

Step 6: The US should support a new search for broader diplomatic solutions in the United Nations involving both ISIS and the
civil war in Syria. One aspect should be greater support for the UN
efforts to negotiate local ceasefires in Syria. Those efforts, renewed
in Aleppo in early March 2015, have led to important examples of
encouraging short-term truces to create humanitarian corridors
and allow humanitarian aid into and evacuation of civilians from besieged areas. That doesn't necessarily mean calling for the opening
of direct talks with ISIS—that is neither practically nor politically
viable in the short term. It does mean working to build a real coalition aimed at changing the desperate conditions that lead ordinary
people, people with power, and people without power, to consider
supporting ISIS.

Even talks with ISIS should not be permanently ruled out.
Jonathan Powell, former chief of staff for then-prime minister and
Iraq war supporter Tony Blair, reminded CNN in October 2014 that

> people forget how long the process leading up to a successful
> negotiation can take. The British government opened up a secret
> channel to the IRA in 1972 and yet the real negotiations only hap-
> pened in 1991–93 when Major opened his correspondence with
> Irish republican politician Martin McGuinness. It takes a long time
> for armed groups to realize that their demands are unachievable
> and to start to consider what else they would settle for.
>
> The same is true of ISIS. No one is going to agree to a uni-
> versal caliphate. But once ISIS realizes they can't win then they
> may be prepared to talk and we need to open a secret channel
> now to give time to establish enough trust to move to negotia-
> tions when the moment comes. There are practical things we can
> talk to them about. The ex-Baathists and ex-Iraqi army offices
> that make up a major part of the ISIS force have genuine griev-
> ances about the way they were treated by the sectarian Maliki
> government. We can discuss with them ways of ensuring Sunnis
> have a powerful voice in a Shi'a majority Iraq.

A viable international coalition will require replacing military
strikes with powerful diplomacy. The US will have to pressure
its ally Saudi Arabia to stop arming and financing ISIS and other

extremist fighters; pressure its ally Turkey to stop allowing ISIS and other fighters to cross into Syria over the Turkish border; pressure its allies Qatar, Saudi Arabia, the UAE, Jordan, and others to stop financing and arming everyone and anyone in Syria who says he or she is against Assad. What is *not* needed is another Coalition of the Killing; what is needed instead is a newly created Coalition of the Rebuilding. Shared opposition to ISIS can provide a new beginning for cooperation between the US and its long-time competitors such as Russia and Iran.

Step 7: Push the United Nations, despite the resignation of two sequential special envoys in 2012 and 2014, to restart real negotiations on ending the civil war in Syria. That means everyone involved needs to be at the table: the Syrian regime; civil society inside Syria including non-violent activists, women, young people, internally displaced, and refugees (Syrian, Iraqi, and Palestinian); the Syrian Kurds, Christians, Druze, and other minorities as well as Sunnis, Shi'a, and Alawites; the armed rebels; the external opposition and the regional and global players supporting all sides— the US, Russia, Iran, Saudi Arabia, the UAE, Qatar, Turkey, Jordan, Lebanon, and beyond.

This could provide a moment for the US to collaborate with Russia on Syria policy, building on the successful joint effort to destroy Syria's chemical weapons and perhaps lessening tensions over Ukraine. A ceasefire and arms embargo on all sides should be the medium-term goal—which will only be possible if the US is prepared to exert serious pressure on its allies to stop arming all their favorite factions, even as pressure is brought to bear on Iran and Russia to stop the flow of arms to the Syrian government.

It should not be forgotten that, at least until mid-2013, despite US reluctance to send arms directly to the rebels, their weapons are mostly US-produced and were sold to Washington's allied Gulf monarchies over the years in multi-billion-dollar arms deals. (France has sold some weapons to Gulf states as well.) All US weapons sold internationally, including to close allies, contain end-use restrictions limiting how they can be used, and whether and to whom they can be resold. There is little doubt that the US could, if it chose, bring an immediate halt to the Saudi, Qatari, and other arms shipments heading to the Syrian opposition forces by enforcing those end-use restrictions, on pain of losing all future access to US arms.

Step 8: The US must be pushed to massively increase its humanitarian contributions to United Nations agencies for the millions of refugees and internally displaced people both inside and fleeing from both Syria and Iraq. Money is desperately needed both inside Syria and in the surrounding countries where millions of Syrians have sought refuge. The US has pledged significant funds, but much of it has not actually been made available to the agencies, and more must be pledged and given.

Syrian Women Know How to Defeat ISIS

A group of Syrian women came together in 2013 and 2014 to discuss how to respond to the crisis facing women and indeed facing their entire country. As reported in the October 2014 Time *magazine article by Kristin Williams and Michelle Barsa of the Institute for Inclusive Security, the Syrian women's proposals are below.*

• • •

More arms and more bombs, they said, are not the answer. They insisted that the only way to fight this extremist threat is to return to the negotiating table and hash out a peaceful political transition to heal the divisions ripping Syria apart.

"Oppression is the incubator of terrorism," one woman told us as the group prepped for meetings with high-level officials in D.C. and New York. Her participation in peaceful protests during the early days of the revolution led to her two-month imprisonment in a four square meter room shared with 30 other women—yet she was adamant: "We cannot fight ISIS except through a political approach."

So what do they recommend? To create stability (which is kryptonite to extremists), Syrian women say three things must happen.

First, humanitarian aid must get to the millions in grave need. Almost three million people are registered as refugees in neighboring countries and over six million are displaced inside Syria. That's in a country with a pre-war population of just under 18 million. Approximately half of the remaining inhabitants live in extreme poverty. In response to this disaster, the UN made an urgent appeal for $2.28 billion just to meet the critical requirements of the internally displaced. So far, Member States have committed only $864 million—a little over one-third of the total. Last month, the UN was forced to cut the delivery of food aid by 40 percent.

Violent extremism thrives in areas where social services have all but disappeared. A woman who serves on the local council of an opposition-held town told us that she fears more of her neighbors may become radicalized because there's no work, no education, and no other opportunities. Women ...[have] first-hand witness of the different needs of zones under government, opposition, Islamic State, or other control. They've seen, for instance, that food baskets can't get into areas blockaded by the regime; in these circumstances, cash transfers are more effective. To reach the greatest number of people, relief agencies should coordinate with civil society and devise humanitarian strategies that reflect these differences.

Second, international actors must encourage local pockets of stability. Beyond funding, a key barrier to humanitarian access is the ongoing violence. Besieged areas are the hardest to reach and most in need. Here too, women have a solution. Though missing from most news reports, a number of local ceasefire arrangements have proliferated throughout the country, often negotiated by civil society actors. In the Damascus suburbs, a women's group brokered a ceasefire between regime and opposition forces. For 40 days before fighting resumed, they were able to get essential supplies into the city. Syrian women are now calling on the UN to not only track these local arrangements, but assign international monitors to ensure parties stick to them. Beyond opening channels for the passage of humanitarian aid, this may also help the parties come closer to an agreement to cease hostilities on the national level. This will require accountability, as these negotiations are all too often used as a tool of political manipulation.

Which brings us to the third, and potentially most important, step: The parties must return to internationally-mediated negotiations and agree on a political solution to the conflict. The last round of talks in Geneva failed, it's true. But this is still the best solution to the burgeoning civil war and the opportunistic extremism that has followed it. Only a unified Syria can beat back the ISIS threat.

Convincing both parties to come back to the table won't be easy. But Syrian women have identified concrete ideas that could help unite disparate factions by encouraging them to cooperate on mutually beneficial activities. For instance, the regime and opposition could coordinate the safe passage of university students between government- and nongovernment-controlled areas to allow them to resume their studies. The women also call on parties to prioritize construction of temporary housing for those displaced by the conflict on both sides. These actions could help cultivate trust between the regime and opposition and encourage popular support on all sides for renewed negotiations.

As important is the construction of an inclusive peace process. One that engages women, but also others who have thus far been missing from the conversation: the Kurds, Druze, youth, independent civil society networks, tribal leaders, and, yes, more radical elements like Jabhat Nusra, who can otherwise spoil the talks from the outside. Without this, no agreement stands a chance.

These three priorities—humanitarian relief, support for local ceasefires, and resumption of negotiations— are not the result of idealistic or wishful thinking. This is not an abstract call by Syrian women to "give peace a chance." It's a plea for policy approaches that are grounded in the lived experiences and long-term goals of the vast majority of the Syrian people.

● ● ●

What can people in the US—separate from the government—do to support movements for freedom and liberation in the Middle East?

The most important thing activists can do—especially in the United States, but in Europe, Japan, and elsewhere in the global North as well—is to build movements that challenge the prevailing war policies of their own governments, that raise the political price at home for going to war abroad. That work takes the form of education, advocacy, and protest. The goal is no less than to transform US policy—from one based on military responses to crises that demand non-military solutions to a policy based on diplomacy, humanitarian assistance, negotiations, and international-law-based alternatives. (See p. 192.)

That includes reminding people in the US about both the global and the US-specific histories of challenging militarism, war profiteering, and violence. The fourth of Franklin D. Roosevelt's "four freedoms," for instance, speaks of the "freedom from fear which, translated into world terms, means a world-wide reduction of armaments to such a point and in such a thorough fashion that no nation will be in a position to commit an act of physical aggression against any neighbor—anywhere in the world." And whether FDR would have described it so or not, for those of us in the United States today, that means starting with the worldwide reduction of *US* armaments.

To accomplish those terribly difficult goals will require anti-war mobilization that engages with people in far greater numbers and far broader politics than those who define themselves as against war or pro peace. It will require inserting opposition to war and to militarism into the very center of every effort under way, every social movement fighting for human rights, for people and the planet, for people over profits, for justice.

Education

At the educational level that requires a campaign to debunk the myth, first propagated by George W. Bush on September 12, 2001, that the only choice is to "either go to war, or let 'em get away with it." Non-military alternatives must be reclaimed as the first choice, the default choice—rejecting the current habit of mentioning non-military solutions only as an afterthought, only after the military attacks begin. That means providing people with the resources to understand what those non-military solutions are.

There must be a willingness to challenge claims such as "you can't use diplomacy, ISIS wouldn't ever talk." The answer includes understanding that, first, some kind of diplomacy is always necessary. Second, it will not start with talking to ISIS directly, but by negotiating initially with those who provide ISIS with the weapons and money to keep fighting, those responsible for creating the conditions that lead some people to support ISIS, or those who justify the brutality of ISIS or other groups. It also means recognizing that some negotiations in Syria have gone forward between fighters at the local level with the goal of establishing local ceasefires, and there may well come a time when ISIS fighters, with or without their leadership, would participate in such talks as well. (See p. 199 for more on how negotiations with ISIS might occur.)

There must be education about the origins of ISIS and its predecessor organizations—how they arose as part of the response to the US invasion and occupation of Iraq. That means teaching and discussing the legacy of US interrogation and torture at Abu Ghraib and Guantánamo, and the consequences of US detention of so many tens of thousands of Iraqis and others during the war, without trial, without rights, without justice. Assessments of military and intelligence officials regarding the lack of efficacy of torture strengthen moral and international law arguments: In 2006, for example, the former head of Army intelligence, Gen. John Kimmons, admitted "no good intelligence is going to come from abusive practices. I think history tells us that. I think the empirical evidence of the last five years, hard years, tells us that."

There must be solid education about what ISIS is and isn't—not to defend or justify its violence, but precisely the opposite: because understanding what motivates such brutality is crucial to stopping it. That may mean learning something about the theological framework that defines the organization, including its roots in Saudi Arabia's Wahhabi form of Islam. But even more important than the religious details, it means learning about why a wide range of people, including many who may be novices in Islamic practice or not even Muslim at all, but who share a powerful sense of individual or collective alienation, of bitter dislocation, of utter hopelessness in their home community or country, end up supporting ISIS. Muslim activists, including religious leaders and Muslims of all degrees of devoutness, who overwhelmingly oppose ISIS and are already playing a huge role in challenging the effect of those challenges in their community, must be supported.

Education and advocacy on Israeli occupation and apartheid, on Palestinian rights and international law, must be continued. While the question of Palestine and US support for Israel are not necessarily at the center of popular debate and discussion across the region now defined as a US "war zone," those issues remain central to public consciousness, opposition to US intervention, and the widespread delegitimation of US-backed Arab leaders.

Writing letters to the editor in local papers, calling in to talk shows on local radio stations, arranging meetings with editorial boards of local newspapers, all can play important roles in educating broader parts of the public. And if a letter to the editor contains the name of a local congressional representative, the letter helps play an advocacy role as well, since members' staff are generally rigorous in tracking anything in print mentioning his or her boss.

The situation in the Middle East and the destabilizing role of the US wars there is certainly complicated. But there are plenty of good resources available—books, films, speakers, online resources—that are useful for study groups, education programs, and individual engagement. Many are included in the resource list at the back of this book. Sharing with family, friends, and co-workers is always a good place to start.

Advocacy

For those who oppose the US war strategy, advocacy work with the US government must be based on a combined inside/outside strategy. That means some people working quietly with some members of Congress (often found in the Black Caucus and Progressive Caucus of the Congress) to make sure that any congressional authorization for war is as limited as possible: restricted to a very short duration, controlled by geographic constraints, strictly limited on who the named "enemy" is. At the same time there must be massive public mobilizations, including petitions, demonstrations, lobbying, to urge a "no" vote from members of Congress and to oppose approval for *any* new Authorization for the Use of Military Force.

The most effective advocacy work comes through collective rather than individual action. So joining existing peace and anti-war organizations, forming anti-militarism and peace contingents within broader campaigns for justice, seeking out like-minded individuals within trade unions, faith-based communities, schools and universities, community and political organizations always provides the best potential. Anti-war and peace organizations are neighborhood or city-based, statewide or national, and often global. Some of the national groups (details in the Resources list) include Peace Action, American Friends Service Committee, Win Without War, Iraq Veterans Against the War, Veterans for Peace, US Labor Against the War, US Campaign to End the Israeli Occupation, Jewish Voice for Peace, MoveOn, Code Pink Women for Peace, Friends Committee on National Legislation, September 11th Families for Peaceful Tomorrows, Military Families Speak Out, and United for Peace and Justice.

Advocacy with the US government means direct contact, claiming as our own the democratic promise of the US Constitution despite the historic challenges to US democracy imposed by the role of corporations and big money in politics. That means returning to the basics of influencing Congress, including bird-dogging them at town meetings and public events, insisting they answer questions about their support for war, or thanking them for their opposition. Initiating and signing petitions is always useful—sign them all, then follow up with direct contact. Even better, send an individual letter, by fax or snail mail, saying the same thing—the individual effort makes it more important. Better still, call your member of Congress to register your concerns. And best of all, request meetings with members or their staff, perhaps when the members are home in their district during recess periods. These are the most effective opportunities for constituents to urge their representatives to hear their arguments.

Contacting members of Congress sometimes seems fruitless. But it is important to remember that even as billion-dollar-funded lobbies demand time and attention from Congress, individual members still have to get the votes every two years to stay in office. That means they can be reached more often than is sometimes apparent—especially by their own constituents. On the question of the US war on terror, there is a potent pro-war influence from key lobbies, including the pro-Israel lobby and most of all the powerful arms manufacturers' lobby. Anti-war organizers can't compete with those wealthy political forces dollar for dollar, but exposing and delegitimizing their influence on Congress is a key component of opposing war. Useful online materials are easily available on the cost of war (National Priorities Project), challenging US war policies (Institute for Policy Studies), the immorality of war (AFSC and Peace Action), the role of Congress and the White House in preventing war (Win Without War), petition drives (MoveOn and Credo), Islamophobia and anti-Arab racism (CAIR and ADC), opposing US military aid to Israel (US Campaign to End the Israeli Occupation), the impact of war on US veterans (IVAW and Veterans for Peace), and more.

The war on terror has also created an unusual partisan mixup. Many Democrats, particularly those in the Congressional Progressive Caucus and the Congressional Black Caucus, tend to be very open to anti-war arguments. But during the Obama administration they also tend to be the most loyal to the president. For those who want to make the right, moral, law-based decision, having constituents at their back demanding they do so is crucial—especially when that decision requires them to challenge their close ally in the White

House. And many Republicans are asking serious questions, albeit from an isolationist rather than internationalist vantage point, about the United States role in the world, and thus are sometimes open to challenging the war. (It's also true that some Republicans, many of whom have never seen a US war they didn't support, are routinely eager to discredit the president on partisan or objectively racist grounds; anti-war strategy needs to be carefully crafted so as not to opportunistically empower those tendencies.)

In some instances advocacy can be strengthened through sectoral relationships built between constituency-based organizations in the United States and their counterparts in the war zones. One powerful example has been the decade-long ties built between US Labor Against the War and the Iraqi Oil Workers Union. Bringing the voices of people who are the targets of US wars and interventions is crucial to humanizing whole populations who otherwise tend to be lumped into stereotyped images of either "terrorists" or "victims"— not people with their own agency, with families and communities, with dreams and ideas. Another example is the work of Iraq Veterans Against the War, whose members continue to partner with various Afghan and Iraqi organizations on campaigns including the demand for reparations in Iraq and better access to medical care for both Iraqi civilians and US veterans of the war.

Protest Campaigns

Politicians who posture about the importance of political solutions while launching military strikes that undermine those same political solutions, and then ignoring political alternatives altogether, must be consistently called out for their hypocrisy.

There is a need for continuing protests against the US wars. In recent years, as the number of ground troops have been reduced and replaced by an escalating drone and special-forces war, public attention in the United States has waned. Keeping the public focused on the wars remains a crucial starting point to building opposition to them.

That includes reminding the public of the costs of war—the 2015 announcement that the Obama administration's war against

ISIS would cost $5.8 billion just for the next year should be at the front and center of campaigns. It can be made more real by linking that cost (through the work of the National Priorities Project) to possible alternative uses of the shares of that $5.8 billion of tax money spent in specific states or cities or the country as a whole—in job creation, health care, education, infrastructure, or perhaps in helping to rebuild the countries US wars have so damaged. Similar tradeoff campaigns can target the $10.54 million that US taxpayers are still paying for war on terror *every hour* since 2001. Or the more than *half a trillion* dollars in 2014 to fund the Department of Defense, an amount that does not include the tens of billions for fighting the actual wars or for maintaining the US nuclear weapons arsenal on high alert—for just one year.

Protest campaigns may or may not choose public demonstrations at any given moment. When education about the costs—human, economic, international law, human rights, environmental—has been effective, when anti-war ideas are popular and strong, protests in the streets are an unsurpassed, vital component of anti-war activism. When a street protest is likely to appear small and marginal, sometimes a return to educational campaigning may be more appropriate.

There is a need for constant campaigns, educational and protest-based, against Islamophobia, making clear that much of the traditional law-enforcement-based strategy for identifying and dealing with potential terrorists is not only failing to solve the problem of ISIS recruitment but also antagonizing whole populations through illegal surveillance, discriminatory arrests and prosecution, racial and religious profiling. Understanding that much of the domestic strategy targeting Arab and Muslim communities is thoroughly linked to carrying out the wars abroad, organizations working primarily against Islamophobia and anti-Arab racism and those based in the communities most affected must be included at the center of anti-war organizing.

Movements against war must be international and internationalist. That means building and maintaining ties with anti-war campaigners around the world, including, though not limited to, counterparts in countries whose governments, often in opposition to massive public opinion, are allied members of the US war coalition. It also means working to give voice to those living the consequences of the US strategy—those whose families have been killed or injured by US airstrikes, drones, bombs, or soldiers; those forced to flee their homes as a result of US-involved fighting; those unable to find work or feed their children because of US policies that have devastated their countries and their economies. And it means working within broader campaigns for justice to help consolidate internationalism as a core value and core organizing principle of every social movement mobilizing to change the world.

Anti-war organizing will never succeed when it is limited to self-defined anti-war or peace organizations. Only when anti-war, anti-militarism, anti-Pentagon-spending themes emerge as one stream in the much wider river of campaigns for racial, economic, environmental justice, and human rights will social movements working to end wars be able to claim victory.

Resources

National (and a few international) Peace and Anti-War Organizations

September Eleventh Families for Peaceful Tomorrows
    www.peacefultomorrows.org
Alternatives (Canada)   www.alternatives.ca
American Friends Service Committee   www.afsc.org
Canadian Peace Alliance   www.canadianpeace.org
Center for Constitutional Rights   www.ccrjustice.org
Code Pink   www.codepink.org
Friends Committee on National Legislation   www.fcnl.org
Historians Against the War   www.historiansagainstwar.org
Institute for Policy Studies   www.ips-dc.org
Inter-Pares   www.interpares.ca
Iraq Veterans Against the War   www.ivaw.org
Jewish Voice for Peace   www.jewishvoiceforpeace.org
Just Foreign Policy   www.justforeignpolicy.org
Military Families Speak Out   www.mfso.org
National Lawyers Guild   www.nlg.org
Pax Christi   www.paxchristiusa.org
Peace Action   www.peace-action.org
Stop the War Coalition—UK   www.stopwar.org.uk
Transnational Institute—Netherlands   www.tni.org
United for Peace & Justice   www.unitedforpeace.org
US Campaign to End the Israeli Occupation   www.endtheoccupation.org
US Labor Against the War   www.uslaboragainstwar.org
Veterans for Peace   www.veteransforpeace.org
War Resisters League   www.warresisters.org
Win Without War   www.winwithoutwar.org
Women's Action for New Directions   www.wand.org
Women's International League for Peace and Freedom
    www.wilpfinternational.org

Books

Benjamin, Medea. *Drone Warfare: Killing by Remote Control*. London: Verso,
    2013.
Bennis, Phyllis. *Before & After: US Foreign Policy and the War on Terror*.
    Northampton, Mass.: Olive Branch Press, 2002.

Dear Readers:

I'm fascinated, as I would guess are all writers who choose a historical setting for their books, by the idea of time travel. And if anyone ever succeeds in ironing the right crease into the fabric of spacetime, I'll be there, standing in line for my ticket!

I'm alarmed, though, to hear physicists say that the outward trip may be easier than the return leg. So, being a careful type even in imagination, I plan to go to a place and time where I would be happy to stay in case gravity abandons me. Forget the Hanging Gardens of Babylon, the palaces of the Pharaohs, the Court of the Sun King. No—for me it has to be the champagne-fuelled, cigar-smoky, jazzy headiness of Paris in the '20s.

More precisely, I've booked my seat at the Théâtre des Champs-Élysées for a performance by the new American sensation in town—the young singer and dancer Josephine Baker. It's the evening of the 21st of May, 1927. An already over-excited audience is further stirred by an unexpected announcement. Miss Baker interrupts her performance to step forward and proudly declare that a young pilot has just crossed the Atlantic Ocean in one hop. Captain Lindbergh landed moments ago, safely, at a Paris airfield.

It's never going to happen to *me*, so I'm doing the next best thing—I'm sending in Joe Sandilands by Argosy from Croyden Airport to enjoy the Paris scene. He will land at Le Bourget a few minutes before Lindbergh—I've always been intrigued by the stranger who stole the aviator's flying hat, and now I know who and why! He may come across Picasso, Matisse, Coco Chanel, the Fitzgeralds, Louis Armstrong, in a crowded Left Bank café. I'm certainly giving Joe the imagined pleasure of meeting and working with the creator of some of the very best detective stories: Georges Simenon. *Amuse-toi bien, Joe!*

—Barbara Cleverly

Praise for Barbara Cleverly's Award-Winning Novels

Folly du Jour

"Cleverly's fine seventh 1920s historical to feature Scotland Yard's Joe Sandilands (after 2007's *Tug of War*) ... [An] engaging sleuth ... A puzzling whodunit." —*Publishers Weekly*

The Tomb of Zeus

"Award-winning author Cleverly debuts a captivating new series.... In the tradition of Agatha Christie, the characters are complex and varied.... Riveting." —*Romantic Times*

"With a spirited, intelligent heroine, a glorious, exotic setting, a clever plot, loads of archaeological detail and a touch of romance, there's nothing not to like in this crisply told first book of a new series by the author of the Joe Sandilands mysteries."
—*The Denver Post*

"The crisp writing and depth of characterization should please traditional mystery fans." —*Publishers Weekly*

"Ellis Peters Dagger winner Cleverly sweeps readers onto the isle of Crete in 1928." —*Booknews* from The Poisoned Pen

"Contains enough deceptive clues to keep readers guessing till the very end... Cleverly draws on a wealth of historical detail and breathtaking scenery while ingeniously weaving ancient mythology, illicit love, greed, long-fueled revenge, and a convincing romantic subplot into an entertaining mystery. For all its complexity, following the threads of *The Tomb of Zeus* makes for a fascinating new literary find." —*The Strand Magazine*

Tug of War

"Despite her mastery at vivid scene-setting, Cleverly never loses sight of the historical puzzle that is central to her story. Simply put, it's a stunner."

—Marilyn Stasio, *The New York Times Book Review*

"Cleverly continues to present fine historical mysteries with complex plots, well-developed characters, and colorful settings. Whether Sandilands is solving crimes in France, Raj-era India or Jazz Age London, he is emerging as one of the most engaging heroes in the history-mystery genre." —*Booklist*

"Impressive... Cleverly maintains the high standards set by earlier Sandilands tales, blending a sophisticated whodunit with full-blooded characters and a revealing look at her chosen time and place." —*Publishers Weekly* (starred review)

"Puzzle-lovers will be appeased by the tale's crafty convolutions."
—*Kirkus Reviews*

"Fans of Charles Todd, take note: Barbara Cleverly's Joe Sandilands series is every bit as good, and in many ways better. *Tug of War,* the sixth book, is simply terrific. It has fine characters and, in post–First World War France, a great setting. But it's the plot, devious and brilliant, that keeps this novel moving.... All this densely plotted, beautifully written history builds into an excellent mystery with a murder and love story at its heart.... A lot of fun." —*The Globe and Mail*

"Cleverly re-creates the atmosphere of the shattered world.... Vivid detail." —*Booknews* from The Poisoned Pen

"Cleverly depicts well the 'tug of war' of her story.... The reappearance of Dorcas Joliffe from *The Bee's Kiss* contributes quite a bit of pleasure, spice and commentary to the story. She is a worthy honorary niece to Joe and an equally worthy partner in sleuthing. Next book, please, Ms. Cleverly." —*Mystery News*

The Bee's Kiss

Nominated for a Macavity Mystery Award for Best Historical Mystery

"Stellar... As always, [Cleverly] scrupulously plays fair, and the careful reader who puts the pieces together will be gratified with a logical and chilling explanation."
—*Publishers Weekly* (starred review)

"*The Bee's Kiss* ... certainly satisfies." —*Entertainment Weekly*

"Intriguing... another enjoyable read." —*Mystery News*

"Cleverly combines a colorful historical setting...with a complex plot and well-developed characters....Make[s] a natural for fans of Elizabeth Peters' Amelia Peabody." —*Booklist*

"Atmospheric...intricately plotted, with red herrings and a denouement that depends on a Lanvin dress." —*Kirkus Reviews*

The Damascened Blade

Winner of the 2004 CWA Historical Dagger Award—Best Historical Crime Novel

"Introduces an intelligent author and an interesting investigator. The Indian setting is expertly exploited and the climactic scenes are full of satisfying twists." —*Morning Star* (UK)

"[*The Damascened Blade*] is set to bring the author into the big league....The writing and accuracy of scene are astonishing."
—*Bookseller*

"This marvelous historical delivers." —*Publishers Weekly*

"This excellent historical mystery gains immediacy in light of the recent events in the region." —*Booklist*

An Old Magic

"Spellbinding." —*The New York Times*

"A pacy and evocative novel. Well-researched historical detail combines with an intriguing contemporary story line. An enjoyable read." —Jane Adams, author of *The Greenway*

"A compelling tale." —Simon Scarrow, author of *Under the Eagle*

"A gripping read . . . unputdownable."
—Sally Spedding, author of *Wringland*

Ragtime in Simla

"Fully developed characters and a convincing portrayal of time and place lift Cleverly's second historical. . . . The author's talents seem capable of transcending any shift in scene."
—*Publishers Weekly*

"Captivating and enchanting. Attractive, magnetic, duplicitous women grab all the best roles in *Ragtime in Simla*. Between the natural beauty of the setting and the seductiveness of the women, it's a wonder that Joe Sandilands gets out of Simla with heart and mind intact." —*The New York Times Book Review*

"*Ragtime in Simla* contains enough scenes of smashing action in and around the marvelously invoked Simla to delight even Rudyard Kipling." —*Chicago Tribune*

"Ms. Cleverly deftly transports readers to an exotic locale filled with intrigue, suspense, and characters skilled in the art of deception. This is a perfect travel companion for historical mystery fans." —*Booklist*

"Cleverly gets credit for a fresh and fascinating setting. She gives her tale a final flip that will leave readers guessing and surely keep Joe Sandilands busy for many books to come."
—*Rocky Mountain News*

The Last Kashmiri Rose
A *New York Times* Notable Book

"Spellbinding debut mystery...embellished by the vivid colonial setting...and enriched by characters too complicated to read at a glance." —*The New York Times Book Review*

"An accomplished debut in a historical mystery that has just about everything: a fresh, beautifully realized exotic setting; a strong, confident protagonist; a poignant love story; and an exquisitely complex plot." —*The Denver Post*

"An impressive debut...an engrossing tale of serial murder. Classic whodunit fans should look forward to Cleverly's future efforts." —*Publishers Weekly*

"A well-plotted...enjoyable read...The atmosphere of the dying days of the Raj is colorfully captured."
—*The Sunday Telegraph* (London)

"A strongly evocative narrative, sensitive characterizations, artful dialogue, and masterly plotting make for an excellent first historical." —*Library Journal*

"A clever debut... The reader will get a strong sense of life in India for the British in the early part of the last century. At the same time, they will be treated to a puzzling mystery that demands their attention and keeps the pages briskly turning."
—*Deadly Pleasures*

"A formidable and likeable first novel. Ms. Cleverly is going places." —*The Literary Review*

"Deftly plotted and filled with unexpected twists, effectively captures the sights and sounds of 1920s India and provides a fascinating look at the social and political climate of the time."
—*Booklist*

"An ambitious, charming first novel." —*The Buffalo News*

"The best mystery I have read in years! The denouement is so good, even the most experienced reader will not guess the ending." —*Mysterious Women*

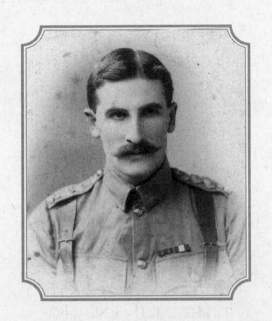

—DETECTIVE JOE SANDILANDS

Folly

du Jour

A Joe Sandilands Mystery

Barbara Cleverly

DELTA TRADE PAPERBACKS

2009 Delta Trade Paperback Edition

Copyright © 2007 by Barbara Cleverly

Published in the United States by Delta, an imprint of The Random House Publishing Group, a division of Random House, Inc., New York.

DELTA is a registered trademark of Random House, Inc., and the colophon is a trademark of Random House, Inc.

Originally published in hardcover in the United Kingdom by Constable & Robinson, Ltd., London, in 2007.

Library of Congress Cataloging-in-Publication Data

Cleverly, Barbara.
Folly du jour / Barbara Cleverly.
p.   cm.
ISBN 978-0-385-34184-4 (trade pbk.)
1. Sandilands, Joe (Fictitious character)—Fiction.   2. Paris (France)—History—
1870–1940—Fiction.   I. Title.
PR6103.L48F65 2009
823'.92—dc22
2008051838

Printed in the United States of America

www.bantamdell.com

9 8 7 6 5 4 3 2 1
Text design by Virginia Norey

for my son Steve
with many thanks for his help,

and for Gary
whose enthusiasm for the Paris Music Hall
was inspiring.

folly

du Jour

Prologue

Paris, 1923

Harland C. White of Pittsburgh, Pennsylvania, shuffled resentfully after his wife, May, through the Egyptian rooms in the Louvre museum. One vaulted stone room after another. You could lose yourself in here. Or lose your mind. He wondered whether this was a good moment to suggest they go for tea on the new roof terrace over the Samaritaine store.

"Say! May!" he called after her. "This is the fourth roomful of sarcophaguses—okay, then, sarcophageeee—we've done. How many more?"

They'd had lunch at Ciro's. The food and wine had made him sleepy, the size of the check had made him grouchy. $1.00 for a slice of melon? $2.25 for a Baby Lobster? Still, lunch at Ciro's was on his schedule. You couldn't go home and not say you'd lunched at Ciro's. Had to be done. Same thing, apparently, with the Louvre.

Maybelle (*May,* since she'd discovered all the girls over here had short names... though it didn't have quite the kick of *Zizi* or *Lulu* or *Kiki*) had come to a halt in front of a huge

dark-painted coffin box and was doing that thing with her hands...Tracing the shapes in the air—hieroglyphs she called them—and silently mouthing the sounds that went with them. Clever girl, May! She'd been to classes. She'd grown chummy with the arty folks at the State Museum. She'd gotten hold of a book called *The Mummy* by some feller called Wallis Budge and had learned—or so she told him...what would *he* know?—to read the sounds out loud. She'd tried to teach Harland to do it but his attention had faded after he'd mastered "*Tut—ankh—amen.*"

"Come look, Harland! This one's kind of special and I can work out the name of the occupant!"

His friends at the Country Club—swell blokes every last one of 'em—had been full of good advice: "So, you're going to Paris? Peppy Paree! Ah! It's the top of the beanstalk— You'll just love it! Give my regards to Harry...and Henry...and Bud at the Dead Rat...and Joe Zelli—now he's a real live wire!"

Two days down and all he'd met were three-thousand-year-old guys who lived in boxes. And here was another introduction coming up.

"*Kham—nut—see,*" said May.

"I'm looking! I'm looking!" he said, trying to lighten the gloom.

"Chump! That's his name. "*Kham—nut—see,*" she intoned again. "High Priest of Ptah."

"Do you *have* to spit your baccy on my brogue, May?" he said, never knowing when to give up.

May ignored him. "At Memphis."

"Memphis?"

"That would be Memphis, Lower Egypt, not Memphis, Tennessee." May could be very squashing.

"Well...whoever...your buddy's just sprung a leak," he

said crabbily. He didn't like the look of adoration on Maybelle's face—the way she opened shining wide eyes and moistened her lips. Never looked at him that way. He pointed to the foot of the upright coffin. "There. He's sprung a leak—or taken one."

The ticking off for loose language he was expecting didn't come. May was staring at the marble floor at the base of the mummy box. He looked again. A dark red-brown glutinous fluid was ponding there.

"Ah! I'll tell you what that is ... it's embalming fluid," said Harland decisively. "Come away, May. Time to move on, I think." He tugged at her arm.

"No, it's not embalming fluid," said May. "It's blood. You ought to know that. I'll stay here. You go get help. Somebody's climbed in there and died."

"But not four thousand years ago ... No, you're right, Maybelle—that's blood. And it's still flowing!"

Oddly, the room guardian wasn't at his post. Nor was the one in the preceding room. What was this—the tea break? He saw not another soul until he came to a grand staircase he remembered. A party of four men, all carrying briefcases and paper files of notes, were coming down, laughing together and chatting in several languages.

"Hey there!" shouted Harland. "Anyone here speak English?"

One of them, a smart-looking Anglo-Saxon type, all floating fair hair and ice-blue eyes, detached himself from the group, responding to the urgency in the American's voice. "I do. Can I help you, sir? Jack Pollock, British Embassy."

"Thank God for that! I need someone to come and

inspect a mummy. There's a High Priest of Memphis, Egypt, down there and he's bleeding to death!"

Jack Pollock should have his name added to the list of live wires about Paris, Harland reckoned. In minutes he'd managed to send for the chief curator, the specialist in Egyptology, the police and a doctor and was relaying what was going on to his party. And all in a babble of English, French, Italian and German.

A crowd had gathered—now where in tarnation had *they* all sprung from?—clustering around the case, gesticulating. They jostled each other in their eagerness to get close to the coffin, and Pollock, using his height and a headmaster's voice, had set them at a distance, firmly requiring Mr. and Mrs. White, as discoverers, to stand by and hold themselves in readiness for a police interview should it prove necessary. He wasn't a man to argue with. In any case, wild horses wouldn't have dragged them away from the scene of discovery. *Their* discovery. This was going to go down a treat at the Club when they got home.

A lively Frenchman was doing a lot of shoulder shrugging and pooh-poohing and Harland made out that he was telling Pollock this was all a load of nonsense and he should mind his own business. Just some fluid, polish probably, spilled by the cleaning detail.

"My dear Marcel," said Pollock, in a kindly voice, pointing to the floor, "*flies* are not, I believe, attracted by polish. I have never seen a fly in the Louvre before. It would take something frightfully delicious to lure them in here. But here, as you see, they most certainly are."

A smart navy-suited *agent de ville*, with képi and baton, swept in and gave orders to clear the room immediately. He waved

his arms about. He tooted his whistle. He made threatening gestures with his baton. He tried to arrest Pollock. Not one of this smart crowd took any notice and he had to content himself with making them all take a step back and sending for reinforcements.

Harland was uneasy. Ghouls! Worse than the flies. One whiff of blood and there they were, mouths open, eyes staring. A doctor bustled in. Was Harland the only one to find the speed of his arrival surprising? No, to give him due credit, the feller himself seemed to be a bit astonished... "I got a message telling me to... Doctor Moulin, from the Institut Médico-Légal, Quai des Orfèvres... Oh, my goodness! Yes, that's blood. And relatively fresh blood. Good Lord, there may be someone still alive in that box. The top must come off at once!"

That was what they wanted to hear. At last—they were to be treated to the bit of theatre they'd all been waiting for.

Six strong men, the policeman and Pollock included, heaved and strained, taking their instructions from the senior Egyptologist who'd hurried down from his office. The box, far taller than the tallest of the men, was lowered flat to the ground on its back and at a word from Pollock, three on each side, they flexed their muscles, ready to lift up the bulky lid.

Before the final revelation, Pollock called a halt and addressed Harland. "I wonder if perhaps the lady might like to be excused this next bit?"

"Naw!" Harland replied. "Maybelle's as tough as my old army boots!" and knew it could have been better expressed.

He and May were the only tourists present. All the rest were—he'd have sworn—academics. Staffers, perhaps. Harland was a salesman and a damned good one. And you didn't make the money he'd made by not being able to read faces. Individuals or in groups. Harland didn't read much

but he read people all right. And this collection puzzled him. It was downright weird! He'd seen a scene like this in one of May's books. It was entitled *The Opening of the Mummy Case*. Earnest professor types gathered round a table, all eyes on the box laid out ready in front of them.

Harland glanced around the faces of this crowd. They'd known just how far they could push the cop. They'd retreated exactly when they had to, conceded no more than was necessary to keep him on board. Thinking as one. Like a good platoon. Struck by his insight, Harland tried but failed to spot the senior officer present. Well, whoever these people were, they knew when to keep quiet.

No one spoke. Harland didn't even hear a gasp when the lid finally went up. He tried to cover May's eyes, but she bit him and he took his hand away. And then, a voice broke the stunned silence.

"Ah. A double occupancy. It's a bit crowded in there, wouldn't you say?" said Pollock, lazily confident. "I think we can safely identify the passenger on the lower deck—and looking a teeny bit ruffled—as the High Priest of Lower Egypt. But—I say—anyone recognise the passenger in first-class accommodation on the *upper* deck?"

"It's Lebreton! Professeur Joachim Lebreton!"

"Ha!"

"Well! Well!"

"'Struth!"

A communal breath was exhaled by the gathering. Wondering looks were exchanged. Most made the sign of the cross. But, strangely, Harland saw not one look of distress or sorrow. One or two even gave—he was certain—a bitter smile.

The doctor took over, sweeping the helpers aside. He summoned the policeman to his side and spoke tersely into

his ear. Harland could follow his gestures and all present could see for themselves what had happened to the professor. He was dead. A wound to the heart. A knife wound, Harland judged. Two years of soldiering in the infantry during the war had taught him all anyone would ever want to know about bullet wounds. This was no bullet wound. The poor guy looked like he'd been bayoneted. Slit down the middle. The body had clearly been propped on its feet at the moment of death because the flow of blood down the front of his beige jacket and trousers had been copious and had ponded in his shoes to overflow into the bottom of the box. Harland thought it must have gathered there in quantities, waited for him and Maybelle to stroll by, and started to seep its way through onto the floor.

Oddly, there was something white sticking out of the dead man's mouth. It looked grotesque and Harland wanted to rush forward and pull it away. The doctor seemed to have the same urge. He chose a pair of pincers from the bag he had laid out open at his feet and tugged at the—cotton, was it? A thin roll of white fabric about two and a half inches wide emerged from the mouth. Moulin pulled again. A further length came out.

"Linen. Mummy bandage," said someone in the crowd.

Another voice specified: "*Ancient* mummy bandage."

"Well—it's outdated rubbish," drawled the Englishman standing in front of Harland, to his neighbour, "what else would we expect the dear professor to spew forth? Let's just hope they won't feel obliged to check the other orifices. I, for one, should have to leave."

A waft of some sweet, spicy scent began to wind its way through the crowd. The inside of his grandpa's old cigar box? Cloves? Cinnamon? Myrrh? What did myrrh smell like? Just like this, Harland imagined. His memory,

triggered, went off with a bang. His mother's apple pie! Suddenly uncomfortable, he reached into his pocket for his handkerchief.

A small gold object fell from the now-bloodstained bandage and landed with a tinkle on the marble at the foot of the Chief Egyptologist. He didn't hesitate. He picked it up and held it aloft between thumb and forefinger. "Gentlemen. I think we all recognise the ugly dog-headed god of Egypt?" he announced. His arched eyebrows, quizzical, superior, assumed a special knowledge in his audience. He could have been leading class.

Harland itched to put up his hand. "It's Anubis," he whispered to May. He knew two Egyptian gods. Ra was the other one.

Maybelle didn't even hear his mistake. She was staring at the gold trinket. She had turned very pale. "*Set!* It's Set!" she hissed in Harland's ear. "I don't like it here. I don't like these people. It's crowded, it's creepy and it's making me nauseous. Get me out, Harland, or your wing-tips really will suffer!"

Serious efforts were made to bar their way. The policeman's hand went to his holster. Orders were yelled in several languages. But Sergeant Harland C. White, survivor of Belleau Wood, supporting his wife with one arm, extended the other, stuck out his jaw and charged for the door.

Out in the main corridor and sounds of pursuit fading, they encountered two newsmen carrying cameras armed with those new-fangled exploding light bulb devices. They were looking about them eagerly.

"Show's back there," said Harland, nodding over his shoulder. "Better hurry, you guys. You've missed the first act."

Chapter 1

Paris, 21st May, 1927

"I know Monsieur will have a most enjoyable evening."

The young woman who'd shown him to his seat offered him a smile at once shy and knowing. She held out her hand for his tip and slipped it swiftly away with a murmured word of thanks. The solitary Englishman hesitated, eyeing the pair of gilt chairs snuggling cosily together in the empty box with sudden misgiving.

"Mademoiselle!"

He detained her with his call as she turned to dart away, and offered his ticket stub again for her inspection. "Some mistake, I think?"

The girl took the ticket and looked with exaggerated care at the number. She was an *ouvreuse*—yes, that's what they called them over here, he remembered. Though what they actually "opened" was a mystery to the Englishman...unless you counted the opening of those little bags into which their conjurer's fingers made the notes and coins disappear.

"No, there is no mistake, monsieur. This is indeed your

box number." She tilted her head and the smile appeared again, this time without the softening element of shyness. "You have the best seat in the house." Her eye ran over the handsome features, the imposing figure, taking in the evening dress, correct and well-cut. She remembered his generosity and paused in her scurrying to cast a glance, amused and complicitous, at the second chair. "A little patience!" she teased. "I'm sure it will not be long before monsieur has company." She took the time to add: "There are ten minutes to go before the curtain rises. And it is no longer fashionable to be late. Certainly not for this show."

She whisked away in a flutter of black silk and a tantalising trace of rather good perfume, leaving Sir George Jardine standing about in something of a quandary.

He had an increasing feeling of unease. He was displaced. He ought not to be here. But the momentary touch of vertigo was chased away by a stab of impatience with himself. With the man he had become over the years. Would he ever be free to lay aside the burden of his training? Years of forethought, political skirmishing, and—yes—out-and-out skulduggery, had imbued him with a watchfulness that was not lightly laid aside, even when he was thousands of miles away from the arena of his intrigues. Here he was, in the pleasure capital of Europe; it was time to let go the reins and leave the bloody Empire to look after itself.

For at least the next six months in fact. George had gone on working after many would have retired, the guiding force, the continuity, behind the last two Viceroys of India. He'd been looking forward to getting away from Delhi, leaving behind the heat, the scandals, the undercover chicanery. It had been a good idea to break his journey at Marseille and take the Pullman up to Paris. Yes, no doubt about that. A

week or two of relaxation and stimulation, before he did his duty by his ageing family back home, had been hard-earned.

A summer in Surrey. He needed to fortify himself. Experience the latest sensations…work up a few stories…bank a few topics of conversation. At home in England one couldn't go on for long talking about India. It pained him to see eyes glaze over when anything other than a passing reference to the subcontinent was made. At the mention of Delhi, people started to twitch and to look anxiously over your shoulder for rescue, but just let drop that you'd been in Paris and they clustered round for news. George determined to have fascinating things to report.

Before taking his seat, he patted his pockets with a familiar sensation of expectation. His opera glasses, cigar-lighter, wallet, spare handkerchief and a roll of currency were present and correct. Along with a folded envelope.

Bit of a puzzle, this.

It had been handed to him the morning after his arrival in Paris—an envelope addressed to him in a careful English hand, care of the Ambassador Hotel. There was nothing in it but a scribbled note and a theatre ticket. For the Théâtre des Champs-Élysées. The clerk at reception had no knowledge of its delivery. No one, George could have sworn, knew that he was to be in Paris this evening. And who the hell was "John"? Which "John" of his acquaintance—and there were many—had, in black ink written:

George, old man—welcome to Paris! Thought you wouldn't be able to resist this. Tickets are like gold dust, so make sure you enjoy yourself. But—there you are—I owe you one! Yrs, John.

A mystery? George had no time for mysteries. His first reaction was of irritation rather than puzzlement. Why on

earth couldn't the wretched fellow have appended his sur-
name? Unless he was so well known to him, it would be considered unnecessarily stiff? A moment's further reflection
and he had it. With a passing embarrassment (was he getting old? losing his grip?) he remembered he had a cousin
called John—though he'd always called him Jack—and that
cousin was, indeed, in Paris, engaged in some clandestine
way in the diplomatic service. And, yes, George did recall
that the younger man owed him a favour. Quite a favour, in
fact. A ticket to the theatre—though the star was the most
talked-of, most scandalous woman in the world—was a
pretty frivolous offering as a counterbalance. Bad form.
George didn't at all object to being sent the ticket but he felt
it was…ah…undignified to mention the moral debt at all.
What are influential relatives for, if not to ease your path
through the career jungle? You accept the leg-up, are duly
grateful and the matter is never referred to again. Well—all
would, doubtless, be revealed. Jack would pop up, late as
usual, and they'd have a laugh together, slightly uneasy to
catch each other enjoying such a spectacle as was promised.
George was glad he'd had the sense to order a tray of whisky
and soda for the interval. They'd enjoy a glass and his cousin
would know that he was expected.

And here he was, the sole occupant of what in London
would have been called the Royal box, the target of lazily
curious glances from the audience gathering below. A public
figure and constantly on parade, George was unperturbed.
He automatically made a gesture to adjust his already perfectly tied black tie, smoothed his luxuriant grey moustache
and eased his large frame into the spindle-legged gilt chair
further from the entrance, thinking to allow easy access for
his cousin when he appeared.

He settled to stare back boldly at the audience, conveying
amused approval. This gathering risked outshining the per-

formers he thought, so brightly glittered the diamonds in the front stalls and the paste gems in the upper gallery. The gowns glowed—silks and satins, red and mulberry and peach apparently the favoured colours this season, standing out against the stark black and white of the gentlemen's evening dress. His nose twitched, identifying elements of the intoxicating blend of tobaccos curling up from the auditorium: suave Havana cigars, silky Passing Clouds favoured by the ladies and, distantly, an acrid note of rough French Caporals.

And every seat taken, it seemed. Definitely *le tout Paris* on parade this evening. George checked his programme again, wondering if he'd misunderstood the style of entertainment on offer. A turnout like this was exactly what you'd expect for the first night of a ballet—he'd been part of just such an audience, tense with anticipation, in this theatre before the war. He'd seen Nijinsky leap with superhuman agility in *The Rite of Spring*, delighting some, scandalising others. George had counted himself delighted to be scandalised. On this stage, Anna Pavlova had thrilled the world with her performance of *The Dying Swan*. And tonight's crowd was seething with expectation of an equally significant display. All was movement: faces turned this way and that, hands fluttered as friends were greeted across the breadth of the hall, places were hurriedly swapped and the unmistakable musical rise and fall of a chirruping French crowd on pleasure bent swirled up to him.

The sounds of such conviviality made him for a moment conscious of his solitary state. Unused to being alone, and certainly never unaccompanied at an evening's entertainment, George swallowed the joking aside he would have murmured to his aide-de-camp. He felt in his pocket and took out a pair of ivory opera glasses. The audience was freely scanning *him*; he'd return the attention and search out

a familiar face among them. The odds were that he knew someone down there. Might note them, wave and see them in the bar after the show perhaps?

A poor haul. His glasses passed swiftly over the barely remembered features of someone he'd been at school with and didn't care to see again. He was probably mistaken...a passing resemblance. And that was it.

He was on the point of giving up when a stirring in the box opposite caught his attention. An usherette had entered to show the occupants to their seats. An inquisitive application of the glasses confirmed that the girl was *his* pretty *ouvreuse*. Obviously i/c boxes for the nobs. A favoured position, most likely. He scanned the scene, watching as a young lady followed her in, clutching her blue and gold programme. The newcomer smiled back at her escort, trailing behind. She waited for him, turning her head in a regal gesture as he tipped and dismissed the attendant and went to stand by a chair, pausing until he came forward to hold it ready for her. As he sat down by her side, she threaded a white arm through his in a familiar way. Ignoring the man, George trained his glasses on her. What a corker! Blonde and flamboyantly pretty. And what quantities of make-up young girls wore these days, he reflected. The tiny pair of glasses was almost concealed in his great hand and he discreetly trained them lower to take in her figure. He smiled. What should he report back to the ladies of Simla regarding the latest fashions? They were certain to ask. He would say that necklines appeared to be retreating southwards while hems were advancing rapidly northwards. Disastrous collision inevitable.

An attractive colour, though, the scrap of silk the goddess opposite was wearing. Colour of a peacock's throat. It glinted in an exotic way, flashing two colours over the void at him. George sighed. Lucky bastard—whoever he was—to

have this girl on his arm! He eased his glasses sideways to take in her companion.

Christ Almighty! George lowered them hurriedly. He dropped his programme deliberately and bent to retrieve it, head lowered, using the seconds floundering about on the carpet to decide what he should do next. This could prove to be, socially, a jolly awkward moment. What bad luck that the only other person he recognised for certain in the whole theatre should be seated exactly opposite him. In clear view. Lieutenant-Colonel Somerton, now a knight of the realm if George had it right, and one-time soldier. Their last meeting had been decidedly an unpleasant one.

But surely the scoundrel would, even after all these years, be lying low, not flaunting himself in a box in full view of the cream of European society? George was assailed by sudden doubt. He risked an eye over the edge and looked again, taking his time. The black hair was as thick as ever, with not a trace of grey as far as George could make out, and the moustache, always the man's affectation, still in place and looking, he thought, rather outdated. The hawk-like features which had struck such terror in the ranks were less sharp and he watched in surprise as the face he had always perceived as humourless softened into a smile when his lady-friend whispered in his ear. Well, well! Steamroller Somerton! George had thought never to encounter him again. And now what? Greet him at once or spend the rest of the evening avoiding his gaze?

He made up his mind. Straightening again and glancing around, he made a show of catching sight of his old acquaintance for the first time and tilted his head slightly in surprise. With a short, stiff nod, unaccompanied by a smile, he acknowledged him and held his eye until the man responded similarly. George made no attempt to extend his courtesy to the female companion. The absent Lady Somerton, he felt,

wherever she was (and it most certainly wasn't Paris), would not have considered it appropriate.

This was one of the dangers you ran in a European capital. Away from the hot-house world of India where you couldn't smile at a girl without running the risk of rumour, you suddenly felt free to turn your long-held fantasies into reality. How appalling for the chap opposite to see that he'd been recognised—caught out—and by a man he had no reason to call his friend. Deeply embarrassing. But it occurred to George that any sympathy he was prepared to expend on the situation would be wasted on a rogue like Somerton. No, it was the girl on his arm who deserved his concern.

He glanced at her again, suddenly shrewd and objective. All appearances were that she was a professional lady-friend, hired by the night. French, he would have guessed, judging by the liveliness of her hand gestures and her confident chatter. Well able to take care of herself—or summon up some protective chap from her murky organisation to do it for her. George was not familiar with the arrangements in Paris. In Simla or Delhi, had such a situation arisen, an aide would have been dispatched and the problem would have dissolved before his eyes.

But he was troubled. He found he could not dismiss the little miss opposite as a world-weary and experienced... what did they call a tart of this quality in France? *Poule de luxe,* that was it! Below all her surface glamour he sensed that she was young—barely twenty, he would have guessed. And, whether dubiously employed or a free agent, she was someone's daughter, for God's sake! Had the silly little thing *any* idea of what she was getting herself into? It would take more than a tap on the cheek with a fan to control Somerton if he turned nasty. George shuddered. The man, he recalled with a rush of foreboding, was rotten to the centre of his being. He couldn't

say "soul"—there was no evidence that he had one. George chewed his lip in irritation.

He should have had the man shot when he'd had the chance.

He stirred in his seat, checked his watch and considered his options. Did he have time to negotiate the lengths of corridor chock-a-block with latecomers on a dash over to the box opposite? And what would he say when he arrived there with the performance about to start? He pictured himself crashing into the box, breathless, perspiring, and in the grip of a Quixotic urge. A ridiculous figure. He had no authority, civilian or military, over Somerton…he would have to appeal to the girl directly. But how would he find the words to warn her? There'd be accusations followed by argument, protests, denials. *Your remarks are slanderous! I'll see you in court, Jardine!* And—heaven forbid!—suppose the girl turned out to be something entirely innocent such as…his niece? George watched surreptitiously as Somerton leaned close and whispered something in her ear, lifting his head slowly and trailing his pomaded moustache lingeringly over her cheek. Almost retching with disgust, George concluded this was no niece.

He pressed down on his armrests and the chair wobbled under him as he prepared to take action. A moment later he sank back in frustration. He never embarked on any course unless his strategy was clear, his tactics well worked out, the outcome predictable and in his favour; the reason he'd survived for so many years when others had not. And he was not about to abandon the careful habits of a professional lifetime on account of a stab of juvenile sympathy. George could foresee the result of any irruption of his into the box opposite. At the best, he'd be ejected by a hurriedly summoned bouncer; at the worst, he'd be trapped over there with the pair of them until the interval.

His conflict was cut short by an arresting fanfare of notes on a trumpet followed at once by a blaring blue jazz riff from the orchestra pit. He was aware of a simultaneous dimming of the electric house lights. The blonde girl across the way opened her mouth in anticipation and wriggled forward in her seat with the eagerness of a six-year-old at a pantomime. George sighed and came to a decision. In the seconds before the light faded, he did what he could. Oblivious of the hush descending on the crowd, he rose to his feet and slipped on his white gloves. He sought out and held the eye of his opposite number.

Imperious, imperial and impressive, over the width of the auditorium, Sir George Jardine delivered a command.

Chapter 2

Abandon target! Withdraw at once!

The soldier's silent hand language flashed, eerily blue in the dimming house lights, across to the opposite box. Unmistakable to a man who had been a fellow officer. On the Frontier, grappling often in hand-to-hand combat with lethally savage tribesmen, officers had learned from their enemy that in close proximity you communicated in silence as they did or you got your head shot off. Would Somerton remember and respond? Or would the man summon up what vestiges of self-respect he still had, to affect ignorance or rejection of the old code? George calculated that he could not depend on touching any finer feeling, on awakening any sense of regimental pride across the void. No—ugly threat was the only weapon left in his armoury. To emphasise his point, he added a universally recognised gesture. He drew the forefinger of his left hand slowly across his throat. *Do as I say or else ...*

At that, Somerton threw back his head and laughed.

Shaking with amusement and hardly able to keep his hands steady, in the moment before the last light went out, he returned the signal: *Message received and understood.*

Bloody French audiences! George remembered they always took their time settling. But the musicians seemed to be well aware of this and mastering the situation. The trumpet solo had silenced most and there now followed, as the last mutterings faded, the last shuffling subsided, a clarinet performance which stunned George with its fluency. Not his style of music at all. Jazz. But he could see the point of it and had been made to listen to the quantities of recordings that had filtered through to Simla and Delhi along with the ubiquitous gramophone. It was one of his party tricks to discuss in an avuncular way the latest crazes with his young entourage. And this was an experience he would want to share with them on his return. What he was hearing, all his musical senses were telling him, was exceptional. He rummaged in his pocket and took out his cigar-lighter. A discreet flick of the flame over his programme gave him the name: Sidney Bechet. English? French? Could be either. Even American perhaps? He'd file the name away. The chap was an artist. Could take his place in the wind section of the Royal Philharmonic any day. Given the right material to play.

He was so absorbed by the music, leaning forward over the edge in an attempt to get a clearer view of the almost invisible soloist, he didn't hear her enter. The presence of a stranger in his box was betrayed by a rush of remembered scent carried towards him on a sudden air current as the door opened quietly and closed again. The effect on George was instant. Memories had ambushed him before he could even turn his head.

The scent of an Indian garden at twilight...L'Heure Bleue, he'd been informed when he'd despatched some gauche young subaltern to make discreet enquiries. The aide had returned oozing information, parroting on about vanilla, iris and spices. George had been gratified and amused that the young man had been received with such voluble courtesy by the wearer. Amused but not surprised; she had always been able to charm...enslave wouldn't be too strong a word...his impressionable young men.

The name said it all. The Twilight Hour. He didn't need to listen to accounts of top-notes and bases. It spoke, for him, in a voice soft as velvet, of the swift, magical dark blue moment between sunset and starlight. But, intriguingly, it brought with it an undertow of something sinister...bitter almonds...the scent of death. George shivered. The scent of a woman long dead. A woman he had mourned for five years. Silently in his heart, never in his speech.

And here, in this gaudy box, in frenetic Paris, the scent seemed as out of place as he was himself. He whirled angrily to confront whoever had invaded his privacy and—idiotically—with a thought to challenge the invader for daring to wear a perfume which for him would forever be the essence of one woman: Alice.

"Alice?"

George's voice was an indistinct croak expressing his disbelief, his raised hand not a greeting but an exorcism, an instinctive gesture of self-protection, as he peered through the gloom, focussing on the dark-clad figure standing by the door. An elegant gloved hand released the hood of the opera cloak allowing it to slide down onto her shoulders. He could just make out, with the aid of the remaining dim light from the orchestra pit, the sleek shape of a blonde head but the face was indistinguishable. Her finger went to her lips and he heard a whispered: *"Chut!"*

In a second, the woman had slid into the chair at his side and had grasped his hand in greeting. She leaned and whispered into his ear: "George! How wonderful to see you again! And how touching to find you still recognise me—and in the dark too! Alice? Am I then still Alice for you?"

"Always were. Always will be. Alice," he mumbled, struggling for a measure of control. He hunted for and caught her hands in his, pressing them together, moving his grasp to encircle both her slim wrists in one of his great hands, his gnarled fingers closing in an iron and inescapable grip.

"And, Alice Conyers, you're under arrest."

Chapter 3

She laughed and winced but made no attempt to struggle. "Let's enjoy the performance first, shall we? And...who knows?...perhaps I'll surrender to you later, George?"

Her purring voice had always, for him, spoken with a teasing double entendre in every sentence. He had dismissed it as a delusion, the product of his own susceptibility, a fantasy sprung from overheated and hopeless senile lust. No one else had ever remarked on it. But the voice he was hearing again, the style, the breathed assumed intimacy—all this was telling him that it was indeed Alice he held in his grasp.

"I do hope you're prepared, George. This can be rather stimulating! The show, I mean! Elderly gents carted off, blue in the face and frothing at the mouth, every evening, I hear. Got your pills to hand, have you? Last will and testament in order? Perhaps you should tell me who to ring just in case..." She broke off at the first twitch of the pearl-grey curtains. The lightly insolent tone was

unmistakable and he remembered how he'd missed it. George swallowed painfully, unable to reply.

With a thousand questions to ask the woman at his side, a thousand things to tell her, he was reduced to silence by the swish of the curtains as they swung back revealing a brilliantly lit scene. George stared at the kaleidoscope of vivid colours filling the stage, a controlled explosion of fabrics and patterns. The set conjured up the interior of a sumptuous Parisian department store—or was it meant to be a boutique on the rue de la Paix? Silks, velvets, chiffons and furs hung draped about the stage, arranged with an artist's eye for effect. After the minutes of darkness, the assault on the sense of sight was calculatedly overwhelming. Another surprise followed swiftly. Set here and there against the background colours, a number of dressmakers' dummies—mannequins, they called them over here—gleamed pale, their pure, sculpted nakedness accentuated by the profusion of clothes behind them. At a teasing spiral of sound from the orchestra the figures came to life and began to parade about the stage.

They were actually moving about! Dancing! George could hardly believe his eyes. He released Alice's wrists at once and cleared his throat in embarrassment. A scene of this nature could never have been staged in London. He tensed, wondering whether he should at once set an example and make noisily for the exit, tearing up his programme and tossing it into the audience like confetti in the time-honoured tradition, snorting his disapproval. Writing off the remainder of what promised to be a disastrous evening. Apparently catching and understanding his sudden uncertainty, his companion put a hand on his arm, gently restraining.

George watched on. Was it his imagination . . . or . . . ? No. He had it right. The girls, without exception, were tall and lovely and—yes—one would expect that of chorus girls. Rumour had it that they were all shipped in from England.

But this bunch were all blonde or titian-haired with alabaster-white skin. After the years of exposure to Indian-brown limbs, this degree of paleness struck him as exaggeratedly lewd. While he was pondering the reasons for this blatant piece of artistic stage management, the girls started on their routine.

To his bemusement the chorus-girl-mannequins were beginning to act out a scene of shopping. They were selecting garments held out for their inspection by a selection of *vendeuses* whose sketchy notion of uniform appeared to be a pair of black satin gloves and a black bow tie. Their clients inspected the garments on offer and saucily began to put them on, layer by layer, tantalisingly and wittily not always in the expected order. It was a while before George realised what was going on and when he did he began to shake with suppressed guffaws.

Alice leaned close and whispered: "A striptease in reverse. They start naked and end up in fur coats. Different, you'd have to admit! You're to think of this as an aperitif," she murmured.

The girls, fully clothed at last, eventually took a bow to laughter and applause and swayed off, flirtily trailing feather boas, silk trains and mink stoles, leaving the stage empty.

The lights went out at once and a backdrop descended. A single spotlight was switched on, illuminating in a narrow cone of blue light, marbled with tobacco smoke, an area of stage front right. It picked out what appeared to be the contorted limbs and trunk of a tree. The drums took up a strong rhythm and a tenor saxophone began to weave in and out, offering a flirtatious challenge to the beat, tearing free to soar urgently upwards.

The shape on stage began to move.

George could have sworn that a boa constrictor was

beginning to ripple its way down the trunk, then he gasped as the tree straightened. A second light came on from a different angle, compelling his eye to refocus. He now saw a massive black male figure carrying on his back, not a boa, but a slim, lithe and shining black girl. George forgave himself for his failure to make sense out of the contorted figures: the girl was being carried upside-down and doing the splits. Her limbs were distinguishable from the man's by their difference in colour—hers, by the alchemy of the blue-tinted spotlight, were the colour of Everton toffee, his gleamed, the darkest ebony. She twined about lasciviously, her body moving in rhythm with the pounding drumbeat, naked but for a pink flamingo feather placed between her legs.

The athletic undulations continued as the spotlight followed the black giant to centre stage. Once he'd mastered his astonishment, George decided that what he was seeing was a pas de deux of the highest artistic quality. Yes, that was how he would express it. But he wondered how on earth he could ever convey the shattering erotic charge of the performance and decided never to attempt it. The relentless sound of the drums, the stimulation of the dance and the overriding pressure of the enigmatic presence by his side were beginning to have an effect on George. He ran a finger around his starched collar, harrumphed into his handkerchief and breathed deeply, longing for a lungful of fresh air—anything to dispel this overheated soup of tobacco, perspiration and siren scents.

On stage, the dancing pair were writhing to a climax. The giant, at the last, determined to rid himself of his unbearable tormentor, plucked the girl from his back, holding her by the waist with one great hand, and spun her to the floor. He, in turn, collapsed, twitching rhythmically.

"Thank God for that! Know how you're feeling, mate!"

George thought, and knew that every man in the audience was experiencing the same sensation. He watched, with a smile, for any sign of Alice's predicted rush for medical attention for the elderly but saw none. To enthusiastic applause and shouts the lights went out, allowing the pair to go offstage and the curtains swished closed again.

"Would you like me to loosen your stays, Sir George?" Alice asked demurely. "No? Well, tell me—what do you make of her, the toast of Paris? The Black Venus? La belle Josephine?"

"Miss Baker lives up to her reputation," he said, ever the diplomat. "A remarkable performance. I'm glad to have seen it."

"And you're lucky to have seen it. This was the first act she impressed the Parisian public with when she arrived here two years ago. Her admirers have pressed her to repeat it for some time and at last they've persuaded her partner— that was a dancer called Joe Alex—to perform with her again. The order of performance, for various reasons, has been changed this evening, you'll find. Word got out, which is why the theatre is packed tonight."

"Is she to reappear?" he asked, trying for a casual tone. "Or have we seen all of Miss Baker that is to be seen?"

"She'll be back. Once more in this half—doing her banana dance—and then again in the second. We're to hear her singing. She has a pleasant voice and an entertaining French accent. Now, George, why don't you sit back and enjoy the rest of the acts?"

George could well have directed the same question at her, he thought. He felt he could have better entered into the spirit of the entertainment had his disturbing companion herself been at ease. But she was not. He hadn't been so distracted by the spectacle that he'd failed to notice the tremble of her hand, the bitten lower lip, the anxious glances around

the auditorium. Troubling signs in a woman he had always observed to be fearless and totally confident. And if Alice Conyers had no fear of the influential Sir George Jardine with his powers to effect her arrest for deception, embezzlement and murder, culminating in repatriation and an ignominious death on an English gallows, then whom *did* she fear? He concluded that there must be, lurking somewhere in this luxuriously decadent space—in her perception at least—someone of an utterly terrifying character.

He followed her gaze. Her eyes, under lowered lashes, were quartering the theatre like a hunter. George sighed with frustration. This refurbished and enlarged theatre now housed, on a good night, up to two thousand souls. And of those, all but two were strangers to him. He wondered how many were known to Alice. And in what dubious capacity? Everything he knew of the woman's past suggested that her associations were likely to be of a criminal nature, after all. And he'd never been aware of a leopard that could change its spots. Good Lord! Could it be that the woman might actually be thinking herself safer in *his* custody than running loose in Paris? That the grip of his improvised handcuffs about her wrists was not threatening but welcome?

Chapter 4

London, 21st May 1927

Croydon Aerodrome. Gateway to the Empire, the hoarding announced.

"Arsehole of the Universe, more like," Joe Sandilands corrected.

It was fear that, eight years after the war, still reduced him to the swearing and mechanically filthy reactions and utterances of the common soldiery. He looked about him, distracting himself from his terror by examining the other lunatics queuing up to experience three hours of danger and discomfort.

Rich, expensively dressed and unrestrainedly loud, they smiled when they showed their passports and plane tickets, keen to be off. They waved goodbye to their Vuitton luggage, their hat boxes, golf clubs and tennis racquets, as a uniformed employee of Imperial Airways wheeled it away on a trolley to be stowed in the hold. Joe clutched his Gladstone bag and briefcase firmly when his turn came to face the

booking clerk, his steely expression discouraging any attempt to wrest them from him.

"My luggage has gone ahead. I'll be keeping these with me," he said firmly, flashing his warrant card. "Work to do during the flight, you understand."

"As long as the light lasts, sir," the clerk agreed reluctantly. "Will you be requiring supper during the flight, may I ask? I believe we have Whitstable oysters and breast of duck on the menu this evening, sir."

Joe tried to disguise an automatic shudder. "Thank you but I shall have to decline." He smiled. "Late dinner plans in Paris." The reciprocal smile showed complete understanding.

"Full complement of passengers tonight?" Joe enquired politely as his tickets were checked and chalk scrawls made on his bags by a second employee.

"No, sir. By no means. Thirteen passengers. You're the thirteenth. We can take twenty at a push but the season isn't in full swing yet. You'll find it pleasantly uncrowded. Fine clear skies reported over the Channel," he concluded encouragingly.

"This lot must be first-time flyers," Joe decided as he shuffled along in file with the chattering group ahead of him to take a temporary seat in a room equipped as a lounge. "They won't be grinning and giggling for much longer." One of his friends, like-minded, had summed up the short flight: "They put you in a tin coffin and shut the lid. You're sprayed with oil and stunned with noise. You're sick into a bag...twice...and then you land in Paris."

The passengers, who all seemed to know each other, swirled around the quiet, dark man absorbed by his documents, offering no pleasantries, attempting no contact. Something about the stern face, handsome if you were sitting to the east of him, rather a disaster if you found your-

self to the west…war wound, obviously…kept them at arm's length. The men sensed an implacable authority, the women glanced repeatedly, sensing a romantic challenge. Everything about him, from the set of his shoulders to the shine on his shoes, suggested a military background, though the absence of uniform, medals, regimental tie or any other identifying signs made this uncertain. His dark tweed suit was of fashionably rugged cut and would not have looked out of place on the grouse moor or strolling round the British Museum. The leather briefcase at his feet was a good one though well-worn, and spoke of the businessman hurrying to Paris. But there were disconcerting contradictions about the man. The black felt fedora whose wide brim he'd pulled low over his eyes gave him a bohemian air, and the gaily coloured silk Charvet scarf knotted casually about his neck was an odd note and, frankly…well…a little outré. An artist, perhaps? No—too well dressed. Architect? One of those art deco chappies? Bound no doubt for the exhibitions that came and went along the Seine.

A pretty redhead wearing a sporty-looking woollen two-piece and a green cloche hat changed places with one of her friends to sit beside the stranger. She leaned slightly to catch a glimpse of the papers which were so absorbing him. Joe wondered what on earth she would make of the learned treatise he was scanning: *Identification of Corpses* by G. A. Fanshawe, D.Sc. (Oxon) with its subheadings of *Charred Bodies, Drowned Bodies, Battered Bodies…*

Aware of her sustained curiosity, Joe mischievously shuffled to the top a printed sheet of writing paper. Under the bold insignia of Interpol, and laid out in letters so large she would have no difficulty in reading them, was an invitation to The Commissioner of the Metropolitan Police, Scotland Yard, London, to attend the second conference of Heads of Interpol in Paris. A detailed programme of lectures and

events followed. Joe took out a pencil and began to make notes in the margin.

She addressed him with the open confidence of a fellow passenger aboard a boat, all companions for the duration of the voyage. "I see you're not on pleasure bent in the capital of frivolity? Er...Commissioner? Should I address you as Commissioner? Is that who you are?"

He grinned and passed her a card. "Not Commissioner, I'm sorry to say. He's the villain who's deputised me to come along in his stead. This is me. I'm Joseph Sandilands. How do you do, Miss...?"

"Watkins. Heather Watkins." And she read: "*Commander* Sandilands. DSO. Légion d'honneur. Ah, I was right! I took you for a military or naval man of some sort. But 'Commander' sounds very impressive!" And she added in a tone playfully inquisitive: "May we look to see 'Commissioner' on your card one day?"

"I do hope not! Annoying my boss is one of my chief recreations. I should hate to find myself at the top of the pyramid keeping order. Who would there be to keep *me* in order? I should have to do it myself!" Good Lord! That was the first time he'd given words to any such feeling. And he'd expressed it in unbelievably artless words to a complete stranger. It must be the fear of the next few hours that was sweeping away his defences, making him reckless.

The arrival of a steward in Imperial Airways livery made unnecessary any further revelations and they were called for boarding. The group, jostling and joking with each other, surged forward. But, at the point of putting her foot on the ramp, the lively and confident Miss Watkins, who had trailed behind finishing a conversation with Joe, balked. She shook her head like a horse refusing a fence, turned pale and began to breathe raggedly. Joe, close behind, recognised the symptoms and put a comforting arm under hers. "Don't worry,"

he said. "And, above all, don't be concerned if the wings appear to wobble alarmingly. They're supposed to do that. Watch them carefully and, should they stop wobbling, then you may start to worry. These big planes are perfectly safe, you know, and the company has an unblemished record. Look—do you see—it's an Argosy. That means it's got four wings, three engines and two pilots. That should be enough to get us through." He wished he could believe all this rot himself. "And, look, Miss Watkins ... Heather ... take this. I find it really helps." He passed her a lump of barley sugar.

A second steward in spanking white mess jacket and white peaked cap welcomed them aboard what he proudly called "the Silver Wing service" and, taking them for a couple, ushered them towards a pair of seats alongside at the rear of the plane.

"Every passenger has a window seat, you see," said Joe, helping her to settle. "Though you can always draw the curtain across, should you have vertigo."

They braced themselves for take-off. It came with the usual terrifying snarls of the engine and bumps along the runway and then there was the stomach-clenching moment of realisation that the machine had torn itself free of the earth and was soaring at an impossible angle upwards. A glance through the oil-spattered glass showed the grey blur of London disappearing below them. Higher up, the sunlight brightened and they caught the full glow of the westering sun gilding the meadows and woods of southern England.

"It will be dark before we arrive, won't it?" Heather Watkins asked, suffering a further pang of apprehension.

"Yes," Joe admitted. "This is technically the night flight, after all. We should touch down just before ten o'clock."

"But how will the pilot ... ?" Hearing the naïveté of her question, Heather fell silent.

"Beacons all the way along the flight route," said Joe confidently. "But while the light lasts, he'll just follow the railway lines. Look—over there!" He pointed out a group of buildings below. "You can see exactly where we are. Do you see—it's Ashford. That was the railway station. They paint the names of the main stations on the roof in big white letters all the way to Paris. They have emergency landing strips every few miles. And even in the dark the pilot can't mistake the Eiffel Tower. It's lit like a Christmas tree!"

Miss Watkins checked every few seconds to see that the wings were wobbling satisfactorily, the railway lines still beneath them and finally began to relax.

"Doing anything interesting in Paris?" Joe asked when he judged she was capable of a sensible reply.

"Oh, the usual things," she said. "Shopping and shows for a few days then we're all off to the south of France. For the tennis tournament." She fell silent.

"Do you observe or compete?" he asked.

"Oh, I play. Not very well. I mean I'm not in the Suzanne Lenglen or Helen Wills league yet, but I'm improving. The boys," she indicated the four young men sitting ahead of them, "are all players. My brother Jim—that's him with the red hair—is the team captain and general organiser. The other two girls are team wives. I'm the odd one out."

"Very odd," Joe agreed. "Most unusual. I've never met a lady tennis player before. One who plays seriously."

"There aren't many of us in England. In France it's thought rather dashing and quite the okay thing to be! We're even allowed to wear skirts up to our knees over there."

She rummaged in her handbag. "Look—here's where we're staying . . . well, you never know. It's a little hotel on the Left Bank. In the rue Jacob. Handy for the bookshops. And a

stone's throw from the police headquarters, funnily enough..." she added with a gurgle of laughter. "It's right opposite the Quai des Orfèvres!"

"I'm booked in at the Ambassador on the Right Bank, handy for the Opéra," he said lightly. "And a few steps away from the department stores. Au Printemps...Galeries Lafayette, funnily enough...One way or another, I think it's very likely in the way of business or pleasure our paths will literally cross again. And if my mental map of Paris serves me well, that'll be just about at Fauchon's, Place de la Madeleine. In time for what they call 'the five o'clock tea.'"

So that was the way to conquer a fear of flying—sit yourself next to a beautiful, athletic redhead and flirt your way there—Joe thought as they began to circle Paris, preparing to land at Le Bourget airfield just to the northeast. He wished he'd suggested something a little less staid than a *salon de thé*. The Deux Magots in St. Germain would have struck a more adventurous note. Well, it was just a few stops on the electric tram and taxis were everywhere.

"How are you getting into the city?" Joe asked. "It's quite a few kilometres distant..."

"Oh, Jim's ordered a couple of taxis. You?"

"A colleague from the Quai des Orfèvres is coming to collect me. In a police car, I expect," said Joe. "All screeching sirens and flashing lights—that would be his style!"

He smiled at the mention of his colleague and relished the thought of the warm greetings they would exchange. Inspector Bonnefoye. Late of Reims. Now, thanks to his undeniable talent and his great charm, promoted to the Police Judiciaire squad in Paris. A useful contact. Relations between the English and the French police departments were not often easy. Joe had made known his plans for attending

the conference and Bonnefoye, with Gallic insouciance, had set about pulling strings and calling in favours, making promises—who knew what?—to get himself appointed to the French contingent at the Interpol jamboree. Not that Bonnefoye seemed prepared to take it seriously. His telephone conversations had been full of plans of an entertaining nature which had little to do with international crime fighting.

The Argosy circled the Eiffel Tower, Joe judged for the satisfaction of the passengers rather than in response to any navigational imperative, then headed off to the northeast and lined itself up, head into the wind facing an illuminated landing strip and made a delicate touchdown. Everyone breathed a sigh of relief.

It was the stewards' odd behaviour that warned Joe. Suddenly unconfident, they advised the passengers to remain seated. "... until we have taxied up to the hangar. There appears to be an impediment on the runway," one of them improvised. The other climbed the stairs communicating with the cockpit to confer with the crew and he returned looking no less puzzled. The doors remained closed. No staff came forward to open the door and release them. And something was going on outside the plane.

Peering through the gloom, Joe saw to his astonishment, shadows moving on the tarmacked runway, lights from torches and flares skittering everywhere. The passengers sat on, docile and puzzled.

Joe got to his feet and, with a calming gesture to the two stewards, made his way down the gangway to the front of the plane. With a bland smile he murmured: "I speak a little French." They nodded dubiously and made no attempt to remonstrate with him. No one ever challenged a man confident enough to make such an assertion on foreign soil, he

found. He nipped up the steps and located the two pilots seated in the open cockpit.

"Captain! Commander Sandilands here. Scotland Yard. What's the problem?"

"Problem? I'll say!" came the shouted reply. "People! It's worse than a football crowd. Look at them! They're standing ten deep up there on the viewing gallery. And they're milling around everywhere, all over the runways. Damned dangerous, if you ask me! And where are the airport staff? Can't move until they've cleared this mob away. What the hell's going on? Some strange French Saturday night entertainment?"

"Oh, no!" Joe groaned. "I think I can guess what's going on! It's Charles Lindbergh! Attempting the transatlantic crossing. It was on the wireless—he was sighted over Ireland this afternoon. Made much better time than anyone expected and I'd guess this mob's gathered to watch him land. We must have beaten him to it by a few minutes. Dashed inconvenient! And we're a huge disappointment to all these idiots on the runway. It's not us they've come out from Paris to see. Ah, look! At last—they've twigged. They're pushing off, I think. They'll leave us alone now."

"Lucky Lindy!" said the captain. "Well, well! Never thought he'd do it! I can see a space now. Sir—would you mind returning to your seat? I think I can get through to the hangar."

Joe made his way back to his place, passing on the news to the passengers as he moved down the aisle. Heather Watkins was thrilled to hear it and at once called forward to her brother: "Jim! I want to stay to see Charles Lindbergh! Take care of my luggage, will you? If we get separated I'll meet you back at the hotel!"

Joe was amused to hear the decisive and energetic girl

emerge from the heap of anxiety he had sat next to for three hours but felt he ought to offer advice: "Do hang on to someone's arm, Miss Watkins. It's a menacing scene out there. Stay close to your group!"

The plane taxied onto an apron by the Imperial Airways hangar and, with no exterior staff in evidence, the stewards opened the door themselves and released the passengers onto the tarmac. They stood, paralysed, unable to negotiate the crowds, wondering which way to turn. Joe's eyes were searching for the familiar form of a police car when he felt his arm seized by a strong hand.

"Joe! I had no idea you were so popular!" said Inspector Bonnefoye. "Welcome to Paris! The car's over there. Let me take your bags." He gestured to a police car parked, lights on, engine running and pointing in the direction of the city with the driver at the wheel. They pushed their way over to it and threw the bags into the backseat.

"Bonnefoye! Never more pleased to see you, old man!"

"But you didn't tell me you were to be accompanied?" Bonnefoye was eyeing Miss Watkins with interest.

"A fellow passenger separated from her group. Miss Watkins," said Joe, surprised to find that she'd followed him, but relieved to see she'd abandoned her notion of staying to see Lindbergh touch down. "I say, would you have room for her? She's bound for the city centre also. Her taxi doesn't seem to have made it through."

"I'm sure I can squeeze Miss Watkins in the back," said Bonnefoye easily, and Joe was amused to hear the automatic gallantry in his voice.

Before they could get in, they were startled by the whining and coughing sound of an engine low over their heads, making for the runway. The crowd screamed and pushed its way to the sides as the monoplane, gleaming briefly silver as it passed between the searchlights, throttled back noisily

and set down on the runway, continuing onwards towards a dark part of the airfield. In evident confusion, the pilot stopped and turned the plane around, nose pointing back to the hangars. But before he had gone far in this direction, he cut the engine abruptly, no doubt in regard for the crowd as people surged back again, risking loss of limbs, unaware of the danger of the scything propeller blades. For a moment the *Spirit of St. Louis* stood in the middle of the trackway, small, battered, oil- and salt-caked and unimpressive once out of its element of air. And then, as the engine spluttered its last, souvenir-hunters moved in and began to pull strips of canvas from the wings, tugging anything that yielded from the framework of the plane. Press camera bulbs flashed and popped, trained on the door.

"For God's sake!" Joe shouted, horrified. "Do something, Bonnefoye! Those maniacs will tear the poor bugger apart! He's been flying solo in an open cockpit for a day and a half over the Atlantic—he won't be in any fit state to face up to a reception like this!"

As he spoke, the two men were already shouldering their way back through the crowd, using their height and aggressive energy to forge their way through to the door. Flourishing their warrant cards in a valiant attempt to keep the masses at bay, they stood together, arms extended, holding an uncomfortably small space free in front of the plane. After a moment, a window slid open and a voice called uncertainly: "Does anyone here speak English?"

"We do!" Joe shouted back. "Captain Lindbergh! Welcome and congratulations! I think it might be a good idea if you were to get out, sir, and we'll escort you to the hangar."

The door opened and the tall figure of Charles Lindbergh appeared, blinking in the spotlights and the flash of the cameras. With a cry of concern, Bonnefoye put an arm under

his shoulders and helped him to the ground, murmuring words of welcome. The pilot was pale and weary and looked much less than his twenty-five years. He stared in dismay at the jostling mass between him and safety and Joe remembered that, by all accounts, the young man was terrified of crowds. Taking his other arm, Joe felt his panic and the stiffness of his limbs and came to a decision.

"Captain, this is an impossible situation you've flown into. Idiotic, unplanned and damned dangerous! If only we could get you over to the hangar...Look—why don't you give me your flying helmet and take my hat instead?"

Lindbergh's eyes brightened with instant understanding. "A decoy? That what you have it in mind to be, sir?"

"Might work. I'm tall. I can keep my hair covered, shout cheerful platitudes in English. That's all they want. In any case, I don't suppose they've any idea what you look like. Anyone in a flying helmet and talking English is going to get the attention of this crowd. Let's give them a run for their money, shall we?"

The American grinned and nodded. "Well, I'd call that a very sporting offer...and good luck to you, sir..."

They ducked down and, crouching under cover of the wing, swapped headgear.

"They'll never think of chasing after a couple," said a confident English voice and Heather Watkins pushed forward. She stood on tiptoe and adjusted the black fedora firmly over the aviator's golden hair. Companionably, she tucked an arm through his. "Right, er, Charles, the hangar's that way. And just by it there's a police car with its engine running and a driver who knows where he's going. How about it?"

They strolled off, unimpeded, and Joe heard with amusement her cheerful voice: "Now—tell me—how was your flight?"

And the laconic response: "Why, just fine—and yours?"

Joe had no time to hear more. He straightened and moved to arrange himself with a tentative wave in the searchlight now trained on the cockpit door, helmet strap dangling provocatively. "Well, hi there, folks! I guess this must be Paris..."

He got no further. In a second he was swept up with a howl of triumph onto the shoulders of two men in the crowd and carried off in parade down the runway towards the terminal building. The throng on the viewing gallery cheered. Joe turned this way and that, nodding and waving to his admirers, shouting the occasional greeting or navigational direction in English. Worse than riding an elephant. His back was slapped repeatedly, his hands wrung, he was lowered and hoisted onto fresh shoulders several times. A painful experience and not one to be endured for long.

Eventually, after spending what he considered an overgenerous amount of his time on this performance, he bent and informed his bearers that after more than thirty hours in the air he needed to have a pee. Urgently. He reckoned they had ten seconds to set him down. It seemed to work. Once his feet were on the ground, he made off at speed towards the hangar, tearing off the helmet as he ran. The front door of Bonnefoye's car opened at his approach and he flung himself inside. Bonnefoye and Miss Watkins were sitting together on the backseat.

"What have you done with our hero?" panted Joe.

"Dropped him off at reception in the hangar. He'll be all right. The American ambassador's taken cover in there with him, offering medical aid, engineering assistance and a bed and breakfast at the Embassy when they can make a break for it. And now, Sandilands, if you've quite finished horsing

around and showing off, perhaps we can extricate ourselves from this mêlée and get ahead of the crowd before they all block the road back into Paris." Bonnefoye looked anxiously at his watch. "If you'd taken many more curtain calls we'd have missed the best of the entertainment at Zelli's, which is where I'm planning we'll make a start."

Chapter 5

Act followed act and George settled to enjoy himself. Music Hall. This was something he could respond to. And the quality of the turns was high—the best the world had to offer, he would have thought, and lavishly staged. He admired especially a slender woman in a tight black sheath, and was moved to wiping a sentimental tear from his eye as she sang of the fickleness of men. He wasn't quite sure about the androgynous creature who swung out over the audience on a Watteau-like flower-bedecked swing and, at the end of the act, peeled off a blonde wig to reveal a man's hairless scalp. Not entertaining. But he enjoyed the lines of chorus girls, performing complex manoeuvres to the split second. Some back-stage drill-sergeant deserved a commendation, George reckoned.

To huge enthusiasm, Josephine Baker made a second appearance just before the interval but this time she sang. Coming forward and involving the audience with a touching directness she warbled in a thin little-girl's voice, strange

but, once heard, unforgettable, of her two loves: *J'ai deux amours, mon pays et Paris* . . .

Everyone including George was enchanted. Except, apparently, for Alice. She leaned over and whispered: "*Two* loves? Is that all she's declaring? Ha! And the other thousand!" Miss Baker bowed and laughed and made her way offstage, the curtain was lowered and the lights began to come on again in the auditorium. Alice started to fidget. Under the pretence of stretching her legs, she moved her chair stealthily back a foot or so and lifted the hood of her cape to cover her head again. Odd behaviour. George wondered whether he should remark on it and decided to give no indication he'd noticed anything strange. If she wanted to tell him, she would tell him in her own good time of whom she was so afraid. But he rather thought it was not her intention to confide in him at all. Do you whisper your terrors to the trunk of a sheltering oak tree when the lightning is flashing all around? No, you stay under its branches looking out, with just the anxious eyes Alice was trying to hide from him until the storm was over. But perhaps there was some revealing reaction he could provoke?

"Ah, the interval already," he exclaimed jovially. "I say, Alice, I was rather expecting my cousin Jack would be with me tonight. I've ordered up a tray of whisky . . . not at all suitable for a lady . . . I'll just speed off and change that to champagne, shall I? Or is there something else you'd prefer? Now, what was that pink drink you used to like?" He started to get up. "Though—we could go and show our faces in the bar?"

Her reaction was instant. She seized him by the arm, trying to hold him in his place. "No! You're quite wrong, George. I'll drink whisky with great pleasure. Don't go off into those crowds; you'll never find your way back and we'll lose minutes of precious time. It's been five years—you must have such lots to tell me. Let's just stay quietly here, shall

we? And talk about old times." And then, with relief: "Ah—here are our drinks."

So—he hadn't imagined her nervousness, her undeclared need to stay close to him. She decidedly didn't want to be left alone up here, ogled by the crowd.

Even the waiter came in for a searching look from Alice and she fell silent, watching his every move until he left with his tip. George poured out two glasses, offering her one of them.

"Let's drink to absent friends," he said, still probing.

She smiled. "So many of them! But I'm thinking of one in particular. Of Joe. Joe Sandilands. My handsome Nemesis. Do you remember? Do you know what became of him?"

"Indeed. A dear friend. Joe's doing well. I follow his career with interest. We've arranged to see each other in London when I move on there. I understand he's gone on dodging bullets and breaking hearts—you know the sort of thing."

Alice gurgled with laughter. "I rather think he broke my bullet and dodged my heart," she said. "But I'm glad to hear he's being a success."

George noticed that she sipped delicately at her whisky, controlling her features to hide her dislike. He decided to torment her. "Not too fond of the hooch, I see? I'd have expected you to down it in one with a resounding belch—seasoned gun-slinger that you are."

He settled back into his seat, pleased to have evoked—and, he was sure, accurately interpreted—an instinctive reaction. The slightest twitch of her right hand towards her right side told him all he wanted to know.

"Don't worry—it doesn't show," he confided. "The bulge, I mean. That cape covers a multitude of sins."

In India, for many good reasons, she'd always gone about armed. He'd met her just after the war when she'd first come out from England. The unexpected inheritor of

an old-fashioned family trading company of international importance, young Alice had set about reorganising the business with dash and inspiration. Her hands on the reins had been firm and capable and she had found many to applaud her performance. For her admirers—and George counted himself one of the foremost of these—Alice was beautiful, talented and enchanting. But the ruthlessness she had inevitably needed to exercise had made her enemies. Enemies who would not shrink from removing her permanently from her post at the head of the company. Her own husband, George remembered, had led this faction.

And, it seemed that for Alice Conyers, though thousands of miles separated her from the scenes of her alleged crimes, there were still people she needed to defend herself against, even here in civilised Paris. She smiled and raised an eyebrow in affected incomprehension at his remark and launched into a bright inconsequential chatter, which she maintained with some skill throughout the interval. A surprisingly easy conversation. She gave every sign of enjoying the gossip he had to lay out and added a few insights and reflections of her own which took him by surprise. "But I had no idea, Alice!" he heard himself exclaiming. "I say—can you be certain of that? Well, I never! Deceitful old baggage! And her daughter was . . . ? You don't say!"

Any third party joining them would have heard a friendly couple talking with enthusiasm and good humour of mutual acquaintances, of experiences they had shared. They were professionals in their own separate ways, the pair of them, George reflected. They could play this game till the cows came home, and often had. But they both greeted the removal of the tray announcing the start of the second half with relief.

At least he would now be able with some confidence to hand her over to the authorities with a warning: "Disarm

her and don't listen to a word she says." Something on those
lines. He doubted that the flics would know what he was on
about if he talked of Circe and her spells, the ensnaring silver sounds of the Sirens. No, better just to say the woman's
got a pistol under her cloak and she's wanted on two conti-
nents.

A considerable feat of engineering, he judged, was what
they were witnessing. To more preparatory blasts of jazz
music, a huge egg of highly decorated Fabergé fantasy, its
shell trimmed all about with golden flowers, began to de-
scend slowly from the great height of the theatre roof and
slowed to hover low over the orchestra pit. After a moment,
the device burst open like a flower, the petals thrust apart
by the person crouching inside. The floor of the golden oval
gleamed and shimmered in the carefully placed spotlights,
a mirror reflecting the figure of the occupant. Josephine
Baker stood, slender, motionless, arms slightly extended
towards her audience with all the naked dignity, George
thought, of the wondrous Tanagra figurines he'd seen
in the Alexandria museum. The same rich earthenware
colour, the same grave attitude and finely modelled features. A goddess.

But then the deity grinned—a very ungodlike smile—
wide and flashing with good humour. Her elbows went out
to her side, akimbo, her legs, apparently disjointed, echoed
the movement, and, twitching frenetically in rhythm with
the band which now belted out a Charleston, she danced.
Shocking, mad but compelling, her movements caused the
only piece of costume she wore—a string of silvery bananas
around her waist—to jiggle and bounce, catching and reflecting the light.

The dance was soon over. The petals of the flower closed

over her and she was hoisted slowly back up into the shadows of the roof, to deafening applause.

More acts followed, thick and fast and with little continuity but all were first rate of their kind. The audience remained appreciative, knowing they were to see one more appearance by the star who always, according to Alice, returned to join the dancing troupe and the other performers for a huge and lavishly dressed finale—the "Golden Fountain."

But this evening they were treated to an extra unscheduled appearance by Miss Baker. In the hour or so between her acts, when she might have been expected to be relaxing in her dressing room, she suddenly, between two turns, dashed onto the stage and came forward to speak into the microphone. The spotlight operator had just followed offstage a handsome young crooner and was taken aback, as was everyone, but recovered to track back and highlight the star. Her stagecraft overcame her excitement and she waited until she was illuminated to claim the full attention of the audience. She looked around the auditorium, her hands extended in the peremptory gesture artistes use to indicate that applause would not be welcome at this moment. Her head flicked from side to side, involving the occupants of both boxes, and she was ready. George listened, breathless with anticipation. He had the impression she was speaking directly to him.

"*Bonnes nouvelles!* Ladies and gentlemen," she said in her warm American voice, "Charles Lindbergh has arrived! The *Spirit of St. Louis* has landed in France!"

The outburst that greeted this simple statement was extraordinary. George put his hands over his ears then took them down again to join in the clapping. Shouts, whistles and cheers rang out. Most of the male members of the audi-

ence, and some of the women, climbed onto their seats, the better to express their enthusiasm. The din went on in many languages as people translated for each other. Americans in the auditorium were singled out for especially warm congratulations.

George's trained observer's eye delighted in identifying the different nationalities' reactions amongst the audience. The unrestrained whooping of the American contingent was unmistakable, the clapping and murmuring of the English a counterpoint and, underpinning all, the squealing, fluttering expressiveness of the French. He wouldn't have expected such warmth from them, he thought, saddened as the nation was by the news that its own French entrant in the race to make the crossing had been lost at sea only a week ago. He wondered cynically whether they rightly understood that the St. Louis whose spirit was now amongst them was a southern American town—and, coincidentally, the hometown of Miss Baker—and not, as they might be forgiven for understanding, a reference to their own saintly king of France.

He leaned to share this thought with Alice, to find that he was once again alone in his box.

Wretched girl! His first feeling of self-recrimination for his careless lapse in attention was followed very quickly by one of intense relief. There was absolutely nothing he could do about it. He luxuriated in the feeling for a moment. She was no problem of his. He pictured her scuttling away to hide herself in a city she'd made her own. He could never find her now. Useless even to think of pursuit. He struggled with a reckless and bubbling joy, acknowledging for the first time the nature of his concern for the woman. Against all his fears, she was alive and had taken the time to show herself to him. The irrepressible thought that

came to mind was: "Good luck, Alice, wherever you're going. I hope you get away with it at the last! Whatever you're up to . . ."

He acknowledged that the glamour had faded from his evening but sat on and admired the last flourish—the ensemble gathering staged amidst miles of golden satin, tulle, sequins, and bobbing ostrich feathers—and clapped heartily as the curtains swung closed for the last time. As the house lights came on, he glanced across to the opposite box to check on the rogue Somerton.

"Ah! So your girl's cut loose too!" he muttered to himself, surprised to see that his acquaintance was alone. Surprised also to find that Somerton was sitting slumped over the rim of the box, fast asleep. "Through all that din?" George was instantly alert. The man's posture was unnatural. No man, however elderly, could have snoozed his way through that performance. Alice's warning words concerning heart-attacks among the susceptible flashed into his mind. Good Lord! The poor old bugger had had a seizure! No more than he deserved but—all the same—what bad luck. And the girl must have gone off to seek assistance.

George gathered himself together, preparing to battle his way to the exit through the still overexcited crowds. He fought against his sense of duty but it won. Suppose the girl didn't speak English? That she didn't know the identity of her escort? That she had just abandoned him to be swept up with the discarded chocolate boxes? His diplomat's antennae for international scandal were sending him signals he could not ignore. The villain was, after all, a baronet, now possibly a dead baronet, and if the gutter press were to get hold of the circumstances, he could imagine the headlines. But the other news of the evening, luckily, George argued with himself, would squeeze the plight of an English aristo-

crat off the front pages. Nevertheless, and cursing his compulsion always to take charge of any delicate or dangerous situation, George hesitated and then, mind made up, turned resolutely to shoulder his way against the tide flowing towards the bar and the exits and headed for Somerton's box.

He gave a perfunctory tap and walked straight in. Somerton was indeed by himself and, to all appearances, fast asleep, head comfortably cushioned on the padded upholstery. George cleared his throat noisily and followed this with a sharp exclamation: "Somerton! Come on, wake up! Show's over!"

The absolute stillness and lack of response confirmed all George's fears. He moved over to the man and knelt by his chair placing a finger behind his right ear where he might expect the absence of a pulse to tell him all. He snatched his finger away at once. He looked at his hand in horror. Black and sticky in the discreetly dim light of the box, there was no mistaking it. With a surge of revulsion, George seized hold of the chair-back to hoist himself to his feet. He had not thought to calculate the effect of his considerable weight being applied in a desperate manoeuvre to the elegant but insubstantial modern chair. It tilted and the body of Somerton heeled over, threatening to land in his lap. The expressionless face was inches from his own, eyes staring open but focussed on a presence beyond George. George's hand shot out in an instinctive attempt to support the back of the lolling head, which seemed about to roll away. A wide slash across the throat had almost severed the head from the rest of the body and quantities of blood had gushed all the way down his shirt and evening dress.

Ignoring the protests of his arthritic old knees and gargling with disgust, George staggered upright, taking the

weight of both the chair and the lolling body against his chest, struggling to right them.

A gasp and a squeal made him turn his head in the middle of this black Keystone Kops moment and he saw "his" *ouvreuse* standing huge-eyed and speechless in the doorway.

Chapter 6

The hammering on the door of his room at the Ambassador Hotel had been going on for a while before Joe Sandilands swam up to consciousness. He looked at his watch. Seven o'clock. The last thing he'd done before his eyes closed was put out the "Do Not Disturb" sign on his doorknob. He'd planned to sleep until midday at least. And now, only three hours after he'd slumped into his bed, here was some lunatic going against all the well-oiled discreet tradition of a French hotel.

Joe cleared his throat and reached for his voice. "Bugger off! Go away!" he shouted. "Don't you know it's Sunday morning?"

A silence was followed by another fusillade. More peremptory this time, sharper. An authoritative voice called out to him: "Monsieur Sandilands. This is the manager here. You are requested to come down at once to the lobby. We have England on the telephone. Long distance and they are holding. Scotland Yard insists on speaking to you."

Joe was alarmed. Always cost-cutting, the department didn't waste money on trunk calls unless they had something serious to impart. He shouted back his thanks and said he'd come straight down to the reception desk.

Minutes later he was enclosed in the guests' phone booth in the lobby taking a call from the assistant commissioner himself. Major-General Sir Wyndham Childs, i/c C.I.D. His dry soldier's voice leapt straight to the point with no preamble.

"Having a spot of bother with the French police… thought you might be able to help out… and how fortunate we are that you're right there on hand. Look—we know you're scheduled to attend the Interpol conference—starting when?—tomorrow. Just put that on hold, will you? We'll send out someone to cover for you and you can rejoin your party as soon as you can see your way through. There's been a rather nasty occurrence. Over there in Paris. One of our countrymen murdered in his box at the Théâtre des Champs-Élysées last night. Knifed to death, I am informed. The French police have made an arrest and a suspect has been detained in a cell at the Quai des Orfèvres, where he's currently giving a statement."

Joe marshalled his thoughts, regretting last night's excesses. "That is sad news indeed, sir. But there's not a great deal I can do. The victim may be English and I'm sorry to hear it, but if, as you say, the murder was committed on French soil it must be the province of the Police Judiciaire. We couldn't possibly interfere…" Joe hesitated. He wasn't thinking clearly. Sir William knew all this perfectly well.

A stifled exclamation of irritation which might have been "Tut!" or "Pshaw!" or even a click on the line startled him into adding hurriedly: "… unless there's something I could do towards identification of the body. Do we know who the unfortunate gentleman is?"

An awkward silence was followed by: "They have a strong suspicion that the deceased is an English aristocrat and ex-soldier. Sir Stanley Somerton."

Joe used the pause following this pronouncement to search his mental records. "Sorry, sir. Unfortunately, I have no knowledge of the man."

"No. I don't wonder." There was no warmth in the reply. "He did spend most of his time travelling abroad, after all. And kept well out of our sphere of activities."

"Have you been asked to send out any members of the family to confirm identity, sir? I'd gladly be on hand to receive them and guide them through the process—it's all rather different over here. The Paris morgue is not a particularly…well…you shouldn't think of sending in someone of a nervous disposition. Perhaps someone at the Embassy could—"

"Stop rattling on, Sandilands! We're sending over his wife. Lady Catherine has been informed and is packing as we speak. She'll be on the noon flight arriving at teatime—you know the score—and I want you to arrange to see her when she fetches up at Police HQ. No need to go to Le Bourget to meet her—the Embassy is taking care of all that. *You* can do the hand-holding business in the morgue."

Joe was encouraged by a lightening in the tone to reply: "Right-o, sir. I'll parade with smelling salts and handkerchief at a time to be arranged. Um…have they told us whom they have arrested for this crime?"

"They have indeed." The assistant commissioner was once again deadly serious. "And this is where you come in, Joe. You will want to be involved in whatever capacity you can contrive for yourself when I tell you that the suspect they've arrested is George. George Jardine. Friend of yours, I understand? When we heard, someone said straight away— 'Get Sandilands out there.'"

Joe mastered his astonishment and disbelief to reply firmly: "Terrible news. But not the disaster you suggest, surely, sir? It must be a misunderstanding... a mix-up with the language... failure to communicate one way or another at any rate—Sir George is a diplomat. And a top one at that! He has immunity. He might have shot dead the whole front row of the chorus and he could be lounging at ease with a reviving cup of tea in the shelter of the British Embassy out of reach of the Law. Why is he in a police cell? This is outrageous!"

"Ah, you don't know... you hadn't heard?" A gusty sigh down the telephone and then: "George no longer has diplomatic status, I'm afraid. He resigned his post a couple of months ago. He's retired. Hasn't quite severed his links— talks of returning—but, officially (and that's all that counts with the French), he's a free agent, no longer employed by HM Government and no longer under the umbrella of diplomatic immunity. Unlisted. A huge loss. One might have expected them to show some respect for his past position and let the matter drop. But the chap I spoke to who seems to be handling the case is one of those heel-clicking martinets you trip across sometimes over the Channel. Brittle. Self-important. You know the type. We're not short of a few over here... Anyway, I see from your file, Sandilands, which I have before me, that you have experience in dealing with this style of Gallic intractability... interpreter during the war, weren't you? We must have a drink when you've sorted all this out— I'd like to hear your slant on old Joffre. Anyway. Mustn't keep you. Get on down there, will you? Let me see... their HQ is at... now where did I...?"

"36, Quai des Orfèvres, sir," said Joe. "Staircase A. I've visited before. Makes our HQ look like Aladdin's palace. I'll do what I can and report back, er, this evening."

"Very well. Oh, and, Sandilands—feel free to reverse the

charges, will you? No expense to be spared on this one. Better take down my home number. Got a pen?"

Joe replaced the hand-set and stayed on in the booth for a moment or two, deep in thought. He went to the reception desk, where the manager was still hovering nervously with a solicitous eye to the English gentleman now revealed to be an agent of the British police force. Joe spoke in a reassuring undertone requesting more telephone time. He needed to put a call through to this number. He handed him a card, carefully avoiding using the word "police." Guests were beginning to trickle through on their way to breakfast in the dining room and Joe recollected that hotel management the world over had a horror of any suggestion of police activity, even benign activity. Luckily Jean-Philippe Bonnefoye's card simply gave his name and telephone number.

Joe went back into the booth and waited through several clicks and bangs for the ringing tone that told him the manager had successfully made contact with the number. Disconcertingly, it was a young woman's voice that answered sleepily. He asked to be allowed to speak to his colleague Jean-Philippe.

"Colleague? If you're a colleague you should know better than to ring him at such an unearthly hour! He's only just gone to bed. Push off!"

He shouted something urgently down the telephone to prevent her hanging up on him and unleashed a torrent of words in which "distress... emergency... international incident..." played a part.

At the words *"entente cordiale"* she finally hooted with derision and gave in. A few moments later Bonnefoye grunted down the phone. He recovered his wits rapidly as Joe concisely and twice over conveyed the information he'd just had from the Yard.

"Martinet?" he said. "Know who you mean. He's a bastard.

But most of the blokes in the Crim' are good guys. Look—
why don't you give me time to get myself organised and I'll
see you down there. I'm not involved...yet...but I can at
least perform a few introductions and blather on about international cooperation. Ease your path a bit. In one hour?
I'll see you at the coppers' entrance. You know it? Good! I'll
just go and soak my head and drink a gallon of coffee.
Suggest you do the same."

The doorman whistled up a taxicab when Joe emerged from
the Ambassador, showered and shaved, and dressed, calculatedly, in conservative English fashion. Thanks to his sister's careful packing, his dark three-piece suit had survived
the journey in perfectly wearable condition. He had put on a
stiff-collared shirt and regimental tie. Sadly, no bowler hat,
which would have impressed them; Joe did not possess such
a ridiculous item of headgear. No headgear at all, since his
fedora was lost somewhere at Le Bourget.

The morning traffic was thick and the taxi, weaving its
way through the press of horse-drawn cabs and delivery
lorries, was making slow progress. Once or twice in his
anxiety for Sir George, Joe contemplated getting out and
racing along on foot. The exercise would clear his muddled
head, the sharp air would purify his lungs and the sight
of Paris, magnificent and mysterious in the dissolving river
fog, would delight his eye, but he decided it might make
better sense to conserve the physical resources left to him
after last night's experiences. He didn't want to ride to
George's rescue sweating, foaming and breathless. Calm,
confident and helpful—that was what was required. In
any case, they were bound to be stunned by his timely appearance on their doorstep, and his title was impressive.
Deliberately so. A "Commander," with its naval flavour, got

attention, largely because no one seemed to have the slightest idea what it entailed or dared to ask; and some even confused it with "Commissioner" and took him to be the face of Scotland Yard.

With so little information at his disposal Joe could not do much to prepare himself for the interview—even assuming he would be granted an interview with the chap in charge. He planned to speak in French from the outset. Occasionally it was an advantage to fake ignorance. Not many English could converse in foreign languages anyway, and the French didn't expect it. Talking unguardedly amongst themselves, they would often reveal useful bits of information, but Joe intended to play no such deceitful tricks on this occasion. Too much at stake. He wanted to raise no hackles. And he wanted no reluctant English-speaking officer with a sketchy knowledge of the case to be pushed forward to handle the communications. Direct access to facts and theories was what he wanted. A face-to-face talk with the martinet. But mostly what he wanted was a chance to see Sir George.

His taxi driver, impatient with his progress on the boulevards, took a chance and nipped down the rue de Richelieu, emerging on the rue de Rivoli at the Comédie Française. They skirted the busy area of the marketplace, unimpeded. The thick traffic from the supply barges on the Seine to the Halles Centrales had been over with some hours before. A right turn at the cross roads of Le Châtelet took them over the bridge and onto the Île de la Cité. And into the ancient heart of the city.

Joe checked his watch with the ornate clock on the side of the Conciergerie as they turned off the quai. The old prison of Paris had the power to make him shudder even on a spring morning. The arrogant grandeur of its exterior, its pepper-pot turrets flaunting a military past, hid an interior

of dismal rooms and thick walls soaked in sorrow. Prison, law courts, police headquarters, medieval hospital, the most magnificent Gothic cathedral in the world—all crowded onto this small boat-shaped island in the Seine, its prow pointing downstream to the sea. Joe constantly expected it to sink under the enormous weight of its cargo of stone architecture.

Five minutes to eight and they were on the island. He'd do it.

What time did the shows end at the Champs-Élysées? About ten? So poor old George had been banged up in the cells for ten hours. Probably had a worse night than he'd had himself. Joe was surprised that he was still in custody. Such was the man's presence, strength of character and charm, Joe would have expected the flics to have bowed him out with an apology and an offer of a lift back to his hotel in a police car. A passing unease tugged at him. At any rate, with his talent for putting everyone at ease and getting precisely what he wanted, George would probably be discovered holding court in his cell and ordering up breakfast.

His taxi passed the imposing Law Court building and dropped him outside the police headquarters. He made his way through to the small courtyard where he counted ten police cars and two *paniers à salade,* empty of prisoners, lined up on the cobbles. Joe wondered briefly as he walked by whether George had been brought here in one of these Black Marias with their metal grilles. They trawled the streets bringing in a nightly haul of vagabonds, thieves, knife-wielding apaches and other villains. George would not have much enjoyed their company.

Bonnefoye was waiting by the policemen's entrance. The two men greeted each other ruefully. A painted sign announced: *Direction de la Police Judiciaire. Escalier A* it added

over an unimpressive door. Ancient, narrow and battered, it would not have looked out of place in any Paris backstreet. The stone slab under the door was worn to a hollow in the centre, witness to the thousands of nailed boots that had clumped their way over the threshold during the centuries. Nostalgically, Joe placed his Lobb's black half-Oxford right in the centre. Putting down a marker for Scotland Yard. Marking out new territory.

Bonnefoye looked at him through bleary eyes. "What a night, eh? I've seen you look sharper!"

"Do I look as bad as you do, I wonder?"

"Twenty years worse!"

Bonnefoye pushed open the door and hesitated. "Are you ready for this?" he asked. "It's a hundred and forty-eight steps up to the fifth floor. And no lift! But I think we may find out what we want to know by the third floor."

The building smelled rather unpleasantly of new paint, old linoleum and stale air, with, far in the background, a waft of coffee. Apart from the swish of brooms, the flick of dusters and the mumbled conversation of the cleaning ladies, it was very quiet. Joe could hear the peremptory toot of a barge on the river and the distant ringing behind a closed office door of a telephone that went unanswered. He silently compared his surroundings to the marble-tiled magnificence of the vestibule of Scotland Yard with its mahogany reception desk manned by helpful, uniformed constables and the ceaseless movement of policemen in and out whatever the time of day or night.

"Where is everyone?" Joe asked as they began to climb the staircase.

"It's early." Bonnefoye shrugged. "Night shift's left and the morning crowd won't get here for another hour."

They stopped off at the third floor and Joe followed his escort into a green-painted waiting room that seemed to

have been furnished by the local junk shop. They settled on two mismatched chairs and Bonnefoye asked for a further report on Joe's telephone conversation. He listened to Joe's brief background details on Sir George and smiled.

"As you say, Sandilands—quite obviously a misunderstanding. I'm sure you'll be able to clear it up in no time. I don't expect that I'll be of much help. I'm very recently arrived here, remember. They don't know my face yet. But I'll do whatever I can. And I'll start by marking your card over the chief inspector. If it's who I think it is, his name is Casimir Fourier and he's an unpleasant bastard. Sour, forties, unmarried, fought in the war, very ambitious. Said to have clawed his way up from lowly origins. What else can I tell you? No known virtues. Except that he's reputed to be very efficient. He has an exceptional record for extracting confessions."

"Confessions?"

"You know our system! You can be discovered by a dozen independent witnesses—and half of them nuns—with your hands about a victim's throat and the state will still demand a confession. The magistrates expect it. It absolves them of any guilt should any contradictory evidence arise after the event. And by 'event' I mean execution. Monsieur Guillotin's daughter still does her duty in the courtyard at La Santé prison. There's no arguing with *her*. I imagine your friend is busy providing Fourier or his deputy with a *procès-verbal* of the events."

"But, taking down a written statement... I can't imagine that would last ten hours, can you?"

Bonnefoye looked uncomfortable. "Depends on whether he's saying what Fourier wants him to say. Perhaps he's not such a cooperative type, your friend?"

"Oh, he is. Very much the diplomat. Experienced. Worldly. Knows when to compromise." Joe grinned. "And he always

comes out on top. But he doesn't suffer fools—or villains—
gladly and your Casimir Fourier may find he's bitten off
more than he can chew if he confronts George. And— let's
not forget—he's not guilty! Hang on to that, Bonnefoye!"

"Wait here, I'll go and tap on the chief inspector's door
and let him know we've arrived." He headed off down the
corridor towards the inspectors' offices.

Bonnefoye returned a minute later. Not at ease. "Fourier's
got your friend in there. As I thought, they're working on his
statement. And not pleased to be interrupted, I'm afraid."
He looked at his watch. "Told me to go away and not to
bring you back before ten o'clock. He'll see you then."

Joe could not keep the annoyance out of his voice.
"Spreading his tail feathers! Showing who's boss! He
doesn't endear himself!"

"Tell you what … pointless kicking our heels here … why
don't we nip out and get some breakfast? The Halles are a
short walk away. The blokes normally go there at the end of
a night shift. There's a good little café where you can get
onion soup, wonderful strong coffee, croissants, fresh
bread…"

Joe was already heading for the door.

He reckoned it was not so much the onion soup that fortified him as the dash of brandy that the waiter stirred into it.
But whatever it was, he returned with Bonnefoye, fully
awake and having got his second wind. They repeated their
ascent to the waiting room and stood by the open door.
Distantly the bell of Notre Dame sounded ten and, taking a
deep breath, Bonnefoye invited him with a gesture to ac-
company him to the chief inspector's room.

The Frenchman tapped on the door and listened. A
peremptory bark was interpreted as a signal to enter. As the

door swung open, Joe was taken aback by a wave of used air, over-warm and sooty, thick with rough tobacco and rancid with perspiration. At a desk too large for the room lounged the chief inspector in his shirtsleeves, tie pulled loosely aside. His stare was narrow and truculent, dark eyes hooded in a sallow face. Joe was gratified to note the dark stubble on the broad jaw. Fourier looked rather less appetising than himself or Bonnefoye and was clearly still finishing off his night's work. Not yet into the new day. He made no effort to greet them, merely watching as they came in to stand in front of him, raising his eyebrows as though to enquire what could possibly be the reason for this interruption to his day.

"A moment, please," he said before they could speak, and rang a bell.

A young sergeant entered from the room next door and looked at him enquiringly. "Do you want me to take over, sir?"

"Not for the moment. I'm still going strong. Good for a few more hours yet," Fourier said, ignoring his guests. "Just check the stove, would you? Oh, and get me another cup of coffee."

The sergeant went smoothly about his duties, pouring out a cup of badly stewed coffee from an enamel pot simmering on the stove and finding a space for it on a tray alongside a green bottle of Perrier water and an empty glass by the chief inspector's hand. No offer of refreshment was made to the men standing in front of him. And as there was no chair in the room but the one on which Fourier sat, stand was all they could do.

All Joe's attention had been for the silent prisoner in the middle of the room but he forced himself not to react to what he saw and turned back to the chief inspector as Bonnefoye performed the introductions. He handed over

his warrant card and waited patiently while Fourier read it with exaggerated care, turning it this way and that. "If he holds it up to the light, I shall certainly smack him one," Joe thought, relieving his tensions with a pleasing fantasy.

"I see. And you claim to be…what am I supposed to assume?…a commander of Scotland Yard?" The voice was dry and roughened by years of cigarette smoke. Joe glanced at the ashtray stuffed full of yellow butts and wondered if he should advise the use of Craven A. Kind to the throat, apparently.

"Your deduction is correct," Joe replied mildly. "I *am* a commander. You may not be familiar with the hierarchy in the Metropolitan Police? I direct a department of the C.I.D.—the equivalent of your Brigade Criminelle—specialising in military, diplomatic and political crime of a nature sensitive to His Majesty's Government. I report to the chief commissioner himself." As well as clarity and exactness, the statement also carried the underlying message that Commander Sandilands outranked Chief Inspector Fourier by a mile.

Fourier dropped the card carelessly onto his desk amongst the disordered piles of papers cluttering the surface. "But a commander who has no crew, no ship and has entered foreign waters. Seems to me you're up the creek without a paddle, Commander." Fourier's hacking, gurgling cough, Joe realised, was laughter and a sign that he was enjoying his own overworked image. "You seem to have a turn of speed at least, though, I'll grant you that! How in hell did you manage to get here so fast? Crime wasn't committed until late last evening."

Joe decided to ignore the slight and respond to the human element of curiosity. "Wings," he said with a smile. "Wings across the Channel. The night flight from Croydon. We landed a second or two before Lindbergh. I was coming

to Paris anyway. I'm to represent Britain at the Interpol conference at the Tuileries." Joe's smile widened. "I'm due to give a paper on Day 3...You might be interested to come along and hear...It's on international cooperation, illustrated by specific examples of Franco British liaison."

A further bark expressed disbelief and scorn. Joe held out his hand. "My card? Would you? I'm sure I saw you drop it into this rats' nest." He kept his hand outstretched and steady—an implied challenge—until his card was safely back in his grasp.

"And now, to business," he said briskly. "Perhaps you'd like to introduce me to your prisoner and outline the grievance you have with him."

At last he felt he could turn and look at George with a measure of composure. Had he reacted at once according to his gut instinct, he would have hauled Fourier over his desk by his greasy braces and smashed a fist into his face.

George was almost unrecognisable. Old and weary, he had been put to stand in the centre of the room, back to the window, in bloodstained undervest and drooping evening trousers. Braces and belt had been taken away; his shoes gaped open where the laces had been removed. A familiar procedure. But used here, Joe guessed, not so much to prevent the prisoner from hanging himself as to humiliate him. One eye was blackened and a bruise was spreading over his unshaven jaw. He seemed uncertain as to how to greet Joe and embarrassed by his own appearance. His slumped shoulders straightened when Joe and Bonnefoye turned to him, and he shifted slightly on his feet, planted, Joe noticed, in the soldier's "at ease" position. But there was nothing easy about George's circumstances.

Joe decided to play it unemotionally and by the book. "Sir! How very good to see you again after all this time. My

sympathy and apologies for the plight in which you find yourself. I'm at your service."

George licked his lips and finally managed, in a ghost of his remembered voice, to drawl: "Jolly good! Well, in that case, perhaps you could rustle up a glass of water, eh? Perhaps even some breakfast? Hospitality around here not wonderful... I've eaten and drunk nothing since a light pre-theatre snack yesterday. Though I discern..." he said, waving a hand under his nose, "that you two boulevardiers have been at it already. Onion soup, would that be?"

Bonnefoye looked down at his feet, unable to meet Joe's eye.

If he gave way to the explosion of rage that was boiling within him, Joe realised he would be thrown off the premises at best, perhaps even arrested and lined up alongside. At all events, he might expect a damning report on his conduct to be winging its way to Scotland Yard in a mail bag aboard the next Argosy, with all the predictable consequences for his future career with Interpol. A passing expression of cunning on the chief inspector's face, the proximity of his finger to the bell on his desk, told him that this was precisely what he was anticipating.

For George's sake, he calmed himself. His old friend, he calculated from the evidence of his senses, had been kept standing here in this ghastly room for twelve hours with no water or food while his interrogator lounged, coffee in hand, taking time off from his questioning through the night, relieved by his sergeant at intervals. Joe imagined Fourier had a camp bed somewhere about the place to which he could retire when the proceedings began to bore him.

Joe glanced with concern at George's legs. Long, strong old legs, a polo player's legs but he was aware of an involuntary

twitching in the region of the knees. There were shadows of exhaustion under his eyes. One of those eyes was almost closed now by the spreading purple bruise. The other bravely essayed a wink. With a stab of pity, Joe determined to make a clandestine but close inspection of the knuckles of both chief inspector and sergeant. Whichever had done the damage to George's face would pay.

Fourier gave him sufficient time to absorb the prisoner's condition and to spring an attack and, as it did not materialise, he added further fuel to Joe's anger. "Breakfast? Not quite sure where *milord* thinks he is... the Crillon, perhaps? As he seems to be prepared to react to *you*, perhaps you could convey my regrets. No information, no refreshment. I can keep him here for a further twelve hours, though I would not like to mar my reputation with the magistrate for speed and efficiency."

The scornful *"milord"* had given Joe an insight into Fourier's character. He had already noted the countryman's accent. He was not experienced enough to identify it, but it quite definitely was not a Parisian voice and it was not the voice of a man who prided himself on his culture, as did most of the Frenchmen Joe had met. This implacable, humourless man could, in a past century, have taken his place on the Committee of Public Safety alongside Danton, Marat, Robespierre and the other bloodthirsty monsters who had spawned the Revolution. Only three generations separated him from his sans-culotte ancestor, Joe supposed. And here was the descendant, still flaunting his traditional twin hatreds: the aristocracy and the English. George was doubly his target.

Joe's fists clenched at his sides but it was Bonnefoye who cracked first.

Chapter 7

Joe had been aware for some time that shame had been doing battle with disciplined deference in his friend. But the young inspector was a Burgundian by birth and possessing the Burgundian traits almost to the point of caricature: merry, deep-drinking, wily and—above all—proud.

Bonnefoye stalked to the desk, seized the Perrier bottle by its elegant neck and proceeded to fill the water glass with the deft movements of a waiter. "The Crillon it clearly is not," he said affably, "nor yet is it the Black Hole of Calcutta."

He presented the glass to George and watched him empty it with one draught, bubbles and all. George handed it back with an appreciative belch.

"Eternally grateful, young man."

"George, this is my colleague Jean-Philippe Bonnefoye. Inspector Bonnefoye," said Joe. "Though not for much longer," he added to himself with an eye on Fourier. Expressionless, the chief inspector had unscrewed the cap of

his fountain pen and was making a note on a pad at his elbow.

Was recklessness a Burgundian characteristic? Or was it Gascon? Joe wondered. Whichever it might be, Bonnefoye was demonstrating it with relish. His next act of defiance was to reach over and ring the bell. The sergeant came in at once. "We need some chairs in here. Fetch three," said Bonnefoye.

"Yes, sir," muttered the sergeant. He looked sideways for a countermanding order, but, receiving none, bustled out.

Another note was scratched on the pad. Fourier's mouth twisted into an unpleasant grimace which Joe was alarmed to interpret as a smile.

A moment later three stacked chairs made their appearance and Joe and Bonnefoye took delivery, lowering Sir George with creaks and groans down onto one of them. They seated themselves one on each side of him, protective angels. Joe sighed. He feared Fourier's pad was going to be overflowing with damning comments before the hour was up. He exchanged a grin with Bonnefoye. Ah, well... in for a penny...

"And now, Fourier, if you wouldn't mind—your *procès verbal*. How's it coming along? The sooner his statement's in, the sooner we can get it to the clerk's office... *le greffe*? Is that what you'd say? And then we can all get out of your hair and you can get back to the business of arresting someone for the killing in the theatre."

"I have him. The killer sits between you," said Fourier in a chilling tone. "Here's what Jardine has confided. Here—why don't you take it. Read it. Come to your own conclusions."

Joe was alarmed to hear the certainty verging on gloating in his voice. He took the meagre account, amounting to no more than two sheets of paper and began to read. He was

quick to pass the report to Bonnefoye, who ran through it and looked up, disturbed.

"Sir George," Joe began, "I'd like you to go through this with me, confirming, if you would, that the chief inspector has not misinterpreted anything you had to say. Add anything you feel has been overlooked. Bonnefoye and I between us ought to be able to hack together something solid. Now... you detail your reason for attending this particular performance... The gift of a ticket, you say?"

"Not actually a ticket," corrected George, opening in the voice of the meticulous witness, "one of those annoying tokens they issue. A sort of ticket for a ticket—you cash the first one in for the real thing when you get to the theatre. It's a ridiculous system for extracting more francs from—"

"Sent to you by a cousin, you say?" Joe set him back on course.

"No, I don't say. Not for certain. I kept the note that came with the token. Fourier has it," he said.

Fourier passed over a torn envelope and a short note.

"John? Just 'John'? Could be anyone, surely? Does this help?" Joe asked.

"No help at all. I must know about two dozen Johns and most of them likely to be passing through Paris sometime during the year. I took it to be my young cousin John who's posted to the Embassy here, though I didn't at first catch on—always call him Jack, you see. These people," George waved a gracious hand in the direction of the chief inspector, "allowed me a phone call at least, though they insisted on doing it for me. They got hold of John Jardine at the Embassy and I'd guess it's due to his efforts on my behalf that you're here, Commander."

"You may also wish to see this." Fourier smiled. He passed over a scrawled report on a sheet of Police Judiciaire writing

paper. "I sent out an officer to interview the gentleman, of course."

Joe summarised the statement, reading aloud: "'Confirm Sir George Jardine my cousin…no knowledge of any gift of theatre tickets. Didn't even know he was in Paris.' Ah. Some mystery there, then. Well, moving on: you arrived at the theatre—"

"Where he was ambushed by a second mystery," Fourier interrupted. "Are you now, in this welcome rush of revelation, going to disclose the identity of the lady who joined you in your box, monsieur?"

Enjoying Joe's surprise, he added, "The *ouvreuse* in attendance on the boxes yesterday evening is a lively young woman and very alert. She it was who discovered your friend in the act of slitting his compatriot's throat. She identified him as the gentleman from Box A across the theatre. She was able to tell us that, moments before the performance started, monsieur was joined by a woman. A Frenchwoman, she thought from their brief conversation, and wearing an opera cape. The hood was up and she would be unable to identify her or indeed remember her face. From the closeness of the chairs in that box, when I examined it, the two knew each other well, I'd say. Or at least were friendly. The bar reveals that both occupants drank a glass of whisky in the interval. And—I would ask you to note—the drinks order was placed before the lady arrived. She was clearly expected. By Sir George."

"George? This is nothing but good news! If we can find this lady, she will provide your alibi, surely? Who on earth was she?"

"No idea! She just turned up moments before the performance started." George's mystification was evident. "A lady of the night, I assumed. Well—wouldn't *you*? Most

probably a gesture from the magnanimous John. Whoever he is. Can't say I approve much of such goings-on! I say—is this sort of behaviour becoming acceptable in Paris these days? The done thing, would you say?"

His words ran into the sand of their silent speculation. Joe paused to allow him to expand on his statement but George appeared unwilling.

He pressed on. "You were not able to furnish the chief inspector with a description of the lady?"

"Sadly, no. She was wearing one of those fashionable cape things...Kept it on over her head. She came in after the lights went out..."

"The lights went on during the interval," Joe objected quietly. He was beginning to understand some of Fourier's frustration.

"Jolly awkward! I mean—what *is* one to say in the circumstances? Any out and out dismissal or rejection is bound to give offence, don't you know! I chatted about this and that—put her at her ease. She didn't have much to say for herself...comments on the performance...the new look of the theatre, that sort of thing. I gave her a glass of the whisky I'd ordered in expectation of a visit from my cousin Jack, who's very partial to a single malt..."

"The lady," said Joe. "What do you have to report?"

"Um...didn't like the scotch but too polite to refuse. She'd probably have preferred a Campari-soda...I think you know the type..." He paused. His mild blue eye skittered over Joe's and then he drawled on: "French. Yes, I'm sure she was French. Spoke the language like a native, I'd say. Though I'm not the best judge of accents. Not perhaps a Parisian," he added thoughtfully. "Cape all-enveloping, as I've said, no clear idea of her features. But—average height for a woman. Five foot something..." He caught Joe's

narrowed look and amplified: "Five foot five. Slim. Well-educated. Obviously from a top-flight establishment. Suggest you start looking there. I expect the chief inspector is well acquainted with these places? In the line of professional enquiry, of course."

Joe hurried on. "Moving to the finale ... You say there was a commotion when Miss Baker announced the arrival of the *Spirit of St. Louis* ..."

"Commotion? It was a standing ovation! Went on for at least ten minutes. Stamping, shouting and yelling! Quite an unnecessary and embarrassing display! And that's when she disappeared, I think. My unknown and unwanted companion."

"And at the true finale—Golden Fountain, you call it?—you observed your acquaintance Somerton to be slumped in his box opposite."

"I feared the worst. Well, not the *worst* I could have feared, not by a long chalk, as it turned out ... Thought he'd had a heart attack. Anno domini, don't you know ... Stimulating show and he'd been twining about a blonde of his own ..." George bit his lip at his faux pas, hearing it picked up in the energetic scratching of Fourier's pen, but he ploughed on: "A spectacular girl—I've given the description."

"Yes, I see it. Remarkably detailed, Sir George. She obviously made quite an impression?"

"The girl thirty metres away was clearly more vivid to Jardine than the one who was practically sitting in his lap," offered the chief inspector acidly.

"Opera glasses, George? ... Yes, of course."

"And she disappeared from her box ... oh, no idea, really," said Sir George vaguely. "Sometime before the finale, that's as near as I can say."

"And you decided to go over there in a public-spirited way to see if you could render assistance?"

"Old habits die hard, you know. Taking charge of potentially awkward situations...always done it...always will, I expect. Interfering old nuisance, some might say."

"Sir George has run India for the last decade," Joe confided grandly, probably annoying the hell out of Fourier, he thought, but he pressed on: "Riots, insurgencies, massacres...all kinds of mayhem have been averted by his timely intervention. A disturbance in a theatre box is something that *would* elicit energetic action."

"As would intent to murder," replied the chief inspector, unimpressed.

"Tell us what happened next, will you? I see that this is as far as you got in twelve hours, despite vigorous encouragement from the chief inspector. No wonder he's looking a bit green around the gills."

George described with accompanying gestures the scene of discovery. The chief inspector scribbled.

At last when George fell silent, Fourier put down his pen, a look of triumph rippling across his features. "And this story meshes splendidly with the eyewitness account we are given by the helpful *ouvreuse*, but only up to a point."

With a generous gesture, he peeled off another police witness sheet and allowed Joe and Bonnefoye to read it.

"The lady says...I say, shall we call her by her name, since she seems to be playing rather more than a walk-on role in this performance? Mademoiselle Francine Raissac states that she came upon the two Englishmen in Box B in the course of her nightly clearing up duties. The man she refers to as 'the ten franc tip'—the large good-looking one (Sir George)—was in close contact with the smaller weaselly one ('the five franc tip') and she took the former to be in the act of cutting the throat of the latter, since the blood was flowing freely between the two, and Sir George, who turned and

looked up on hearing her scream, was covered in his compatriot's blood.

"The men were alone in the box, the partner of the five
franc tip being no longer present. Mademoiselle Raissac declares she is unable to furnish us with a full description of
the lady. She had never seen her before. She remembers she
was young—less than twenty-five years old—and had fair
hair. Mademoiselle Raissac further declares the girl must
have been speaking French since she (Mademoiselle Raissac)
was not conscious of any accent. Mmm..."

"A second elusive fair beauty. How they cluster around
you Englishmen! I do wonder what the attraction is,"
scoffed Fourier.

As George seemed to be about to tell him, Joe changed the
subject with a warning scowl. "I should very much like to see
the corpse," he said, "and hear the opinion of your pathologist..."

"But certainly," agreed the chief inspector. "And perhaps
you would also like to examine the murder weapon? Oh, yes,
it was discovered. At the feet of the corpse on the floor of the
box where Sir George dropped it. A finely crafted Afghani
dagger." He turned and looked for the first time at George.
"I understand, Jardine, that you were, at one time, a soldier
in Afghanistan?"

"A long time ago," said George. "As was Somerton. We
both served for a spell on the North-West Frontier. The
blade was most probably his own. He had a fondness for
knives. And a certain skill with them. It definitely wasn't
mine. I have an abiding aversion for them. I favour a Luger
these days for self-protection. Though I make a point of
never going armed to the theatre. Too tempting to express
an over-critical view of the performance. And these closely
tailored evening suits— anything more substantial than a
hatpin completely ruins the line, you know."

Joe was reassured to hear a flash of the old Sir George but was becoming more anxious for his safety as the sorry tale evolved. His old friend, the man he admired and trusted above all others, was in serious trouble.

Fourier clearly didn't believe a word he said and was looking out for a quick arrest. Possibly within the twenty-four-hour limit he prided himself on achieving. If George had killed this man, Joe was quite certain Somerton had deserved it. But he determined to know the truth. His compulsion was always to go after the truth using any means at his disposal; he had no other way of functioning. And having found out the truth? And supposing it didn't appeal to him? He smiled, recalling the wise words of an old member of the Anglo-Indian establishment...what had been her name?...Kitty, that was it. Mrs. Kitson-Masters.

"What could be more important than the truth?" he'd asked her one day some years ago in Panikhat, at a moment when he was being, he remembered, particularly officious, annoyingly self-righteous. And, gently, she'd replied: "I'll tell you what: the living. They're more important than the dead and more important than the truth." And, as long as George was among the living, Joe would lay out all his energy and skill to keep him there.

But there was bargaining to be done. Agreement to be reached. Feathers to be smoothed and arms to be twisted. Joe grinned. He was going to have to discount the pathetic and confused old person sitting next to him and call on all the skills he'd learned from the man he'd first met as Sir George Jardine, Governor of Bengal, Adviser to Viceroys and discreet Spymaster of India.

And the first of these skills had been: never lose your temper, and the second: deploy what Joe had always thought of as a type of mental ju-jitsu. Identify and assess your opponent's strength and, under the guise of accommodation and

reason, use its energy against him to propel him arse over tip onto the nearest dung-heap.

He turned a tentative smile of relief on Fourier when he looked up from the notes which were now flowing fast from his pen.

"I'd say this is going rather well, wouldn't you, Fourier? But if you're thinking the magistrate is not going to be happy to accept so much conflicting and inconclusive evidence without the underpinning surety of a confession—well, then, I'd be the first to agree with you."

Fourier scowled at him suspiciously.

Joe leaned forward in his chair, hands on his knees, fixing his opposite number with a keen stare. He spoke to him with quiet force. They could have been the only two people in the room. "I'm an ambitious man, Chief Inspector," he confided. "You've seen my card. You are aware of how I am currently...placed—"

"*Poised*, I'd have said," interrupted Fourier.

Joe smiled. "As you say...'poised' will do very well...poised for advancement. I make no secret of the fact that I have my eye on the directorship of one of the more interesting divisions at the Yard. 'Assistant commissioner' would not be out of the question. There is much competition, many excellent candidates. Not a few are military men who know how to plan an effective campaign. I expect it's the same over here? And it's the man who can forge a reputation for himself who will win out. The one who can make himself stand out from the rest. 'Ah, yes—Sandilands. Isn't he the bloke who cleared up that killing in Paris?' I believe I have a nose for an interesting, attention-grabbing case. And we have one here!" He paused for a moment to allow his excitement to be caught on the other side of the desk.

Fourier yawned.

"A front-page, sell-every-copy story that could rival the

Whitechapel murders. On both sides of the Channel. It has everything one could ask for! Pretty girls, daggers, gallons of blood spilt in the most spectacular of settings...And— cherry on the cake—the victim is a *rosbif*—an Englishman for whom we need feel no sympathy. Probably got no more than he deserved...I challenge you to invent three possible head- lines for this case. Go on, man!"

Joe took out his notebook and pencil and began to scrib- ble. Before Fourier had a chance to call a halt to his games, he rushed on. "Got it! I've got one for the English press. Not sure that it will do much for you. You'll have to invent your own. *Death du Jour*," said Joe. "What do you say?"

"Not bad. I'd use something a bit longer and more dra- matic—that's the style of our papers. They like to involve a famous person: *Did the Black Venus witness the Angel of Death?* They're bound to pick up the fact that the star of the show could well have been onstage at the very moment when Jardine struck the blow—only a few feet away as it happens," Fourier speculated.

George tensed, preparing to object, but stayed silent, aware of Joe's tactics.

"They might use: *Throat-slashing at the Folies...*" Fourier went on with ready invention, and it occurred to Joe that his mind had already been running in just such a direction. He wondered if George, his mentor, had seen it? Joe had rightly guessed the chief inspector's imperative, his motivation. He'd judged Fourier's craving for advancement to be at the same time his strength and his weakness and, by ascribing the same ruthless ambition to himself, Joe had made it appear acceptable in his eyes. More than acceptable—commend- able. He had bracketed them together, two like-minded cyn- ics ready to exploit a situation for their mutual benefit. Somerton, Sir George, even Bonnefoye, were marionettes, their strings in the hands of two hard-eyed professionals.

Joe wasn't quite there yet but he was on his way to using the power of Fourier's forward rush to kick him into space.

"Two Englishmen fight to the death for the favours of mysterious *fille de joie*. Plea for the blonde beauty to come forward." The chief inspector was enjoying himself. He shrugged. "Well, these news editors—they'll say whatever they like. Of course, sometimes they respond to a confidential suggestion in their ear."

He looked at the clock and glared at Sir George. The obstacle between him and his story. "Pour the man another glass of water, Bonnefoye," he said. "It seems to loosen his tongue."

"Fourier, may I have a word in private?" Joe asked.

He left the room with the chief inspector, a companionable hand on his shoulder. They returned a minute or two later and Joe went to stand almost at attention by Fourier's desk, alongside him and facing the other two men.

Fourier cleared his throat and gathered up his documents. "Gentlemen," he said, "the commander and I have come to a decision. In order to pursue the case further, I will be releasing the prisoner from police custody into police custody. Jardine is to be handed over to Sandilands with the assurance that he will not attempt to leave the city. I retain his passport and his documents. I require him to attend for a further interview as and when I deem it necessary."

He rang the bell. "Sergeant—the prisoner's clothes are to be kept as evidence. Can you find an old mackintosh or something to cover the mess? And you may bring his shoelaces and braces back. Gentlemen—go with the sergeant. He will walk you through the process of signing out the prisoner. Oh, and, Commander—your request to examine the corpse—I grant this and will leave instructions at the morgue accordingly. Now—Bonnefoye! I'm not au fait with your schedule . . . Remind me, will you?"

"Mixed bag, sir. The suspected poisoning in Neuilly—toxicology report still awaited. The body under the métro train—no ID as yet. And there's last night's floating *bonne bouche* dragged from the St. Martin...And the conference, of course." He smiled blandly back at the chief inspector.

"Then I recommend that you get yourself back on track at once." Fourier added with menacing politeness: "Your contribution to the proceedings has been noted."

Joe thanked him and, taking advantage of the spirit of burgeoning cooperation, asked if he might fix a time to escort Lady Somerton to the morgue for purposes of identification. Fourier was beginning to see the advantages of having an Englishman on hand, Joe thought, as his response was quick and positive. His own response would have been the same. The dreadful scene of the widow wailing over the remains was always the one to be avoided, particularly when the grieving was being done in a foreign language. It added an element of awkwardness to a situation requiring sympathy and explanation. Fourier seemed to have no objection to passing on this delicate duty. They eyed each other with a gathering understanding and a mutual satisfaction.

The unanimous verdict burst from the three men as they reached the safety of the courtyard below:

"Arsehole!"

"Qu'il est con!"

"Fuckpot!"

Without further exchange or consultation, they quickly made their way out onto the breezy quayside, where George came to a standstill, content to stare at the river traffic, enjoying its bustling ordinariness. He listened to the shouts, the hoots, the throbbing of the engines; he narrowed watering

eyes against the brilliance of the spring sunshine dancing on the water. He waved and shouted something teasing at a small terrier standing guard on a passing barge. It barked its defiance. George wuffed back and laughed like a boy in delight. An escapee from one of the circles of hell, Joe judged. A night in clink with Fourier for company would make anyone light-headed.

With something like good humour restored, Joe began to lay out a programme for the rest of the morning. He was interrupted by Sir George. "The hotel can wait," he declared. "Now we're free of this dreadful place, I want some breakfast! Some of that soup wouldn't come amiss. Where did you get it?"

Joe eyed his dishevelled state and was doubtful; George was looking even less appetising in the bright light of morning. He could have strolled over to join the dozen or so tramps just waking under the bridge a few yards away and they'd have shuffled over to make room for a brother. But at least the worst of the bloodstains were hidden under a dirty old wartime trench-coat two sizes too small.

Bonnefoye was more confident. "Excellent idea! Looking as you do, we won't take you to a respectable café. Au Père Tranquille—that's where we'll go. Back to the Halles, Joe. It's a workman's café—they'll just assume Sir George is a tourist who's fallen foul of some local ruffians. Or an American artist slumming. Wait here by the gate—I'll flag down a taxi."

After his second bowl of soup with a glass of cognac on the side, a whole baguette and a pot or two of coffee, George's colour was returning and his one good eye had acquired a sparkle.

"I'm curious! Are you going to tell us, Joe," Bonnefoye asked, "what precisely you said to the chief inspector that

made him change his mind? Rather a volte-face, wasn't it? I could have sworn he was all set to have another go at harrying Sir George. Perhaps closing his other eye?"

"No, no! You're mistaken, young man," said George. "I tripped and banged my head against a corner of the desk. But—you're right—I have a feeling I was about to execute the same tricky manoeuvre on the other side. What *did* you say, Joe, to turn him through a hundred and eighty degrees?"

Joe stared into his coffee cup. "I merely suggested that if Fourier had it in mind to apply the thumbscrews, he might like to know that Sir George had been for years a soldier in the British forces, battling the bloodthirsty Afridi, to say nothing of Waziri tribesmen in the wilderness west of Peshawar. I enquired whether he was aware that George had at one time been captured by the enemy and subjected to torture of an inventive viciousness of which only the Wazirs are capable. Rescued in the nick of time, more dead than alive after three days in their hands, but having divulged no information to his captors. Not a word. Name, rank and number and that's it. Surely Fourier, during his physical inspection of his prisoner, had remarked the scars on his back, the dislocation of the left shoulder, the badly repaired break to the ulna...? I think he decided at that point that any action he was planning against such a leathery old campaigner was a bit limp in comparison."

"Good Lord!" said Bonnefoye faintly, inspecting Sir George with fresh and wondering eyes.

"Joe! Come now!" George reprimanded. "Ulna? Wasn't aware I had one... Are you quite certain that's not one of Napoleon's victories?" He turned confidingly to Bonnefoye. "It wouldn't do to believe everything this man tells you," he advised with a kindly smile for the young inspector. "He enjoys a good story! Keen reader of the *Boy's Own Paper,* don't you know!"

"Oh, I see!" Bonnefoye was embarrassed to have been caught out so easily. "Well, for a moment, Commander, you had me fooled too! But then, I was always a sucker for tales of derring-do." Bonnefoye looked from one to the other, suddenly wary and mistrustful of these two Englishmen who seemed to share the same lazily arrogant style, the same ability to look you in the eye and lie.

He flicked a speculative glance at Joe. Surely he was aware? Could he possibly have been taken in by that performance in the interview room?

"And now—back to your hotel, George," said Joe. "Where are you staying?"

"Hotel Bristol. Rue du Faubourg St. Honoré. D'you know it?"

"Ah, yes. Handy for the British Embassy. Well, a bath and a change of clothes and about twelve hours' sleep are all on the menu. And when you wake up, there'll be a policeman by your bedside waiting to take down your statement. Leaving out the invention and prevarication, this time. No more lying! Nothing less than your *uncensored* revelations will do. And the policeman will be me."

Chapter 8

As they approached the hotel, George became increasingly agitated. In his hatless, beaten-up state he had been receiving some questioning looks from the smartly turned-out inhabitants. One lady had even crossed the road to avoid encountering him.

"I say, you chaps," he said fifty yards short of the Bristol, "better for everyone if I don't cross the foyer looking like this. I'd be an embarrassment to the management as well as to myself. There's a side alleyway they use for deliveries to the kitchens. I'll use that. I know my way about. I'll nip up in the service lift. See you in my room. That's 205."

He would listen to no argument and slipped away without a further word.

Joe and Bonnefoye pressed on to the Bristol and requested the key. Bonnefoye produced his badge and asked the maître d'hôtel to summon a doctor and send him up with the utmost discretion.

Once over the threshold of his own room, George rallied

and tried again to dismiss his attendants. "No need to wait on me, you chaps. No need at all. I can manage. I'll see the medic if he appears, for form's sake, but—really—no need of him. Let's keep the fuss to a minimum, shall we?"

"No khitmutgars here," said Joe cheerfully, pushing past him into the room. "Not even a valet. You'll have to make do with us. Jean-Philippe—run a bath will you, while I hunt out his pyjamas and dressing gown. Is this what you're using, George? This extravagantly Oriental number? Good Lord! Now, just sit down will you, old chap...you're teetering again...and you can start peeling off that disgusting vest."

Bonnefoye returned from the bathroom lightly scented with lavender to catch sight of Sir George in his underpants, slipping a purple silk dressing gown around his shoulders. He stood still and exchanged a startled look with Joe. When George had disappeared into the bathroom he hissed: "Sandilands! That mess on his back! Scars? Weals? What in hell was it?"

Joe was recovering from his own astonishment at the brief glimpse he had caught. "Good Lord! It seems I wasn't exaggerating. I was just retelling an old story that does the rounds in India. I had no idea it was accurate."

"Tough old bird," murmured Bonnefoye. "Fourier had no idea what he'd run into." And then: "He never would have signed a confession, would he?"

"No," said Joe. "But that doesn't mean he has nothing to confess. There's something wrong with all this. He's hardly begun to explain what he's involved in. I think he's been lying to the chief inspector but, if he has, there'll be a damned good reason for it. Fourier couldn't beat the truth out of him and we, my friend, must use other methods. As soon as we've got him settled I'm going back to the morgue to take a look at the man at the bottom of all this—our mystery man, Somerton. No—no need to come with me—I'll report back.

You should go back to your duties, Jean-Philippe—I've taken up too much of your time already."

"No one will notice. I was given a couple of days to prepare for the conference. Unfortunately, I can't get out of that and I'll have to turn up and show my boss my grinning face, I'm afraid. You can telephone me at the number you have at any time—if I'm not there someone will take a message. It's pretty central...Left Bank...nothing very special but my mother's happy there. The rue Mouffetard—do you know it?"

Joe knew it. A winding medieval street of old houses, market stalls, cafés and student lodgings, one of the few to escape the modernising hand of the Baron Haussman.

"Just southeast of the Sorbonne? Near the Place de la Contrescarpe?"

"Exactly. You need the Place Monge métro exit. Let me write the address on the back of the card I gave you."

Joe was amused. "You don't give out your address to all and sundry?"

"Matter of security," said Bonnefoye. "Mine!"

"You have an apartment?" Joe asked.

"No. It's my mother's apartment. On my salary it will be some time before I can afford to rent one of my own. You have to pay fifteen thousand francs a year for a decent place in Paris. It's the foreign invasion that's put up prices."

"Invasion? You'd call the tourist influx an invasion, would you?"

"Hardly tourists! Ten thousand semi-permanent residents have flooded in, mostly American, some British, all keen to take advantage of what they consider the low prices in France and all able to pay more than an ordinary copper for a decent place. Do you know how I've spent my time, this last month? Sorting out cases of grievous bodily harm and damage to property on the Left Bank. The *indigènes* of

Montparnasse have started to show their resentment of the way the Yanks have taken over whole quartiers. They don't like the way they buy up cafés and turn them into cocktail bars, they don't like the food they consume or the way they consume it... they don't like their loud voices... they don't like the way they look at their girls... You know the sort of thing. It'll only take a spark to blow the lid off. Might try raising that with Interpol."

The hastily summoned doctor examined Sir George and passed him as perfectly well—suffering from shock, naturally, as one would, being the victim of a street robbery, and from the obvious contusions but otherwise nothing to be concerned about... Nothing broken. No—a very fit specimen for a man of his age, was the reassuring verdict. All the same, the doctor grumbled, attacks like this were growing more frequent. And on the Grands Boulevards now? Tourists to blame, of course. A honey pot. Too easy and tempting a target for the local villains. It was quite disgraceful that a respectable gent like the patient couldn't return from the theatre to his hotel along the most civilised street in the world without being beaten up. Where was the police presence in all this? the good doctor wanted to know.

A complete rest with plenty of sleep was his prescription. Of course, there was always the danger at any age of a delayed reaction to a head wound. Was there someone they could summon to sit with him... just in case... a compatriot perhaps would be most suitable in the circumstances. He left his card and took his leave.

"A nurse?" Joe, eager to dash off to the morgue, was impatient at the doctor's request. "Is that what he's suggesting? Where on earth do we dig up a nurse at a moment's notice?"

Bonnefoye grinned. "This you can leave to me, Joe. I think I can work my way around the problem." He took out a small black notebook and began to flip through the pages.

"You go off and interrogate the corpse. You'll find all well when you get back."

On the ground floor a lean-faced man in his mid-thirties, unremarkable in sober city clothes, was waiting for a friend. He watched Joe step out of the lift, cross the lobby and greet the doorman. He looked at his watch, shrugged and decided to abandon his assignation. Following Joe outside, he stood patiently by, next in line. He heard Joe speak to the driver of the cab: "Île de la Cité. Institut Médico-Légal." The man smiled and walked back into the lobby.

Joe was admitted with courtesy into the Institut. Sombre, forbidding and dank, the building was everything Joe expected of a morgue and forensic pathology department combined. He was going to have to return in the evening escorting Somerton's widow and he wanted to be certain that he could find his way about, to be prepared to answer any questions she might have. The usual run of grieving relatives tended not, on first confrontation with the corpse, to be particularly searching with their queries. A combination of feelings of loss and the oppressive atmosphere of the viewing room were enough to reduce them to an inarticulate silence, a nod or a shake of the head or, at best, a few muttered words, most frequently: "Did he (or she) suffer?"

Somerton certainly suffered. But not for long, Joe estimated, staring down at his corpse. The pathologist in charge of the case who had officiated at midnight the night before had returned, he now told Joe, straight after breakfast to continue his examination. Le docteur Moulin was wearing the white overall, cap and gloves of a surgeon and

was as cheerful as the depressing circumstances allowed. His intelligent brown eyes were the only source of warmth in the whole building, Joe thought. He was expecting Joe and looked only briefly at his identification before leading him past three other livid corpses laid out in a row to a marble-topped channelled table where the body of the Englishman was laid out.

"Were you gentlemen acquainted?" asked the doctor, extending a hand to Somerton.

"Not in the slightest. I'm here to investigate, not identify. He has been named by the man who discovered the body and his papers confirm his identity. The widow, Lady Somerton, is on her way and will attend this evening to sign any documents you may present. Before she turns up, I'd like to familiarise myself with the details, so that I can guide her through it, if you have enough to go on…"

"Oh, yes. More to do, of course, but peripheral to the police enquiry, I'd say. I shall be obtaining a toxicology report, checking stomach contents—the usual—but the cause of death I think you'd agree is pretty obvious."

Joe stared with pursed lips at the body laid out on the slab. He was struck by the way in which the hair and moustache, retaining their luxuriance and dark colour, were at odds with the waxen flesh from which the humanity seemed to have drained away. What was the dead man telling him? What could he possibly learn from the already decaying features of a man he'd never seen alive, had never heard speaking? Joe recalled a phrase the usherette had used in her statement: "*Visage de fouine.*" Weasel-faced. Yes, he could see why she might say that. The sharp nose and chin in a narrow face offered a contrast with George's broad and handsome features. The expression and animation of the living man would also most probably have coloured the girl's impression of him and on this Joe would never be able to form an

opinion. The eyes were closed, the thin, well-shaped lips set in a tight line.

The five franc tip, Joe remembered. What a frightful epitaph!

The knife slash that had killed him went from ear to ear. Cleaned and closed, it was still a fearsome sight. Joe could only imagine the shattering effect on George of discovering his friend—dead? dying?—with blood pumping by the pint from the gaping wound.

"Have you any views on how the wound was administered?" Joe asked.

"I have. Dealt from behind, I'd say. I understand the victim was watching a performance at the Folies? In a box either by himself or accompanied by a young lady? A question for the police to clear up. Obviously, if she was sitting or standing next to him the lady would be drenched in blood. When she went to the *vestiaire* to retrieve her coat, someone would have noticed her state."

"He's quite a tall man, the victim?"

"About five feet ten inches and, though he must be in his mid-fifties, his musculature is in good condition."

"Difficult to subdue a man of that height unless you are yourself taller and more powerful, you're thinking?"

"As are you, Commander. He's hardly likely to oblige by standing there, sticking out his chin and closing his eyes! A man like this would have fought back against a *perceived* assailant." The pathologist pointed to the hands and forearms. "No signs of wounds received during self-defence, you see. No attempt to repel a knifeman. It's my theory that his attacker came up behind him while he was still seated, seized him—possibly left hand over his mouth—and slashed and sawed his throat from ear to ear. Standing behind your victim, you would not be showered by his blood, which would be projected out and down. You then allow the body

to flop forward onto the padded edge of the booth, where the obliging upholstery absorbs most of the litres of blood. Velvet, quilted over cotton wadding, I understand."

"And if you're a careful killer," added Joe, "and I'm sure our man was just that, you'd have taken off your opera cloak and put it on the peg by the door, murdered your victim and then put your concealing cloak on again before leaving. If you've timed it just right, your exit will coincide with the moment everyone is streaming out of the theatre." He knew that moment. Everyone preoccupied with his or her own immediate plans . . . taxis, supper, romance. No one wanted to catch the eye of a stranger in the crowd.

Joe went to fetch a chair, placed it at the foot of the marble slab and sat down on it. "Doctor, would you mime the action of the killer as you judge it to have been carried out? I'll be the victim."

"Of course. And, in the pursuit of authenticity—a moment—I'll just fetch the weapon."

Moulin bustled away into his office, returning with a cardboard box filled with material conserved from the corpse. "We're holding all this until the police and the magistrate are satisfied. You know the routine?" He waited for Joe's nod and went on: "The personal effects will be returned to the next of kin. Not sure they'll want to keep this as a souvenir, though," he said, producing from a paper bag a dagger with an eight-inch blade and a carved ivory hilt.

"I'd like the lady to take a look, if she can bear it," Joe said. "Just in case she can identify it as her husband's own property."

"You can take hold of it," said Moulin, offering it by the point of the blade. "It's been tested for fingerprints and cleaned up. No prints, by the way. It had been wiped clean— just some unusable smears left."

Joe took the object with distaste. "Afghan." He turned the

blade flat and slid it over the back of his hand, slicing through a few hairs. "Sharp as a razor."

"It would need to be to go quickly through such an amount of muscle and gristle. The throat is not an easy option. But it is quick and sure. Think of pig-killing. In my village they always go for the throat. And a pig's flesh has more or less the same density and resilience as a man's. This knife went upstairs to the laboratory for inspection. Under the microscope you can see the signs of the use of a sharpening implement on this blade. Very recent sharpening was done. Perhaps with the killing in mind?"

"Ah? A workmanlike tool. Not a cheap blade but not lavishly produced for display, I'd say. It's not as ornate as many I've seen. An inch or so shorter than most. Discreet. An efficient killing blade."

"Indeed. Now, this is what I think happened. For the record—I'm five foot eight inches tall, so we're possibly looking for someone two to four inches taller. And almost certainly more powerfully built." The doctor took the knife in his right hand. He mimed taking off his cloak and hanging it up then he moved silently behind Joe, who leaned slightly forward in the attitude of someone engrossed in the performance on the stage below.

"Ah! In the dark and with your head tilted forward like that it's not so easy to get a hand around your mouth. I'm going to change my plan slightly," said Moulin.

He grasped Joe by the hair and pulled his head back, applying the dagger blade to his exposed throat. Joe could not repress a shudder as the cold steel gently touched the skin behind his left ear.

"Yes, that's how it would have been done!"

"What about the noise, Doctor? Would he have had time to let out a scream?"

"Oh, yes. Think of any pig you've ever heard being slaugh-

tered. They manage a few seconds of hideous squealing before their voice box is cut. It must have been done at a moment of intense surrounding noise."

"I agree. The finale?"

"Yes. Clapping and cheering and, these days, with such a large foreign element in the audience, you tend to hear whistles and squeals of a very un-French nature. And that theatre is the largest in Paris. There must have been close on two thousand people creating a din. Now, if his companion for the evening had been there *during* the murder she would have been an accomplice or—if a witness—would have been, I presume, made off with—eliminated?—by the guilty party. In some other place, at some other time, as there were no signs of further violence in the box, I understand. I would fear for the young lady's safety, wouldn't you?"

"Accomplice? Witness? Not necessarily," said Joe. "She might have been the killer. What would you say?"

"A woman?" The doctor was taken aback. "Physically it's certainly possible, I suppose... if she approached him from behind as I've demonstrated. You'd need a considerable rush of energy—determination, hatred..." His voice tailed off doubtfully.

"You don't like the theory?"

Moulin smiled. "No more than I observe you do, Commander! We both know this is not a woman's method."

"True. In my experience, when women plan a murder—and from whatever rank of society they come—they choose more subtle methods. Poison and the like. Anything from rat poison to laudanum. When the killing is done on the spot and the result of an overriding urge, or a desperate attempt at self-protection, they use the nearest weapon to hand—usually a domestic tool which, depending on their circumstances, may be a frying pan... a silver sconce..."

"Contents of a theatre box not much use, I'd have thought. Could you throttle someone with all that gold braid?"

"I wouldn't want to try it. No. Someone chose to take this dagger into the box and use it. And leave it behind for all to see. This particular dagger. It's distinctive. Meaningful. Personal, I'd say. The victim had fought in Afghanistan, his fellow soldier tells me. There's a possibility that it may be from his own collection. Carried there by the victim himself and turned against him in an unpremeditated attack?" Joe sighed. "Much work to be done yet, I'm afraid."

Rising from his chair, Joe was struck by a sudden thought. He walked over to the corpse and lowered his head to sniff the improbably dark hair. He looked up and said: "Pomade?"

Moulin joined him and repeated the process. "Certainly," he agreed. He sniffed again. "Unpleasant. Not French. Much too heavy. I'd say something like Bay Rum, wouldn't you? And it's sticky." He took off a glove and tested a strand of hair between thumb and forefinger.

Joe did the same. He peered at the crown of the man's head. "Well-barbered hair, though a little long for most tastes, I'd have thought. Plentiful and would give a very good grip to anyone choosing to sink his fingers into it. As you demonstrated. Left parting and—look—it's disordered on top. Could have happened involuntarily at any moment after the death, of course, during the manhandling of the body by the authorities. But if your theory's right, Doctor, the killer must have had a disgustingly sticky left hand—and not sticky with blood. It's not much but . . ."

He accepted Moulin's offer of soap and water and towel in a side room and they washed their hands in a companionable silence together, each deep in thought. "I thank you for

working through all this with me, Doctor," Joe said, walking back to pick up his briefcase. He hesitated and then made up his mind to ask: "Shall I hope to see you later on today when I bring the widow Somerton? Or will you have handed over to a colleague by then?"

Moulin smiled. "I shall arrange to be here, Commander. More dead than alive myself by that hour but..." He shrugged. "You'll find me here. I'm very bad about delegating. Particularly when a case has caught my attention as this one has."

Emerging from the depths of the stone Palais de Justice building, Joe experienced again a rush of relief and pleasure. He took a minute or two to raise his face to the sun, to breathe in the not-unpleasant river smell, to be thankful that he wasn't laid out on a slab or filed away in one of the steel drawers that lined the walls. He'd taken a liking to Moulin—an admirable man, professional but not stuffy. A brother. But he did wonder how he managed to stay sane working in that chill, haunted place. Above all he asked himself how bearable would be the claustrophobic effect of those thick walls on a recently widowed Home Counties lady. He looked at his watch and calculated that she was in mid-air over the Channel, delicately refusing the oysters most probably.

Lunch! Suddenly hungry, Joe decided to make for a café and find something he could eat within half an hour. The Place St. Michel was just over the river. Food over there on the Left Bank was cheap and quickly prepared. The customers were mostly students and Joe enjoyed the informality, the laughter and the sharp comments he heard all around him. He settled at a pavement table on the square and decided to order a croque-monsieur. Always delicious

and quick to produce. He wondered what to drink with it and thought his usual beer might finally send him to sleep. A bottle of Badoit or a plain soda water might be more—

Soda! Campari-soda! The shock of realisation was so intense he looked furtively around him to see if anyone was conscious of his reaction to the sudden thought. Ridiculous! These chattering strangers, even if they'd been looking in his direction, wouldn't have given a damn for an Englishman whose startled expression was that of a man who'd just remembered—too late—his wife's birthday.

"Campari-soda"! George had been trying to pass on a message and he'd missed it. Pink and decadent, light but lethal. And always, for him, to be associated with that woman.

George had been attempting to let him know he'd spent the evening trapped in a box with a viper.

Joe, all appetite vanished, chewed his way through his sandwich and planned his next move. Looking around him, he remembered that he was just a few steps away from the rue Jacob and he frowned.

Good Lord! It seemed a week ago he'd met that redhead on the plane. What was her name? Heather, that was it. And she was staying at a small hotel down there. Raking his memory, he had a clear impression he'd promised to meet her again, though he'd left it all a little vague. He doubted she was the kind of girl to sit in her room waiting for him to contact her but, all the same, it would be too rude to do nothing. He could at least explain that he'd run head-first into the most frightful bit of trouble and wouldn't be at liberty to enjoy Paris with her as he'd hoped. Paying his bill, Joe strode off down the rue St. André des Arts and crossed over into the rue Jacob. He wandered along until he found a pretty flower-bedecked hotel whose name rang a bell.

The receptionist at the Hotel Lutèce admitted he had a

guest of that name but Mademoiselle Watkins had gone out over an hour ago and—no—she had not said at what time she expected to return. With some relief, Joe scribbled a note and left it in her pigeon-hole.

And now, he was free to concentrate on a second lady who'd caught his attention. He took out his notebook and checked the address he'd hurriedly memorised from the chief inspector's interview sheets and copied down later. An address in Montmartre. He looked up and north, seeking but not finding, for the press of rooftops, the gleaming white dome of the Sacré Coeur, presiding over the huddle of cottages, mills and cabarets that made up the old village on the hilltop. Too far to walk in the time he had. Joe went back to the Place St. Michel and picked up a taxi.

"*Montmartre. La rue St. Rustique,*" he said. "*Le numéral 78.*"

"Another liar!" he thought, and began to plan how best he could lay a trap for her.

Chapter 9

Joe decided to tell the driver to drop him in the Place du Tertre in the heart of Montmartre. The cab moved off easily northwards, threading its way according to Joe's directions, along the Right Bank, taking a westerly route through Paris's most spectacular streets and on up the rue d'Amsterdam. They turned onto the boulevard de Clichy, which wound like a necklace along the wrinkled throat of the ancient village on the hill.

As they crossed the Place de Clichy, he glanced at the billboards of the Gaumont Palace cinema with its imposing Beaux Arts façade. *Le plus grand cinéma du monde,* it announced. Today they were offering a matinée programme, a repeat showing of a pre-war thriller: *Fantômas III. Le mort qui tue.*

Fantômas. Part Three. The Murderous Corpse. One of a series of horror stories that had swept France. Joe was not a fan. He'd stopped reading them after the second book, when he'd worked out that the Emperor of Evil whose sadistic

exploits were recounted always escaped the law. At the end of every story one implausible bound set him free from the clutches of the tenacious policeman who'd vowed to bring him to justice. Joe lost patience with the good Inspector Juve. But he was a human like Joe, overworked, mortal and fallible and fighting a hydra-headed, superhuman essence of wickedness. A completely implausible villain, for Joe. He much preferred Professor Moriarty. Though *he* had shown a tendency to survive unsurvivable plunges into waterfalls.

They attacked the hill by way of the rue Lepic, lined with market stalls. Progress up the cobbled streets was slow. They were impeded every few yards by two-man push-and-pull handcarts whose pushers and pullers stared in disdain at any motor vehicle attempting the steep incline, taking their time, demonstrating defiance. The worst blockage was caused by a two-wheeled cart being pulled along by an ambling old horse. His sole interest was in the contents of the nosebag he wore and he eventually ground to a halt outside a grocer's shop. La Bordelaise looked prosperous, its windows bright with bottles of wine and oil, baskets of olives and dangling saucissons. Sticking his head out to assess the delay, Joe was caught by the scent of roasting coffee beans. On impulse he called to the driver to wait and dashed into the shop. A moment later he climbed back into the taxi with a fragrant bag of beans in his hand.

He paid off his taxi in the Place du Tertre and looked about him, getting his bearings. He strolled off along the north side of the square, getting a feeling for his surroundings. More strident than it had been in its heyday half a century ago when Pissarro, Cézanne and Renoir had sat at their easels on exactly this spot, painting the crossroads scene. More self-consciously colourful, tricked out, alluring, completely aware that it had something valuable to sell. Itself. Montmartre was a tart. But people fell for her

charms every time. And he was gladly allowing himself to be seduced.

The gaudy square was surrounded by poor streets. He turned left into one of them. Here, the children playing in the street were ragamuffins like the ones in the East End of London. Barefoot, some of them, all scrawny but cheeky enough to shout rude comments at a stranger. He brushed aside offers to shine his shoes, take him to a jazz bar and other more dubious propositions. He skirted around ball games and dodged urchins swinging out across the pavements on ropes suspended from gas lamps—a dangerous game of bar skittles in which the passer-by risked losing his hat or, at the least, his dignity. Joe, in a moment of playfulness, could have wished he was wearing a top hat for them to aim for and quickly took himself in hand. Such a spurt of frivolity was not appropriate. He blamed it on the freshness of the air up here on the hilltop, the blossom, the new leaves, the wad of bills in his pocket and a feeling that all was possible. He gave the lads his police stare, put on a show of knowing exactly where he was going and they left him alone.

Every narrow street he looked down called to mind a scene already captured in paint or waiting to be captured. He turned a corner into the rue St. Vincent and found himself following a few paces behind a figure from the last century. In baggy black suit and wide-brimmed gypsy hat, guitar slung across his back, a *chansonnier* strolled on his way to perform perhaps at the Lapin Agile. Conscious that he was wasting time, Joe tracked him until he disappeared into the dilapidated little cottage, his entrance marked by raucous cries of welcome and a burst of song. For a moment Joe paused, tempted to go into the smoky depths. He remembered that in an earlier age it had been known as the Cabaret des Assassins.

Who would he see in there if he slid inside and took a table?

He narrowed his eyes and pictured the scene. Letting his fancy off the leash, he saw: Picasso...Apollinaire...Utrillo...Jean Cocteau...and he grinned. He probably wouldn't understand a word of the conversation! Avant-garde, fast-living, arty...But he knew who would understand and almost turned to share his thoughts with young Dorcas. He felt a stab of regret that his adopted niece who'd trailed through France with him last summer was not by his side. She'd have felt at home here. She'd have greeted the gypsy guitarist and talked to him in his own language. Her raffish father, Orlando, must have spent hours drinking and yarning with his fellow painters in this picturesque hovel, judging by the quantities of canvases it had inspired. And his daughter was probably on first name terms with half the clientele!

He looked at his watch. Better left for another day. Yes, he'd come back some other time. With Dorcas. Why not? He reminded himself to find a suitable postcard to send to her in Surrey. But a different girl was higher on his agenda today.

He had work to do. A self-imposed task but tricky and not one to be attempted light-heartedly. Not heavy-handedly either, though. He looked around and caught sight of a flower seller's stall on a corner of the square. Five minutes later, armed with half a dozen of the best red roses the seller could provide, done up in a silver ribbon, he locked onto his target.

Everyone who could be outside on that May afternoon was out on the pavement. The concierges of the lodging houses had settled in chattering groups, shelling peas, their chairs obstructing the pavements. From open doors behind them drifted the fragrant smell of dishes cooking slowly in some back room. Mothers fed babies or crooned them to sleep.

Around a corner to the north of the square he came upon the faded blue sign he was looking for: rue St. Rustique. The

oldest street in the village and quite probably the narrowest. The three- and four-storey houses had known better days. Shabby grey façades retained interesting architectural features: elegantly moulded architraves graced doorways, Second Empire wrought-iron grilles added dignity to windows whose shutters stood wide open onto the street. Bourgeois net curtains gave seclusion and an air of mystery to the interiors.

Joe located number 78. The patch of pavement in front of the house and the cobbled road as far as the central gutter were freshly cleaned. A broom was propped against the wall to the right of the open door, two large pots of daisies stood to attention and an eye-watering waft of *eau de javel* leapt from the interior and repelled him. Joe read the sign painted in art nouveau letters above the door's architrave: *Concierge*.

He froze. There she was, filling the doorway, barring his entrance. Redoubtable. Cerberus? The Cyclops? He reckoned he had about as much chance of getting past her and into the building as he would have had facing up to one of those monstrous guardians. She stood, four-square, bulldog face peering at him over gold half-moon spectacles. She was holding a pile of letters to the light and shuffling through them. Sorting out the residents' afternoon post, he guessed, and she was not counting on being disturbed. She was dressed like a badly done-up parcel; her clothes were all in shades of brown, shapeless and hanging in layers to her mid-calf. Here the tale of sartorial disaster was taken up by a pair of drooping socks and bulging slippers.

Joe did not often find himself at a loss for words and was angry with himself for hesitating to address her. He regretted now the bunch of roses in his hand. What a twerp he must look.

"Yes? Who are you?" Her voice would not have disgraced a sergeant major.

The challenge provoked a military response. He stood at

ease in front of her with what he hoped was an air of languid confidence and managed a tight smile. "An English gentleman to see Mademoiselle Raissac. I understand she lives here." He began to reach into his pocket for his warrant card.

She stopped him with a gesture. "She's not seeing callers today. She's not well. Come back tomorrow." The concierge turned and, as an afterthought, seized her broom as though she thought he might run off with it. She made to go back inside.

"Police! Wait!"

That claimed her attention. She came towards him. "Shh! Keep your voice down! This is a respectable street," she hissed at him. "Police? *Again?* She's given a statement. Can't you leave her alone?"

"I will see her here, discreetly, in her own room, for half an hour or I will haul her off to the Quai des Orfèvres for a rather lengthier interview. I'm quite certain neither you nor the young lady would relish the appearance of a *panier à salade* outside your front door, madame." Joe was not at all certain that one of these sinister motorised cells would be deployed at his request for the conveyance of one suspect but the old dragon appeared impressed by the threat.

"You'd better come in then . . . sir. And you can show me your proof of identity." Her voice would never be capable of expressing deference but at least it was now verging on the polite. "You can wait in my parlour while I go up and see if she's prepared to see you. Through here."

She took him to her two-roomed *loge* on the ground floor off the hallway and offered him a hard-backed chair. The small room, which served as both kitchen and living room, was sparsely furnished but neat and well polished. A few ornaments twinkled on the mantelpiece above an open fire on

which a blackened pot had been left to simmer. Monsieur's supper no doubt.

She wiped her hands on her pinny and reached for the warrant card he held out to her. Every aspect of it came under her searching eye and finally: "Well, it's good that the flics are taking a serious interest in this tragedy. Bit unusual, isn't it? Not something we're used to round here—courtesy visits from the Law with roses in its hand. Have a glass of water while you're waiting, young man. You look overheated," she said, surprising him, and poured a glass from the tap. "Don't pull that face! No need to be fussy! Paris water is good water."

Joe drank gratefully, puzzled but relieved by her change of attitude. On a whim, he reached into his pocket and took out the bag of coffee beans. "For you, madame. I hope you can drink coffee?"

The tight lips twitched slightly and she took the bag from him, squinting at the label. "From La Bordelaise! I can certainly drink that! Thank you very much." She set it down on a dresser beside the polished copper funnel of a coffee-grinder and went to summon her lodger. In the doorway, she turned and spoke to him over her shoulder in her clipped, machine-gun phrases. "Francine is a good girl. Never been in trouble with the Law. She works every hour God sends. As good as a daughter to me. And she's still reeling from the shock. You're to treat her with respect."

Joe's saluting arm twitched in automatic response to the tone.

As her slippered feet thudded up the staircase, he eyed the coffee. A sop to Cerberus? It still seemed to work.

A sleepy face peered round the door at him, focussed blearily on his card and, after a delay calculatedly long enough to

register her protest, she opened the door with a grudging: "You'd better come in, I suppose."

Her room was untidy and, Joe thought at first glimpse, perfectly charming, though he would not have relished the task of carrying out a detailed search of the premises. The afternoon sun streamed in through the window illuminating, on the opposite wall, an open armoire densely packed with dresses of all colours and fabrics. They spilled out to hang in bunches on hangers along the picture rail. A treadle sewing machine with a piece of work still clamped across the needle plate stood under the window to catch the light. Against one wall of the single-roomed apartment was a bed, made up and covered with a gold brocade eiderdown. A low table held a row of unwashed coffee cups and one or two baker's shop wrappers covered in crumbs and patched with grease.

Once he was inside, she rounded on him. "*Two* interviews in as many hours? What's going on? I'm a witness, not a suspect! Couldn't you leave me alone to get over it? And why are they sending me the handsome inspectors? Is this a new tactic? Are there any more of you lurking round the corner? I'm not in the chorus line, you know! Though you seem to think so—are those for me?" She seized the roses and went to put them in a jam jar that she filled with water from the wash basin in a corner of the room. "Doesn't it cross your mind that you might be ruining my good name? Arriving here with flowers? Wish I'd got dressed ..."

Francine Raissac was wearing a creased white silk dressing gown embroidered—and rather richly embroidered—with black and red dragons. Her eyes were puffy and last night's mascara smudgily outlined her dark eyes, giving her the comical air of a cross panda. Joe said as much and she looked at him first in astonishment, then with a flash of amusement. He rushed on while he had this slight advantage. "*Handsome*

inspectors, did you say? I thought I was the only stunner they could field...?"

"The previous one was better," she said, looking closely at him, giving the question her serious attention. Her response told him the light approach was probably the effective one. "You're very nearly handsome. But you're older and you don't have a Ronald Colman moustache."

"Ah! I think I recognise my colleague, Inspector Bonnefoye?" said Joe, trying to keep a tetchy note out of his voice.

"Jean-Philippe." She managed a tease and a confirmation in one word. "You mean you didn't know he was coming here?" she asked. "Doesn't the right hand know what the left's getting up to at the Sûreté? Or aren't you speaking the same language?"

"We have different roles," Joe said, recovering from his surprise. "My questions will not be the same as his. He has other fish to fry."

"Ah, yes, of course. I understand that."

"I am, as you've noticed, English. I'm representing the interests of the gentleman who was taken in as a suspect."

"Not the interests of the *murdered* Englishman, then?" she asked sharply.

"His interests also," Joe hurried to add. "Indeed, I am shortly to meet his widow and conduct her to an identification of the body. An inconvenience to the French authorities and an embarrassment to us that what may prove to be a quarrel between two of my countrymen should be played out on French soil. I am doing what I can to assist the Police Judiciaire and working under the auspices of the British Embassy, of course. Interpol also, of which—"

"All right... all right! You're a big shot! Got it! Will Your Eminence deign to take a seat?" She heaved an armful of fabrics off a sofa and Joe lowered himself onto it.

"Oh…carry on then! I'm listening. I suppose I should be grateful they've not sent old sourpuss…the chief inspector…um…"

"Fourier?"

"That's the one!" She rolled her eyes. "He interviewed me at the theatre. Looks and talks as though he's sucking an acid drop."

"You take, I detect," he said with a grin, pulling a straight pin from under him, "more than an amateur interest in couture?"

"I'm sure you're not here to count my dresses and check their provenance." She sounded slightly on her guard. "I'll tell you straight, Mr. Detective, that every last frock you can see has been acquired legally. Working in a theatre, they're easy to pick up, if you know the right people. Did you know there's a whole workshop underneath in the basement, sewing away day and night? I go down there sometimes and chat to the girls. They're always pleased enough to hear news from the world above! The show clothes aren't much use to me, of course—all ostrich feathers, tulle and lamé—but the girls pass on the occasional remnant that I can use.

"The stars are my best source. Now—Josephine! She's incredibly generous and if you know just when to show your face—as I do—she'll shower you with stuff she doesn't want or gowns she's only worn once. We're much the same size and sometimes she asks me to model a gown for her to help her make up her mind."

So that accounted for the head-hugging hairdo with the over-sized curl slicked onto her forehead. Francine had a dark complexion for a Frenchwoman, Josephine had a light skin for a black American. The two girls met somewhere in the middle. But the conscious attempt to mirror the looks of the star was more than just flattery. Josephine must have found it useful to see herself from a distance in this bright

young woman. And the thought came to him: "Probably enjoys her company too."

"You get on well with the star?"

"Yes, I like her. We French *do* like and admire her. It's the Americans—her own countrymen—and the English who give her a rough time. Her dancing is too scandalous for some and she's black. There are those—and some are influential people—who'd like to see her closed down and put on the next liner home. Not the French. We don't care at all about her colour. And her morals…" Francine shrugged. "Well, that's up to her, isn't it? She's entertaining and stylish and we love her for it."

"I expect she suffers professional jealousy—one so successful at such a young age? What's the name of the Queen of Paris Music Hall? She must be feeling a bit miffed!"

"Mistinguett? Yes, she's a rival but she's big-hearted, you know. Reaching the end of her career…she must be in her fifties, though she still has the best legs in Paris! She can afford to rise above it. But there are two younger stars, French, both, at the Casino de Paris and the Moulin Rouge, who hate Josephine's guts. She's rather stolen their thunder. Either one might have hoped to inherit Mistinguett's ostrich feather crown as *meneuse de revue*. And one of them has a very wealthy protector. A banker. You'd know his name. He sends his Rolls-Royce to the stage door for his little mouse every night!"

"Does Josephine mind? All this antipathy?"

"Too busy enjoying herself. I'd say she doesn't give a damn! In fact," she added dubiously, a sly, slanting question in her eyes, "those close to her think she doesn't care *enough*. For public opinion or her own safety."

Joe seized on the word: "Safety?" he murmured.

"Everyone thought when she had her accident last year—"

"Accident?"

"Not actually. It could have been nasty...In one of her acts, she's lowered in a flowery globe down over the orchestra pit. A breathtaking bit of theatre! Luckily she'd decided to rehearse in the damn contraption before the actual performance." Francine shuddered. "She was on her way down from the roof in this thing when one of the cables jammed. That's what they said. A mechanic was sacked afterwards and everyone heaved a sigh of relief. The globe suddenly tilted over and swung wide open. She *ought* to have been thrown out into the pit. But she's a strong girl with fast reactions. She jumped for one of the metal struts and hung on like a trapeze artist until someone could get up into the roof and haul her up again."

"Good Lord! What would have happened if she'd fallen?"

"She'd have been dead. Or so badly injured she'd never have walked again."

"Dangerous place, the theatre."

And a breeding ground for all kinds of overheated nonsense, he reckoned. Scandal, exaggeration, petty jealousies. He was allowing his own tolerance of gossip to put him off track and guided Francine Raissac back onto the subject he wanted to pursue. "These clothes the generous Miss Baker gives you—where do they come from?"

"Gifts. They arrive at the theatre in boxes for her to try. If she doesn't like something, she'll tell me to take it away. I found her knee deep in Paul Poiret samples the other day. Wonderful things! She'd just had an almighty quarrel with him and was throwing the whole lot away. Before she'd even tried them on!" The girl was filling the space between them with irrelevant chatter, taking her time to get his measure, he guessed. And, unconsciously, going in exactly the direction he'd planned to lead her.

"Does she have a preferred designer?"

"Hard to say. I doubt if she can tell one style from another. She hates turning up for fittings so they take a chance on what she'll like and send her lots of their designs, hoping she'll be seen about town wearing them... *I* think Madame Vionnet suits her best and Schiaparelli... her bias cut is very flattering... Lanvin... of course..."

"And your outlet for these dazzling couture items?" he asked. "I'm assuming you don't acquire them simply to decorate your room."

"I send them on to my mother. She has a little business in Lyon. We started it together when my father died. *Location de costumes*—but not your usual rag and bone enterprise. We're building up a well-heeled client list—plenty of money about down there. Industry's booming and it's a very long way from Paris. Everyone wants a Paris model for her soirée!" She indicated her sewing machine. "I can undertake adjustments here at the source if I have a client's measurements. Then the lady's box is delivered and she tells her friends it's straight from Paris—just a little confection she's had specially run up for the Mayor's Ball or whatever the event... And the label—should her friend happen to catch a glimpse of it—has a good deal to say about the success of her husband's enterprise. And *her* taste, of course. We rent out things by the day, the week. A surprising number we sell."

"I'm talking to someone with a keen eye for fashion, then? Someone acquainted with the work of the top designers of Paris?" he said, raising an admiring eyebrow.

"I'm sure you didn't come here to talk fashion," she said doubtfully, "but—yes—you could say that. I could have been a mannequin if I'd been three inches taller. If I'd been five inches taller I could have been a dancer. But I'm not really interested in 'could have been.' I'm a going-to-be," she said with emphasis. "Successful. Rich. I haven't found my niche quite yet. But I will." And, angrily: "It won't, of course, be in

the professions or politics or any of the areas men reserve for themselves. We can't vote…we can't even buy contraceptives," she added, deliberately to embarrass him.

"But some girls have the knack of attracting money and don't hesitate to flaunt it…Does it annoy you—in the course of your work—to be seen in rusty black uniform dresses when the clientele are peacocking about in haute couture?"

"No. Why would it? The black makes me faceless, invisible. The work is badly paid—no more than a starvation wage—but the tips are good. Men are so used to being greeted by old harridans with scarlet claws whining for their *petit bénéfice,* they are rather more generous to me than they ought to be. Sometimes, I flirt with the older ones," she said with a challenge in her look. "And, before you ask—no, I don't take it any further. But they toy with the illusion that it might develop into an extra item on the programme and tip accordingly. No man wants to be perceived as a tightwad."

"A five franc tip?" he reminded her.

The eyes rolled again. "I pitied that girl!"

"Ah, yes. Now tell me…the dress she was wearing…"

She put her hand over her mouth and stared at him over it. "Ah! So you really *did* come here to talk fashion! Well, I talked myself into that, didn't I?"

"You did rather," he agreed. "So, come on! Expert that you are—I think we've established that much—tell me all. You divulged almost nothing to the chief inspector. What was it now…? Under twenty-five and fair? Oh, yes? Bit sketchy, I thought. Huh! Your poor old ten franc tip with his rheumy old eyes gave a fuller description of the disappearing blonde from thirty yards away! A seam by seam account of her gown! And he wouldn't know his Poiret from his Poincaré…I want to know everything about her appearance

and—perhaps more important—why you chose to pull the wool over Inspector Acid Drop's eyes."

She went to sit at the bottom of her bed, demurely adjusting the belt of her Chinese gown, tucking up her bare feet under her. Joe swallowed. "Man Ray, where are you? You should be here with your camera, fixing this moment," he was thinking, seized and dazzled by the theatricality of the scene. This girl with her high cheekbones, sleek black hair, snub nose and huge, intelligent eyes made Kiki of Montparnasse look ordinary. He reined in his thoughts. She was also deliberately distracting him, making time to weigh his question, possibly to plan a deceitful answer. After a further diverting shrug of the shoulder, she began her account.

"Well, for a start—it was expensive—eight hundred francs at least, probably more. That shot silk fabric—there's not a great deal of it about yet and the designer who's been using it this season is Lanvin. Her shoes were Chanel T-straps. Blue satin. Her opera cloak was silk. Midnight blue. She shopped about a bit, this girl, but it was all well put together. She was carrying it under her arm—the cloak. When she came up the stairs. Her escort hung it up at the back of the booth. They often do that. Sometimes it's to avoid tipping at the *vestiaire* but with the box clientele it's usually to avoid the queue to pick it up at the end." She gave a twisted smile. "The gentlemen don't like to be kept waiting at this stage of their evening. Now, I did manage to catch a glimpse of the label on her cape. It was a Cresson. Rue de la Paix."

"Are you able to give me a description of this garment—an idea of the fabric?" he asked unemphatically, pencil poised.

She thought for a moment, and deciding apparently that the information was routine and could not harm her in any way, chose to cooperate. He noted the details. In a show of helpfulness which told him he was almost certainly heading

down a cul-de-sac, she even got up and walked to a basket overflowing with fabric remnants. Stirring them about, she finally produced with an exclamation of triumph, a piece of heavy silk. Dark blue silk.

"Not this exact fabric but—very nearly. Her cloak was made of some stuff like this."

He thanked her and put it away in his pocket.

"And—Cresson…Lanvin…Chanel…you say. These are all impressive names you mention, I think?"

"The very best."

"With a distinguished client list?"

"Of course."

"And if I were to traipse along the rue de la Paix to the boutiques of those you've mentioned and apply a little pressure or charm or cunning I might find the same name coming up?"

"If you choose to waste your time like that…I wouldn't bother. Some of these houses are hysterical about piracy. And they're always wary of having their clients snatched by a rival. The *vendeuses* are well trained and they have a nose for wealth." She looked at him critically then smiled. "You're an impressive man but you don't look like the kind who'd spend a fortune indulging his girl!"

Joe regretted his meagre half-dozen roses.

"Far too clever. I think you'd have considerable trouble extracting the information."

"So—you're going to point out a short-cut?"

"Why should I? The girl had nothing to do with the murder. And this answers your second question. It wasn't *her* I found covered in blood. She was working for a living. If she'd been willing to give evidence she'd have hung about, wouldn't she? But she had the sense to leg it. I'm not going to make her life difficult for her by involving her with the flics. They're shits! And they have a hard way with *filles de*

joie. There but for the grace of God and all that...If things
don't go so well for me—well, that might be the next step.
Who knows? Cosying up to old farts like the five franc tip
isn't my idea of a career, but I'm not stupid. I see lots of girls
making a lot of money that way. I've had my propositions!
And I see it sometimes as an easy option. A good deal of un-
pleasantness for a short time but the rewards are good."

"Francine, don't think of it!" Too late to snatch back the
instinctive exclamation.

While he looked at his feet in confusion and she smiled
in—was it triumph or understanding?—the attention of
both was caught by plodding footsteps on the stairs. The
concierge's peremptory voice called out: "*La porte!*" and
Francine went to open it. Joe got to his feet, fearing that his
interview was about to be cut short, ready to repel the intru-
sion, but instead he hurried forward to take the tray she was
carrying from the old woman's hands. He carefully balanced
the weight of the silver coffee pot, two china mugs, a jug of
milk and a plate of Breton biscuits, adding his own thanks
to those of Francine: "Oh, Tante Geneviève, you shouldn't
have!"

The dragon looked around and, apparently happy with
what she saw or didn't see, cleared the top of the table to
make way for the tray, gathering up the dirty cups and wrappers, grunted, and went out.

"I don't have much experience of concierges," said Joe,
"but I'd have thought room service of this kind is a bit out
of the ordinary? Did I hear you claim that lady as a relative?"

"I call her 'Aunty' and I've known her forever, but she's
my godmother. Her husband was wounded in the war. Has
never worked since. They scrape a living. My mother would
only agree to my continuing to live alone in the wicked
city if I was under someone's wing." She smiled and added
thoughtfully: "And she was quite right. It's not always

convenient to have a mother hen clucking after you, but the advantages are considerable. My rent is fair, not extortionate as it can be for most young girls trying to live by themselves. No spirit stoves allowed in the rooms, of course." She looked around at the quantities of fabrics festooning the room. "And this would be a fire hazard if I attempted to use one. So—occasionally, she brings me coffee. Inspector Bonnefoye rated one too." Francine sniffed the coffee as she poured it out. "But not as good as this! Mmm! Moka? And no chicory!" She looked at him with fresh speculation. "The old thing's brought out her best for the English policeman. Now, what on earth did you do to provoke this attention?"

They sipped the coffee appreciatively for a moment or two and then Joe said mildly: "So—your attempt to pervert the course of justice by withholding vital information (six months in La Santé if Acid Drop were to find out) was occasioned by a feeling of solidarity for a fellow working girl? No more than that? Am I expected to believe this?" He left a space in which she was meant to reflect on her predicament and assess his power to carry out his threats, veiled, as they were, by a charming smile and delivered in a pleasantly husky voice. "But loyalty is something I can understand. It is my motivation also in pursuing this case," he confided. "The suspect, Sir George Jardine, is an old friend of mine, a distinguished public servant, a much-decorated soldier and a man of impeccable honour. He is not a man to sink a dagger into the throat of a fellow officer, to hear his death rattle, to soak up his blood."

Fearing he was raising George's virtue to an unbelievable height, he paused.

"Are you telling me such a man never killed before?" she said, cynically. "Come on! A politician and a soldier? To me that combination shrieks power and violence. I saw him—you forget. He is a man capable of killing." She sur-

prised him further by looking him in the eye and adding: "Like *you*."

Joe was alarmed by the accuracy of the girl's insight. "He's a competent man. Such a messy killing is not his *style* at all. Completely implausible. If circumstances ever forced a man like Jardine to contrive the death of a fellow man—and I can't imagine what they might conceivably be—" he lied, "he would do it from afar . . . He would not do it before an audience of two thousand. And—I can tell you—he would not be discovered floundering about with blood on his own hands."

"Exactly! You're getting there! From afar—you've said it! Perhaps the victim was no pushover? A soldier might be expected to fight back? Your elderly friend not too keen to get close enough to sink a blade in him? I wonder how much your Sir George laid out for the distancing? Money can take you anywhere in this city, Inspector. If you know where to go. The right address. A thousand francs will buy you a night of passion you never dreamed of . . . If your desires are of a more sinister nature, the same sum will buy you a death."

Chapter 10

"And if all I hear is correct, both may be obtained at the same establishment," she whispered.

"*Établissement?*" he queried, apparently not understanding the word, and waited for her explanation. A trick he must use sparingly, he thought. She was clever and would soon realise that, in offering a simplified and expanded version of her comments, she was giving away more than she had intended. He listened carefully to her reply and nodded his understanding.

She made an effort not to look about her and Joe was aware of a lowering of her voice even though they were unobserved. Was this done for effect? He thought he'd better be prepared to reserve judgement on Mademoiselle Raissac.

"If this is an agreement you're offering, Inspector," she went on, "I have to accept, but I want your assurance that it will not be known that this information comes from me. Nor will I involve others. They don't like loose ends. They cover their tracks and they don't leave witnesses."

"They?" he questioned lightly. "Did you mention a name? Did I miss it?"

"They have no name but they have a reputation, amongst those who need to know these things, for efficiency and even"—she shuddered— "a certain style."

"What are you suggesting?" He glanced around at the couturier's silk and satin confections. "An element of *design* in their deaths? Bespoke killing? Made-to-measure murder?"

"Don't scoff! You have no idea!"

The words burst from her, raw and vehement. What emotion inspired them, he wondered—fear, despair or fury at his wilfully obtuse comments? He had a knack of making people fizz with rage when he chose to use it. Anger frequently knocked down carefully erected defences and left his suspect exposed. But this girl had not yet reached that pitch. Her emotion—whatever it might be—was still surging and gathering. In an anxious effort to impress on him the gravity of her situation, the gestures accompanying her words became intense and urgent.

"If they found out I'd spoken of this . . . I'd be discovered dead, with my mouth sewn up with scarlet thread and a pair of scissors through my heart. Do you understand?"

He affected dismay. "Am I to suppose, then, that the elimination—shall we now call it 'assassination'?—of Somerton was a *commercial* undertaking? That someone approached the nameless organisation you have in mind and ordered up his death?"

"Yes. The dead man was probably lured there by this blonde girl, who at an agreed moment abandoned him to his fate. At the finale, I'd guess, the killer entered and cut his throat, leaving the knife behind. They usually take the weapon away with them. This knife must have been significant, wouldn't you say? I caught a glimpse of it. They picked it up with a handkerchief from the floor at the man's feet. It

looked foreign to me. And it wasn't a zarin, which is the most popular knife in use in Paris."

"Zarin?"

"It's like a stiletto. The street gangs use it. For ripping and stabbing. Like this." She held an imaginary weapon in her hand using a backwards grip and demonstrated. Her face was impassive but her breathing was increasingly fast and shallow.

"I've seen just that action somewhere," he said vaguely.

"Well, this weapon was no zarin. It was short...fancy carved hilt."

"Ivory. Very distinctive. The dagger in this case was from Afghanistan," he said calmly. "A country in which Somerton had served some years ago, before the war." He calculated he was giving nothing away. It would be all over the newspapers tomorrow. And her response would tell him what he needed to know about Mademoiselle Raissac. Would she fall for the stimulus of the exotic blade he was offering and be inspired to spin out her story?

Yes, she would. Her eyes gleamed, her hands fluttered in expressive embroidery of her tale: "Well—there you have it, then! You should be looking for someone with a grudge going back to that time. A clear case of vengeance—wouldn't you say? Someone with enough money and enough hatred, after all these years, to have the man very publicly killed. Payback for something murky in the past? That's what the scene would have shown if your poor old friend hadn't stumbled into the box prematurely. And now he's got himself arrested and it all looks like an exhibition of jealous rage between two old codgers who ought to know better. A fit of rage that got out of hand."

She considered for a moment and added: "They might not like that. An expensively staged act of retribution reduced to a sordid squabble. The customer who paid for his bit of theatre might not be entirely satisfied at the outcome."

"Not sure where you're going with all this. *He*—whoever *he* is...Client of *them,* perhaps?—can hardly say: 'Excuse me—may we see that bit again—from the top?' can he? It's not a dress rehearsal we've been treated to! More of a live—or rather *death*—performance."

She scowled. "Nothing I can say will make you take this seriously. I've said enough. I've said too much. Who knows what he's deciding at this moment? What they are planning? You'd better leave now. But before you go—I'll remind you of our bargain. What was it? Six months in La Santé or spill my guts? Now, the question is, do I trust a policeman? (Am I naïve?) An English one? (Am I barmy?)" She put her head on one side and considered. "No. I'm not stupid. And I'm not taken in by an affected lack of understanding that comes and goes, or by a handsome face and a pair of grey eyes that, with a little guidance, could find my soul. I'm going to take you for an honourable man. I couldn't serve time in prison. Not even a day. I know what it's like. The river...or the canal...would be my way out of that. So, unless you want my death on your conscience, you'll keep your word."

It was not the moment to tell her that so far she'd revealed nothing he could use. *He...They*...Nonsense. But sensing that she was still working her way through to offering something he stayed silent.

"Look, can I ask you to do something for me before I give you the one bit of information I have that may help you? By coming here you've put me in danger. You must do what you can to put things right! No effort on your part involved! Agreed? Good."

Ten minutes later Joe emerged into the sunshine. He looked around him, a man in an unfamiliar street, getting

his bearings. He appeared oblivious of the passers-by though he was noting them through eyes narrowed against the sun: the two men strolling down the middle of the road, the tramp scavenging for cigarette butts in the gutter, the fashionably dressed young hostess on her way to her shift at one of the jazz clubs. Any one of them could be disguising an interest in a man leaving Mademoiselle Raissac's apartment. Joe loitered on the doorstep as he'd promised Francine he would. She leaned briefly from the window, hitching up the shoulder of her silk gown, and called down to him: "Darling—I should have asked—can you make it two hours later next week?"

As a bonus, Joe made a show of adjusting his trousers with a louche smirk. Francine ducked back inside the room, unable to hold back a burst of throaty laughter. He looked at his watch, sighed with satisfaction and made off back to the square, whistling.

Better to compromise her good name rather than her neck, she'd judged. He'd been impressed by Mademoiselle Raissac. Mannequin? Dancer? No. Her modest stature might have deprived the boutiques or the Folies of her talents—but it was the stage of the Comédie Française that was the true loser. She would have graced any one of Molière's plays. Dorine in *Tartuffe*? Perfect! What a performance the girl had put on for him! Emotion threatening to overflow at every verse end.

Charming girl, but she'd clearly been watching too many overblown dramas—onstage and backstage. Probably spent her spare time at the matinées in the Gaumont cinema, terrifying herself watching the adventures of Fantômas, Emperor of Evil. Joe shuddered as he recalled the image on the posters, known all over the world, but very particularly French in flavour: a mysterious gentleman, elegant in evening dress, inhuman green eyes glowing through his

black mask, stalked a city-scape of Paris with giant strides. His left hand, kid-gloved, cupped his chin thoughtfully, as he selected his next victim. His right hand, slightly behind him, held in a backwards grip a blood-smeared dagger. And the grip was the very one Francine had demonstrated with such vigour. He wondered whether her storytelling was a part of her character, her way of enlivening an otherwise hardworking but humdrum life, or whether she was making a special effort to mislead the police.

The young nightclub hostess he'd marked down earlier must have doubled back. He was disconcerted to find her suddenly in front of him, coming towards him. How had she slipped by? He was getting careless. A few more strides and she was face-to-face with him on the narrow pavement. With an exclamation of apology Joe stepped to the side. But he chose to hop to the unexpected side, away from the road. Put out by his clumsiness, she dodged. They got in each other's way, setting to the side and back again, partners in a country dance, disguising their impatience with embarrassed smiles. She began to speak to him. "I wonder if monsieur is looking for an encounter of a more intimate nature?" she murmured, and then the familiar, shyly delivered *"Tu viens?"*

Joe relaxed. A streetwalker after all. All was well. Training made him keep up his pretence of Englishman eminently satisfied by his experiences in Montmartre and he said politely: "Awfully sorry, my dear. Couldn't possibly! I'm afraid you've picked just the wrong moment . . . if you understand me? Ha! Ha! Some other time?" He rolled his eyes in an expression meant to convey both satiety and anticipation of a pleasure deferred and walked on.

Francine's nervousness must be affecting him. "They don't leave witnesses," she'd said, wide-eyed. Once round the corner, Joe's pace increased. Belatedly catching her anxiety,

he broke into a trot. Witness? He was thinking of another witness who'd had a clear view of the murder box. The chief witness, you might say, and one who had yet to make his full testimony. One he'd personally removed from the protection of police custody and left behind asleep in a hotel room. He began to run. Had he abandoned, unguarded, a loose end to be tidied up?

Chapter 11

With a crowded lift just taking off upwards from the lobby, Joe ground his teeth and dashed for the stairs. He arrived panting and took a moment outside the door of George's room to ease and check the Browning revolver in his pocket and to put his ear to the woodwork.

"Liar!" George's voice boomed. "You're not getting away with that! Lying cheat!" he added.

Joe burst in, revolver in hand.

"Oh, I say! Great heavens! Don't shoot! I was just about to come clean anyway!" Heather Watkins put her hands in the air and shook with laughter. The playing cards she was holding began to slide from her hands and flutter onto the counterpane between herself and Sir George.

George was sitting up in bed, rubicund with rage or good humour or bruising, it was hard to tell. He was crisply dressed in nightshirt and dressing gown. "Ah! Commander!" he said. "There you are. What an entrance, my dear fellow!

As you're positively bristling with authority, you may as well arrest this young lady. Cheating at cards is the charge."

"What...what in hell's going on here?" Joe blustered, slipping the Browning away in confusion.

"Good afternoon, Joe. I see you are well," said Miss Watkins, primly ignoring his loose language.

"But...Heather...You weren't at your hotel when I called..."

"I imagine not. I was summoned this morning by Jean-Philippe to come to the assistance of a fellow countryman. He's very persuasive, your French friend, Joe." She smiled and Joe saw for the first time that she had a very pretty dimple in her left cheek. "Well, in less time than it takes to tell, I was here receiving instructions in the nursing care of a distressed old gentleman." She waved a hand at George, who put on a pathetic face. "Not so old, not very distressed and I'm not so sure about the gentleman bit of the billing either. He's ruthless when it comes to cards! We were playing Cheat. Do you know it?"

Joe could only nod in reply.

"I was told to bring a book and to expect to sit by his bedside while he slept and be there, all cool hands, reassuring smile and soothing words when he woke. Which I was led to believe might be in eight hours or so. Hmm! It was difficult to get him to agree to go to bed at all and he only slept for three hours and then snapped awake. It's taken a lot of ingenuity and force of character to keep him where he's supposed to be—in bed," she huffed in a nannyish way.

The warm smile she exchanged with her patient told Joe all he needed to know about the developing relationship.

"An inspired idea! And what luck Jean-Philippe had your telephone number, Heather," he said innocently. "Thank you indeed for giving up your day to ride herd on my old friend. Did the inspector tell you—we had to wrest him from

the hands of the Police Judiciaire who were determined to wring something—anything—from him by means of the third degree?"

"He did!" Heather reached over and squeezed George's hand. "Monsters! If I ever get hold of that dreadful Fourier, I'll give him what for! If only I could be trapped in a lift with him with a tennis racquet in my hand! How *could* he? And Sir George already distressed by the death of his friend... So unfeeling!"

George grimaced, trying and failing by a mile to look pitiable. "Well, Joe, with all this female sympathy deployed, how could I not have perked up and made a full recovery? Miss Watkins has been wonderful! A breath of crisp English air in all this overheated foreign nonsense." He looked sideways at Joe and added: "And—as it seems you're counting, Joe— she's been good enough to give *me* her address too. Her address in England. Look forward very much to continuing our acquaintance, my dear," he said, turning to Heather, "when you get back from your tennis tournament. You must tell me all about it... show me your medals, swap gossip from the Riviera. I shall want to know the truth behind that liaison we were speaking of..."

"The gigolo and the English countess...?"

"Shh! Discretion, my dear Miss Watkins!"

"Of course!" Heather Watkins stood up and began to collect her things together into the small travelling bag she'd brought with her. "Well, it would seem my work is done here, for the time being at any rate. Look, Joe, Sir George, I consider myself on hand if required, for the rest of my stay in Paris. Don't hesitate and all that..."

"Heather, you don't have to rush off?" Joe began.

Her eyes twinkled as she looked from one to the other. "I'm quite certain you have things to discuss. Serious things. Crime things. I'm very happy to go about my business,

which—you won't be surprised to hear—involves a quick trip to the Galeries Lafayette. I saw a darling little day dress in their window on my way here in the taxi."

After an affectionate goodbye to George she tucked him up again under his covers, ran a hand over his brow and spoke gently to him: "Why don't you try to take another forty winks now that Joe's back? You're quite safe, you know."

She paused, bag in hand, by the door, and Joe went to open it for her and show her out. "Hang on a minute! Gosh, I wouldn't make a good agent, would I—I nearly forgot! Jean-Philippe told me to tell you he'd be back by French tea-time…"

"Five o'clock, then." Joe grinned.

"Oh…and you might like to tell him that he was quite right to warn me about attempted incursions by strangers."

Suddenly chilled and alert, Joe asked quietly: "What was that, Heather? Are you saying someone tried to force his way in here?"

"Not force, no," she said thoughtfully. "Much more subtle. And I'm probably being over-suspicious in the light of Jean-Philippe's warning… Well, you can judge, Joe. About a quarter of an hour after he'd left, there was a tap on the door. I looked around. George hadn't gone to bed—he was in the bathroom with the door shut. Avoiding me, I think. Hoping I'd go away. The bed was made up, the room neat. I chucked that mucky old trench coat away behind the chair, picked up my bag, looking for all the world as though I'd just that minute arrived, and opened the door a crack. There was a stranger there. A man. Thirties? Forties? French, I'd say. Dressed in black jacket and trousers. Room service, you'd have said. Except that no one had called for room service."

"Go on!" Joe could hardly bear the pause as she marshalled her impressions.

"Well, I took the initiative. 'Yes? Who are you and what do you want?' I said in English.

"'Reception, mademoiselle, I have a message for the gentleman,' he said. He was trying to speak English. And doing it well, I thought.

"'What gentleman?' I asked. And without looking up at the number on the door I said: 'This is room 205. You must have got the wrong number.' At this point I opened the door properly... didn't want to appear to be hiding anything... or anybody. His eyes darted... yes, they darted... inside. I thought for a moment he might try to get in so I squared up to him, barring his way.

"'Sir George Jardine,' he said. 'It's very urgent. I must deliver the message directly and into his hand.' He was holding something in his right hand, which was stuffed into his trouser pocket, I remember.

"'Well, I'm sorry about that,' I said. 'But, hard luck—you'll have to enquire elsewhere. I've just been shown to this room, which of course has been vacated. There's no one under the bed—I always check. Silly, I know! And now if you wouldn't mind—I'm just about to take a bath. Look—obvious question, but—you *did* check with Reception before you came up, didn't you? Perhaps,' I suggested helpfully, 'your Sir John was here last night? But he's not here now. Perhaps they gave you the wrong floor? Yes, I'd go back to Reception and ask them what on earth they think they're doing. They'll set you straight.'"

Joe must have been looking shocked. With a wary eye on him, Heather asked anxiously if she'd done the right thing.

"Exactly the right thing. Wonderful presence of mind, Heather!"

She was encouraged to ask quietly: "Who was he, Joe?"

"I've no idea," he said, and, displeased by his answer which, though true, was unsatisfying and unworthy for a girl who had, by her quick thought and courage, most probably saved George's life, he added: "Someone sent to tidy up a loose end, I fear. Thank God you were here, Heather, holding the gate!"

When Heather had left, Joe turned from the door to survey the loose end. Sir George had fallen fast asleep again and a gentle, rhythmic rumbling suggested it might go on for a few hours.

Thoughtfully, Joe picked up the deck of cards and put them away, then settled to write up some notes in his book. He had depressingly little. He drew arrows from one word to another, isolated some in balloons, began again. Times might prove vital, he felt, and reconstructed the day as accurately as he could from several perspectives. He looked again at his material, searching for links, threads, coincidences even, and finding none. The only words that compelled his attention were the words Francine had used: "He...They..."

And an address in Montparnasse.

At precisely five o'clock, Joe was waiting by the door and heard Bonnefoye's quick rap and his voice identifying himself. He entered, seemed reassured by the peaceful scene and said as much.

"Yes, old mate, and it's by the grace of God and Miss Watkins that George there is sleeping the sleep of the just and not the just dead. Why didn't you tell me you knew his life might be at risk? I'd not have left him!"

"What! You mean to say...? But tell me, man!" Bonnefoye's dismay was acute.

Joe repeated Heather's account of her sinister visitor and Jean-Philippe groaned. "And, coming after my interview with Francine Raissac, who raised not a few suspicions in my mind, I've been sitting here, imagining horrors."

"But I didn't seriously expect anyone to try to get in," said Bonnefoye. "You know me—careful, exact, always taking precautions..." Joe wondered whether he really did know Bonnefoye. "I thought... just in case those buggers at head-quarters decided to change their minds—not unknown!— and re-arrest Sir George, we'd give them the runaround for a bit. Good girl, though! I say—I would think twice about playing tennis against her, wouldn't you?... or any other sport, come to that. I told her to repel boarders, yes. And I took the precaution of asking them at Reception to cancel George's booking. Said he was shaken up and going to stay down the road at the Embassy and all enquiries should be sent there. Meantime, my friend Miss Watkins would be pleased to take the room for the next two days. I gave them her details. It ought to have looked right in the books. The management know who I am," he said thoughtfully. "They wouldn't annoy the P.J. And I can't see them divulging de-tails of an English guest to anyone. Large part of their clien-tele are British diplomats. They wouldn't want to upset one.

"But, Joe, what's all this about Mademoiselle Raissac? What were you doing over there in Montmartre? And what's the connection?"

"Like you, I saw from Fourier's notes that the girl was only telling a part of the story. In her job, she would be able to give a far more detailed description of the disappearing witness. She was hiding something. I thought I'd get over there and find out what it was before she disappeared her-self."

Joe recounted his interview, down to the last detail of his confrontation with the streetwalker. "Well, that's me. And now—do tell—what did *you* and your moustache manage to charm out of her?"

Bonnefoye looked aside shiftily, Joe thought.

"Not charm. No time for charm. Living up to the rough-tough image of the P.J., I'm afraid. And I had some bad news to impart."

"What have you got on her? She seemed to me, if not innocent exactly, at least uninvolved in shady goings-on?"

"She's a law-abiding woman—your impression was right. Agreeable and hardworking. And very protective of her younger brother, who is none of those things. We have nothing against Mademoiselle Raissac, but young Alfred has a sheet as long as your arm."

"Good Lord! She didn't mention him. A Parisian?"

"Lives in the thirteenth arrondissement. On the fringes of the student quarter. Bad area. Full of thugs and villains. Thirty years ago, he'd have been running with a gang of apaches."

"Apaches? Why do you French always speak of those villains in a hushed tone? Dead and gone, aren't they? Nothing but a musical-comedy memory?"

"I looked up the word one day," said Bonnefoye. "Couldn't think why French gangsters should be named after a tribe of North American Indians...you know—Geronimo's mob. And, after a while, you realise you've left it too long and it becomes impossible to actually *ask* anyone without being laughed at. It's from a native word, *àpachu*, meaning 'enemy.' And the tribe in question was notorious for the savagery and boldness of its attacks. They had a certain style."

There it was again, that word. Francine Raissac had used it, hadn't she? Or had he used it himself?

"And a dashing image was what the Parisian apaches aimed for! They wore hats with visors pulled low over their

faces, red scarves, polished boots, waistcoat, black trousers and a stiletto. A uniform. Liked to see themselves and their exploits all over the front pages of the press. They swore undying loyalty to each other and, though gangs fought each other all over Paris, they'd always join forces to take on the police. There were those who found that sort of skul-duggery attractive. Smart. Some romantic fool wrote a poem about them. It's suspected that they actually hired themselves out to stage knife fights on the pavements in front of particular cafés to attract customers. Nothing like a little frisson with your absinthe!

"And they had a very short way with informers. They didn't take bribes and they didn't squeal. Vermin! But styl-ish vermin. They disappeared in the war. Swept up for can-non fodder. And now it seems they've been reborn."

"The sons of the apaches?" Joe's voice was laced with irony.

"Just so. They're alive and kicking on the fringes of the boulevards. And this lot are tougher and smarter and less conspicuous. They don't advertise themselves and they avoid being written up in the press but the crime figures speak for them. Never stray south of the Boulevard St. Michel after dark, Joe!"

"And poor little Francine has a brother mixed up with this crew?"

"Francine doesn't acknowledge her brother. Claims to have cast him off. Never mentions him. Did she mention him to you? No! She pretends he doesn't exist. But I've seen the records. She's always there in court pleading for him with the magistrate, bailing him out, when things go wrong for him. I think he's used up a lot of her money. Drug user when he can get his hands on the stuff. Do anything for the price of the next shot...you know the sort of thing. But if he's not in the centre exactly of the criminal underworld, he

hears things that ripple out. Might have passed them on to his sister. That's probably the stuff she was spinning into a tale for you. The framework of a few authentic details and a lot of embroidery on top—she's good at that. Send the impressionable copper away thinking he's heard something useful from a helpful citizen when all he's got is a headful of nonsense."

"Not a very flattering picture but I do hope you're right," said Joe soberly. "Because the alternative might be to suppose that Heather and George were standing a whisker away from the stilettos of the sons of the apaches."

Bonnefoye laughed silently.

"But before you write off my fishing expedition as a trip down the garden path, answer me this—is there any reason why Francine Raissac might decide to confide in a bloke like me? I didn't invoke my charm particularly, nor did I resort to strong-arm tactics...A little light coercion, perhaps, but nothing she couldn't have seen through and side-stepped if she'd wanted to. I'd say she was playing my game. Why would she choose to pass on to a man she's never met before and a foreign policeman at that, a piece of information that might be vital to the solution of last night's murder?"

Bonnefoye was silent, tugging at his moustache, unable to meet his eye.

"What reason?" Joe insisted.

Finally, "Listen," he said quietly. "I told you I had three urgent cases on my books?"

Joe nodded.

"I was supposed to shelve them or delegate them until the end of the week for this conference. But, you know how it is..."

Again Joe nodded. "Can't be done. Especially when you see threads running through them which fresh eyes might not be able to connect."

"Right. Well, one of them involves this hooligan brother, this Alfred. It's thought he was in a fight with three or four other men down by the Canal St. Martin. Some bargees reported a scuffle and screams. Nightly occurrence! No one took much notice. Alfred disappeared on that night and hasn't been seen again since. His sister reported him missing. She was supposed to be having coffee with him as she always does on a Sunday afternoon—passing on some of her wages no doubt. She gets paid on a Saturday. He didn't turn up. She made an incursion—brave girl—into his territory and caught hold of one of his pals. He told her nothing but the terror in his reaction, she reports, was enough to make her fear the worst. And then, late last night, before I came out to meet you at the airport, on my desk, a note from the morgue.

"A body of a young man fished from the canal. No identification but the description fits Alfred."

"Have you had time to go and see it?" said Joe.

He had a memory of walking past three dripping bodies on slabs on his way to view Somerton. "The night's catch," the pathologist had commented. "A poor haul."

"No. Been too caught up with your business, Joe."

"Cause of death? Is it known?"

"Oh, yes. It was very clear. And it wasn't drowning." Bonnefoye's sentences were growing shorter and shorter as his tension increased. "The ultimate cause of death was a stiletto to the heart."

"Ultimate?" Joe picked up the word.

"Yes. That's what killed him. Finished him off. But before he died, his lips had been sewn together. With a length of black cobbler's thread."

Chapter 12

Joe groaned and put his head in his hands.

Not histrionics, he thought, but hysterics or verging on it. Francine Raissac had been mourning her brother, still raw from the inspector's description of his death, bruised, no doubt, by what Bonnefoye called "his rough-tough image," when the English policeman had come bumbling in on his two left feet, making, with insouciance, silly remarks about her panda's eyes. Eyes swollen not, as he'd unthinkingly assumed, by interrupted sleep but by grief. Mascara smudged by tears.

Joe tormented himself and Bonnefoye by insisting on going over some of his worst remarks. "'Bespoke killing...made-to-measure murder,' I said! Can you believe that? How crass! How hurtful!"

"How were you to know? You weren't, Joe! And with all that sewing equipment about the place—I have to say—rather an apt if unfortunate image. Now stop this!"

"She hinted at it, you know...said she might herself be

discovered with her mouth sewn up with—I think she said scarlet—thread. And scissors in her heart. She was using the facts of the death you'd just dropped into her lap to illustrate something—something she was frightened to disclose but…"

"I think her grief pushed her to tell you too much. She didn't tell me, she was still stunned. Gave me nothing. I've seen this before. Shock makes them clam up. Then the anger begins to build up. By the time you got to her and flashed your understanding eyes at her, the desire for revenge had taken over and she was ready to pop. You were treated to her explosion and didn't have the facts to help you to make sense of it. But her insinuations—that there's a clandestine assassination agency with a flair for the dramatic out and about and doing business in Paris —what do we make of *that*? Ludicrous, surely? And it has no name. What in hell *would* you call it?" He grinned. "Shakespeare & Co.? No, that's been used. Bookshop, I think. How about: Death by Design?"

"Bonnefoye, there are two corpses laid out side by side in the Institut Médico-Légal. Alfred Raissac and Sir Stanley Somerton, unlikely morgue-mates. Knifed to death the pair of them, and they're not laughing with us."

"Sorry, Joe." He sighed. "Sometimes it's the only way through the nastiness. But it's not like you to be such an old misery guts? La belle Francine seems to have had quite an effect on you. Always a danger with these girls."

"No, Jean-Philippe! That's the problem. She isn't just one of 'these girls.' I thought she was a very fine young woman. And I'm deeply sorry that I must have—albeit unconsciously—offended and upset her at a distressing moment in her life."

"Hard to avoid that in this job," commented Bonnefoye. "Always offending someone. But—look—put her out of your

mind and concentrate on the most important character in all this. We've hardly given *him* a thought since it started."

"Yes, of course. Somerton. The victim. The moment George wakes up I'm going to want to know exactly how the two are connected. There's something he's not told us. George is an accomplished liar. It's not like him to do it *badly*. That's what concerns me. But, if he hasn't told us, can you blame him?—we haven't got around to asking him yet. Though I'm sure old Fourier must have made the attempt."

They both turned to the bed where, from his pillows, George gave a fluttering and extended snore. They waited for him to turn and settle again before they continued their hushed conversation.

"While you're filling in background on Somerton, I'll go off and take a look at this address in Montparnasse," said Bonnefoye. "The one Francine confided. I'm getting to know that area quite well. I'll be able to make more sense of it than you would, I imagine. Oh—and don't forget you're due to escort the Lady Somerton to the morgue."

He took out a notebook and checked a page. "A message came to headquarters. I ring in every hour and there's usually something for me. Six o'clock at the British Embassy. Can you pick the lady up there? The Embassy's just down the road from here. Very convenient. Oh, they stipulated number 39, rue du Faubourg St. Honoré. That's the residence of the ambassador—not the offices next door. That gives you forty minutes to smarten yourself up. No time to go back to your hotel . . . Why not borrow one of Sir George's shirts? You're about the same size. He's got a drawer full of them over there. And a hat? Never did get your louche fedora back but you'll find something suitable if you look in the wardrobe.

"And look, Joe . . ." Bonnefoye weighed his next announcement, suddenly unsure of himself. "You'll probably

think I'm overreacting to circumstances...put it down to Gallic hysteria if you like...but I think we should move Sir George out of here. To a safer place."

"I agree. Sensible proposal," said Joe. "What do you have in mind?"

"The rue Mouffetard," he said. "My mother's apartment. She's used to soldiers. My father and uncles were in the army. She'll take good care of him. I'll take him out the back way through the kitchens. When you've finished at the morgue why don't you come along and check his accommodation? He's technically in your custody, after all! It's above the baker's shop halfway down. Got a map? Here, let me show you..."

"Before you start dressing to impress the widow, Joe, why don't you get acquainted with my razor?" George's jovial voice was brisk. Not in the least sleepy. "No newfangled patent safety razor on offer, I'm afraid. I always use an old-fashioned cut-throat. You must pardon the expression in the circumstances."

Bonnefoye shrugged and grinned and went with the smooth efficiency of a valet to select a shirt.

"Let me mark your card, Joe." This was the old Sir George, good-humouredly in charge, presiding. "Now, the present ambassador is the Marquess of Crewe. Can't help you there. Never met the chap. Though I was well acquainted with his predecessor. Hardinge. Viceroy of India for many years. And a good one. Anyway, play it by ear and if it seems appropriate to do so, convey my respects and good wishes to whoever seems to be expecting them...you know the routine, Joe."

"I don't suppose the top brass will be parading for a mere Scotland Yard detective and a widow on a lugubrious mission, sir."

George pursed his lips for a moment, assessing the social niceties of the situation. "You're probably right, my boy. Six

o'clock. Dashed inconvenient time for them to be landed with handing a distraught old lady over to the bluebottles. They'll be preparing to welcome guests for whatever shindig they've got planned for tonight. Sociable lot at the Embassy! Always some sort of soirée on. You'll probably find they've tethered the old girl to a gate post outside, awaiting collection.

"No, Bonnefoye! Not that one! Wherever did you get your training? He's not bound for the golf course! Find a boiled shirt, my dear chap! Yes, that'll do. Collars top left. Grey felt hat in the cupboard. Nothing grander. Don't want to look as though you've turned up for the canapés."

At five minutes to six Joe stood, getting his breath back, in front of the Embassy, transfixed by the perfection of the Louis XV façade. Balanced and harmonious and, in this most grandiose quarter of Paris, managing to avoid pomposity, it smiled a welcome. He almost looked for George's gatepost but of course there was none. An elegant pillared portico announced the entrance; doors wide open gave glimpses of figures dimly perceived and moving swiftly about in the interior. As he watched, electric lights flicked on in all the windows of the first two floors. The reception rooms. Obviously a soirée about to take place.

He collected his thoughts and strode to the door.

The liveried doorman barely glanced at the card in his extended hand. "You are expected, Commander. Will you follow me?"

He passed Joe on into the care of an aide in evening dress who came hurrying into the vestibule to shake his hand. "Sandilands? How do you do? So glad you could come. Harry Quantock. Deputy assistant to the ambassador. You'll have

to make do with me, I'm afraid, sir. His Excellency sends his greetings—he's at the moment rather tied up with the string band." At the upwards flick of an elegant hand, Joe caught the sounds of a small orchestra essaying a piece of Elgar somewhere above their heads. The deputy assistant grimaced. "French band, English tunes...not a good mix. I sometimes think they do it on purpose."

"Still seeking revenge for Waterloo?" suggested Joe. "Ouch! I'd surrender at once."

"We won't hear them in the red salon; come with me." Quantock led him across the impressive space in front of them. Airy, well proportioned and sparely decorated. *"Le hall d'entrée,"* announced his guide with a perfect accent.

Joe had an impression of cool grey and white marble tiles leading the eye to the graceful curve of a great staircase. The delicate wrought-iron handrail outlining it sparkled with gold and bronze, promising further wonders as it wound upwards.

Quantock leaned to him and confided: "Most of the refurbishment was done with impeccable taste by Napoleon's favourite sister. And there she is—Pauline Borghese."

Joe nodded in acknowledgement as they passed her portrait. The young princess, slim and lovely in her high-bosomed gown, was as handsome as her house.

"Pity about the curtains, don't you think? Red velvet!" Quantock was shuddering. "Too Edwardian for words! And the theme continues through here in *le salon rouge.*" He paused by a closed door. "Your charge, Lady Somerton, is in here, taking sherry and flirting with the Duke of Wellington. They *will* do it! His Grace still exerts a certain power over the ladies."

Joe entered a room richly decorated, in contrast with the restrained hall. In the centre, a gleaming round mahogany

table stood precisely in the rosette of a deep red turkey carpet and was overhung by a stunning chandelier. Gilded mirrors applied to each of the red walls reflected the flickering lights of candles in sconces, and in the middle of all this magnificence Joe had to hunt for the figure of Lady Somerton. She was standing at the end of the room, empty sherry glass in hand, still, black-clad, almost a shadow. She was looking up at a portrait. Transfixed, she did not hear them enter.

As they drew near she began to speak: "Arthur Wellesley. The Iron Duke. Now, there was a man one can admire! So handsome! So competent! I'm just surprised, after what he did to the French, that they allow us to display him, Mr. Quantock."

"His Grace was himself ambassador for a year here in 1814, immediately before his victory at Waterloo, your ladyship," Quantock reminded her. "And therefore takes his rightful place on these walls." He performed the introductions. "May I refill your glass? And how about you, sir? Would you like some sherry?" He went to pour the drinks himself from a sideboard, tactfully leaving Joe to continue the conversation.

"His quality leaps from the canvas, don't you agree?" she continued, determined, apparently to hear his views.

"It's all in the nose, I believe," said Joe, annoyed that the widow appeared far more interested in Wellington than in himself.

"I beg your pardon? The nose, did you say?"

"Yes. Look at it. An ice-breaker! A promontory! Your hero could have fought a duel with Cyrano and they would have needed no other weapons."

At last she smiled. "Noses. In the Bois. At dawn. I'd have put my money on the duke."

Her attention caught, Joe moved easily into the routine of

expressing sorrow for the death of the lady's husband. His smooth sentiments were graciously received, helped along with sighs and sips of sherry. Quantock politely sought the most recent information on the tragedy and Joe gave him an acceptable and highly edited account. The task before him was to point this uncertain dark horse at a rather taxing fence and he wanted to avoid scaring her off. Without appearing to do so, he studied the widow, assessing her strengths and qualities. Exactly what he was expecting. Apart from her age. She was middle-aged, possibly as much as forty, but at any rate, more than a decade younger than her late husband. Quite a normal age gap in military families. He could imagine that, with promotion in mind—possibly colonel the next step—Somerton had been taken on one side by a superior officer and advised to marry. And, one summer, on home leave, he'd met and courted this woman. What had she said her name was? She'd rather particularly during the introductions corrected young Quantock. "Lady Somerton no longer," she'd informed them. "With Sir Stanley dead and the title gone to his son, my daughter-in-law is the present Lady Somerton. I am now to be addressed as *Catherine*, Lady Somerton." The voice was educated, Home Counties.

Her face was pale, enlivened by a gallant touch of rouge along the cheekbones. Quenched but pretty. Her hair was light brown, not greying yet, her eyes hazel. She'd chosen her dress well. Black, of course, but silk and well cut. The drama was relieved by a double strand of pearls around her throat and matching pearl earrings that peeped out just below her bobbed hair.

Joe enquired amiably and sympathetically about her flight over the Channel. She declared she'd enjoyed it but he set her brave comment against the betraying rise and fall of her pearls as she failed to restrain a gulp. The conversation,

which was never going to be an easy one, felt as discordant as the strains of the Gallic version of "Nimrod" filtering along the corridor and all three were relieved to draw it to a close.

Harry Quantock escorted his guests back to the front door where, to Joe's surprise, an Embassy car was waiting for them. A manservant hurried forward with Madame's cape and Monsieur's hat. After routine farewells, Quantock handed Catherine Somerton into the backseat, closed the door and turned to speak softly to Joe: "His Excellency will be keen to hear the outcome of this business, you understand, Sandilands?" A light smile softened the command. "As will Jack Pollock. Sir George's cousin. He sends his respects and good wishes. He'll be in touch."

The morgue, illuminated as it now was by electric bulbs, was all the more sinister. The light had the effect of deepening the many dark corners, emphasising the roughness of the walls and highlighting things better left in the shadows. Like shining a torch in the face of an old whore, Joe thought. Disturbing and unkind. But at least they were not faced, on entry, with a line-up of freshly delivered corpses to pass in review as had been the custom from the Middle Ages to the recent past. All the bodies apart from one had been filed away in the sliding steel cases along the back wall, Joe was relieved to see.

Dr. Moulin was still at his post and waiting for them. He greeted Joe warmly and the two men went into their routine. Dignified and considerate, he checked that the lady was prepared for the sight of her husband's corpse. Catherine Somerton hugged her cape about her, clutched her pearls, shivered and nodded.

"Do you think we might take a look at Exhibit A before

we begin?" Joe asked, and Moulin nodded his agreement.
The dagger was produced for her inspection.

She made no attempt to handle it but looked at it carefully and turned a cooperative face to Joe. "I'm sorry,
Commander. I've never seen it before."

"Did Sir Stanley keep a collection of knives at home?"

"Ah. Where *was* his home? We had no such objects in the
house in Kent. But you should be aware, Commander, that
my husband lived for many years in India. He had a passion
for the country that I could not share. I joined him there for
the first year of our marriage but the climate did not agree
with me and I returned. He could have amassed a collection
of such artefacts and I would be unaware of their existence.
This is, I take it, the very blade that did the deed?"

Joe and Moulin murmured in unison.

She peered at it more closely, then shook her head. On the
whole, a good witness, Joe thought. When the doctor moved
to the head of the sheeted figure she moved with him and
stood waiting on the other side. Joe watched her carefully as
the cover rolled downwards to the waist. There was at first
no reaction. Finally, she drew in a deep breath and whispered: "That's Somerton. My late husband." And, as Joe had
predicted, there came at last the inevitable question: "Tell
me, Doctor, did he suffer?"

The doctor also was prepared for this. But he was a scientist, not a diplomat and he gave an honest reply. "His death
must have come very quickly, madame. He did not linger in
pain. But the wound—you may see for yourself—is a savage
one, almost severing the head. The initial assault would
have caused a degree of pain, yes."

"Good!" said the widow, suddenly bright. "But however
painful it was, it could never have been painful enough!"

In the stunned silence, she rounded on the corpse and for
a moment Joe felt his muscles tense. Fearing what? That she

was about to inflict a truly painful blow of her own? Incredibly—yes. The doctor had put out a restraining hand. She gestured it away impatiently and went to stand close by the head. She bent and spoke directly to the corpse, her lips inches from his ear: "I hope you're in hell, you rotter! I hope that Lucifer in person is turning your spit. Look at you! Oozing your stinking essence onto a slab in a foreign dungeon! Dyed hair! Pomaded moustache! You lived—a disgrace; you died—a disgrace!"

She took a step back and gave her last, formal farewell: *"Down, down to hell; and say I sent thee thither."*

Joe was uneasy. The vehemence was spontaneous but the quotation from *Henry VI* had been, he calculated, prepared with some forethought. The whole outpouring appeared the distillation of years of resentment. He looked again at the dead face, softening in decay and speculated on the qualities that could provoke such hatred.

The widow collected herself and struggled for a more level tone, addressing the two men: "You may have his remains burned or whatever you do. I don't want to take them away with me or have them posted on. Send the bill to the Embassy. And now, if you're ready, Commander...? We must be on our way."

She threaded her arm through Joe's and turned for the last time to her husband, unwilling even now to let him go in peace, her parting words meant for him: "I have an engagement on the Champs-Élysées. At Fouquet's."

She began to drag Joe towards the door, calling out still over her shoulder her taunts: "Champagne...foie gras...asparagus...the first of the wild strawberries..."

Joe paused in the doorway and looked back at the startled doctor, mouthing silently: "Not with me, she hasn't!"

Chapter 13

She swept out ahead of him and stood by the car door until he opened it. When they were settled inside she gave him his instructions: "Tell the driver I'll drop you off before he goes on to Fouquet's. Where would you like to be set down, Commander?"

Without waiting for his answer, she took a velvet bag from the deep pocket of her cape and fished about until she found a small flacon of perfume. "Do you mind if I apply something a little fresh? I'm quite sure I must smell of—what was that fluid? Ugh! Formaldehyde, would it be? That stink?"

"Death and bleach, Lady Somerton," said Joe tersely.

He addressed the driver, who was sitting patiently waiting for instructions. "Driver—would you take me across the river onto the Left Bank, please? I'm bound for the Place de la Contrescarpe. Do you know it? And then, the lady requires to be set down in the Champs-Élysées. She will direct you."

The big car moved off and Joe reeled at an over-enthusiastic application of perfume. Rose and sandalwood? Chanel's Number 5 was easily recognised. And what had Mademoiselle Chanel saucily said about her creation? "Perfume should be applied in the places where a woman expects to be kissed." Joe watched in fascination as Catherine Somerton dabbed the contents of her tiny flacon behind her ears, at the base of her throat and when she thought he'd turned to look out the window, he saw, in the reflection in the glass, her forefinger steal down into the hollow between her breasts to lay a seductive trail.

For whose nose? For whose lips? Joe smiled to himself. He hoped Fouquet's had got the champagne on ice.

The car rolled to a halt, held up by the press of early evening traffic fighting its way across the Pont Neuf onto the island. On an impulse Joe spoke to the driver again. "Look—I'll get out here. With the traffic as it is, Lady Somerton will find herself late for her assignation in the Champs-Élysées if she makes a detour to drop me off. I'm happy to take a taxi."

She made no demur, not even noticing his slight reproof, even thanking him for his consideration. Mind elsewhere. Impatient to be off. In the advancing headlights her eyes flashed, her pearls gleamed and although nothing about her appearance had substantially changed, Joe suddenly saw, where had been the downcast widow in her weeds, a sophisticated woman, elegantly dressed and eagerly looking forward to an adventure.

"Give my regards to the duke," he called to her before he slammed the door shut. "I trust his olfactory powers will be in fine fettle this evening." He enjoyed her puzzled expression.

Joe watched the car crawl away again and turned on his

heel, trotting back across the bridge to the morgue. Hoping he wasn't too late.

The lights were still switched on. Moulin was there, putting away instruments and equipment, when Joe burst in. He seemed pleased to see him.

His cheerful voice echoed the length of the room, dispelling the shadows. "Oh, hallo, there! You managed to escape? I'm glad of that! Wouldn't want to find *you* on one of my slabs with a mysterious mark on your throat. It can be pretty poisonous, the bite of *Latrodectus mactans,* I've heard. The Black Widow Spider. Its venom is thought to be sixteen times more virulent than the rattlesnake's."

"I leapt out of the car! If I weren't so exhausted, I'd have been tempted to go along to Fouquet's, bribe someone to give me a table in a corner, and lurk to see who she's got caught up in her web!"

Moulin eyed Joe with concern. "You *do* look all in, Commander. Come and have a mug of coffee in my lair. I've just put a pot on. Put your feet up for a bit. Get your breath back and ask me the question you've passed up an evening at Fouquet's to come back and ask."

They sat clutching mugs of strong coffee in the small and calculatedly bright study across the corridor from the morgue building. Not so much a study as a retreat, an affirmation of his humanity, Joe thought, looking around with pleasure. And wouldn't you need one! He'd sunk gratefully into the depths of one of a pair of old-fashioned armchairs piled with cushions and topped off with lace antimacassars. Thoughtfully, Moulin kicked over a footstool for him. The

room had probably, in its first use, been some sort of torture chamber, Joe calculated, but no signs of a lugubrious past lingered after the determined application of rich lengths of drapery to the walls, Tiffany shades to the lamps, rows of books and a gently puttering gas fire warming the room. On a desk and smiling out into the room, the silver-framed photograph of a very pretty dark-haired woman. The ticking of a deep-throated clock soothed Joe to a point where he had to shake himself awake and take a sip or two of his coffee.

Under the influence of the strong brew, the good company and fatigue, Joe recounted his day to a pair of willing ears. But the warm smile, the understanding comments and the ready humour dried up at the mention of Francine Raissac's flight of fancy. Joe caught the sudden stillness.

"Yes, that's what I've come to ask. I try not to leave any accusation unchecked, however ridiculous it sounds on first hearing. The girl's theories began to sound less crazy when I heard—from another source—that her brother is a customer of yours. Filed away in a steel drawer, I should think? Fished out of the Canal St. Martin."

"Alfred? Drawer number 32," said Moulin. "She hasn't been in to identify him yet. Poor girl! It's all deeply unpleasant, I'm afraid. I've taken the waxed cobbler's twine out of the lips so it doesn't look quite so frightful but I can't obliterate the wound altogether. The lad was very young. But physically in rather bad shape. Emaciated. Taking drugs, I shouldn't wonder. And are you saying you see a connection between this poor specimen of humanity and an organisation run by some sort of super criminal? A Fantômas reborn?" Dr. Moulin laughed and pointed to a shelf of lurid novels over the desk. "I have the whole collection, you see! You're very welcome to help yourself if you like."

Joe shivered. "I gave up after the second book. Too utterly terrifying for a law enforcer like myself. Fantômas, if I re-

member rightly, never died," he explained. "He's immortal—a god of Evil. Nightmare! But yes, I wouldn't mind taking a look at the third one in your line-up. *Le mort qui tue,* I think it's called."

Moulin gave him a startled look and counted along the shelf, extracting the book he'd mentioned. "Here you are. I shall leave the gap there! I'm going to insist on having it back, then I can be sure you'll come again and entertain me with a further episode in your horror story. Will you have a little brandy in your coffee? It can strike chill in here in spite of my efforts to dispel the gloom!" He reached behind a row of leather-backed novels and found a bottle of cognac.

"I think you can guess what I'm going to ask," said Joe seriously. "Inspectors each have their own case loads. Three corpses is what Bonnefoye's got on his books at the moment. They may not have the time to exchange theories with each other, or see anything but their own narrow picture of crime in the city... *You* would see it. You examine all—very well, most—of the bodies. They pass through your morgue and under your scalpel for an hour or two—a day possibly—and you move on. But you see the wider landscape of murder..."

"I know where you're going with this. And I know you don't want to wait while I dig out screeds of notes, sheets of records—all of which are available, by the way—so I'll ask—will memory be a good enough guide? It will? Let me think, then..." He got up and wandered to his stove, pouring out more of the liquid inspiration.

"Over the last four or five years? Is that enough? That's as far back as my current appointment goes."

Joe nodded, thankful that his notion hadn't been dismissed out of hand with a pitying shake of the head.

And then he waited, unwilling to press Moulin, understanding that this was the doctor's first and alarming overview of the crime pattern.

"Like your Jack the Ripper—a killer in series—but yet quite unlike him. The victims in his case were all of the same profession, sex and situation. They—and the killer most probably—were living within a few doors of each other. The Paris corpses I have in mind are male and from varied backgrounds, they're of different nationalities, killed over a period of years and in vastly different scenarios. No one would dream of linking them together as a group because apart from their being male—which the victims of violent death predominantly are—they have only one thing in common—a totally fanciful notion. In Francine Raissac's head, in yours and now—in mine! Curse you! No, it won't do, Sandilands." He shook his head in an attempt to dismiss ideas too shocking to entertain.

"And there's the question of motive," he persisted into Joe's silence. "Motive could be guessed at in most of the cases. Or should I say motives? They were varied but run-of-the-mill."

"Financial gain, provocation, revenge, hatred..." Joe started to list them.

"Yes, yes... a bit of everything. And I'm not sure it tells us much in these cases."

"Would you like to bring some of them into the daylight again—just as a matter of speculation, of course," Joe encouraged.

"No, I try rather to forget them." Moulin stirred uneasily and turned up the fire a notch. "Working here—you'd think I'd become—if I wasn't already—some sort of automaton. I haven't. I don't think I could do the job adequately if I had. I feel something for each 'customer,' as you call them. And bury a little bit of myself with each one." He smiled to see Joe's eyes flare with concern. "Don't worry! I shall know when to stop!"

Moulin pointed to the row of thrillers. "You're not to think, on the cold winter evenings between postmortems, I allow my imagination to be fired by these things! Lots of people you might admire enjoy them! Jean Cocteau, René Magritte, Guillaume Apollinaire, Salvador Dalí ... Blaise Cendrars called them 'the Aeneid of Modern Times'!"

"And you can add to your list of playwrights, poets and artists: Sandilands of the Yard," said Joe comfortably, sensing that the learned doctor was slightly embarrassed to be caught out in his enthusiasm.

"Very well—you're prepared, then? To explore a really outlandish idea?"

Joe nodded.

"Before we start, I must insist—no notes! This is just a chat between two weary men whose brains are ticking over faster perhaps than they should. Agreed?"

"Agreed," said Joe.

"In 1924, the body of a priest was found. I remember it was the night before All Saints' Day. Your Hallowe'en, I believe?"

Joe nodded again, saying nothing. He sensed that it would not take much of an interruption to put Moulin off a track he was plainly uncomfortable to be following. The man was a scientist, after all. Rational. Logical. Not given to fervid speculation. Intolerant of ridicule.

"I wondered later if that was significant. The man was dangling by a noose to the neck on a bell-rope. The rope was the one that hung from the bell tower of the curé's own church. The tolling started in the early hours of the morning, as the body swayed—in the breeze? It was a windy night ... Or from a push? We don't know. The sound went unregarded for an hour or so as the good citizens of the well-to-do faubourg huddled deeper into their goose-feather

eiderdowns. They might have decided he'd committed suicide—not unknown in the priesthood—had it not been for
his other wounds. His robe had been slashed from neck to
hem and was heavily bloodstained down the front. His male
member had been cut off. Before death."

"Revenge for some kind of abuse committed by the
priest?"

Moulin shrugged. "I would expect so. No one ever came
forward with accusations, let alone evidence. Case closed.
Unsolved. The Church, in any case, was glad enough to hush
it up.

"And then, later that same year, a rich industrialist whose
name I'm certain would be familiar to you died in bed. Not
his own bed, but that of a common prostitute in a pic-
turesquely low quarter of the city. The lady was absent and
never surfaced again. The corpse of our louche old money-
bags was discovered naked, tied up with scarlet velvet rib-
bons to the bedpost—hands and feet. He'd died from an
overdose of hashish. The gentlemen of the press had been
alerted before the police and were instantly on the scene
with their flash bulbs. Everyone was horrified. Except for
the man's five sons. They were now to inherit his fortune,
clear of any fear of premature depletion by the extravagant
young actress whose charms had led him, a month or so previously, to propose marriage."

Joe gave a wry smile. "Next?"

"Last year. Picture the Eiffel Tower. A favourite jumping-
off point for the suicidally minded. The body of a young
man falls from a crowded viewing platform to splatter itself
all over the concourse below. It happens every month. No
one sees anything. No one is aware of any suspicious circumstances. The man's fiancée, the spoiled daughter of one
of our prominent politicians, is aghast. 'But why the Eiffel

Tower?' she sobs. 'The very place where he declared his love and asked me to marry him!' She is distraught. She is inconsolable. But her best friend reveals—spitefully perhaps?—that the boy in question had, in fact, changed his mind since the tryst on the tower and decided to marry *her*. The first fiancée was, luckily, far away in Nice on holiday with her family at the time of the death and could not possibly be involved in any dirty work."

"This is a mixed bunch of motives I'm hearing," said Joe.

"And here's one for the connoisseur! I've saved the best for last! But, for me, it was the *first* in the sequence, I suppose. Though it wasn't for some weeks that I realised I'd had a pretty strange experience. In 1923. Newly appointed to the Institut and rather overawed by the big city, I wasn't quite sure what to expect—except that everything would be faster, more exciting, than I was used to in Normandy. I got a phone call from upstairs telling me to grab my bag, jump into a police car and get over to the Louvre. To the Egyptian rooms on the ground floor. Pandemonium when I got there! And something very odd going on. An American couple alone in one of the galleries had come across a pool of blood at the foot of one of the mummy cases. You know—those great big ornate coffin things . . . weigh a ton . . ."

"I know them."

"When I got there—ten minutes after receiving the call—the body hadn't even been discovered. It didn't strike me as strange until later, mesmerised as I was by the quality of the communications in the city: phone, telegraph, police cars standing at the ready outside . . . 'So this is the modern pace!' I thought. 'Must keep up!' And there was a lot of activity to distract me at the museum. A whole chorus of academics—curators, Egyptologists, students—had assembled to see what was going on. Newsmen weren't far behind!

"Luckily, a British official of some sort who happened to be leaving a meeting was collared by the distraught American who'd just avoided putting his foot in something very nasty, and this Briton, using the several languages he spoke, backed up by—shall we say— a certain natural authority…" Moulin paused and grinned apologetically at Joe.

"Arrogance, you can say if you wish," suggested Joe easily. "We learn it on school playing fields—or charging enemy machine gun nests armed with a swagger-stick and shouting: 'Follow me, lads!' But I can imagine what you're going to say and—I'd have done the same, I'm afraid."

"Well, the Englishman took charge. Jack Pollock, his name was, and thank goodness he was there."

Joe had reached automatically for his notebook but, remembering his promise, he relaxed.

"He calmed everyone down and sent for all the right people. A policeman was on the spot to see fair play, I remember."

"And you found a body in the case? Dripping blood onto the floor? Not very well hidden?"

"No. I think it was meant to be found. And the finding was timed…orchestrated, you might say."

"Who was in the box?"

"Two bodies. Below: the rightful occupant, a High Priest of some sort, and on top: an alien presence. A professor of Egyptology. Stabbed. Messily. The killer knew enough about knife work to ensure that the body drained itself of blood. Weapon? A type of butcher's knife, I wrote in my report. Something capable of stabbing and ripping open. A pig farmer could advise, perhaps? It was never found. But we did find, in the throat, and sucked right down into the breathing passages of the deceased, wads of linen bindings. Ancient linen. Taken from the body of some other mummy. He'd been forced to swallow the stuff."

"Deeply unpleasant!" Joe could not contain his revulsion.

"That wasn't the worst. I say, you won't arrest me if I make a confession, will you, Sandilands?"

"Good Lord! Depends what you're confessing. If you want to tell me you're the mastermind behind all this, I'll have you in cuffs at once!"

Moulin smiled, got to his feet and went to take a small box from a shelf. "I'm going to show you something I stole. From an evidence file. It comes from the scene of the crime."

He handed the box to Joe, who raised his brows in alarm on catching sight of the contents.

"You can handle it. It's been sterilised."

"Why would you need to do that?" asked Joe, cautiously.

"I removed it from the bloodied bandage lodged in the throat of the corpse of Professor Joachim Lebreton. It was sticky with various body fluids and an oil that had been used to ease the descent of the fabric down the tubes."

"Charming!" Joe took the golden object gingerly and held it to the light between finger and thumb. "An amulet?"

"No. Not my job, of course, to establish the provenance of exhibits but no one else seemed interested enough to do it. In the police report it's listed as 'imitation gold medallion, value 5 francs.' It would have been chucked out after a year, but I was curious enough to preserve it. Oh, it's not valuable. It's not even ancient. A modern copy—gilded. Crudely done. Anyone with a bit of tin, a chisel and a pot of gold paint could produce the equivalent. Any *mouleur-plaquiste* could churn them out by the hundred. But you'd need to know your Egyptology. This is a bona fide, head and shoulders portrait, you might say."

"It's a disgusting image! Whoever *is* this fellow? Or is it an animal?" Joe peered more closely. "It seems to be half god,

half bad-tempered greyhound. I know just enough to recognise that it's *not* the rather stylish *jackal*-headed god, Anubis."

"You're right. But he is a god all the same. And at one time widely venerated in Egypt. It's the son of Ra and brother of Osiris."

Joe shook his head. "We're not acquainted. Don't particularly wish to be."

"You show good taste! His name's Set. Set murdered his brother and scattered his body parts all over Egypt. He debauched his own nephew Horus. In his capacity as Lord of the Desert, he had the power to stir up terrible storms. For the Ancient Egyptians, Set was utterly terrifying—the embodiment of Evil. The God of Evil."

Joe put the gilded trinket back into its box. "I'm bringing no charge, Moulin. Let's just keep the lid on him, shall we?"

Moulin, smiling, agreed. "And why don't you take him away with you? I think I was just hanging on to him until someone who knew what he was about took an interest. You know, Sandilands, I think the purpose of that thing was to drop a hint as to motive for the crime. Out of the victim's mouth came evil? Something on those lines? Again—no suspect was ever arrested. But, bearing in mind the closed circumstances, you'd have to say—an inside job. The man had many enemies. Archaeologist himself, he'd been ruthless in his acquisition of artefacts and had plundered his students' and his fellows' learned works for his own glory. He'd wrecked promising careers by his vitriolic criticism, his sly innuendoes. At least fifty academics must have raised a glass on hearing about the circumstances of his death. Now, they couldn't *all* have been present at the discovery of the body but, Sandilands—a good many *were*. It never occurred to anyone pursuing the case to ask why so

many experts, all known to the deceased, were right there on the spot."

The doctor fell silent. Then: "There was a moment... When the amulet emerged, it dropped to the floor. Someone fainted at the sight of it and had to be taken out and I had the strangest sensation... I was acting in a drama. Onstage. Pushed on into the middle of a scene and left to improvise my part. The crowd—who should never have been allowed to remain—weren't a crowd. They were... *an audience*. An *invited* audience."

Moulin took a deep breath, relieved to have unburdened himself. "I say, Sandilands, does any of this make sense?"

"Certainly does. My friend Sir George was himself pushed in, almost literally, onstage, last night to perform the same function. And he *was* actually sent a ticket to the event! But, being an Englishman of a type you recognise, he bustled in rather too actively and got himself arrested for the murder. But, Moulin—four cases, in as many years? Is that all?" Joe asked. And, tentatively: "If this were some sort of syndicate—shall we say?—taking commissions to carry out crimes spectacular to the general public or crimes deeply satisfying to the one who orders them up, well—we are rather assuming a business, I suppose. And businesses exist to make money. Not sure I'd take the enormous risks involved for the return. Are you? What must they charge? One killing per year? Overheads, knifemen, underlings to pay? Hush money! It wouldn't work."

Moulin's expression was grim. "There are many more than four possibilities. I didn't want to over-face you with detail but, if you can give me a week, I'm sure I can make out an expanded list for you. And there might be as many as twenty cases on it. Some less uncertain than others. And that's just Paris. What do we know of other towns? But I

agree with your unstated thought—it's not just the financial returns, is it? There's an underlying sense of ... enjoyment?"

"A sadistic indulgence?" Joe said. "And with an added element of self-forgiveness—a twisted feeling of justification for the crimes. Someone else has paid for this. Someone else supplied the ingenious requirements of the death—the means, the scenario. So—someone else is to blame. The brain which devised the murders, the executive producer if you like, holds himself no more to blame than the dagger that came bloodstained from the heart of the victim. The guilt can be as easily washed away as the blood. Am I being fanciful?"

"I've no training in psychology!" said Moulin. "So you must put your theory to others. But I have to say I've travelled that same path, Sandilands."

"And the latest victim, congealing in one of your drawers? I wonder who dialled up *his* death?" Suddenly decisive, Joe said: "I'm going to find out who's behind the mask, Moulin. Whose hand held the Afghani dagger *and* whose voice asked for it to be done. I'm going to have 'em both. I can't go back four years in a foreign country, crusading for belated justice but I can get to the bottom of this one that's landed in my lap. And I'll only get close to the truth by digging up the nastier bits of Somerton's past. Not much chance the widow will confide but I know a man who I can persuade to cough up some details."

Sensing that his guest was ready to leave and on the point of exhaustion, Moulin got to his feet. "Wait here, Sandilands, while I nip out and whistle up a taxi for you. Oh, and thinking of the rogue Somerton ..." He tapped the cover of the book Joe was still clutching. "*Le mort qui tue.* Read the title again. That's *le mort*, not *la mort*. Dead man— not Death itself. The corpse that kills. Be warned! Have a

care for your friend. We don't want an innocent man, blundering in on a sorry episode, to pay for his well-meaning interference on the guillotine. I suspect this man, Somerton, has caused enough havoc in his life. I don't want to think that, from the depths of the morgue, he has the power to kill again."

Chapter 14

He chose a dark side street behind the Place de la Contrescarpe to pay off his taxi. Feeling mildly foolish but in no way allowing this to make him lower his guard, he waited in a doorway until he was sure he hadn't been followed. When he was fully confident, Joe wandered into the small square lined with cafés and restaurants. The aperitif hour was swinging to a close and the tables were rapidly filling with diners. He browsed the menus displayed on boards outside or scrawled on the windows and made his choice. The Café des Arts, being the biggest and noisiest, had claimed his attention and he went inside to the bar, ordered a Pernod and paid for a telephone connection.

He'd committed Bonnefoye's number to memory and destroyed the card and, in his state of fatigue, hoped he'd got it right.

The same lively female answered his tentative: *"Umm... allô?"*

"There you are! Just in time for supper. You know how to get here? Good. See you in two minutes! Bye!"

No names, no details, he noticed. And none asked for. Whoever she was, Bonnefoye's female was well trained. And hospitable.

Joe was conscious of the unusual honour the inspector was doing him and Sir George by extending this invitation to take shelter in his own home. The French rarely asked friends to dinner at their flat or house. Friendships were pursued in the café or restaurant or at shooting weekends in the country. If the Englishman's home was his castle, the Frenchman's was a keep with the drawbridge permanently up to repel invaders and visitors.

Bonnefoye had been surprised and enchanted with his first taste of British hospitality the previous winter. Welcoming the Frenchman on an official visit to London, Joe had taken responsibility for the young officer and invited him to spend a long weekend with him at his sister's house in Surrey. An instant love-affair had flowered. The English family had fallen for Bonnefoye at first sight and Jean-Philippe had been equally smitten. He probably considered he was in Joe's debt in the hospitality stakes but Joe was, nevertheless, surprised and charmed by the gesture.

And concerned. The man kept his address a close secret and doubtless for excellent reasons. Joe had no intention of bringing danger within his orbit. He was keeping up his guard. He ambled around the square again, marking his exit, and when he was sure he was unobserved, he slipped off into the rue Mouffetard. A lamp-lighter was moving down the street creating romantic pools of light and Joe hurried to get ahead of him, hugging the shadows. He was looking for a baker's shop. In the alleyway to the side of it he found a door which opened at his tap.

He was greeted by Bonnefoye, who closed and bolted the

door behind him. "We've got him settled in," he told Joe as he led the way up a flight of stairs. "All's well! Through here—it's a bit crowded and you'll have to share a room with me if you want to give the Ambassador a miss tonight. I gave Sir George our only guest room."

Sir George was sitting at a kitchen table shelling peas. He was under instruction from a middle-aged woman who, with her striking dark looks, could be no other than Bonnefoye's mother, and he appeared to be doing well at his task. His manicured thumbnail was slicing along with skill, making short work of the pods. When his mentor turned to greet Joe, he stuffed a podful of peas into his mouth and was sharply rapped on the knuckles.

"Now add the spring onions and the butter...more lettuce leaves on top...tiny drop of stock...don't drown it... and there you are! Put it on the stove. Back burner...So glad to meet you at last, Commander!" The voice from the telephone. Youthful, bossy and eager. "I'm running a little late this evening and I've had to call up reinforcements." She flashed a devastating smile at George. He grinned and mumbled a greeting across the table, content to take a back seat in the proceedings.

Madame Bonnefoye was much younger than George— perhaps fifty years old but, in the way of Frenchwomen, still attractive. She whisked off her grey pinafore to reveal a black widow's dress enlivened by a pink scarf draped at the neck. Bonnefoye's father, he had told Joe, had fallen at Verdun.

"Jean-Philippe! A glass of wine for the commander! It's one from our home village in Burgundy. We bring it back in quantities. You boys have ten minutes to exchange information before you present yourselves at table. It will be a very simple supper: I made some soup to start with, then the butcher had some excellent veal which will be good with

George's *petits pois à l'étuve*, followed by cheese and, since Jean-Philippe tells me you Englishmen are fond of sweet things, I've got some chocolate éclairs from the pâtissier."

Joe decided he'd died and gone to heaven and, as he'd always thought it might, heaven smelled of herb soup and rang with a woman's laughter.

He went to sit in the small salon of the apartment with Jean-Philippe, listening to the chatter from the kitchen. George's stately but adventurous French sentences rolled out, to be punctuated by sharp bursts of amusement and exclamation from Madame Bonnefoye.

"First things first," said Joe. "Security. I'm as sure as I can be I wasn't followed here. You?"

"Sure. But we mustn't reduce the level of precaution. A message came by telephone late this afternoon. From Miss Watkins, I'm afraid. One of my staff took it down and I've translated it but I think it's very clear. All too clear!" He passed Joe a scrap of paper.

> *My new boyfriend very keen! He even came shopping with me. Was compelled to go on the offensive. He has a two-inch red scar on his left jaw.*

Joe was aghast. He picked out the word which most alarmed him. " 'Offensive,' she says?"

Bonnefoye cleared his throat. "This ties in with a report we had from the Galeries Lafayette," he said. "To be precise— from the ladies' underwear department. A customer lodged a complaint against a man she alleged was following and threatening her. Two assistants, who remarked the young lady grappling with a tall man in a dark overcoat, went to her aid and attempted to detain him. Unfortunately, he was able to effect an escape."

"And the scar? I hardly dare ask!"

"...was already a feature of his physiognomy before he encountered Miss Watkins."

"Thank goodness for that! But we should never have involved her."

"I agree. And it's too late now to *uninvolve* her." Bonnefoye sighed. "But look—if these people are as good as we think they are, they'll make enquiries and discover that she has absolutely no connection with Sir George and leave her to get on with her hearty tennis life. They'll assume that she was just spooked by an over-zealous piece of shadowing. He'll probably get a ticking off from his boss—should have had more sense than to follow her into the lingerie section. And Miss Watkins has certainly got closer—physically at any rate—to the tool they're using than we have."

"That scar? Any use to us?"

"Yes, could be. I've reported it to the division that keeps our Bertillon records. All marks of that kind are listed, classified and kept on card. If the chap has committed a crime before, his features will be on file and indexed. They ought to be able to come up with a few suggestions.

"The thing that's worrying me, Joe, is their apparent preoccupation with Sir G. They seem to have him in their sights. But why? Did he see something he's not told anyone yet? Does he know something he ought not to know? You'll have to grill him. I can't seem to get near him. Any attempt on my part at putting a few questions gets batted aside—with the greatest good humour, of course. Genial, avuncular, smelling of roses—and he's as slippery as a bar of soap. But tell me—how did you get on with the widow?"

After a draught or two of the Chablis he was handed, Joe launched into an account of his evening.

"She was off to Fouquet's, eh?" Bonnefoye was entertained by the thought. "I'll make enquiries. We'll know to-

morrow who she met, what they ate, what time they left and where they went afterwards! Are you thinking—there's one lady who is delighted that old Somerton was done to death?"

"She told me she had no idea her husband was in Paris— they hadn't communicated for years. And, of course, she was hundreds of miles away from the scene of the crime..." Joe began dubiously.

"Well, if your mad theory about the crime-order-catalogue business is correct, she *would* be. That's the whole point of it. They have the telephone in England and the wires run as far as Paris, remember."

"Not sure she fits the frame," said Joe. "Glad enough, yes, to be rid of the old boy. As, indeed, might be the *son* I discover she has. The one who succeeds to the title. And who knows what else! We might check on *him* and the size and nature of his inheritance. But why would she or he or they bother with all the palaver? I mean, the showmanship element? The theatre...the dagger. I watched her examine the knife. I'll swear it meant nothing to her. She was curious, fascinated even, in a ghoulish way, but there was no flicker of recognition. Just an element of his past life she'd rather not think about. Why didn't they simply have him pushed under a bus or off a bridge? And why wait all these years?"

Bonnefoye shrugged and poured out more wine. "Still— glad enough to have them as suspects two and three. I like to collect a good hand."

Joe raised a questioning eyebrow. "Your first suspect?"

Jean-Philippe was suddenly grave. "Sir George, of course. I don't like it any more than you do but the man's up to his neck in whatever's going on. You'd have to be blind not to see that."

Joe produced the doctor's copy of *Le mort qui tue* from his pocket and slapped it down onto the table between them.

"Look at the title, Jean-Philippe. If we work with your suppositions, Sir George will die. An innocent man guillotined for a corpse we haven't the wits to account for. Somerton will be the death of him, and with our cooperation. I can't shake off the feeling that someone's pulling our strings, playing the tune we're dancing to. And that puts my back up! The pathologist, Dr. Moulin, had some interesting observations to pass on. He's formed theories which support Francine Raissac's strange ideas."

He took the small box from his pocket and revealed the contents. "Exhibit B. He passed this on too. And listen, will you, to the story the doctor had to tell."

Bonnefoye listened, wholly involved in the story, turning the gold amulet between his fingers, his face showing fascination and revulsion at the ugliness of the features of the god. Finally: "The God of Evil, you say? Brother of the good god, Osiris? And his murderer?"

"Yes. Set was worshipped throughout Egypt for many centuries. But as a god of goodness. He and Osiris were peas in a pod. But then, apparently, he turned to wickedness and was struck off everyone's calling list. His subsequent career plumbed the depths of iniquity, you might say. A recognisable myth—in many cultures you find a reference to the evil obverse of a coin. Cain and Abel...And take Lucifer—after all, the name means 'Bringer of Light.' He started off on the side of the angels. *Was* one of the angels."

Bonnefoye picked up the crime novel and began to riffle through its pages. "Have you seen it yet? The link between your book and your amulet?"

Joe shook his head.

"Good stories, these! The theme still fires the imagination, you see? Down the centuries and right through into the twentieth."

Joe didn't quite see.

"The evil Fantômas is pursued in each story by a police inspector from my own outfit, the Brigade Criminelle, no less. Inspector Juve, the good guy! And no prizes for guessing Juve's secret identity. He's the long-lost twin brother of Fantômas."

"Juve and Fantômas, Osiris and Set?"

"Two minutes, boys! Heavens! Is this how you waste your time? The Série Noire? Don't you have enough real-life crime to occupy your time? And who's your ugly friend? Not sure I want *him* in my drawing room."

"He's the man we're looking for, Maman, and who's looking for us! Let me introduce you—he's the God of Evil. And our nameless killer, I think, now has—according to Joe—an identity. Let's call him Set, shall we?"

Madame Bonnefoye considered for a moment and then said soberly: "Well, if Set comes calling, he'll run into some fire-power! Your Lebel, Jean-Philippe, the pistol I see the commander has on his right hip, the Luger Sir George has tucked in his upper left-hand inside pocket and my soup ladle. Come to table now!"

After a long and delicious meal, Jean-Philippe's mother herded the men back into the salon with coffee and brandy, closed the door on them and began to clatter her way through the clearing up.

Sir George put on an instant show of affability and frank cooperation. "Now—I'm sure you chaps must have a question or two of your own to…" He was expansive, he was slightly wondering why they had held off for so long from questioning him. He knew he was cornered.

"Indeed we do, George, and this time you're not ducking them," said Joe firmly. "People's lives—including, I do believe, your own—depend on your answers. So you must stop

all this bluffing and circumlocution and come clean. I will know if you're lying. Now, I have a list of questions to put to you."

Sir George nodded.

Joe decided to catch him off balance by launching an easy throw but from an unexpected quarter. Start them on the easy questions; establish a rhythm of truthful responses and the slight hesitation before a lie is told will be picked up by a keen ear.

"John Pollock?" he said. "Or Jack Pollock—whichever you prefer. Tell us about him."

"Cousin Jack? Oh, very well. Son of my father's very much younger sister, my aunt Jane, who married a man called Pollock. Only son: John Eugene. He was never a friend, you understand. Twenty-year age gap. Looks on me more as an uncle. Little Jackie! A delightful child! Clever boy and with the Jardine good looks! He must be in his mid-thirties by now. He's working in Paris, as you remember from Fourier's notes. He was keen on a diplomatic career when he came out of the army and I was able to put his name in front of someone who was, in turn, able to give him a leg up. Find him a niche, you might say. And they haven't regretted it. Doing well, by all accounts. Haven't seen him since a year or two after the war ended. 1921? Possibly. I remember he wasn't looking too sharp then—recuperating in London. But he had a good war. Quite the hero, in his way."

"Your cousin sends his regards and promises he'll be in touch."

"Good. Good. I look forward to that."

"I'm afraid we'll have to tell him any meeting between the two of you will have to be put on hold. Officially you're in the custody of the Police Judiciaire in a lock-up somewhere on the island. No one but the three of us knows you're here and that's how it must remain until we've cleared you."

"Very well. Sensible precaution. He'll be the first to understand and approve. Very security-minded, naturally. Next?"

"Now, sir." Joe gathered his thoughts. The next bit was not so straightforward. "I'm hoping you feel able to supply us with the name of someone who witnessed your appearance at the theatre and can vouch for the fact that you were in your place across the width of the hall when the murder occurred—assuming it to have happened during the finale?"

"Yes, I do. Been thinking about it. Racking the old brain, you know. And the name's come back to me: Wilberforce Jennings."

"Who?" Joe was startled. This was not what he was expecting. He'd been leading George to expand on the information he had slid into—or allowed to escape into—the conversation in Fourier's office. Joe's mind was running on a beautiful and unscrupulous woman with a penchant for Campari-soda. And murder and blackmail and extortion and deceit. But here was Wilberforce Jennings stealing the spotlight.

"Old school chum. 'Willie,' we called him. I was surprised to see him. You know how you gaze around the audience to see if there's anyone you know—well, there was. Jennings. The most frightful little creep, I remember, and I may have completely misidentified him, but he was in the sixth row of the stalls, at the end of the row. No idea whether he recognised me. You could always ask, I suppose. If you can find him. He may have allowed his gaze to rest on me in the concluding moments."

"When he could be looking at la belle Josephine and a hundred chorus girls wearing not so much as a bangle between them? Worth a try, I suppose. You never know your luck," said Joe doubtfully. "Can you oblige, Bonnefoye?"

"Easy. We have access to records of every foreigner using

accommodation in the city. There are about six hotels the English prefer to use. We'll try them first."

"And now, George, we've got you in your box... The chairs—pulled into a companionable huddle... the tray of convivial drinks served and consumed. Tell us about your mystery guest. Who was she? Why are you twisting about in an effort to keep her identity from Fourier?"

Irritated by George's dogged silence, he tried a full assault. "Alice Conyers paid you a visit, did she? Yes, I knew she'd survived. Though I had no idea she was in France."

"It's hard to imagine, eh, Joe? You're expecting your cousin and there bobs up at your elbow a girl you thought had died in terrible circumstances five years ago. I was never more surprised! She seemed well and happy and sent you her fond regards."

"She has good reason to remember me with fondness," said Joe bitterly. "But why did she show herself to *you*? I always thought the two of you were pretty thick but... all the same..." Too late he heard the tetchiness amounting to jealousy in his voice. "A risky manoeuvre on her part, I'd have thought," he said more firmly. "You could have arrested her!"

"I did. She escaped." George was breezily defiant.

Joe snorted in exasperation. "Sir, are you saying you had the woman in your grasp and you let her loose?"

"That's about it. Yes. And, Joe, that's exactly where I want her—on the loose. At liberty, to go where she pleases."

Into the astonished silence he set about his explanation. With rather less than his usual confidence, he spoke: "I've resigned my position, you know. I'm free for the first time in my life of duty, protocol, intrigue, politicking of any kind. I'm not so old I can't enjoy the rest of my life. Got all my faculties and bags of energy. Knees not wonderful but I hear they can do amazing things in Switzerland with knees.

Funnily enough, at the very moment when *you* might say my life was hanging by a thread, I've realised the value of it. It came to me on the bank of the Seine this morning. I'm going to make good use of whatever years are left to me and I'm not starting on them by taking the life or liberty of another. Especially not a woman like Alice, whom you rightly surmise I have always held in esteem and affection."

The expression in the blue eyes he turned on Joe was, for once, not distorted by guile, amusement or cynicism. The eyes were direct and piercing and Joe found it hard to meet them. How could he accuse George of negligence in letting Alice Conyers go free when he'd done exactly the same thing himself five years before?

"And last, before you fall asleep, my boy, you'll be wanting to hear about the rascal Somerton. Do try to concentrate. You really ought to know what it was he did to make a mighty number of people want to stick a dagger in him. Including yours truly!"

Chapter 15

George took a fortifying swig of his brandy and lapsed into thought.

"Look here, chaps," he said finally, "I know you're both men of the world and violence is your stock in trade, so to speak, but what I have to tell you is shocking and offensive. In the extreme. You must be prepared. It may be that, when you understand the kind of man he was, you'll be less eager to pursue his killer. A plague-infested rat...a striking cobra...Somerton...the world would always be well rid of them.

"He was commanding officer of a military station in the north of India. Before the war. Known to me—we'd met briefly during a tour on the frontier and I'd formed a dislike for the fellow then. The affair I'm about to mention was hushed up to avoid bringing disgrace on the British Army at the time so—if you'll excuse me—I'll respect that and give you no names, no pack drill.

"You'll know, Joe, that when outfits turn rotten, you al-

ways find the cause of it is the commanding officer. And
Somerton's was a rotten outfit. Oh, outwardly crisp—their
drill and appearance could never be faulted. Indeed, in the
way of such men, he was a stickler for detail, regimentation.
So, the fact that he was running a brutish, bullying crew
moulded by him in his own image, was likely to be overlooked. They were never seriously tested militarily—I'm
speaking of the period before the war when there was always
the danger of units turning soft through inactivity and
boredom—so I can't speak for their fighting qualities. After
the event, the whole corps was broken up and dispersed. I
presume they went to France and many must have perished
on the battlefields, along with the rest of the army of the
day. I'm probably the only man left alive who would be willing to tell the tale, but there must be many more who remember and will always stay silent.

"There was a native village on the outskirts of the station…usual arrangement. Many of the local men undertook
work for the army. One day the rubbish collectors, going
about their business, found a body on the rubbish tip. It was
the corpse of a young girl from their village. They all recognised her. She was the daughter of the dhobi—the laundry-
man." Sir George was uneasy with his story, his delivery flat
and deliberately uninvolving. "They thought at first she'd
been torn apart by jackals. The station doctor was summoned.
Fast turnover of doctors in that unit. They never stayed long
before asking for a transfer, and this one was newly arrived. He
involved himself before consulting the commanding officer.
Had the body brought in for examination.

"The girl had been the victim of multiple assaults. Of a
sexual nature. She'd been raped. Many times. Also beaten
and cut with a dagger and, finally, strangled. She was twelve
years old." George's head drooped and he seemed unable to
carry on.

Joe and Bonnefoye could find no words to encourage him.

"Somerton tried to cover it all up. No need of a report for such a matter. Who was lodging a complaint? The father? Pay him off! A few rupees would close his mouth. But the medical officer was made of stern enough stuff to stand up to him. He sent in a full report to Somerton's superior officer and he sent a copy to me."

"Was a proper investigation conducted?" asked Joe.

"I insisted on it. I put my best men in to get to the bottom of it and when I heard what they'd discovered I took steps. They found that the girl had been sent—against her will and against custom—into the camp to deliver items of laundry urgently needed by the C.O. Women never ventured near the place as a rule—the men had a reputation for savagery of one sort or another. The poor child must have been terrified to be given the errand, but girls in that country obey their fathers. She'd delivered it to Somerton's quarters. She'd been seen going inside and coming out again. This was the story my men picked up from every witness. A word-perfect performance, they judged. Too perfect. Rehearsed. They went to work and after some days finally found sitting before them at interview a young chap fresh out from England and as yet untrained in the ways of that regiment. He spilled the beans.

"Put his own life in danger, of course, by his assertions, and we had to take him away directly to a place of safety and hold him in reserve for the trial. He stated that the girl had indeed come out of the C.O.'s quarters, but thrown out screaming and bleeding and in great distress—by Somerton himself. Some of his men had gathered round on hearing the din and our recruit had been horrified to hear his instructions: 'She's all yours, lads, if you can be bothered!'

"Our chap ran away and hid and no one was aware that

he'd seen anything, but he was able to give a full list of those involved. We had the names and rolled it up from there. The men had bragged about it to each other openly afterwards. They never knew exactly who had shopped them. It wasn't difficult to get a confession from most of them."

"And you left him alive, George?" said Joe quietly.

"A court martial was held and he was found guilty. Kicked out of the army with every ounce of parade and scorn they could muster. A pariah for the rest of his days. I thought that was punishment enough. At the time. I wish now I'd had the bugger shot. I could have arranged it."

"Why did you hold off?" Bonnefoye wanted to know.

"The fellow had a wife and young son back home. And, on the whole, a cashiering makes less of a splash than an execution." He sighed. "Discretion, always discretion."

Suddenly angry, he burst out: "And now see where discretion and pity have landed me! In danger of losing my head because the silly bugger's got his comeuppance! And *I* didn't even have the satisfaction of plunging a dagger into his snake's heart! It's a thankless task you two fellows have got on your hands. If you find out who ordered up this assassination, I shall have to ask you to congratulate him before you slip the cuffs on."

"He *didn't* kill Somerton, did he?" Bonnefoye commented when Sir George, finally exhausted, had excused himself and gone off to his room.

"What makes you change your mind?"

"At the end, when he lost his temper and spoke without restraint...I believed him when he said he would have plunged the dagger into the man's heart. He would have done just that. Quick and soldierly. He'd quite forgotten for the moment that Somerton had died from a gash from ear

to ear. I can't see Sir George sawing away like a pork butcher to bleed a man to death, can you?"

"No, I can't. But I'll tell you what, Bonnefoye—the wretched man's gone off to bed leaving us with a mass of things to do tomorrow. I say, will you ...?"

"Yes. I've arranged for a deputy to take my place and bring me notes of the conference afterwards. I'll be of far better use to international crime-fighting if I pursue this case actively. We'll allocate tasks in the morning ... Though I leave the Embassy to you—I think you have the entrée!"

"And, speaking of entrées—your evening, Bonnefoye. How did you get on in the Boulevard du Montparnasse?"

"Ah, yes! Mount Parnassus, home of Apollo and the Muses! Well, there was music and verse, certainly, but it wasn't at all classical. The address Francine Raissac gave you turned out to be a jazz café. And, you know, Joe, I'd have gone in there anyway! The music I heard as I was passing was irresistible. The performers were a mixture of black and white. There was a guitar, but a guitar played very fast, a violin and a clarinet and something else I can't remember ... a saxophone? Odd assortment of instruments—you'd swear they only just met and put it together. But brilliant! And the crowd was loving it."

"Did it have a name, your café?" asked Joe, intrigued.

"Oh, Lord! Some animal ... They're all called after birds or animals, have you noticed? Le Perroquet ... Le Boeuf sur le Toit ... L'Hirondelle ... Le Lapin Agile ... And here's another one—Le Lapin Blanc—that was it. It's a bit further out than the Dôme and not as far as the Closerie des Lilas."

"What sort of people were in the crowd? Did you know any of them?"

"No one on our books, if that's what you mean. Upright citizens, I'd say. Large number of Americans—you'd expect it in that part of Paris. Poets, painters, photographers and

their models and muses all packing the place out. Sixth arrondissement bohemian, to use an old-fashioned word! But
living up to it—you know, a bit self-conscious and not the
real thing. Every client looking over his shoulder spotting
the latest outrageous artist. And every outrageous artist
looking over *his* shoulder spotting the *mouchards* from the
police anti-national department. Who's likely to be snitch-
ing on *them*? The local commissariat is still on the alert for
extreme views of one sort or another. Marxism, Fascism, in-
tellectualism. Dadaism. Is that a word? They especially don't
like that! We're supposed to be on the watch for it. Not sure
what we're expected to do with it if we find it..."

"Anyone spot you?"

"No, indeed! I thought I blended in rather well. And no
one was making inflammatory statements. The clientele
weren't annoying anyone when I was there. Usual mixture of
thrill-seekers and thrill-providers. Well-heeled but quirky.
Silk scarves rather than ties, two-tone shoes, little black
dresses and cocktail hats—you'd have felt very much at
home, Joe."

"I'd never wear a cocktail hat to a café," muttered Joe.

"Unless you were going on somewhere. No... the seediest
customers were a couple of gigolos... nothing too flamboyant... and a pair of politicians. The rest were businessmen,
rich tourists and poseurs, I'd say. It's obviously the place to
be seen this month."

"Nothing unusual? No dope? No under the counter absinthe?"

"None that I noticed, and I notice more than most. The
only odd thing, and it didn't occur to me until I was on the
point of leaving, was that two of the men had gone off
into the back quarters, separately, and neither had come
out again. I followed the second of them after a discreet
interval. Cloakrooms, as you'd expect. The gentlemen's

accommodation was impressive—as good as a top hotel—
and I'd assume the ladies' was of equal comfort. Nothing
untoward going on. The man I was pursuing was not in the
room. He'd disappeared. Alongside the cloakrooms was a
carpeted staircase."

"You didn't resist?"

"Whistling casually, I followed on up to a landing. A table
with a lavish display of flowers and three closed doors. No
numbers. They each had a—fanlight?—a pane of glass over
the top. Well, I judge the management have some sort of
mirror system in place because the middle door opened at
once, before I'd even knocked, and a maître d'hôtel type appeared. Large, ugly, unwelcoming but exquisitely polite.
Well trained. He sent me straight back downstairs. I was
trespassing on private property, apparently."

"Some sort of house of ill-repute, are you thinking? A
house of assignation?"

"Yes. Something in the nature of the Sphinx, which is
close by—just off the boulevard by the cemetery. There's a
call for it. Tourists seeking thrills and well able to pay over
the odds for their indulgence. And citizens come over from
the affluent Right Bank into the Latin Quarter in search of a
slight frisson of danger, a whiff of spice, but not the out and
out dissolution on offer round every corner in Montmartre.
Another attraction is that the *maisons d'illusion* of this type
guarantee anonymity. From a perfectly innocent meeting
place, thronged with people—like the jazz club—clients present themselves, are checked and gain entrance through an
antechamber. They leave through a different door. All very
discreet. You could run into your brother-in-law who's an
archdeacon and you needn't blush for your presence there.
You'd be just another fan of that wonderful saxophonist."

"This Sphinx you mentioned...?"

"...is generally reckoned the top of the tree. It's reputed

for the calibre of its girls. They started with fifteen and now have about fifty. Beautiful, of course, but also well-educated and charming—good conversationalists. Many of them—or so it's said—have aristocratic pretensions: Russian princesses, Roumanian countesses, English nannies."

"Top drawer stuff!"

"And it's fresh and modern. Forget the red plush decadence of the Chabanais and the One-Two-Two! The Sphinx is avant-garde, art deco... Good Lord! It's even air-conditioned! It's the sort of place where responsible fathers take their sons for their first serious experience with the fair sex."

"And our nameless establishment over the White Rabbit jazz club may have set up as a rival?"

"Perfectly possible. There's an increasing demand. Every luxury liner disgorges thousands of eager sensation-seekers. Restaurants, theatre, night spots—they've never been so busy. And of course the brothels are going to cash in too. The Corsicans who used to run this side of life have suddenly lost authority and the market's ripe for the taking. The North Africans are moving in but there's a strong challenge from the lads of the thirteenth arrondissement. They're flexing their muscles, getting Grandpa's zarin down from the attic and are ready for the fight." Bonnefoye became suddenly serious as he added: "But more than knives. Some of them have guns they didn't turn in after the war ended. And the men themselves... they're not untried lads. They survived the war. They're trained killers. Killers who perhaps got used to the excitement of war and miss it?"

"But if the guard dog was told not to admit a clean-cut and clearly solvent chap like yourself—well, that's a bit strange, isn't it? I'd have expected them to have dragged you in the moment you stuck your head over the parapet."

"Yes. I was quite miffed! I went back down into the bar and got myself a drink. Found myself next to the two I'd

marked down as politicians—I vaguely recognised one and, since they were talking about government grants on animal fodder in Normandy, I think I got that right. I'd parked myself next to the two most boring men in the room! I knocked back my vermouth and was on the point of leaving when the conversation next to me started to break up. It's always worthwhile listening when goodbyes are being said. People say things with their guard down that perhaps they ought not to—and more loudly."

"Like—'Remember me to your brother and tell him to count on my help. The Revolution's next Tuesday, is it? I'll be there!'"

Bonnefoye grinned. "In fact, my man said, 'Remember me to your wife. Her soirée's next Saturday, isn't it? I'll be there!' It was the bit he added that was worth hearing. At least I *think* it was worth hearing. You must be the judge. He leaned over and in a hearty, all-chaps-together voice said: 'I'm just off to the land of wonders...interested? No?' And he walked out through the back door."

"Say it again—that last bit," said Joe uneasily. "The bit about wonders. Where did he say he was going?"

Bonnefoye repeated his words in French: "...*au pays des merveilles*..."

"*Au pays des merveilles*," murmured Joe. He was remembering a book he'd bought for Dorcas the previous summer to help her with her French reading. It hadn't been well received. "Gracious, Joe! This is for infants or for grown-ups who haven't managed to. It's sillier than Peter Pan. I can't be doing with it!" His mind was racing down a trail. He was seeing, illuminated by a beam of hot Indian sunshine, a book, fallen over sideways on a shelf in an office in Simla, the cover beginning to curl, a peacock's feather marking the place. The same edition. *Alice au pays des merveilles. Alice's Adventures in Wonderland.* Alice.

Surely not. He knew what Dorcas's judgement would have been if he'd confided his mad notion: "Sandilands in Fairyland."

The idea would not go away. Alice Conyers, fleeing India, Gladstone bag stuffed with ill-gotten gains of one sort or another, stopping over in Paris—might she have used her formidable resources to set herself up in a business of which she had first-hand knowledge? She might well. Bonnefoye waited in silence, sensing that Joe was struggling to rein in and order his thoughts.

"Tell you a story, Bonnefoye! At least Part One of a story. I think you may be about to make a bumbling entrance with me into Part Two. As the Knave of Hearts and the Executioner, perhaps?"

Bonnefoye was intrigued but scornful. "That's all very fascinating but it's as substantial as a spider's web, Joe!"

"But we'll only find out the strength by putting some weight on it, I suppose. Your face is known there now. My turn to shoot down the rabbit hole. It's my ugly mug that they'll see leering in their mirrors next time! And, if Madame's there, I think I know just the formula to persuade her to let me in. There's something I shall need...Two items. Didn't I see a ladies' hat shop down there in the Mouffe? Two doors north of the boulangerie? Good. What time do they open, do you suppose?"

Chapter 16

Harry Quantock was again performing front-of-house duties at the Embassy. He recognised Joe at once and greeted him breezily.

"Good morning, Commander! Good morning! We got your message and it's all laid on. Come along to the back quarters, will you? You don't merit a *salon rouge* reception to-day," he teased. "Much more workaday surroundings, I'm afraid. Jack Pollock's expecting you in his office. Being on the ambassador's staff, an attaché, if you like, at least he's housed in relative comfort."

Joe was shown into a ground-floor office at the rear of the building, looking out onto a courtyard garden. It was high-ceilinged, wood-panelled and stately. The walls were studded at intervals with sepia photographs of pre-war cricket teams. Joe noted the progression from public schoolboys to the undergraduates of an Oxford college whose first eleven was outstanding for its striped blazers, striped caps and ugly expressions. These were followed in the line-up by examples

of the University side. The only touch of modernity was a black and gold telephone sitting on a mahogany desk next to a silver vase of spring flowers. A tall window was open, letting in the scent of lilac blossom and the sound of traffic rumbling along the Champs-Élysées.

The attaché was seated behind his desk thumbing through a file, one eye on the door.

Joe was prepared for a family resemblance but, even so, he was taken aback by the young version of Sir George who leapt from his seat and bounded across the room to greet him with a cheerful bellow. Pollock's handshake was dry and vigorous, his welcome the equal of—and reminiscent of—that of any large yellow dog that Joe had ever met.

"You'll have a cup of coffee, or do you prefer tea, Commander? Tea? Harry—could you...? Let's sit down, shall we? I won't waste your time—busy man—I'll just say how sorry I am that you've been dragged into this mess, Sandilands. Lucky for us you were here on the spot, or in mid-flight to be precise, when all this burst over our heads. But—first things first—how are the Varsity doing?"

"Varsity? Doing?" For a moment, Joe was perplexed.

"The Surrey match," Pollock prompted. "First fixture of the season."

"Ah, yes. Last I heard, I rather think they were losing 3–1 at half-time."

The stunned silence lasted only a second. Pollock threw back his head and laughed. "Of course—Edinburgh man, aren't you? Like my old relative, George. And how you must be cursing him! He might have expected to get into some trouble or other by taking a box at the Folies—might even have been relishing the thought—but surely not trouble of this magnitude. Never heard the like! He has told you that the ticket didn't come from *me*, has he? Good! I wouldn't like it assumed that I was remotely responsible. Not my

style! But, I say, Sandilands—if I didn't send the fatal billet—
are we wondering who did? It must be someone, apart from
myself, who knew he was going to be in Paris and is aware of
our relationship. It could only be known through an ambas-
sadorial contact—here in Paris, in London or in Delhi, I suppose."

"You've just narrowed it down to a thousand people,"
said Joe. "Thank you!"

Jack Pollock grinned, leaned over the desk and added: "I
can narrow it more usefully to someone who knows that
there's no way in this world my cousin would have recognised my handwriting. I'd swear the last sample he had was
the gracious note I wrote in appreciation of the mechanical
tiger he sent me when I was at school!"

Pollock's eyes twinkled at the memory. He looked at Joe,
friendly but calculating. "Wonderful contraption! With a
bit of devilish skill, a dab or two of honey and lashings of
schoolboy callousness, I contrived to get my tiger to snap up
flies!"

"The Tipu Sultan of the Lower Third?"

"Exactly! I was allowed to demonstrate it on Sundays after tea. George had taken me to see the original life-sized
tiger at the Victoria and Albert—you know—the one Tipu
had made...His tiger was in the act of eating a British soldier. I'll never forget the roars and screams it emitted when
someone wound it up! And the way the victim's arm
twitched as the tiger held him in his jaws!"

Joe laughed. "George would know how to please. He has a
certain magic with children. I've watched it working."

"Pity the old feller has none of his own," said Pollock,
suddenly serious again. "What a waste of many things." He
snapped back into the conversation he had himself interrupted. "But the note—I have no reason to suppose he'd

recognise my scrawl. We were never frequent—or even regular—correspondents. Distance and the exigencies of the war rather put paid to intimacy of that kind. And the transition from uncle-nephew to equal adult cousins has never had a chance to take place. Not sure how it will all pan out . . . we'll just have to wait and see."

Joe listened to the outpouring of eager speculation and confidences, smiling and agreeing.

"Now, tell me—what have you done with him? I'm assuming you've put the boot in imperially and sprung him from whatever hell-hole they'd banged him up in?" The question was put abstractedly, Pollock's attention on the tray of tea a manservant carried in. "Just set it down over there, will you, Foxton? Milk or lemon, Sandilands?"

"Milk, please."

Returning to the first question he'd been asked: "I'm afraid not," said Joe carefully. "Still incarcerated, I'm sorry to say. Reasonably comfortable, I insisted on that, but still in a lock-up on the island. The authorities appear to be unimpressed by Sir George's standing. I shall have another try later today. It may come down—or rather up—to a personal representation from the ambassador himself."

Pollock was angry. Whoever said that blue eyes could only be cool should see Pollock's at this moment, Joe thought. They blazed. "What impertinence! Poor old George! He must be let out before the end of the day. Ring in and reassure me he is comfortably settled back in his hotel—where's he staying? The Bristol? Of course. Well, the moment he gets there I'll go and see him. And you, Sandilands—where are you staying?"

"I'm at the Hotel Ambassador on the Boulevard Haussman."

Pollock made a note.

"And all went well with the widow yesterday? Thank you for undertaking that unpleasant task!"

"Unpleasant perhaps, but not the harrowing experience it most often is. The lady seemed not particularly grieved to find her husband dead." Joe wondered how far he could pursue this line but the slight nod of agreement he received from Pollock encouraged him. "In fact she emerged from the identification scene a changed woman, I'd say. Reassured. Confident. Feeling a certain amount of release, no doubt? She was looking forward to an evening's assignation at Fouquet's with a companion whose identity is as yet unknown to us." He caught the echo of deadly police phrasing and added: "Give a lot to know who the lucky chap was!"

"Oh, I think I can help you with that!" said Pollock, enjoying the intrigue. "Doubtless the gentleman she sat next to on the plane—her travelling companion. Her constant companion for the past year, I understand. A Major Slingsby-Thwaite." Pollock lowered his voice though there was no risk of his being overheard. "Between you and me—bit of an adventurer! But then . . . perhaps that's exactly what the lady's after—a bit of an adventure—after all those bleak years of being married to a murderous swine. I take it my cousin has filled you in on the activities of the unlamented Somerton?"

"I've had a pungent account of the case. And agree with Sir George—the man got no less than he deserved. But you seem to be very well informed as to his movements, Pollock? Why does His Britannic Majesty's Government take such an interest in an ex-this, a disgraced-that? A wandering has-been?"

"Current nuisance! For many a year. We've always kept tabs on him, watched his movements around Europe. Passed him on to the next chap with a sigh of relief. The man made many enemies—he was always likely to be a target

for revenge or embarrassing mayhem of one sort or another. And a thorough cashiering, though well-deserved, doesn't, in my experience, turn a villain into a saint overnight. 'Off with his buttons!' is in no way as effective as 'Off with his head!'"

Pollock frowned for a moment and looked at Joe with speculation. "You may not approve, of course. But I see you are a military man. You must agree with Richard the Third when he was having his problems with...now, who was it...?"

"Lord Hastings, it was, who provoked that famous order for execution, I believe," said Joe, coming to his rescue. "In Shakespeare's play."

"Quite right! Someone ought to have advised Sir George similarly at the time— 'Off with his head!' Overtly or covertly if necessary. Either method easily available in that locale, you understand. No questions asked. Death closes all. George slipped up there. When they're given the sack, some of these villains take the honourable way out of their situation—the revolver and the brandy on the terrace after a good dinner, a friend's steady hand on the elbow—but the ones who go on fighting the judgement—you need to keep an eye on *them*. Trained soldiers, used to command, wily and unscrupulous—can cause havoc if they take it badly! Even in death, the wretch Somerton's causing problems. And it all happened on my watch! I'd have thought he was harmless enough boxed up at the Folies. Glad he's gone!"

"As perhaps may be his son? I understand that Somerton was a baronet? So, the title is a hereditary one and will pass— has already passed—down to his only son."

"Yes. The world now has Sir Frederick Somerton to reckon with. An effortless way of acquiring a degree of nobility. Though a tarnished title. And one some might not be eager to parade. I'll look into all this. The contents

of the will, if the man left one, are not yet known. I'll inform you if anything interesting comes up. Are you thinking that the young man got fed up with waiting for his absent reprobate father to drop off the twig? Young Frederick can't have been easy, aware that the old man was roving about Europe, spending the family fortune. I understand this to have been quite sizeable at one time. Perhaps he decided to hurry things along a bit? Makes sense to me. He'll have an uphill task, trying to burnish up the family name again, though. Old Somerton left quite a stink behind him!"

Intrigued by the nuances of speech and the unusual ideas they hinted at, Joe felt himself steered into asking with more familiarity than he would normally have assumed: "How are you placed, Pollock—dynastically speaking?"

He seemed ready enough to reply. "I'm not impressed by dynasties, successions, and all that family rubbish. I suppose I take that attitude from my father. My mother—oh, it's well known—married beneath her, as they say, and my father brought me up to be very dismissive of all that inheritance nonsense. I went to a Good School where the other boys merely confirmed me in my prejudices. On the whole, the grander the nastier, I concluded. But—the system seduces us all, I suppose you'd say. Did I refuse my cousin's offer of a recommendation to the right person? No. And I have to confess, Sandilands, that..." Again he lowered his voice, taking Joe into his confidence, slightly embarrassed at what he was about to reveal. "...there's a chance...a good chance...that there'll be an honour in the offing for me before very long. Knee on the velvet cushion, sword on the shoulder, 'Arise, Sir John' stuff! And, do you know—I shan't feel inclined to turn it down. I'll have earned it. It will be my own achievement and will owe nothing to a scheming old

ancestor having pleased some capricious monarch in the dim and distant."

"So, if we were making a book on the runners and riders in the Somerton slaying, we'd be giving short odds on the new baronet?"

"I'd certainly leave him on the list until we have more information. And his mother. At slightly longer odds, of course. Any more suspicions?"

"Vague ones. Tell me, Pollock—there's been a suggestion that the whole thing was staged deliberately to be witnessed by Sir George ... or for the delectation of someone else in the audience. What's your opinion on that?"

Pollock frowned. "A bit far-fetched but not out of the question, I suppose," he replied cagily.

"I wonder if it had occurred to you that there might be a similarity with another crime scene you were dragged into some four years ago? I only mention this because the officiating pathologist at both crimes turns out to be one and the same—efficient fellow called Moulin."

Pollock's face livened at the name. "I remember. Yes, indeed. Good man! Effective and businesslike. And the scene was in the Louvre, of all places! Good God, is it really four years? To me it's as clear as if it happened yesterday. Did he fill you in ... ?"

"Yes, he gave me the details of the discovery of the body, the means of killing, the identity of the corpse and so on. But the most interesting thing he had to say was that, in common with that of Somerton, the murder was undertaken as a form of display to an invited audience of Egyptologists and academics, all who had reason to hate the man. Did you have the same feeling, I wonder?"

"Certainly did! The whole event was—well, just that!—an event. Apart from the representatives of law and order,

there were three of us non-combatants, so to speak, caught up in the sorry scene. A very nice couple of Americans who raised the alarm when they caught sight of the blood pool under the coffin box—and me."

"What on earth were you doing in the Louvre? Did anyone orchestrate *your* movements on that day?"

"Do you know—that thought never occurred to me! No ... I'd say it was impossible. I was newly at the Embassy. Relatively low ranking, of no significance in this context. Has George told you how I spent the war years? No? Well, knowing something of Egypt, and speaking a few languages, I was posted into Intelligence there. I picked up first-hand experience of the tricky political situation in the country. Powder keg! Wanting its independence from Britain, France, Italy, Turkey and every other piratical nation that thought it had a claim on its archaeological resources, to say nothing of its strategic and geographical advantages. After demob, which came at very long last—always one more dispute to preside over—it was thought I could use the skills I'd acquired on the ground here in Paris.

"I owe my present position to George—were you aware of this? When I got here I found that the war was still being fought out amongst the archaeological cliques! And that's what I was doing at the museum that day. On neutral territory, away from embassies, we were having a meeting, trying to reach an agreement between four nations growling like dogs over a bone. Well, several thousand bones, as it happened. A whole newly discovered burial chamber. And the digging rights were in dispute. Not as straightforward as you might expect—many borders were still being negotiated in those days after the war.

"We'd come to something approaching a position all could accept and were gratefully on our way home when we were accosted by a frightfully concerned American who

thought he'd discovered someone bleeding to death in a coffin case. Well, I assume the doctor who arrived shortly after that has filled you in?"

He paused, marshalling his thoughts. "Moulin did not mislead you. I agree with him. There was something very strange going on. I was so occupied with keeping the peace I was perhaps a bit slow to catch on. It wasn't until later at police headquarters ... The Americans—the Whites—fled. The wife was feeling ill. Got clean away. But their consciences overcame them afterwards and they duly reported to the police, who set up the interview and took their statement. Mr. White asked particularly if I could be present to help with the language. A sensible arrangement and a task I was pleased to carry out. Very nice people, as I said. He was an army sergeant who'd been decorated for bravery on the Marne, I believe. I've never understood why they call those Yanks 'doughboys,' have you? Most unfortunate. Conjures up images of puffy-faced, spotty youths, soft to the touch. This man was as hard as a well-seasoned oak beam. And smart. We talked later, off the record, so to speak, and he put his ideas to me. I had to agree with him. He'd seen more than I had and made better sense of it. And his wife's insights were even more acute!

"Sandilands, the audience were there by invitation, I'd swear it. Someone had arranged the whole thing. A ringmaster of sorts. Set the scene, knowing it would go down well. A much-hated man had got his just deserts."

"Would it be too fanciful, do you think, to assume that this, um, ringmaster had gone on cracking his whip? Organising spectacles of this kind? Perhaps this wasn't the first? Perhaps it wasn't the last?" Joe suggested tentatively, as though the idea had just occurred to him. He spoke with the diffidence of one putting such a ridiculous suspicion into words.

Pollock was astonished. Then he smiled. "You didn't know? Well, how could you be expected to know? Just nipped over the Channel for a few days...no access to records...Oh, I do beg your pardon! How rude of me! It's just that...you've shown such insight...delved so deep in no time at all—the temptation is to assume Scotland Yard is omniscient. It takes a diplomat with fingers in many pies, a nosy bugger like me, someone with months to reflect on it, to get the full picture."

Joe's easy smile showed that he was not at all put out by Pollock's frankness.

"The murderer was indeed in the room. Enjoying his little show. When I thought about it, I was only surprised he didn't take a bow or lead the applause."

Pollock became suddenly serious and Joe caught sight of the tenacity and moral muscle that lay beneath the insouciant surface. "There were several nationalities involved, you understand, Sandilands. At least three Englishmen present and participating. There were men I had had dealings with in the past and with whom I could expect to deal in the future, men whose hospitality I would be accepting, men on whose goodwill I would have to count. But I hadn't been so long in the business that I no longer cared whether the hand I was shaking had blood on it. I made a few enquiries, put two and two together and came up, I believe, with the right answer."

"You have his identity?" Joe tried to keep his voice level.

"Certainly have! And the excellent Maybelle White confirmed my suspicions!"

Chapter 17

Joe waited, allowing him to savour his moment of intrigue.

"The murderer wasn't concealing himself or his motive with very great care. What a show-off! I expect *you*, sharp fellow that you are, would have been waiting by the door to finger his collar."

The ball had been patted back into his court and Joe wondered whether he was being tested in some mildly playful way. Readying himself to provide an entertaining belly-flop, he slipped a hand into his trouser pocket and checked that what he was seeking was there. He remembered the details of Dr. Moulin's story and plunged in. "It was, of course, the jocular prestidigitator who pulled the gold amulet of the god Set out of his victim's mouth! Rather in this manner..."

Joe flourished the trinket he'd palmed, holding it between finger and thumb, enjoying Pollock's astonishment. This was followed swiftly by a burst of laughter.

"You've got him! Good Lord! I never would have expected to see that piece of nonsense again! Wherever did you come by it? And the murderer produced it that day in front of that learned crowd, just as you've demonstrated! Probably with a wink for his admirers, but I'll never know—he had his back to me at the time. And, like everyone in the room with the exception of Harland C. White, I was able to interpret the symbolism of the gesture: here was a man who was opening his mouth one last time to Spew Out Evil. Mrs. White had a good deal of interesting remarks to make about the Egyptian burial rite of 'The Opening of the Mouth' but we decided that line of thought might be a little over-adventurous."

"And what's become of your ringmaster?" Joe asked. "Your entrepreneur of crime? Is he still flourishing? I should very much like to talk to him. Is he still here in Paris?"

"In a manner of speaking, yes, he is! He's in Père Lachaise. The cemetery. Committed suicide last year. Down in the south somewhere . . . Cannes, that's it. Left a full confession. More tea, Sandilands?"

Joe accepted a fresh cup using the mechanical gestures to disguise his surprise and disappointment.

"The murder in the Louvre wasn't the only thing he had on his conscience." Pollock shook his head, in distaste. "A really terrible man! Almost the equal of the man he'd had done away with. Two of a kind! But then, the profession, which it now claims to be, has always attracted unscrupulous rogues of all nationalities. And all ranks of society. From Napoleon to the ten-year-old native tomb-robber."

After a carefully calculated interval, Joe put down his teacup and began to draw the interview to a close, thanking Jack Pollock for his help and interest: formulaic phrases cut short by Pollock's bluff response: "Think nothing of it, old

chap!" His warm hand reached again for Joe's and gripped it firmly. "If there's anything—the slightest thing—I can do, I'm your man. Keep me informed, won't you?"

At the door he paused. "French views of Law and Order not the same as ours, you know. Stay alert, Sandilands!

"And where have you decided to have luncheon today? May I recommend somewhere?" he asked as they crossed the hall on the way to the front door. "At your hotel? The Ambassador, I think you said? Excellent reputation for its cuisine! Good choice!"

So. Moulin and Francine Raissac—and he swiftly added himself to the list—had fallen victim to an over-coloured story, a lurid crime-novel notion of villainy. Relief and disappointment were flooding through Joe, fighting for control. Of course Pollock's theory was correct, and it was supported by a confession. The scene at the museum had to have been staged by a man with influence enough to clear rooms, to lure in the victim, to have him dispatched with all that chilling ceremony, to arrange for an independent witness to stumble on the body, and to have the insider's knowledge to invite just the right people to participate in the finding. No one but the Americans and Pollock was there by chance.

The whole presentation had been a work of art. A labour not of love but of hatred. And, with a final directorial twist, the case had been solved and brought to a conclusion by the perpetrator himself. Very proper. Inevitable. The death had occurred down south in Cannes and Moulin had not been aware or involved. "I've saved the best till last," the doctor had told him. And the best—the most astonishing—case in the series of unexplained crimes now proved to have been no

such thing. A one-off. Solved. Case closed with Père Lachaise finality. And, with that key element dislodged, the whole house of cards tumbled down.

Joe surrendered to relief. And yet he was left feeling foolish. He was still saddled with the problem of assigning responsibility for Somerton's killing and had wasted a precious day. But at least now he could concentrate on the motive he had originally thought most likely: vengeance. And he could probably discount the unlikely phone calls from the Somerton residence in England to an undisclosed agency in Paris: "The name's Somerton. You'll find him at the Crillon... Dagger would be most suitable... How much? You *are* joking, of course? Ah, well... I suppose it will be worth it..."

He could forget about Sir George's presence being an element in the planning. It was most likely that there had been no planning at all. Perhaps some Anglo-Indian, retired from the army, someone with a grudge against the man, had seen him lording it in a box at the Folies accompanied by an attractive young girl and this had been the trigger for a vengeful act of fury. It was the unconsidered flaunting of power and position that could incite lesser men to rage. Many men had come back from India with daggers in their possession. They might, with all the alarming stories of the revived apache gangs, have chosen to carry a knife from their collection instead of the more usual swordstick as a means of self-defence in this dangerous capital.

Joe wondered wearily if he could ask Bonnefoye to release names from the information he knew the French police kept on foreigners residing in the city, permanently or temporarily. Hours of patient checking would be called for and he was very far from certain that such a request would be taken seriously by the police authority. In any case, Fourier would

have lost patience long before results were available and re-arrested George.

But, looking on the bright side, Sir George was no longer to be considered the target of some mysterious Set or Fantômas figure, stalked through the streets of Paris by a scar-faced acolyte. And Joe could now return safely to his hotel without slinking along like a polecat. He badly needed to change his clothes. Toothbrushes and other essential items had been provided by the industrious and early-rising Madame Bonnefoye and he had spent a comfortable night in a pair of Jean-Philippe's pyjamas, but he wanted to touch base.

But what of Heather Watkins? Her encounter had been with a flesh and blood menace. Twice. Could the shadowing of Miss Watkins be explained by the girl's obvious attractions? Her vivid hair and fresh Celtic looks would always attract masculine attention, he thought. It had attracted *his*. He knew that many men on the lookout for just such loveliness haunted the foyers of even the best hotels. Perhaps she was being pursued by some theatrical impresario? To be recruited into the ranks of high-kicking chorus girls? She had exactly the right height and athletic appearance. And he didn't doubt that, like every other English girl he knew (always excepting Dorcas Joliffe, of course) she'd been to ballet classes. Bonnefoye had confessed that certain nameless limbs of the government actually kept lists of spectacular girls—attractive and good conversationalists—who might be summoned to escort visiting royalty or the like about the city. Joe wasn't quite sure he believed him. At the worst, she might be the target of the gangs of confidence tricksters who ran the "badger games" from hotel lobbies. Beautifully dressed, well-spoken and plausible, the female bandits they employed would lure men freshly arrived and looking

forward to adventures with a sob-story or an involving smile and in no time they'd have the gold out of their pockets—and their teeth.

He reined in his thoughts. Nonsense! There were more loose fragments of tinsel swirling about in this kaleidoscope than he could pull into focus at the moment and he was not going to lose track of a single element. The face of Francine Raissac had stayed with him. He remembered clearly her terror. Her warnings. He'd take her seriously and he'd listen to Pollock's parting words of advice and stay alert.

He performed his automatic checks for surveillance as he strolled along the rue du Faubourg St. Honoré, but with no sense of urgency. If anyone cared to follow him from the Embassy to his hotel, they were welcome to do so. He paused in front of the window display in one of the book-shops along the street, decided they probably didn't have what he was looking for and moved off. Finding what he wanted a few yards further on, he went in and spent a few minutes examining the stock before he made his choice.

The receptionist at the Hotel Ambassador greeted him and told him a telephone message had just arrived for him. Joe took the note. A brief one from Bonnefoye.

We have Wilberforce. Has agreed to meet Fourier at 11.30. Be there!

Joe telephoned to congratulate Bonnefoye on his speed of performance.

"Not difficult! He was at the third hotel on our list. Having breakfast. Confirms he was at the theatre that night

and says he'll be pleased to be of help. I'll see you both at Staircase A?"

Joe, freshly bathed, shirted and suited, met Bonnefoye at the entrance to police headquarters and waited with him for Jennings' taxi to drop him off. The man stepping out was easily identified by his English overcoat, bowler hat and rolled umbrella. Bonnefoye suppressed a snort of laughter at the image of propriety the man presented as Joe stepped forward to enquire: "Mr. Wilberforce Jennings, I presume? How do you do, sir. Commander Sandilands of Scotland Yard liaising with the Police Judiciaire. May I introduce my colleague, Inspector Bonnefoye?"

Jennings relaxed on hearing Joe's suave voice and shook hands with each man.

"This is to do with the killing at the theatre, night before last, eh? What? Not sure I can be of much help. I know people always say they saw nothing but, in this case, it's absolutely true! I saw nothing of the killing, that is!"

Joe allowed him to chatter on nervously as they crossed the courtyard. These forbidding surroundings would give anyone the jitters—even a man fortified by a bowler and a brolly. At the door to Staircase A, he turned to Jennings, reassurance in his voice. "Don't be alarmed, sir. Just a few questions to be put to you by the French chief inspector in charge of the case. He's obliged to cover all bases, you understand? Explore all avenues."

Jennings nodded vigorously to indicate he understood this calming drivel.

"Many people are being interviewed—one of them may have seen something he was not aware that he had seen. Just answer the questions carefully. I will be on hand to translate."

Chairs, Joe noted, had been provided in Fourier's office. The files and papers were aligned in rows. After introductions all round, he and Bonnefoye settled in a group with Jennings between them, facing Fourier and a sergeant who was taking notes at his elbow.

"I say! However did you know I was there? Clever of you to find me! I shall have to hope my wife is less vigilant than the French police, eh? What? I read about this sorry affair in the papers. Fellow Englishman knifed to death, they're saying. And that's the extent of my knowledge, I'm afraid. I've never met the dead fellow. I was in the stalls. Thought you might like to see my ticket stub."

Fourier looked carefully at the number on the ticket. He took a pencil and a sheet of paper and in a few quick strokes sketched out a floor plan of the theatre. He placed it on the desk in front of Jennings. "Can you confirm you were sitting where I have marked an X?"

"Yes. You've got it exactly!" said Jennings. "I say—you know your way about, Chief Inspector! A regular yourself at the Folies, are you then?"

Joe didn't attempt a translation.

"I now add two boxes," said Fourier, supplying them. "Take my pencil and mark in the box where you understand the murder to have taken place."

Jennings obliged.

"Well done! Quite correct! Box B." Fourier's attempt at bonhomie was unconvincing. "Now, tell us who and what you observed in that box."

Jennings' account was disappointing. He was quite obviously doing his best but his best was not pleasing Fourier. An unknown man (dark-haired), an unknown girl (fair-haired), had been noted before the lights went out and again when the lights came on again in the interval. Between and after those times—nothing of interest.

"Of course, had one only known, one would have…" Jennings burbled. "Tell you what, though! Why don't you ask the chap opposite? May I?" He took the pencil again and marked Box A. "Now, if you can find *me*, I'm jolly certain you can find *him*. He had a perfect view of the deceased. And he knew him," he announced.

"And I understand the witness in Box A was known to you also?" said Fourier with mild interest.

"I say! This is impressive! Yes, he is known to me. Only seen him once or twice since we were at school together—reunions and so on—but there's no mistaking that nose. Jardine. It was George Jardine. I'll bet my boots. Something important in India, I believe. Showing off as usual. In the Royal Box. But where else? Wouldn't find *him* rubbing shoulders with hoi polloi in the stalls."

"And you think he was acquainted with the man opposite?"

"Oh, yes. Undoubtedly. They were *talking* to each other."

Fourier stirred uneasily. "Across the width of the theatre, sir? Talking?" His strong witness was showing signs of cracking. He looked to Joe to correct his interpretation but Joe shook his head.

"'Communicating,' I ought perhaps to have said. Exchanging messages. Just the sort of showy-off Boy Scout stuff Jardine would have indulged in. He always enjoyed an audience, you know. Incapable of fastening his shoelaces without turning round to acknowledge the plaudits of the crowd."

Joe summarised this and added, "Fourier, may I?"

Fourier spread his hands, amused to delegate.

"Would you mind, Jennings, demonstrating the form this communication took?"

"Certainly. As the lights were being lowered…" Jennings got to his feet and went to stand, back to the wall, looking

down at an imagined audience. His face froze in a parody of George's lordly style. "He put on his white gloves..."

On went the gloves.

"And then he did this sort of tick-tack nonsense with his hands."

The hands flashed rhythmically, fingers stabbed, thumbs were extended.

"You'd have thought he was leading the Black and White Minstrels in the show at the end of the pier. People were beginning to think he was the first act."

"And did the man opposite take any notice? Did he reply?"

"Yes. Same sort of thing but a shorter response, and he wasn't wearing gloves so it wasn't so obvious. I thought, at that moment, it was a game. Yes, I was sure it was a game. He was laughing, joining in the fun."

"You *thought*?" asked Joe, picking up the tense.

"Yes. Changed my mind when I saw the *last* gesture, though!"

"Describe it," said Fourier.

"He did this," said Jennings.

Face twisted into a threatening mask, he gave a flourish of the hand and trailed the forefinger slowly across his throat.

No one spoke. The sergeant stopped writing. Fourier turned to him and advised: "Sergeant, why don't you put down— 'The suspect was observed at this point to make a life-threatening gesture announcing his intention of cutting the victim's throat.'"

The sergeant noted it down.

Jennings knew enough French to take alarm at the twist Fourier had put on his words. "Look here! That's a bit strong, don't you know! Sandilands, put him right! I wasn't implying that...Oh, good Lord! He wasn't in my House,

but I didn't come here to drop old Jardine in the quagmire…"

"Did you not?" drawled Joe. "Well, you've made a very
good fist of it. But before we ask you to check and sign your
statement, just tell us, will you—what was the reaction of the
second man playing this game? Did he appear alarmed? Did
he seem menaced by Jardine's gesture?"

"Well, no. Not at all. Most odd. He laughed. Damn near
slapped his thigh, he thought it was so funny."

When Jennings had been thanked and escorted from the
premises by the sergeant, Fourier turned to Joe and
Bonnefoye with a pitying smile. "The case firms up, it
seems," he said. "And unless you two are about to produce
some late entrant like a jack-in-the-box to surprise me…"
He left a pause long enough to annoy the younger men.
"No? Well, there is one more amusing little excursion I've
laid on for you."

He gestured to his sketch of the theatre layout. "Forget
the audience. What no one else seems to have observed is
that there were a hundred or so other potential witnesses
and all much closer to the scene of the murder at the moment of the murder. The cast! Lined up for the finale, their
eyes would have been on their audience. They say that Miss
Baker herself is always acutely aware of the reactions of the
crowd before her and responds to their mood. Dark, of
course, out there, I should imagine. Up to you to see how
much you can make out. How close the boxes are to the
stage. Which performer was standing underneath.

"I've arranged with the man in charge—Derval's his name,
Paul Derval—for you to be given an hour to scrounge
around before the matinée performance this afternoon. I
guaranteed you wouldn't get in anyone's way. He'll send

someone to open up for you if you present yourselves at the stage door. That's about it…Jardine behaving himself, is he?"

He started to collect up his papers. As they reached the door he said: "Oh, I fixed a ten-minute interview for you with Mademoiselle Baker. Thought you'd make a better impression on her than I would. She wants to help, apparently. Tender-hearted girl—keeps a menagerie of fluffy animals in her dressing room backstage, I'm told. She was upset to hear some admirer had bled to death while she was singing her heart out a few metres away. See what you can do.

"We may be getting closer to that headline," he added with a chuckle as they left.

Chapter 18

"Some time to kill before our two o'clock tryst in the avenue Montaigne." Joe emerged with relief into the sunshine. "The theatre's not all that far from my hotel... Why don't I take you to lunch there first—Pollock assures me the cuisine is excellent. And I think we've earned it! But first—a short walk. What *is* it about this place"—he stabbed a thumb backwards over his shoulder—"that makes me want to burst out and run ten miles in the fresh air?"

"Fourier?" grunted Bonnefoye. "Medieval architecture... medieval mind? Know what you mean, though. Which direction do you want to take? I'll gladly trot alongside."

"Let's cross over into the Tuileries, cut through the gardens and make for the Place Vendôme."

"Why would we want to do that?"

"Off the Place Vendôme, running north towards the Opéra, we'll find the rue de la Paix. Not a street I've frequented much. Wall to wall with *modistes*, I'm told."

He took Francine's scrap of blue fabric from his inside

pocket. "Well, you never know. This is from the House of Cresson, according to Mademoiselle Raissac. It's a lead we ought to follow up. It may take us to the beauty who showed a clean pair of heels before the show ended. Think of it as Cinderella's slipper, shall we?"

"Not *we*, Sandilands. They would be instantly suspicious of two men arriving with a strange enquiry." He looked at Joe, then tweaked the sample from his fingers. "I'll deal with this. You can loiter outside, window shopping. I suggest the jeweller's. That's safe enough. You're choosing a ring for your girlfriend."

It took a considerable amount of confidence to put on a routine such as Bonnefoye was demonstrating, Joe thought, in this smartest, most exclusive of streets. There *were* men to be seen entering the salons but they followed, dragging their heels, in the slipstream of their smartly dressed wives. Their role was clear: parked in a little gilt chair, they were required to smile and admire everything they were shown until, finally catching a nod and a wink from the *vendeuse*, they would come to a decision and pull out their wallets. The solo flight Bonnefoye was contemplating was daring. Professional, well-disciplined and having the sole aim of charming large sums of money from rich and fashionable women, the elegant assistants Joe caught glimpses of through the windows were truly daunting. They moved about with the easy arrogance of priestesses tending some vital flame.

Bonnefoye looked smart enough—he wore his good clothes well—but he would be entering hostile territory. He watched the young inspector's reflection in a shop window opposite the gold and black façade of Maison Cresson as he straightened his tie, tilted his straw boater to a less rakish angle and strolled inside, humming an air from *Così fan tutte*.

He was in there a very long time, Joe thought suspi-

ciously. He saw Bonnefoye emerge finally, scribbling on a page of his little black book. He slipped it away into his breast pocket. Joe sighed. An address had been added to his list. But whose?

"Another success, Inspector?" he asked. "How did you manage it?"

"Two successes!" Bonnefoye gave a parody of his best slanting Ronald Colman smile to indicate method. "But the one that concerns you, my friend, is the identification of the fabric. It wasn't easy. Sacrifices had to be made! There's a good café just around the corner. Why don't we walk on and have our second coffee of the day?"

They moved off out of the sight lines of the salon.

"A charming girl greeted me...Delphine...I told her I was desperate. I wished to buy something special for my mother—for her birthday. And the trouble with rich spoiled old ladies...I was quite certain Mademoiselle Delphine would understand...was that they had everything. I had noted (sensitive son that I am!) on a recent visit to the theatre that she had been very taken with a certain evening cape being worn by a blonde young lady. I produced the swatch at this point. A dear friend of mine—the comtesse de Beaufort—had advised me that such a garment might be found at the Maison Cresson."

"A moment, Bonnefoye...the countess? You've lost me! Who's this? Does she exist?"

"Of course. And I know the lady to be a devoted patron of this establishment—Cresson labels right down to her silk knickers! I arrested her husband two months ago for beating a manservant nearly to death. The countess was duly grateful for the brute's temporary removal from the family home. And the suggestion of intimacy with a valued customer impressed Delphine. She was very helpful. She

identified your scrap—though claims the stuff they use to be of better quality. Twice the weight and a richer dye, apparently. She remembered the garment for a very particular reason. They had designed and sold no fewer than four as a job lot, a highly unusual procedure, and all in the same size and fabric. The capes had been commissioned by a certain customer with whom they do a good deal of business. To reproduce a copy for my mother, it would be only polite to seek permission, of course."

"Understandable. The thought of *five* examples of a designer piece out and about in Paris would horrify your Delphine. Suppose the ladies all chose to wear it at the same occasion? The reputation of the House for exclusivity would be ruined! Have you noticed, Bonnefoye, that we men all try to look alike, toe the fashion line, cringe at the thought of looking different, but a woman would die rather than be seen in the same get-up as one of her friends?"

"Exactly! So why on earth would they want so many cloaks? Not kitting out a nunnery, do you suppose?"

Bonnefoye produced his book again and flipped it open. "Delphine was very happy to undertake the negotiations on my behalf. I'm certain she didn't take me for an haute couture pirate or anything of that nature but, all the same, the training prevailed. No address was forthcoming, I'm afraid." He grimaced. "And I even went to the length of ordering one of those things. There on the spot! I heard myself selecting twilight blue silk. Grosgrain. Lined with pigeon's-breast grey."

"Shantung?"

"Of course. Have you any idea of the cost? A month's pay! But I thought I ought to underline the urgency. Birthday next Thursday, I said. It seemed to work!"

"That—or the appeal in your spaniel's eyes, liquid with filial affection?" said Joe.

"We have a saying—*A good son makes a good husband.*

Perhaps that's what Delphine was thinking? But whatever it was, it did the trick. She swayed over to the telephone and asked for a number. I memorised it."

They settled at a café table outside on the terrace and ordered coffee.

"The temptation," said Joe, "of course, is to nip straight inside and use their phone. See who answers...but..."

"We could do that. I have ways of tricking identities out of people who answer their telephones. Ordinary, innocent people, still slightly bemused by the new device on their hall tables. I wouldn't expect any success if we're dealing with a criminal organisation. And if I mumbled, 'Sorry—wrong number,' or 'Phone company—just checking,' and cut the connection, it might alert them."

"I don't want to be boring," Joe began tentatively, "but in London—"

"*And* here in Paris!" said Bonnefoye. "We have the same facility. It's not so exciting as establishing a direct contact with a suspected villain, but I'm about to go inside and ring up a department on the fourth floor at the Quai. They hold reverse listings of all the numbers in Paris." He took out his book again. "Won't be a moment."

Joe was drinking his second cup of coffee before Bonnefoye emerged again. In silence he passed the notebook across the table to Joe.

"Ah! I think we might have been expecting this," said Joe, smiling with satisfaction. "Let me teach you another London expression, mate: *Gotcha!*"

Vincent Viviani strode smartly down the avenue Montaigne towards the Pont de l'Alma. He was glad that his schedule had led him back to this part of Paris. He'd make time in his day to go and have a look at his favourite bridge over the

Seine. Not being a theatre-goer, he found little to bring him to this increasingly smart area. Like everyone else passing by, he gave a swift, unemphatic glance at the three-storey art nouveau façade of the Théâtre des Champs-Élysées. Overblown, sweet-toothed, but perfect for its purpose, he supposed. Offering rich men the chance of parting with large sums of money for the privilege of gawping at acres of jiggling, gyrating female flesh—of all colours now, it seemed. He flicked an interested eye sideways, following the two men on the opposite side of the road. They ducked into the alley that led to the side door of the theatre. Stage-door johnnies? Yes, they looked the part. At least the boater was a good attempt. Vincent wasn't sure the grey felt would open many doors.

He pressed on without a break in his stride down towards the bridge. The bridge itself wasn't much but he'd always been fascinated by the four stone figures that decorated it. Once, when he was a small boy, his father had brought him here and pointed them out. He'd thought that's what a soldier's grandson would like to see. He was right. Vincent had been enchanted by the four Second Empire soldiers. The Zouave was his favourite. He stood, left hand on hip, neatly-bearded chin raised defiantly against the current, swagger in his baggy trousers, tightly cinched jacket and fez.

His father had been pleased with his reaction. "*Les Zouaves sont les premiers soldats du monde,*" he'd said. "That was the opinion of General St. Armaud after the Battle of Alma when we licked the Russians. And your grandfather was one of them. A *real* Zouave. Not one of the ruffians they recruit from the east of Paris these days—no, he came straight from the mountains of Morocco . . . Kabili tribe. Second regiment, the Jackals of Oran. No finer fighters in the world."

Vincent had signed on as soon as they would take him. He'd managed to see action in North Africa before the war

broke out in Europe. He'd been a seasoned hand-to-hand fighter like the rest of his men, wearing just such a flamboyant uniform. A lieutenant by then, he'd slashed, burned and bayoneted his way through the forests of the Marne at the beginning of the war, realising that he and his regiment were finished. The red trousers, the twelve-foot-long woollen sash, the red fez, all cried, "Here I am! Shoot me!" And the Germans, lying holed up in every village, wasted no opportunity. He'd witnessed the arrival of the British gunners, coming up late to their aid. Not creeping or dashing along—marching as though on the parade ground, camouflaged in their khaki clothing, stern, calm, standing firm when the sky above them was exploding. Machines of war.

And, of course, his regiment had adapted. They'd been kitted out in *bleu d'horizon,* issued with more suitable weapons. He'd survived until Verdun. He'd been there at the storming of the fort of Douaumont. He'd been collected, one of a pile of bodies and sorted out at the last minute by an orderly more dead than alive himself, into the hospital cart instead of the burial wagon. Months later, he'd come back to his old mother in Paris and she'd seen him through the worst of it. And he was flourishing. Not for Vincent a nightly billet under a bridge with the other drunken old lags. He had his pride and as soon as he had his strength back he'd got himself a job. It had taken a stroke of luck to get him going but he was in full-time employment. Employment that demanded all his energy and used all his skills. What more could a retired soldier ask? The pay was better than good, too, and his mother appreciated that. She had a fine new apartment. When he'd told her he was in the meat industry, she'd not been impressed but she'd accepted it. Something in Les Halles—a manager in the transport section—she told her friends. Out at all times of night, of course. She didn't know he was still soldiering.

He smiled and strolled the few metres down to the Place de l'Alma where he greeted the old lady keeping her flower stall by the entrance to the Métro. He spent a few rare moments idling. Paris. He never took it for granted. After the grey years of mud and pain, the simplest things could please him. The walnut-wrinkled face and crouched figure of the flower seller, surrounded by her lilies and roses, beyond her the glinting river and the Eiffel Tower, so close you could put out a hand and scratch yourself on its rust-coloured struts, this was pleasing him.

His smile widened. He'd buy some flowers. And he knew exactly which ones to choose.

"Two inspectors and both speaking French? Monsieur Derval understood that we were about to receive a visit from a gentleman of Scotland Yard. I was sent along in case there were language problems. I do not represent the theatre, you understand, but I speak English. Simenon. Georges Simenon. How do you do?"

Joe handed his card to the young man. "Monsieur Simenon? You are French?" Joe asked.

"No. Belgian." The man who greeted them at the stage door was reassuringly untheatrical, Joe thought. Of medium height and soberly dressed in tweeds with thick dark hair and a pale complexion, he looked like a lawyer or an accountant. Although not far into his twenties, Joe judged, he had already developed a frowning seriousness of expression. But the lines on his forehead were belied by a pair of merry brown eyes, peering, warm and interested, through heavy-framed spectacles. A strong, sweet smell of tobacco and a bulge in his right pocket told Joe he'd been passing some time at the stage door waiting. He seemed genuinely pleased to see them.

"Everyone else is doing what they usually do an hour before the matinée. You may go wherever you please in the building—just try to keep out of the way as far as you can. I'll come with you. You'll be needing a flashlight, I think. And a guide. I know where the light switches are. Front of house is empty—the orchestra drag themselves in at the very last minute. The cast are thumping about backstage. Clattering up and down stairs and being drilled by Monsieur Derval. Soon they'll be screaming and yelling, tearing each other's hair and stealing each other's lipstick! Oh, and you're expecting to see Josephine?" He paused for a second, and continued with a slight awkwardness. "Can't promise anything as far as she's concerned, I'm afraid. Not the most reliable . . . In fact, she's usually late. She's not arrived yet and may well drift in, still eating her lunch, and go straight onstage. We'll just have to wait and see. I'll give you a call when she gets here."

He seemed to tune in to the two policemen's puzzlement. "You must be wondering what I'm doing here, answering for the star? Wonder myself sometimes! I'm not an employee of Josephine's—more of a friend. I'm a journalist, in fact. I met her last year when she arrived, fresh off the boat. I was a stage-door admirer, I'm afraid, turning up with a bunch of roses. She talked to me. I discovered she knew not a word of French." He smiled. "Her English isn't wonderful either! She was an instant success and, as you can imagine, began to receive sacks full of mail. Every day there were invitations from some of the grandest people you can imagine, offers of hospitality of one sort or another, gifts, proposals of marriage—thousands of *them*. And, of course, the poor girl was unable to answer a single one of them. Couldn't even manage a thank-you note for a diamond necklace or a De Dion-Bouton! I began to help her out. She'd tell me how she wanted to reply, I'd put it into suitable French—or English—and see that the notes were sent off."

"You're her secretary?"

"It's not that formal. No. As I said—I'm a news reporter. And I'm a friend who writes for her. But—to business. I expect you'd like to inspect the scene of the crime first? The box? It hasn't been used since the killing. Nor has the other one. All entry barred. The police squad didn't spend a great deal of time up there..." His voice was slightly quizzical. "Commissaire Fourier in attendance. The big gun! They hauled off the corpse and the weapon—and a suspect they claim to have caught red-handed— gave firm instructions to leave the site alone and that's the last we've seen of them. Wondered when you'd be back...There must be much still to discover...Have they made an arrest? Have they charged their Englishman with murder? Did they have any success with the fingerprinting, do you know?"

"*Which* branch of journalism are you employed in, monsieur?" asked Joe with the air of one who knew the answer.

"Crime," he replied, smiling.

"Then you'll never be without material in Paris," said Bonnefoye acidly.

"And we're working on the assumption that the suspect they carted off is an innocent man," Joe felt bound to assert.

"I never thought otherwise," Simenon said graciously.

Their guide switched on the house lights and the inspection began. Joe and Bonnefoye opened up the two boxes and tick-tacked rude messages to each other over the void, agreeing that Wilberforce Jennings' account was probably entirely accurate. The reporter went obligingly to occupy a position centre stage, confirming that he had a clear and close view of Joe in one and Bonnefoye in the other box, sight limited

only by the available light. With nothing of note in Jardine's box, the three men gathered at the murder scene and looked about them. The grey upholstery with its sinister dark stain was witness to the exact spot on which Somerton had breathed his last.

Simenon waved a hand at the walls, where patches of graphite from the finger-printing brush stippled the paintwork. "Dozens, you see! Not one of them bloodstained. I expect the ones they've taken belong to the world and his wife—and his mistress; everyone who's been in here since it was last cleaned. And the knifeman could have been wearing gloves. Not much of a tradition with us, I understand, Inspector—fingerprinting? Chances are, if they can pick up the murderer's prints on these surfaces, they'll have no records to compare them with. You'll have to catch him first and then match them up."

Joe took the flashlight he was offered and trained it systematically along the walls, since it seemed to be expected of him. He wasn't hopeful that this murderer had left a trace of himself behind. He wasn't likely to have paused to decorate the walls with his calling cards, but he had to come and go through the door. Yes, the door, if anything, would be the most revealing, Joe thought, and said as much.

"Unless he had the forethought to leave it ajar," murmured Simenon. "And shove it open with his foot. That's what I'd have done. He was right-handed, I assume? Is it known?"

Bonnefoye nodded. "And Somerton's lady friend who nipped off early could have ensured it was left open when they entered—had to have a draught of air or some such excuse, so he could push it open with an elbow."

"Indeed? Mmm...So he's in and out with no need to touch anything with or without bloodied hand or bloodied glove?"

"Wouldn't he have closed the door behind him in anticipation of his private moment? Instinctive, you'd think," said Joe, "covering your back?"

"A man with cool nerves would chance it. With the finale going on...star on stage...no one's going to be prowling about the corridors. And his back could have been covered by his blonde conjurer's assistant keeping watch outside, holding his cloak ready to slip over any bloodstains he might have on him.

"You know—I think the man probably *wasn't* wearing gloves..."

Joe was enjoying the man's musings. "Yes. Go on. What makes you say that?" Joe asked.

"Not their style. It's a tricky manoeuvre slicing through flesh—muscle and gristle. They like to have complete control of the blade in their fingers. I've witnessed a demonstration." He shuddered. "They'll tell you a gloved hand can slip. And why bother when it's easy enough to wipe the blade afterwards? It had been wiped clean?"

"It had," said Bonnefoye.

"There you are, then. No gloves."

"But tell me, monsieur: *they*? Who might *they* be? Do they have a name and number? An address, perhaps? Where they might be reached?"

"The professionals. *You* must be aware of them, Inspector. You clear up their nasty little messes often enough."

"The gangs of the thirteenth arrondissement? The sons of the apaches, I've heard a romantic call them." Bonnefoye grinned at Joe.

"No, no! Those buffoons are window-dressing! Practically a sideshow for the tourists. Did you know you can hire them by the hour to stage a knife fight in the street, right there on the pavement in front of whichever café is opening

that week? They even have stage names: Pépé le Moko! Alfrédo le Fort! Didi le Diable! La Bande à Bobo. Two rival gangs will fight it out with blood-curdling oaths and threats, egged . on by their molls. And all to an accompaniment of delighted squeals from the clientele. Then, after a suitable interval," he looked slyly at Bonnefoye, "on they come—the *hirondelles,* the swallows flashing about in their shiny blue capes. The boys in blue sweep up on their bicycles and confront both gangs who, miraculously, always seem to turn around and join forces against the flics. Oh, it's a pageant! You could put it on at the Bobino! The bad boys always know exactly the moment to disappear down the dark alleys, leaving really very little blood behind them. Just a few spots for the *patron* to point out to his customers. These—as you might expect—are quite unscathed but have worked up quite a thirst in their excitement. No—this is not their work. And no, I can't give you any names. They have none."

"Is what we're hearing your theory or your evidence, monsieur?" asked Joe, intrigued.

"I've told you what I do for a living. To report on crime, you have to be close to the criminals. As close as they will allow you to approach. I know, or think I know, a good many people who are known to you also—by reputation. I've shared a drink with them...talked to them...drawn them out. I have friends in some pretty low places! Brothels, opium dens, absinthe bars...Sometimes they shoot me a line for their own benefit. But even their lies and false information can give much away if you're not taken in by it...are prepared to analyse it. I'm aware of what they can do—of what they have done—but I have no name to offer you and would not offer if I knew it...The last man who let his tongue run away with him was found two nights ago in

the canal with his mouth stitched up. They have a brutal way with those who would ... *vendre la mèche* ... ?"

"Sell the fuse?" said Joe, puzzled. "Oh, I see ... Give away the vital bit? Squeal. Inform."

"The warning is reinforced periodically. Whether it's called for or not, I sometimes think," he added with chill speculation.

"Is that all you have for us? A portentous warning empty of any substance?" Joe's voice was mildly challenging.

The reporter was spurred to make his point. "There's a small group of villains—six at the most. Deadly. Discreet. For hire. When the Corsican gangs folded their tents and moved on after the war, a central core of bad boys, the survivors, stayed on. Licensed to kill, trained and encouraged to kill, they came out on the other side of it ruthless, skilled and, above all, older and wiser. They regrouped themselves. They're careful. And that's most unusual; gangsters have a touch of the theatrical about them as a rule ... they like to have their names known, their exploits vaunted ... there are even songs made up about some of the more flamboyant villains! But the men I have in mind are silent. Or else they're being run by someone capable of imposing discipline on them. And when they work, it's not in public, for a handful of francs in front of a Saturday night audience of voyeuristic merrymakers, it's for thousands, in the dark. In secrecy. In anonymity."

"Well ... Well, well!" said Joe. "No name, perhaps, but every man has fingerprints. And he can't change those every six months. You roundly declare our chap was not wearing gloves? Let's see what we can do, shall we? Perhaps the officers who worked here on the night of the crime have, inadvertently, recorded his prints. Though, amongst this profusion of sticky dabs, they are not aware of what they have."

Bonnefoye stared and sighed. "So many! It's going to take a month to process this lot. If they haven't given up already. And—really—are they going to bother when they have so many of Sir George's on the victim's chair?"

"Ah! *Le pigeon! Le gogo!*" was Simenon's verdict on Sir George, and Joe was encouraged to hear it.

"The 'patsy,' you might say. Our supposition also."

The beam of Joe's flashlight illuminated the last section of the wall, to the left of the door, passed on and then jerked back again. "I wonder if we can reduce the area of search?"

He moved closer to a powdered print on the left door-jamb. "Here's a remarkably sticky print, wouldn't you say? Just look at the detail there!"

"Not blood?" said Bonnefoye.

"No, not blood. The greasiness is pomade! Hair grease. I had some of that muck on my fingers yesterday. It's the pathologist's theory that the killer seized Somerton by his hair with his left hand from behind to hold his head in the correct position, and then slit his throat with his right hand. So, his right hand might well have been covered in blood and he was obviously at some pains not to touch anything with that but, possibly leaning out to check the corridor was free, he placed what he thought was his clean left hand here…" Joe extended his hand without touching the wall into a natural position and found he had to move it up an inch. "Tall man," he commented. "Just over six feet tall? Bonnefoye? Could you…?"

"As soon as I can get back up to the lab! Focussing! That could save them a bit of time!"

"That policeman! Is he still in the building?"

The voice boomed out from the rear of the stage. Urgent. Powerful. Alarmed.

"We're up here, Monsieur Derval," Simenon called back. "Just finishing in the box. I have two inspectors with me— one Police Judiciaire, the other Scotland Yard."

"The more the merrier. Bring the Grand Old Duke of York as well if you've got him. Quickly! To Josephine's room."

The figure exited at speed, stage left, pursued, Joe would have sworn, by all three Furies.

Joe checked his watch.

Their escort turned an anxious face to them and he muttered something abstractedly, indicating that they should follow him. So evident was his concern, Joe speculated that the young man's relationship with the star was warmer than he had declared. It wouldn't have been surprising. Josephine was rumoured to enjoy a vigorous and fast-changing series of romantic involvements. But if the reporter had been a fixture in her frantic life for over a year, he must occupy a position of some trust and intimacy.

He led them at an ankle-breaking pace down staircases and along narrow corridors, burrowing always deeper into the vast unseen reaches of the theatre. They swept through gaggles of girls, practising steps and formations in any space they could find, skirted around others standing rigidly enduring the pinning up and repair of flimsy costumes. Someone threw a tap shoe along with a curse at them as they blundered by. Finally, they climbed a spiral staircase which brought them out on the level of the dressing rooms. The first three rooms were crowded with dozens of girls with sweaty towels round their necks, offering greasy faces to over-bright mirrors, dipping fingers into pots of Crowe's Cremine or peering closely to apply layers of Leichner make-up. They were screeching at each other in English, breaking off to shout louche invitations to the three men as they hurried by. All perfectly normal behaviour. Joe felt he could

have been backstage at the London Palladium. Nothing untoward going on here.

At the end of the corridor, a group of three men stood
guard in front of the closed door of the star's dressing room.
They were agitated. They did not wait for introductions.
One, the director, Derval, who'd boomed at them from the
stage, put a hand on the doorknob.

"Come in quietly! No fuss, please! We haven't disturbed
or touched anything. We'll stay outside until you call us.
This is Alex, our stage manager. He found her." He nodded
to one of his companions. "He went to check whether she'd
arrived yet."

Simenon frowned and chewed his lower lip but said nothing.

"You'd better go in with them, Georges," Derval added,
touching the man's shoulder gently.

She was lying in the middle of the room, on her front on the
floor with the back of her glossy black head to the door. Her
high-heeled shoes had fallen off. They were green satin, exactly matching the shining cocktail dress that had slid up,
revealing brown thighs and strong calves. Joe at first wondered whether the room had been ransacked. Everything
was in disorder. Clothes and stage costumes hung from
every picture rail and spilled from open couturiers' boxes lit-
tering the floor, towels were draped on every chair back.
There was a stench, overpowering and at first inexplicable. A
potent cocktail of death and dung. Joe wrinkled his nose,
trying to identify the elements. A farmyard? A zoo? And
then he noticed the menagerie. In cages and boxes, small animal faces pushed forward, grunting, growling, mewing,
sensing their presence, eager for attention. Dog, cat, two
rabbits, a small goat, a leopard cub asleep on a cushion in a

cardboard box, and—Good Lord!—a snake, thankfully securely boxed.

Well that at least explained the trail of cereal of some sort that had spilled from the dead girl's hand all over the carpet. She'd dropped a bag of pet food and must have been preparing to feed her animals when she was attacked.

The reporter had rushed forward and sunk to his knees beside her before they thought of calling a warning, touching her sleek head with a caressing hand. "She's dead," he whispered. Then he recoiled and froze, eyes starting. He gasped and cursed and, taking the body by the shoulders, turned it over.

Chapter 19

It was Joe's turn to draw in his breath in surprise. "It's not her ... No—that's not Miss Baker!"

He stared at the face and added, "No scarlet thread. Thank God for that at least." His gaze lingered uncertainly. "But all the same, there's something odd here ... something missing ..."

"You're right, though. It's Francine," said Bonnefoye. "Francine Raissac." He moved to the body with quiet authority. "Would you both move aside?" Bonnefoye checked for signs of life and shook his head. "Dead—and very recently. Within the last half-hour. After a second's inspection, I'd say she'd been strangled. No—wait a moment—neck broken. Better leave that to the pathologist. But what on earth was she doing here? By herself in the star's dressing room? All dolled up for a party but feeding the animals? It's unreal!"

The reporter, visibly shaking from the shock, had taken a pipe from his pocket and was attempting to hold a match

steady enough to light it. "No, you're wrong. Everyday scene. The girls were very thick," he started to say, between puffs. "Josephine liked her. They were always giggling together. She had the run of the place."

"I understood from Francine herself that she often modelled new outfits for Josephine. They're the same size and I suspect Francine may have worked hard at acquiring the new fashionable Baker look. Not difficult with her dark skin and hair," Joe said.

"She would choose clothes for Josephine to wear after the show. Josephine always goes on somewhere after she's performed. She's tireless, you know! Usually to a nightclub. To her own, first of all. Chez Joséphine, it's called. In the rue Fontaine. And then on somewhere else. Bricktop's more often than not. She's not *captivated* by fashion as Francine is . . . was—she takes her word for it that what she's picked out for her will be just right for whatever party she has in mind." The words spilled out, a confusion of thoughts and tenses, a reaction to the relief he clearly felt. Relief that the dead girl at his feet was not Josephine but also guilt that, in these circumstances, he could be feeling relief at all. He collected himself. He stared at the body and frowned in pity. "Francine always got it right. This green satin gown is probably the one she'd selected for whatever Josephine was planning for this evening.

"And she used to come in before work to see to the menagerie." Simenon waved a hand with distaste in the direction of the animals. "Josephine adores them but she isn't all that consistent in her care . . . no more than she is with people, I suppose. Francine couldn't bear to see them go without attention. She even cleaned up after them and took them for walks. The ones that *can* walk. I suspect Derval slipped her a little extra for her trouble. She never stopped working, that girl."

They watched in fascination as Bonnefoye in total silence poked and prodded his way through a textbook examination of the corpse. Joe was determined to extract as much information as he could from the man who was so close to both girls. For Joe, listening to witnesses' early reactions was more important than firing off the usual series of routine police questions. And he'd never met a witness so involved and so insightful, he thought, as this man. He would encourage him.

"Are you thinking that this may be—if indeed it is murder we're looking at—a case of mistaken identity? Finding Francine, looking as she does, in Josephine's clothes, going about what ought to be Josephine's chores, perhaps with her back to the door, one can understand that a mistake might have been made."

"They're really meaning to kill Josephine, you mean? I had feared as much." He took two deep puffs on his pipe and the atmosphere in the room thickened further. "She has enemies, you know. Quite a lot of them are American. Successful, opinionated, liberated black girl that she is—that's too much for some of them to stomach. I was with her at a dinner party the night before last—we were celebrating the arrival of Lindbergh. Some oafish fellow countryman announced in ringing tones across the table that black girls where he came from would be in the kitchen cooking the food, not sitting at table eating it with civilised folks. I think sometimes it breaks her heart. Strong heart, though."

"And, I've heard—enemies in the theatre," said Joe. "Rival ladies wishing to be the paramount star in the Paris heaven. Ladies with influential lovers, prepared and able to indulge them."

"She nearly died when that device she comes down from the roof in misfired. Death trap! There was a fuss and they sacked someone. But there never was a serious enquiry.

Certainly no one called the police in." He looked at Joe across the body, startled. "It could have been arranged. Someone could have been paid to foul up the works."

"The most spectacular exit ever on the French—or any other—stage, that would have been," said Joe thoughtfully. And with a memory of Fourier's avid face, "What headlines! *Black Venus plummets head-first into death pit.*"

"*Dea ex machina.* It was just a rehearsal, thank God. But it could have gone to performance, you know. I might have been in the audience, witnessing the death with my own eyes," murmured Simenon with a shudder. "What a waste of an opportunity! Because, I can tell you, it's not an article I could ever have written."

Joe believed him and was glad to hear him say so. And yet Joe was, while struggling with his shock, touched by a feeling of resentment. He could find no comfort in the realisation that this was not the star lying dead at his feet. There was no need to mourn Josephine. But this was Francine, the girl he had flirted with, sipped coffee with, and, by his unwitting clumsiness, annoyed the hell out of only yesterday. He'd liked and admired her. More than that. He flushed with guilt as he acknowledged he'd been planning a further meeting with Mademoiselle Raissac. In fantasy, he'd taken her to a performance at the Comédie Française—more her style than the cabaret, he thought—and then he'd walked with her along the Seine and dropped in at the Café Flore for a brandy before...well...whatever Paris suggested.

He looked again in sorrow at the chilling flesh and realised how much of her attraction had sprung from her movements, her light gestures, the slanting upward challenge offered by her dark eyes. He remembered her head tilted like a quizzical robin and now permanently tilted, it seemed, at that angle by a broken neck. The last throaty, gurgling laughter he'd provoked by his clowning beneath

her window in Montmartre replayed in his memory. Stylish and intelligent. He was saddened that such a girl had thought it necessary to copy the looks of anyone, even an entertainer like Josephine. The thought startled him into a gesture.

"Bonnefoye! There *is* something wrong here!" He bent and looked closely at the dead face. "Her hair. Look, there—d'you see?—it's been cut. Raggedly. She had a kiss curl on her forehead, I'm certain, when I met her yesterday. You know—one of those cowlick things ... stuck down on her forehead like Josephine."

"*Une mèche rebelle*," said Simenon. "Yes, she had. There's a pair of scissors—over there on the floor." He went to peer at them, carefully refraining from touching them. "And there's a black hair trapped between the blades." He looked back at Francine. "She's cut it off. Perhaps that was yesterday's fashion?" Concerned, he went to the waste basket and turned over the contents. "No hair." He checked the crowded surface of the dressing table. "No hair anywhere."

With mounting dismay, Joe pointed to the girl's mouth. "Her lipstick's badly smudged." He touched her cheeks gently. "And her face is puffy."

"Time for the opening of the mouth ceremony?" said Bonnefoye quietly. "What did you say, Joe? Release the *ka*? Let's do it, while we can—before rigor starts to set in!"

He delicately ran a finger between her lips and slid it under her top teeth. With his other hand he tugged gently on the lower jaw and the mouth sagged open. The fingers probed the inside of her mouth and drew out the contents.

With an exclamation of disgust, Joe spread his handkerchief on the floor by the corpse to receive the damp bundle.

Bonnefoye poked at it. "A wad of currency and ..." He flipped the folded notes over, revealing the contents wrapped tightly up in them. "There it is—the curl of hair."

He sat back on his heels, confused and defeated. "Now, what the hell are we supposed to make of that?"

"*Mèche!* That's what we're meant to understand!" Simenon's voice was urgent, trying to stifle triumph. "It's a play on words! It means 'kiss curl, strand of hair' but it's also a candle wick...or a fuse. And if someone informs on you in criminal circles you'd say: *on vend la mèche.* They're selling out. Selling information. They got the girl they wanted, you know. It was Francine they intended to kill. No mistake!"

"And the choice of currency, I believe, was not random," said Joe bitterly. "Significant, would you say? That the notes are *English* ones? Have you noticed? Those elegant white sheets of paper are English treasury fivers. They're saying she sold out to *me.* To the English cop. They've crammed in ten of them. Fifty pounds! No expense spared on the death of a little Parisian *ouvreuse*? More money than she ever had in her life."

He turned away to hide his sorrow and anger.

Simenon's eyes flashed from one policeman to the other. "Ah. Little Francine whispered more than she ought to have done into a sympathetic English ear, did she? Alfred? He's the connection. He talked to *her* and she talked to *you,* Sandilands. Brother and sister both got their rewards, then. They're suspicious of family relationships. One sees why. Word of this will be on the street by the end of the day. And people like me will be silenced for another year." He turned to Joe and finished quietly: "Whatever you charmed out of her, keep it to yourself, will you? I don't want to hear. Not sure it's even safe to stand next to you."

Joe began to pull himself together and turned again to the body, though he noticed the younger men looked away, unable to meet his eye, alarmed by his expression. For a fleeting moment, the two sides of his face came together,

disconcertingly in harmony, uniting to give out the same message. A message of fierce hatred.

Joe made the sign of the cross over the dead girl and knelt, tugging down and straightening the hem of the green satin dress. "Even in death, she looks beautiful," he murmured. "She'd be pleased to be making her last appearance in something special. Not her black uniform. What is this little number do you suppose, Bonnefoye?"

"I know what this is. I checked the label. It's a Paul Poiret. Her favourite."

The three men gathered at the door pausing to adjust their expressions, regain control and prepare for the flood of questions waiting for them in the corridor.

On the point of leaving, Simenon took a parting glance around the room, then, one element of the chaos evidently catching his attention, he pointed and exclaimed.

"Look! Over there! That's how he got in!"

Chapter 20

They followed his pointing finger to a lavish bouquet of two dozen large white lilies abandoned behind the door and beginning to wilt on the floor. The smell of death. Funerals and weeping. Joe had seen too many lilies.

Bonnefoye sighed. "A special delivery! They must be three feet high! Walking along behind those, no one's going to notice your face or challenge you. 'Who are you and what's your business here?' Pretty obvious, I think. You'd feel silly asking!"

"And flowers arriving at the stage door—it's a daily occurrence. There's usually someone on duty to receive them, though, and bring them on here to her dressing room."

"I'm thinking this must have been a particularly forceful delivery boy," said Joe. "Too much to hope there's a card with them, I suppose?"

Bonnefoye checked and came up with nothing more than a shrug.

"Well, gentlemen, are we ready to face the crowd?" asked Joe.

Information, explanation and requests for back-up followed in an intensive quarter of an hour. Derval hurried away to carry out Bonnefoye's instructions.

"I hope you don't mind but, in the circumstances, with the performance about to start, we've kept all this quiet," said the stage manager, assuming authority. "Josephine turned up five minutes ago, strolling down the corridor, munching on a ham sandwich, cool as you please. God! I nearly fainted! We guessed what had happened and when Derval could get his voice back he told her there'd been an accident in her room, a spillage...Had to get the cleaners in...When we could reassure her that her animals were all safe she agreed to borrow a costume, use the general dressing room and go on as normal. She doesn't make a fuss...used to bunking up...gets on well with the girls. Goodness only knows what I'm going to tell her when she comes off! She was very fond of Francine, you know. We all were."

Joe launched into an angry outburst. "Then you should take better care of your staff, monsieur! Where is your security in all this? A murderer walks in from the street and kills what he assumes to be the star? What next? One killing on the premises, I will call chance, two, a coincidence. But three? That's known as enemy action! If you call us back here for a further crime I shall send Commissaire Fourier to arrest *you*! Good day, monsieur."

Joe and Bonnefoye each felt his arm taken in a firm grasp and they heard Simenon's voice in their ears growling: "The bar's open! Come on, lads—we all need a brandy. This way!"

"It's not your fault. I'm talking to both of you! I haven't got the whole picture by any means, but I see enough to say: I

can see you're both knocked sideways by that girl's death—more than professional concern calls for, perhaps? I don't know what more you could have done or shouldn't have done and why you should hold yourselves responsible, but it wasn't *your* hands around her throat. Hang on to that! All you can do now is find those hands."

"And break every last bone in each one," muttered Bonnefoye viciously. "Slowly and one at a time. Then stamp on both of them." Catching sight of Joe's wondering look, he added, "Excuse me. My uncle was in the Foreign Legion."

They had found a quiet corner behind a screen of potted palms and were sitting, heads together, sipping generous measures of cognac, half an hour before the doors opened to admit the crowds.

"It seems that, unwilling as we were to believe it, what we've got is a double—at least—murder, carried out, gangland-style, to punish informers and send out a warning," said Joe. "Alfred and Francine."

"You said you knew about Alfred?" Bonnefoye asked the newsman.

"Her brother? Rumours only. Nothing for certain. Feel like telling me?"

Bonnefoye obliged.

"...So it would seem to me that these clever dicks not only punish but signal ahead the identity of their next victim," Joe summarised heavily.

"See what you mean," said Simenon. "All that stitching done on Alfred was a very personal warning to his sister."

"She perceived it as such. Yes."

"And her own death is meant to carry with it a threat to the next name on their list?"

"Oh, good God! Those English banknotes, Joe!" said Bonnefoye. "It was more than a cocky way of saying, 'Look,

this was all your fault. She sold out to *you*, you English copper.'"

"Yes. I'm afraid so. Though they got that wrong. The notes they provided from their own resources. She had nothing from me but a red rose, a cup of coffee…and a laugh." With an effort, he pulled himself together and battled on: "I think the next name on their list is Joseph Sandilands. As Simenon here has remarked—I'm not safe to stand close to, and I take the comment seriously. I've no intention of being the death of anyone else in this hellish chain. I think we know the source of the infection. Let me go in and lance the boil."

"What! You know who's responsible for all this? Then why are you sitting here on your bums…excuse me…?"

Joe and Bonnefoye exchanged looks.

"Are you quite sure you want to listen to this?"

Simenon looked from one to the other doubtfully, then his curiosity overcame his wariness and he nodded.

"Very well. A further theory that we dismissed out of hand, I'm afraid," said Joe. "Perhaps we should reconsider. Alfred was involved with the nameless crew you have mentioned to us. He became addicted to drugs and, we must assume, less reliable on account of that. Confused, lacking judgement…desperate. Perhaps the reason they wanted to get rid of him? These soldiers appear to maintain an absolute discipline. He remained close to his sister—dependent on her—and, as they rightly feared, had confided information to her. Not exactly key information—I suspect he was something of a fringe figure…messenger boy…back-up. But information we"—he glanced at Bonnefoye —"have been able to make use of. An address," he added vaguely.

"Look—we know nothing for certain. We merely have a fervid imagining that there may be an assassination service

operating from these premises. One of rather special quality."

"Do you know who's running it?" Caution overcame eagerness and Simenon hurried to add: "Don't give me a name."

"We couldn't anyway. No idea. There obviously is a mind devising and controlling all this nastiness and, whimsically, we've called him Set after the Egyptian God of Evil. But that's since proved to be a distraction."

Joe told him of Dr. Moulin's theory which had been shot down by Jack Pollock's evidence.

Simenon stirred excitedly and began to stuff his pipe again. "You're saying the villain who committed the murder in the Louvre confessed to it and died by his own hand, thus breaking the continuity? He didn't take responsibility for any of the others?"

"Not yet known for certain. Pollock is a good authority but I'll check the records. Shouldn't be difficult."

"Then, consequently, the series of deaths the pathologist recalls must all be personal, unconnected acts of imaginative staging? Not impossible, of course. Most murders are impulsive but boring, spur of the moment stuff... the push downstairs, the carving knife through the heart over the Sunday roast... Not many would have the confidence or the patience to kill as you've described. Though I can imagine the satisfaction. There's this editor I've worked for who's just asking to be... Never mind! Tell me—when, in Moulin's chain of suspicious events, did this Egyptian one occur? Do you know? The *first* he was aware of? So the concept died with him? Hmm... But there *is* a thread, you know... stretching all the way from the Louvre, forward to poor Francine. This obsession with the mouth. Things, revelatory things, spilling out."

"I shall keep my mouth shut," said Joe lugubriously. "At all times."

"I'd say you'd got their message," said Bonnefoye. "And so have I. I'm going to put you on the next Silver Wing service back to London. Gagged and bound if necessary."

"If you're looking for a feller, always try the bar first." The voice was female, joking and warmly American.

Simenon had shot to his feet a second before the other two men were aware of her presence. He introduced the two policemen to Miss Baker and went off to fetch her a glass of mineral water.

Like and yet unlike Francine. Joe was startled to see she was wearing a silk Chinese dressing gown, very like the one the French girl had been wearing in her room in Montmartre. Seeing the girls side by side, no one would have confused them, but from a distance or an odd angle or from behind it would have been all too easy to take one for the other. Judging by her lightness of tone and her smiles, no one had hurried forward to tell Josephine the truth of what lay behind the closed door of her dressing room. Cynically, he calculated they would not reveal it until the end of her performance. The show would go on, regardless of Francine.

"Two fellers? Well, how about that! Joe and Jean-Philippe? Say—I'm sorry I'm late! Long night! Didn't get to bed till six. Louis played until four in the morning! Can you imagine! And no one walks out of a Louis Armstrong performance. Have you heard him play? Come! Tonight! Pick me up here and we'll make a night of it," she said, batting eyelashes flirtily at Bonnefoye.

For a moment, Joe was so disconcerted he could not remember why on earth they were seeing her. The three men exchanged glances, silently and shamefacedly acknowledging that they'd get the best information out of Miss Baker if

she remained for the moment in ignorance of her friend's death.

Josephine herself came to their rescue. "That poor old gent!" she exclaimed. "I hate to think the guy was up there dying...could have been just above my head...while we were wiggling our way through that last Irving Berlin number. Why would anyone want to *do* that? At a show?"

"We were wondering, Miss Baker," said Joe, "if you could recollect anything—anything at all—of the occupant of what I'll call the murder box."

"Sure. I'll try. Can't say I'd remember any old night. But this was special. Lucky Lindy made it, did you know that? Someone rushed in with the news and I went on in between numbers and announced it. Crowd went wild! And so they should! What a feller! I remember looking up at both boxes. But you'll have to tell me which one the dead guy was in."

Joe touched her right hand and said, "From the stage, he would have been on this side."

"Okay. Up there." She looked up to her right, and extended her finger, fixing the imagined box. "Got it. Not that it makes a heap of difference, ya know—I could have been seeing double! Two gents. Wearing tuxedos, the both of 'em, and each with a girl. All snuggled up hotsy-totsy. Nothing out of the ordinary. Clapping. Seemed to be having a good time..."

She sipped her water with a smile of thanks for Georges and thought hard. They waited in silence. "Can't say I noticed anything odd about the fellers but the *girls*..."

"Yes?"

"Yeah...that *was* kinda strange...I was struttin' about, leading the applause. Watching *them* watching me. Everybody was getting very excited about the flight. Clapping and whistling and screeching like you'd never heard but they were

talking to each other as well, smacking each other on the back, standing on their seats. Gathering together into one big shout of congratulations. But not those girls."

"Girls?"

"Yeah, the two of them. You'd have sworn they were agreeing with each other. Exchanged a look and turned and left. Without a word. No goodbyes. No nothing. It was choreography. And I know choreography! The men were left on their lonesome for the finale." She frowned, doing her best to call up her fleeting impressions.

A good witness, Joe thought.

"The one you say died . . ." Out came the right hand again. "I last had a glimpse of him halfway, I suppose, through the finale. I don't have a lot to do in that routine—just prance around in gold feathers—and I remember being something put out—he was looking at his watch! Turning it this way," she held up an arm and demonstrated, "towards the stage lights, you know, to get a look at it. And he stared across at the other box. I was beginning to think we were losing the audience. Feller looked as though he couldn't wait to take off."

"Strange behaviour?" murmured Joe.

"Well, exactly! Lord! If a hundred naked girls—and me!—can't knock his eye out, whatever will?"

"A good question, Miss Baker. What better entertainment can he possibly have wanted?"

Bonnefoye looked curiously at Joe, who had lapsed into silence, and he seemed about to speak but he was interrupted by Josephine, who, half-rising, was drawing the conversation to a close. "Still, sorry to hear the old goat died."

"Don't be," said Bonnefoye, getting to his feet. "The man was more of a cold-hearted snake and he got off lightly. Don't give him another thought."

* * *

Simenon showed them to the side door and said goodbye. "You will let me know how all this turns out?" he said hesitantly. "I've been most intrigued..."

"And helpful," said Bonnefoye. "We've been interested to hear your insights, monsieur." He hesitated for a moment. "Look. You're a crime reporter. You must be keen to see how we live over there at the Quai? Take a peek inside? Have you ever been? Well, why don't you come over and see me there when this is all over? I'll fill you in. My turn to give *you* the tour!"

"Bit rash, weren't you?" Joe commented as they walked away back into the avenue de Montaigne. "Fourier won't like that."

"Sod Fourier! I can swing it! Anyway—with the ideas you've been stuffing into his head, a newsman might be just exactly what he wants to encourage...'Now, my dear Simenon, just take this down, will you?' Chaps like that are very useful to us. They're a channel. They're not exactly informers but—well, you heard him—he talks to people who'll accept a glass from him and open their mouths but who wouldn't be seen within a hundred yards of a flic. They can pass stuff to the underworld we can't go out and shout through a megaphone. He seemed to be able to take a wide view of things. Man of the world."

"And quite obviously something going on between him and the star, wouldn't you say?"

"Oh, yes, of course. Good luck to them! How did he say they met? Stage-door johnny, didn't he say? Just turned up on the off-chance?"

"Yes. But not empty-handed," said Joe thoughtfully. "Said he brought her a bunch of roses. Roses...lilies..." He looked about him. "We're a long way from a florist's shop

here. But there must surely be some enterprising merchant out there catering for star-struck young men on their way to the theatre?"

"Place de l'Alma," said Bonnefoye, turning to the right and walking towards the river.

"Lilies? Two dozen? Yes, of course. Not every day I shift two dozen in one go! Lucky to get rid...they were just on the turn. I told him: 'Put them straightaway in water up to their necks.' Must be nearly two hours ago. That's right—the bell on the Madeleine had already rung two. But not the half past...

"What did he look like? Oh, a handsome young chap!" The *fleuriste* turned a toothless smile on Joe and cackled. "To my old gypsy eyes at least. Rather like you, monsieur. Your age. Young but not too young. Tall, well set up. Dark skin. Southern perhaps? North African even? Mixed probably. Sharp nose and chin. Well dressed. Nice hat. Lots of money.

"You'd need lots of money to buy all those lilies! His wallet when he took it out to pay for them was stuffed! Wished I'd asked double! He didn't really seem interested in the price. Some of them haggle, you know. This one didn't. Paid up, good as gold.

"Scar? Can't say I noticed one...I did notice the bristles, though. He's growing a beard. It'll be a fine black one in a few weeks' time.

"Where? Oh, he walked back up the avenue towards the theatre." The old woman grinned. "Probably spotted some young dancer on the front row. He'll certainly impress her with those flowers, anyway!"

Sensing they were about to close up the interview, she re-called their attention: "Do you want to know what he was doing before he came to my stall?"

A further five francs changed hands.

"He was wandering about on the bridge. Looking at the statues," she said. "Now, gentlemen, I've got some lovely red roses fresh in from Nice this morning if you're interested..."

"Heard enough?" said Bonnefoye, using English, in a voice suddenly chilled. "She's scraping the barrel now." And then: "He's not exactly hiding himself, is he? He must have known we'd trace him here to this stall."

"He's watching us at this moment," said Joe, managing by a superhuman effort not to look around. "Down one of those alleys, at one of those windows. Under the bridge even."

Bonnefoye carefully held his gaze and Joe added: "So, let's assume that, just for once, it's we who have the audience, shall we? And give him something to look at."

He turned to the flower seller. "Thank you, madame. I'll take two dozen of those red roses from Provence."

The old woman stood and moved a few yards to watch them as they went down to the river. When she saw what they were about, she shook her head in exasperation. Idiots! Mad foreigners! Had they nothing better to waste their money on? They'd taken up their position halfway along, leaning over the parapet, and, taking a dozen blooms each, were throwing the roses, one at a time, downstream into the current.

She pulled her shawl tighter about her shoulders and crossed herself. She watched on as the swirls of blood red eddied and sank. How would those fools know? That what they were doing brought bad luck? Flowers in the water spelled death.

Chapter 21

Bonnefoye had returned to the Quai des Orfèvres to pass on instructions for the fingerprint section and to check whether they'd made any progress with the Bertillon records of scarred villains. He'd been reluctant to let Joe turn up unaccompanied at the jazz club on the boulevard du Montparnasse, offering, as well as his own company, the presence of a team of undercover policemen in reserve.

Joe had reassured him. "Don't be concerned . . . Just think of it as a visit between two old friends . . . Yes, I think I can get in. I'm prepared." He patted his pocket. "A bird has led me to the magical golden branch in the forest. I only have to brandish it and the gates to Avernus will swing open. As they did for Aeneas."

Bonnefoye had rolled his eyes in exasperation. "The gates can swing shut as well. With you inside. And I'm not too certain that Aeneas had a very jolly time. Full of wailing ghosts, Avernus, if I remember rightly. If you're not out by eight,

I'm storming the place. I mean it! Now, here's what I'm offering..."

Joe waited until six o'clock, when the crowds hurrying in through the door made him less conspicuous. He went to the bar and ordered a cocktail. He asked for a Manhattan and threw away the cherry. A Manhattan seemed the right choice. The combination of French vermouth and American bourbon, spiked with a dash of bitters, was in perfect harmony with this atmosphere. Throaty, fast Parisian arpeggios studded a base of slow-drawing transatlantic tones and the band also seemed to be an element in the blend. Setting the scene, in fact, Joe thought, as he listened eagerly. Excellent, as Bonnefoye had reported.

A black clarinettist doubling on tenor saxophone was playing the audience as cleverly as his instruments this evening and there was a jazz pianist of almost equal skill. A banjo player and a guitarist added a punchy stringed rhythm. Not an accordion within a mile, Joe thought happily. Generously, the instrumentalists were allowing each other to shine, turn and turn about, beating out a supporting and inspired accompaniment while one of the others starred. To everyone's delight, the pianist suddenly grabbed the spotlight, soaring into flight with a section from George Gershwin's *Rhapsody in Blue* and Joe almost forgot why he was there.

Damn George! If it hadn't been for his officious nosiness, Joe could have been here, plying Heather Watkins with pink champagne, relaxing after a boring day at the Interpol conference, just a couple of tourists. She'd have been laughing at the new cap he'd bought and flattened onto his head, wearing it indoors like half the men in the room. Instead, he was crouching awkwardly, sitting slightly sideways on his

bar stool to disguise the bulge of the Browning on his hip and hoping that no friendly American would fling an arm around him, encountering the handcuffs looped through his belt at the small of his back.

He glanced around at the crowd. Not many single men but enough to lend him cover. The one or two who appeared to be by themselves had probably chosen their solitary state, he reckoned. He saw two men line up at the bar, released from the company of their wives whom they had cheerfully waved off onto the dance floor in the arms of a couple of dark-haired, sinuous male dancers. What had Bonnefoye called them? Tangoing tea-dance gigolos. Everyone seemed pleased with the arrangement, not least the husbands. On the whole, a typical Left Bank crowd, self-aware, pleasure-seeking, rather louche. But then, this wasn't Basingstoke.

He enjoyed the clarinettist's version of "Sweet Georgia Brown" and decided that when he spiralled to a climax, it would be time to move on.

He ducked into the gentlemen's room and checked that, as Bonnefoye had said, it was no more than it appeared, and waited for a moment by the door he held open a finger's breadth. No one followed him. A second later he was walking up the carpeted stairs towards the three doors he'd been promised at the top on the landing. And there they were. The middle one, he remembered, was the one behind which the doorkeeper lurked.

The building itself was a stout-hearted stone and rather lovely example of Third Empire architecture seen from the exterior. But it had been drastically remodelled inside. The original heavy wooden features had been stripped away and replaced with lighter modern carpentry and fresh bright paint. Entirely in character with the new owner, Joe suspected.

He fished in his pocket for his ticket to the underworld,

thinking it might not be wise to be observed digging about as for a concealed weapon at the moment when the door-keeper turned up. And the mirrors? Just in case, he offered his face to the fanlight, grinned disarmingly, and waited for Bonnefoye's promised monster.

A moment later the door opened and he was peremptorily asked his business by a very large man wearing the evening outfit of a maître d'hôtel. Bonnefoye, for once, had not exaggerated. The attempt to pass off this bull terrier as a manservant could have been comical had he not seemed so completely at ease in his role. He was not unwelcoming, he merely wanted to know, like any good butler, who had fetched up, uninvited, on the doorstep.

Joe held out the book he'd bought that morning.

"This is for Madame. Tell her, would you, that Mr. Charles Lutwidge Dodgson..." He repeated the name. "...is here and would like to speak to her."

It's very difficult to avoid taking a book that someone is pressing on you with utter confidence. The man took it, looked at Joe uneasily, asked him to wait, and retreated, closing the door behind him.

A minute later, the door was opened again. He saw a slim blonde woman, giggling with delight and holding out her arms in greeting.

"Mr. Dodgson, indeed!" She kissed him on each cheek. Twice.

"We can all make use of a pseudonym at times," he said, smiling affably and returning her kisses. "Good to see you again, Alice."

The giant appeared behind her, a lowering presence. She turned to him and spoke in French. "Flavius, my guest will hand you his revolver. House rules," she confided. "I see you still carry one on your right hip, Mr. Dodgson."

Joe traded steely gazes with Flavius as he handed over his

Browning. The man's head was the size of a watermelon and covered, not in skin, but in hide. Cracked and seamed hide, stretched over a substructure of bone which had shifted slightly at some time in his forty years. Wiry grey-black hair sprouted thickly about his skull but had been discouraged from rampant growth by a scything hair cut. It was parted into two sections along the side of his head by an old shrapnel wound. Or a bayonet cut. His hands resembled nothing so much as bunches of overripe bananas. Joe wondered what pistol had a large enough guard to accommodate his trigger finger.

"Thank you, that will be all Flavius," said Alice daintily. "I'll call you if we need to replenish the champagne."

"Or adjust the doilies," said Joe.

"May I just call you, as ever—Joe?" she said, switching back to English when her guard dog had stalked off on surprisingly light feet. She held up the copy of *Alice's Adventures in Wonderland,* with a peacock's feather poking out from the pages as he remembered it on her shelf in Simla. The hat maker in the rue Mouffetard had been puzzled and amused by his request that morning and had refused payment for such a small piece of nonsense, but it seemed to have worked. Alice was still laughing. "Do you know—I never did get further than the page marker? I got quite bogged down in the middle of a mad tea party!"

"The reason most of us leave India," Joe suggested.

"Yes, indeed! But, as you know, it wasn't boredom that drove me away! I was having a happy time. It was Nemesis in the shape of a granite-jawed, flinty-eyed police commander who chose to delve too deeply into my business affairs."

Joe decided to bite back a dozen objections to her light summary of a catalogue of murder, theft and fraud. "Not sure I recognise *him.* Shall we just say something came up and you had to leave India in a hurry?"

"*You* came up, you toad! And here you are again, doing what toads do! Now the question is—shall I step on you and squash you or invite you inside and give you a kiss?"

"I think it's *frogs* that are the usual recipients of osculatory salutations," he said cheerfully.

Alice groaned. "Still arsing about, Sandilands? Can't say I've missed it! But come in anyway."

He followed her trim figure along the corridor. Dark red cocktail dress, short and showing a good deal of her excellent legs. Her shining fair hair, which had been the colour of a golden guinea, he remembered, was now paler, with the honey and lemon glow of a *vin de paille*. It was brushed back from her forehead and secured by a black velvet band studded with a large ruby over her left ear. Had her eyes always had that depth of brilliant blue? Of course, but in the straitlaced society of Simla, she had not dared to risk the fringe of mascara-darkened lashes. She still had the power to overawe him. He found himself looking shiftily to left or right of her or down at her feet as he had ever done and was angry with his reaction.

"Joe, will you come this way?" She turned and, stretching out her right hand, invited him to enter a salon. Distantly, sounds of the jazz band rose through the heavily carpeted floor and he realised they must be directly over the jazz café. She closed the door and they were alone together.

"Champagne? I was just about to have a glass of Ruinart. Will you join me?"

"Gladly."

She went to a buffet bearing a tray of ice bucket and glasses and began to fill two of the flutes, chattering the while.

"Cigarette? I'm told these are good Virginian...No?" She screwed one into the end of an ebony holder and waited for him to pick up a table-lighter and hold the flame steady

while she half-closed her eyes, pursed her scarlet mouth and drew in the smoke inexpertly. Joe read the message: English vicar's daughter, fallen amongst rogues and thieves and ruined beyond repair, yet gallantly hanging on to some shreds of propriety. He was meant to recall that, for someone of her background, smoking was a cardinal sin. He smiled. He remembered her puffing away like a trooper at an unfiltered Afghan cigarette in Simla.

"Five years?" she asked, her thoughts following his, back into the past. "Can it really be five years since we said goodbye to each other on the steamer? You're doing well, I hear. And I hear it from George, of all people. We met at the theatre the other day. Did you know he was in Paris?"

"Yes, I did. But tell me how *you* knew he was going to be here, Alice."

"No secret! You know my ways! In India I was always aware of who exactly was coming and going. It's just as easy to keep track of people over here if you know the right man to ask. And the French are very systematic and thorough in their record keeping. A few francs pushed regularly in the right direction and I have all the information I need at my fingertips or rather in my shell-like ear…" She glanced at a telephone standing on a table by the window. "Bribes and blackmail in the right proportions, Joe. Never fails. Tell me, now—how did you find George? Is he all right? I heard a certain piece of nastiness was perpetrated after I left the theatre. I'm guessing that's why you're here?"

Alice shuddered. "I blame myself. If I hadn't shot off like that, he would never have gone over and got himself involved with all that nonsense. Look, Joe, I'd rather not break surface and I'm sure you can understand why but if he's desperately in need of help, then—oh, discretion can go to the winds—the man's a friend of mine. I do believe that. I always admired him. If I can say anything, sign anything, to get him

out of that dreadful prison, then I will. That *is* why you're here, Joe?"

"No, it's not. And—don't concern yourself about George. No action required—I'm sure I can manage."

"I'm assuming he is still over there on the island?" she asked less certainly. "Or have you managed to get him out?"

"He's in police custody," said Joe, looking her straight in the eye. Alice had, he remembered, an uncanny way of knowing when she was being told a lie. And she was likely to have developed such a skill leading the dubious life she'd led. He wouldn't have trusted himself to tell her anything but the truth. "Still in the hands of the French police," he said again. "He's not enjoying the downy comfort of the Bristol, which is where he ought to be, but I'm pleased for him to be where he is. For the moment. I don't believe Paris to be an entirely safe place for him. I've persuaded Commissaire Fourier, in charge of the case, to go more easily on him—the chief inspector seems to think he ought still to have the use of medieval methods of extracting a confession as well as the medieval premises."

"Poor, dear George! You must do what you can, Joe!"

"Of course. I visit every day. I'm happy to report the bruises are healing. He enquired after you when I saw him this morning. Wanted to know that you are well and happy."

"Ah? You will reassure him, then?"

"Can I do that? Tell me—what should I report of little Alice in Wonderland? Business good is it?"

For a moment she was taken aback. "My businesses always do well. You know that, Joe. Until some heavy-footed man comes along and stamps them into the mud."

He decided to go for the frontal attack. "So—how do you get on with the management of the Sphinx? Your competitors can't have been too enchanted when you came along and set up here in their rabbit patch. Have you come to

some amicable agreement? Equable share of the lettuces? They have a Paris bank underpinning them financially, I understand. I wonder how you manage, Alice? A single foreign woman?" He shook his head. "No. Wouldn't work, would it?" And, abruptly: "Who's your partner?"

He saw the moment when she made up her mind. Alice hadn't changed. She was behaving as she had done years ago. Why not? It had deceived him then. Wide-eyed, she was about to plunge into a confession to a sin she knew would revolt him, a sin in his eyes so reprehensible it would distract him from and blind him to the deeper evil she must keep hidden at all cost.

"Very well. I see you've worked it out. I run a brothel. The very best!" She made the announcement as though she'd just made a fortune on the stock exchange and wanted him to share in celebrating her good luck. "Even you, old puritan that you are, Joe, could hardly object. My clients are the cream of society. The richest, at any rate... They demand and I supply the loveliest girls, dressed by Chanel, jewels by Cartier, conversation topics from *The New Yorker*."

"I understand. Expensive whores. Is that what you're dealing in these days? But, of course, you learned a good deal from Edgar Troop, Brothel-Master Extraordinaire, branches in Delhi and Simla."

"These girls aren't whores! They are *hetairai*—intelligent and attractive companions!" Pink with anger, she put out her cigarette, creasing her eyes against the sudden flare of sparks and smoke. Calculating whether she was wasting her time in self-justification. "You are not in England, Commander. Are you aware of the expression *maison de tolérance?*"

"I have it on my information list, just above *magasin de fesses* and *abattoir*," he said brutally. "'Knocking shop' and 'slaughterhouse', to translate politely."

"Tolerance!" she replied angrily. "These establishments are exactly that—*tolerated*—not hounded out of existence by hypocrites like you. As long as the ladies succumb to their weekly health check—the doctor visits—we break no rules. So, if you've come to threaten me, I'm not impressed. If the Law can't close down those abattoirs in the rue de Lappe, they're hardly likely to turn their attention on *me*. Not with the list of habitués I have... *députés*, industrialists, royalty, diplomats... senior police officers," she finished triumphantly. "*You* will be seen leaving. You may be sure of that! I may even send your superior a photograph to show how his pet investigator adds to his expenses."

Her lip curled as she played with an amusing thought. "Though, in the manly English way, he'd probably summon you to his office to compare notes."

"Probably," Joe agreed, the further to annoy her. "Tell me—where do you recruit? I can't see you standing in line with the other pimps at the Gare du Nord?"

"My girls are top drawer! Your sister was probably at school with some of them..." she added defiantly. "Some of them I found in the music hall line-ups, some had just run away to Paris for excitement, some are escaping violent men in their lives... Not many openings for unsupported girls in these post-war days, you know. Men have flooded back and elbowed women out of the jobs they'd found in fields, factories and offices—"

"Spare me the social treatise, Alice!" Joe growled. "You look ridiculous on that soap-box, champagne glass in hand, a hundred quids' worth of ruby over your left ear and twenty girls on their backs down the corridor, working for you."

If she attacked him now, as he was hoping, he could have the handcuffs on her without a second thought. He'd find it easier than requesting politely that she extend her hands.

"Very well," she said, ignoring his gibe, and added angrily

to annoy him: "Starry-eyed romantic that you are, I know you'll not believe it when I tell you—some of my girls actually don't at all mind the way of life. They're paid well and cared for. *I* care about them and their welfare. They're fit and happy. See for yourself if you like. An hour or two on the house? No? Well, perhaps you can accept another glass of champagne?" She put out a hand.

He nodded, looking at her with stony face. "Why don't you let me do that?" He went to the sideboard and refilled his glass, taking the opportunity of positioning himself between her and the door.

"And is *she* well and happy, the little miss who was encouraged to enter the wild animal cage with Somerton the evening before last? The bait you hobbled for the tiger? Did you warn her about the character of the man she was to entertain?"

Alice laughed. "Watch out, Commander! Your soft centre's oozing out of that hard crust! Something you have in common with Sir George. Makes me very fond of the pair of you! My girl wasn't in the slightest danger. I was on hand."

"Because you knew it was never intended that she should finish the evening with him. At a given signal the two of you donned your silken cloaks and disappeared into the Paris night. Or did one of you—both?—lurk behind to ensure the killer had easy access to the box?"

"How the hell?"

"A wardrobe of four midnight-coloured cloaks—I'm guessing that your girls, or a small picked unit of them, are actively involved in the other branch of your operation here. A sort of alluring Flying Squad? An undercover ops unit? You were always a showman, Alice. You enjoy playing games. And reading novels. Inspired by *The Three Musketeers*, were you? Well—listen!—this is where it all gets terribly serious."

He put down his glass on a low table and stood ready to knock her to the floor if she tried to get past him or move towards the bell. To his surprise, she retreated away from the door and went to stand, a hand on the mantelpiece at the other end of the room. He followed her, careful to position himself ready to block her exit.

"I've got handcuffs in my pocket. Real steel ones, not forgiving flesh and blood ones. They'll be round your wrists and I'll be pulling you with me down the stairs and out into the street before you can say 'knife.' And I'll hand you straight over to the lads of the Brigade Criminelle who are waiting below. You can sample the accommodation at HQ for yourself. Not sure which of the murders you'll confess to but eventually you will confess. I don't imagine even your partner's influence spreads as far as the inner reaches of the Quai des Orfèvres. He wouldn't be trying hard to ride to your rescue, at any rate, I'd guess. And you'll have lost again, Alice, to a man who's made use of you. He'll wait, knowing you won't give him away, because by doing so, you implicate yourself. He'll sit it out until the storm's blown over . . . until the guillotine at La Santé has silenced you permanently and then he'll start up again. Madams are ten a penny. He can probably raise one from the ranks with no bother at all."

"I'm not sure what you expect me to say. How can I respond to these maunderings? Partner? Who is this partner you rave on about?"

"The head of the assassination bureau. The undertaker of delicate commissions. Murder with a flourish. That partner. Or should I say—boss? Two compatible services under one roof. The White Rabbit, the jazz club, and its escape hole up here into Wonderland—your part of the organisation, I would expect, and then there's the other. The Red Queen, I suppose we could call it. Wasn't she the one who rushed around calling 'Off with his head'? Or didn't your perusal of

the text take you that far? She was quite insane, you know, and incapable of discriminating. Innocent or guilty, it didn't matter to her. Heads rolling was all she cared about. And so it is with your partner in crime."

His voice hardened. "I've seen his handiwork. Somerton's head was damn near severed. A youth of sixteen had his living lips stitched together. His sister had her neck broken and her mouth stuffed with banknotes because someone thought she'd spoken to me. Three deaths in as many days! You're sheltering Evil, Alice!"

"By God! You haven't had time to put all this together! Who've you been talking to?" She looked wildly around the room.

"You'll be safer with me in my handcuffs, so stop looking at the bell. Every street urchin, every tramp under the bridge, will know by this evening what you've been up to. It'll make the morning editions. The authorities may turn a blind eye to whoring but they still disapprove of murder. From this moment, you're a liability. Perhaps if I left you running loose he'd devise in his twisted, sick mind a way of bumping you off in a spectacular and appropriate way. Let me think now! What could it be? Found strangled with a silk stocking in the bed of Commissaire Fourier? I like that! I'm sure I'd be amused by the headline. Kill two nasty birds with one stone. Alice, you're finished here. Yes, you're safer with me."

She was looking at him in horror. Distanced. Shocked. But still calculating. "Safer with you? You're mad!"

"Possibly. Leaves you with a narrow choice, Alice. You walk out of the front door with a mad puritan and negotiate your future career or stay behind with a mad sadist and die. Which is it to be?" He looked at his watch. "A taxi arrived just a minute ago in front of the jazz club. I expect your sharp ears picked it up?"

She turned her head very slightly to the window. The

thick cream and black curtains and closed shutters reduced the traffic noise on the boulevard to a low murmur.

"It's sitting there with the engine idling. We can be inside it and away into the night in thirty seconds."

Alice had never been indecisive. The last decision he'd seen her take had been witnessed by him down the barrel of a gun. A gun trained on him.

"Top left drawer of the sideboard," she said. "There's a Luger in there. 9 mm. It's loaded. Eight rounds. Safety's on. You're going to have to use it."

Chapter 22

"Your guard dog's standing right outside, isn't he?"

"Yes. He's as tough as he looks and he understands English. That's why I lured you down to this end of the room. Laugh a little, Joe. If you go on snarling at me, he'll come crashing in."

She gave a peal of laughter that sounded genuine enough but he couldn't bring himself to join in. "You won't be allowed to leave here alive, you know. I don't think we ever expected you'd come here . . . just walk in. Flavius will have sent a message by now . . . To the boss. I'll be expected to entertain you—to keep you on the premises until he gets here. He'll want to think up something original for *you*. It's high time the police had a warning shot across their bows."

Joe decided to ignore her bluster and concentrate on the present danger. "Tell me about him quickly, your Flavius. Is he a one off or is he at the head of a pack?"

He looked again at his watch.

"He's from the south. Not bright but quick enough.

Vicious. Ex-Foreign Legion. Knife or gun, he doesn't mind. He'll have one of each in his hands at the moment. He's right-handed. He'll use the knife if he can—we like to avoid noises up here—but if he has to, he'll shoot you with his pistol. It's fitted with a silencer. He's top house dog but there's a security staff of four more always on the premises. They are wolves. Two North African, two Parisian. Armed. They have discreet house guns for indoor work. Beretta 6.35s. Last year's model. At the first sign of trouble, two will go out through the back exit and circle round. Two will come straight down the main corridor to back up Flavius."

"Where are they all at the moment?"

"Flavius is right there, as you guessed, at the door. The others?" She shrugged. "Playing cards in their room. It's ten yards down the corridor to the left. Playing with the girls, given half a chance. They won't be expecting trouble at this early hour and the girls won't be busy. We like to keep the staff sweet."

Joe went to the sideboard. "More champagne, m'dear?" he asked in a louder, drunken voice. "Jolly good drop of fizz you keep! What?" He clinked a glass against the bottle at the moment he pulled open the drawer. It opened silently. He took out the Luger.

"It's fully loaded. I did it myself," she mouthed.

Joe checked it anyway.

She shuddered as he reached behind his back and took a pair of handcuffs from under his jacket. "I borrowed these from a colleague," he murmured. "I think I can make them work. Do I need to put them on you?"

"No. I'll be more use with my hands free. And don't forget we have to get out through the club. They're not used to seeing women in cuffs. And they're not very fond of the police. They might object."

He slipped them back through his belt.

"Come closer to the door but stay well to the side. I don't forget he's got my Browning. If he fires that into the room the bullet won't stop until it hits the towers of Notre Dame. Remind me—which way does the door open?"

"Inwards."

"Listen! When I nod, you're to squeal. Not loudly. Enough to encourage him to come in to investigate. Okay?"

"Ready."

Joe took a deep breath then nodded.

Alice squealed.

Joe waited one second then blasted the door with four rounds. The wood splintered as the bullets tore through the flimsy structure. A lozenge pattern of blackened holes marked out a target area two feet square which would reach from throat to abdomen on a six foot two inch man standing at the door.

If, indeed, he had been standing at the door.

Joe heard no scream or oath. Not even a grunt.

Crouching to the side, he listened. Not a sound. No time to wait. The wolves would be slamming down their cards, saying "What the hell was that?" or murmuring "Excuse me, ma'am" and unsheathing their Berettas. Covering the door space with his gun, Joe reached out, turned the knob and flung the remains of the door open into the room.

Alice made a little wuffling sound in her throat.

Flavius was utterly silent. His huge body lay collapsed, sandbagging the doorway, still pumping out blood from at least two wounds. No screams because the highest and first of the bullets had shot out his throat.

Alice was faster than Joe. She leapt straight at the obstacle, scrambling in high satin heels over the twitching body. Joe followed. As they reached the door to the stairs Alice

fiddled with the bolt and double lock, and a gathering roar rumbled down the corridor after them. As the door yielded, Alice took off down the stairs.

Joe turned and raised the Luger. He watched the door Alice had mentioned, waiting. The door creaked open and the snub-nosed barrel of a pistol started to slide out. Joe fired. The gun crashed to the ground. Someone howled in pain. Joe fired again blindly through the wood. Two bullets remaining. He waited a heartbeat and fired them off, warning shots down the length of the corridor, then wiped the gun and threw it back towards Flavius's body. He turned and leapt, three steps at a time, down the stairs. Alice had already disappeared.

When he reached the entrance to the jazz club he paused and listened. The music had stopped, women were shrieking, men shouting. He was in greater danger of being torn apart in a mêlée of angry jazz fans, he calculated, than from the wolves.

He turned and backed into the door, bumping it open. He held up both hands, clearly unarmed, and gestured with a hand towards the stairs, a soldier indicating an enemy position. He yelled, "*Au secours!* Help!" He looked over his shoulder, eyes wide in alarm, and shouted into the horrified silence: "Hell! A feller goes to the john and World War Two breaks out over his head! What sort of joint *is* this?"

Two hearty Americans leapt to his rescue and dragged him backwards to safety into the café. All three of them were instantly caught up and struggling in the general surge towards the exit.

God! It was there! Joe hadn't heard and really didn't believe in Bonnefoye's promised taxi but there it was, as he'd described it, panting and choking at the kerbside. A petulant

Alice was locked in the back. Bonnefoye was leaning non-chalantly against the driver's door. He greeted Joe as he dashed up and unlocked the rear door.

"Do you mind, Joe? Sitting in the back? Standard proce-dure when we're carrying a dangerous prisoner. The lady took me for the driver. Understandable, as I was sitting at the wheel. Jumped in and told me to drive to the Gare de Lyon. In quite a hurry. Peremptory, even. Promised me a re-ward if I arrived on bald tyres! Another woman fleeing your company? What on earth do you say to them, Joe?"

He climbed in behind the wheel and turned off the en-gine. "Well, now—what do you have to tell me, Joe?"

"Four others on the premises, you say?" Bonnefoye was calm, enjoying the moment. "We found the rear exit and covered it. There's a *panier à salade* round there blocking the alley and ten of our best boys raring to have a go. A section of the Vice Squad are on their way as well. They'll go in and clear up. Um ... heard the noise. Are we likely to put our feet in anything up there, Joe?"

"I'm afraid so. One rather large casualty, bleeding copi-ously. Not our man—the doorman. Name's Flavius. Not that he's answering to it. Problem with his throat."

"It was self-defence!" Alice spoke up firmly. "He was threatening me and the commander had to shoot him."

"Much as I dislike contradicting a lady," said Bonnefoye pleasantly, "I have to say I think you've got that wrong, madame. Your guard was shot by one of the other bits of scum you keep about the place with the house gun. I expect if we search carefully we'll find the ..."

"Luger," supplied Joe.

"... Luger, yes. Wiped clean? Yes, of course. And we'll es-tablish that the fracas was no more than a fight over a girl.

The usual. We'll just have to wait and see which one confesses to what, won't we? But I'm sure one of them will be
only too pleased to assume responsibility. Do you want to
stay and see the fun, Joe, or shall we take off for the Quai?"

"Hold on a moment," said Joe, still getting his breath
back.

Alice had shrunk away from him as he pushed himself
into the backseat alongside.

He stared at her and burst out laughing. "Two minutes
ago this woman, you'd have sworn, was on her way to the
Ritz, sporting the last word in cocktail frocks! And now
look at her! Milady de Winter! Fully caped. Booted and
spurred probably too, if I could be bothered to check.
And"—he kicked a soft leather bag she'd pushed away behind her calves—"packed and ready for the weekend, I see.
Now where were you off to, I wonder?"

"Not planning on helping us with our enquiries," said
Bonnefoye with mock resentment. "I was watching her. She
tore into the café and spoke to the barman. He handed that
stuff to her from under the bar."

"My exit bag. I always have it to hand," she explained
sweetly.

"And what were you intending to do at the Gare de Lyon,
Gateway to the South? From where so many adventures
start?" Joe asked. "Return to your old haunts on the
Riviera?"

"Change taxis? Head north . . . or east . . . or west," she said,
tormenting him. "You'll never know. Not sure I do myself.
Joe, are you ever going to introduce me to your charming
young colleague? He seems to have the advantage of me."

"No. You don't need to know him. You just need to do as
he says."

He had counted on annoying her, but Joe was taken
aback by the fury in the glare she directed at him.

A small black police car screamed to a halt a few inches in front of them.

"Here he is," said Bonnefoye. "My associate in Vice. I'll just leave you for a moment while I fill him in, then we can leave. We'll make for a nice quiet place and put a few questions to the lady. If she answers correctly and reasonably, it may be that she can go free—after signing a statement, of course. If we're concerned by what she has to say then she may have to proceed as far as Commissaire Fourier. Won't be a minute."

"How long will he be?" Alice's voice was strained. He could hardly see her face. She had flung the hood over her head and was shrinking down into the upholstery. Her eyes were scanning the crowds milling about on the pavement. "We must leave now, Joe! Call him back! He—*you*—have no idea...!"

Joe was reminded of George's remark about Alice's strange behaviour. "...eyes quartering the room like a hunter," he'd said, and then corrected himself: "No—more like the prey. There was someone out there in the auditorium..."

And there was someone out there at this moment on the pavement, coming closer. He began to catch Alice's fear. He spoke softly to her. "Alice, we are surrounded by at least a dozen assorted flics. You're quite safe. For the moment."

She looked at him, incredulous. "You think that will stop him?"

Uneasy, he muttered, "Damn! I haven't got a gun. I really did remember to wipe the Luger and drop it a suitable distance from the body. And—oh God!—I didn't get my Browning back. No time, even if I'd thought of it."

Alice bent and fished about in her bag. "Here. Take this. It's only a .22 but it's a little more effective than pointing a wagging finger."

He took it warily, resting it along his thigh between them, finger on the trigger.

"You make me nervous, Alice," he said finally. "As nervous as you made Sir George on Saturday night at the theatre? And for the same reason perhaps? I'm afraid for my life. *Should* I be afraid for my life? What are your instructions this time? The same as last? Kill the Englishman?"

She looked at him, eyes darkening with suspicion inside her silk hood. "What on earth do you mean?"

"I mean that I *know*, Alice. I know that you'd gone to the theatre that night, not for the pleasure of seeing Sir George again, but to kill him."

Chapter 23

"To kill him. At the very least, to participate in his killing."

She swallowed but remained silent, still staring through the windows.

"Sir Stanley Somerton was never the target, was he? His death has brought freedom, much relief and even unholy joy to a good number of people but it was never intended, was it? No one put cash in an envelope and asked for *him* to die? Am I getting this right, Alice?"

She nodded her head. "As usual."

"Do you want to know how I guessed?"

"No. Not particularly. I assume you to be omniscient."

"Well, I'll tell you anyway. Because I shall enjoy the satisfaction of making you and your filthy organisation aware that you've been tripped up by no more than a couple of bystanders, neither of them connected in any way to the murder that went wrong but both sharp-eyed, observing

accurately and passing on their observations to those who could make sense of them."

Alice appeared not to be listening. "Where's your friend? God! Now where's he off to? Do we have to wait for him?"

"The star of the show, Miss Josephine Baker," Joe pushed on, "was kind enough to grant us an interview. She's a responsive girl who feeds off her audience, is aware of them and their moods. She remembers that evening particularly because the routine was broken. Lindbergh flew in and she took it upon herself, being from St. Louis, to invite the audience to celebrate with her. She was aware of you, Alice, and your young employee in Somerton's box. She was aware enough of the two men to tell me the boxes were a mirror image of each other. Two elderly gents, two blonde young women with them. She didn't even know which man had died. Left or right, they were much the same to her. It made no difference to the star but it was life or death for one of those men. And then it struck me. For me, the kaleidoscope suddenly shifted and settled into a different pattern when she said that.

"And, taken with the strange behaviour of Somerton, the behaviour reported both by Sir George and a treacherous school friend of his who happened to be in the audience, it all began to pull together. They said the same thing. George, compassionate man that he is, attempted in the only way open to him to ensure—not the virtue—but the well-being of your little tart across the way. Before the show started and you showed up, he got to his feet and in soldier's hand language told Somerton to back off. 'Or else!' he added. Accompanying his threat by a very familiar gesture. This!"

Joe performed the slow dragging of the index finger across the throat.

"George was relieved to see his old enemy signal: 'Message received and understood.' He was puzzled, though not dis-

turbed, by the man's further reaction. He fell about laughing. The witness in the stalls, Wilberforce Jennings, told us
that Somerton 'damn near slapped his thigh, he thought it
so funny...'

"And it was funny. In the circumstances. Very. Ironic
might be a more accurate word, as no one but Somerton
would have been genuinely amused by the gesture. Because
George was the one who was supposed to die and in exactly
the way he'd mimed—by the slicing of a dagger across his
throat. And the man who supplied the dagger, chose the
killing place and the time, and paid for the assassination
show was Somerton *himself*. George's prophetic gesture
added to the gaiety! The cherry in the cocktail!"

Joe didn't care that she was barely listening to him. His
outrage pushed him to try to make an impression, to make
her admit an understanding. Regret and shame were out of
the question, he supposed.

"The vile Somerton discovered that Jardine, the man
who'd disgraced him and ruined his life—as *he* saw it—was to
be in Paris at the same time as himself. He wanted the satisfaction of watching while his old enemy was filleted in front
of his eyes. But a solitary viewing is not an entirely satisfac-
tory experience for a man like Somerton. He wanted to share
it. He arranged to be seen, flaunting female company of the
choicest kind, knowing that this would annoy Sir George.
And he intended that his companion should join him in
witnessing a real-life bit of theatre."

"You know that's not what happened, Joe."

"No. And I'm wondering what went wrong—or should I
say right? It seems to me that someone threw a sabot into
the works and put all the cogs out of mesh. Are you going to
tell me?"

"Me! It was me! You know that! *He* didn't tell me, for
once, the name of the target, as he usually does. Sometimes

he allows me a veto when he's getting his schemes together. He trusts my judgement. But in this case, he must have been offered a great deal of money and he didn't care to hear my objections." Alice paused and bit her lip, still working through her reasoning. Not quite happy with her thoughts, Joe guessed. "He might have expected me to balk at killing off someone I knew from India. And he was right. I would never have agreed to harming George. He confided in Cassandre—that's the girl's name—and set up the whole theatre episode with her. The assassin had been told to kill the Englishman in Box A, the one sitting alone. The client himself would have one of our girls with him, a protective marker, so there was no chance he would get it wrong.

"Cassandre consulted me about the outfit she should wear that evening and I discussed it with her. I was concerned that I'd been sidelined in this—suspected Cassandre herself of making a try for my own position. No such thing—the girl was just as much in the dark as I was. I got the whole thing out of her. It wasn't difficult, she assumed I knew. I was horrified. I knew nothing of this Somerton but I did know I wasn't going to let Sir George die. I thought by arranging for the other man to be killed in his place, I could put it down to a ghastly mistake on the part of the knife-man. And there'd be no client left behind to complain that he hadn't had his show, after all! No consequences!

"At the appointed time—the killing was fixed for the moment when the applause for the finale rang out—I left and went down the stairs. I met our man coming up and berated him. 'Idiot! The bloke you want is over the other side! B, not A. Don't you listen? Or don't you know your alphabet? I'm with this chap, can't you see? The other, the dark one, is the one sitting by himself. Go quickly!'

"Cassandre had got away by then, leaving the door ajar,

and the fiend got in and did the business. So long as he had someone to carve up, he wouldn't give a damn. If someone had made a mistake it wasn't his fault. He would put it down to a management mix-up. He isn't paid to think. But stupid Sir George! Why the hell did he have to go over and foul everything up?"

"Because he's got what you've never had, Alice—a kind heart and a conscience. But . . . here comes Bonnefoye at last. Just time to say—thank you!" He scrabbled around for her hand and lifted it, cold and trembling, to his lips. "For those dim glimmerings of human kindness, I thank you."

"Dim glimmerings? Fool! I saved his life! And now see where it's got me, my human kindness! Sharing a taxi with two rozzers and on the way to prison."

"You took your time," Alice accused Bonnefoye. "Can we go now?"

"Fun's nearly over," he reported, settling back in again and easing out into the traffic. "Didn't entirely go to plan. A problem. Apart from the corpse—four armed security, you said? We've got three of them. Two dead, two injured, trying to shoot their way out. They loaded the lot into the police ambulance and headed off for the Quai. At the first halt, corner of the boulevard, one of the wounded leapt from his pallet, bashed the attendant on the head and jumped out into the traffic. He's covered in blood—his or someone else's. We should be able to pick him up with no trouble."

Alice groaned. "You're saying you've left one of the wolves on the loose? He'll go straight to . . ." She teetered on the edge of a name.

Finally Joe had thought she was about to give him what he wanted but she caught herself in time. Losing patience,

he said: "To whom, Alice? Who *is* this bogeyman you're so frightened of? Who's out there? How many of them?"

"Not many. He likes to keep it small. Very small now, but there are always men available to swell the ranks. There's the one you've allowed to escape, the knifeman, and the boss. But they've got a network that runs all through Paris. And beyond. They'll track us down wherever we go... Where *are* we going?"

"Yes—where *are* we going?" Bonnefoye repeated. "I'm just the driver, madame. Better check with the gentleman."

"Follow that ambulance!" said Joe, suddenly coming to a decision. "I wonder if you knew... in times of danger, the Parisii tribe who settled here—before the Romans arrived and spoiled things for them—would make for the central island and pull up the drawbridge, so to speak. We'll do the same. Île de la Cité, please, driver."

"Oh, Lord! Not Fourier, Joe! Not sure I'm quite prepared for that yet!"

"I'm certainly not! No, I have in mind a different location. In the law enforcement buildings, but not involving a trip up Staircase A. A quiet spot... none quieter. We're off to the morgue!"

Moulin was already gowned, gloved and masked, standing ready. He was accompanied by three young assistants, similarly clad, sorting through trays of instruments. At their approach, he removed his surgical mask and gave them a puzzled smile of welcome. "I was just on my way out for the evening," he grumbled. "Under this," he indicated his white starched gown, "I'm dressed for the opera. We were alerted by telephone. Rush job on. Someone warned us to expect incoming dead."

"Ah, yes," said Bonnefoye. "That was me. Sorry to foul up

your evening, Doctor. Gangland fracas in the boulevard du Montparnasse. They'll be a few more minutes yet. They were told to drop the wounded off at the hospital before coming on here. When you check your laundry list, you'll find you have three bodies, unless another succumbed en route. There's one commander and two soldiers. Gunshots, all three."

"Ah. Anything to do with you?"

"It's all right, Doctor. The commander, a person with the proportions of a small whale, died first with not a scrap of police-issue hardware in him. Luger bullets from the house gun. That's what started it all. The other two … were reckless enough to fire on the officers sent to arrest them."

"I say, excuse me, but is this an entirely suitable conversation for a lady's ears?" They heard the slight reprimand in his voice as Moulin turned a concerned face to Alice. She had been standing listening, not, apparently, looking for a formal introduction. "I'm sorry, mademoiselle? Madame?" He broke off with a bemused and reproving glance at Joe.

"Don't worry, Moulin. The lady's seen and heard and, indeed, perpetrated much worse. May I introduce you to a genuine example of *Latrodectus mactans*? We're here seeking sanctuary. Her life may be in danger—from the villains who are responsible for all this mayhem. I don't think they'll be looking for her in the morgue. Though that is where they'd *like* to see her. She has certain confidences of an intimate nature she's bursting to make, confidences including the identity of the gentleman we have been calling Set."

"Indeed? *Set*? I wondered if he'd bob to the surface again!"

"The interview is to be an informal one, for the moment. Moulin, I wondered if we might impose on you for an hour? May we borrow your room?"

After a flash of astonishment, the doctor did not hesitate. "Certainly. You remember the way? Coffee's on the stove.

Help yourselves. Oh, and before you go off, Bonnefoye, Sandilands—a word with you, please. Something's come up about Somerton...Ah! Here's our delivery!"

They settled Alice in the armchair furthest from the door and positioned themselves in front of her, Joe to her right, Bonnefoye perching on the footstool to her left. She smiled slightly, watching their manoeuvres. "What a simply ghastly room!" she said, staring around her with a particular look of distaste for the tacked-up theatre posters. "Don't you think? Looks like Quasimodo's idea of a snuggery. Dr. Moulin's? How can he bear it?" She removed the antimacassar from her chair between delicate fingers and dropped it to the floor.

"He doesn't like it any more than you do, but people will keep sending him corpses to be dealt with," said Joe, angrily. "This is his attempt at a retreat from your handiwork. Six bodies you've fed him over the last three days...how can *you* bear it? The alternative is Fourier's office. Shall we take you there? It's not far. No lace frou-frous there, no common thespian mementoes to curl your toes and shrivel your sensibilities. Spartan, you'd say. Entirely functional decor. But what you *wouldn't* like is the spot marked in the centre of the room where he will make you stand."

Alice shrugged her shoulders, unimpressed.

"And stand...and stand...Have you any idea how much stress that puts on the body after a few hours? George is still suffering. So, be thankful you're sitting in an overstuffed armchair being served with coffee, talking to two understanding chaps making notes."

"I'll have mine black with one lump of sugar, please, Inspector," she said, capitulating. "And you can put your thumbscrews away. I'm going to talk to you. Look on this as

a practice run. You must advise me regarding the contents of my official statement. If, that is, you are still requiring me to make one when I've got to the end of what I have to say. You may be begging me to tear it all up by the time I reach that point. And hustling me aboard the next transatlantic liner with my head in a bag."

Relishing their sudden wariness, she added: "No, gentlemen—you won't be pleased."

Chapter 24

"The Zouave, I'll start with him," she said, accepting a china mug of coffee.

"The knifeman, as you call him, though he's more versatile than the name suggests. He was in the same regiment as the dear departed Flavius. Yes, I think you've detected that there's a military thread running through all this. I met him nearly five years ago when I arrived here from India. Alone and friendless and trying to establish myself in a hostile city..."

She caught Joe's eye and went on hurriedly: "The man tried to rob me! There in the boulevard, in broad daylight. A scarecrow! A heap of rags and bones, he suddenly appeared in front of me with his hand held behind him, like this..."

She got to her feet and with a frisson, Joe recognised the apache gesture.

"He put his other hand out and demanded that I give him money. He wasn't thinking clearly or he'd just have snatched my whole bag and run. He seemed on the point of

collapse…wobbling rather. I realised he was incapable of running anywhere. The man was at death's door. Desperate. I opened my bag as though to look for money and took out the gun I always keep by me. You still have it in your pocket, Commander. He wasn't worth a bullet, I thought. Certainly not worth the time it would take making statements, having my pistol confiscated and all that rigmarole, so I hesitated. And then he did something rather extraordinary. He brought his knife hand forward and showed me it was empty. Too poor even to possess a knife. And then he smiled, his chin went up and he saluted. I could hardly make out what he was saying at first but he repeated it. 'Vive la France!'

"He thought he really was living his last moment. 'Don't be so silly,' I told him. 'When did you last eat?' I took him to a pancake stall. He wolfed down about six. I made him walk ahead of me to a park bench and sat him down at the opposite end. Perfectly safe—I had my gun in my pocket, covering him the whole time. He told me his story. Perfectly ghastly! He'd drifted back from the war, where he'd been badly wounded, and was searching for his mother in Paris. He hadn't seen her for eight years. He'd been reported missing, presumed dead, and she'd moved on. He was destitute. Dying of neglect. A common story. They sweep up a dozen like him from under the bridges every morning. But there was something about this one…the tilt of his chin, the glare in his eyes. It was like finding a rusty sword by the wayside. If I polished it up, sharpened it, I would have a weapon worth owning."

"So you bought yourself a Zouave, Alice? For an outlay of six pancakes? Were you aware of the reputation of these men? I'd be more comfortable in the close proximity of a mad bull terrier with a stick of ginger up its backside!"

"I had a use for his skills. I know they are fierce, implacable,

terrifying fighters and none more effective with a knife. And there was someone in my world at that time that I needed to terrify. I gave him food, drink, money and a purpose in life. I asked him to undertake a small task for me in return. He was happy to repay my kindness. Loyalty is another of their virtues, you know. And he has never been asked to do something he has not been delighted to do. Clean work compared with what his wartime commanders expected of him. He reestablished himself and in time introduced some old army acquaintances. They became the core of my organisation."

"*Your* organisation?" asked Joe.

"Yes. Initially it was mine. I bought the premises in the boulevard du Montparnasse. Girls need protection, you know that. And I needed to show a tough face to the world to make it understood that my affairs were not to be interfered with. There was a power-shift going on at that time. Corsicans killing each other, North Africans moving in...an unsettled and dangerous time for one in my business."

"Alice, couldn't you have set yourself up in a tea shop and bought a pair of poodles?" Joe burst out.

Alice and Bonnefoye both turned a pitying glance on him.

"A cup of tea brings in one franc," said Bonnefoye. "A girl, between a hundred and a thousand. A dirty business but a calculatedly short one, I'd guess. Five years...I'd say you were pretty well poised to make off with your ill-gotten gains?" he guessed.

"I am," she said with a confident smile.

"So—tell us about the moment when *your* organisation became *his*."

"Ah! A sad story! And one you will have heard many times before. I became friendly with one of my clients. Overfriendly. I fancied myself in love with him. He reminded me

very much of someone I had been fond of in my past, and I allowed him to get too close to me. He also was recently arrived in the city, finding his feet, totally without female companionship. Someone introduced him to the establishment. We were a comfort and a support to each other."

Joe was remembering just such a confession in a moonlit garden in Simla when she'd talked of a man she'd loved, and he wondered.

"I was rash. I confided in him. But why not? He gave me good advice and he brought me more clients—he's a well-connected man. I told him one day, for his amusement, of a fantasy shared with one of my girls...Thaïs, it was...A regular customer of hers had whispered in her ear. They do. And my girls are required as part of their job to pass on their confidences."

"God! I'd like to get a look at your little black book, madame," Bonnefoye chortled.

"Clients assume—perhaps you will know the reason for this, Inspector—that the head on the adjoining pillow may always be disregarded. The woman, by nature of her employment, must be empty-headed, deaf or have a short memory. None of that is true.

"Thaïs told me that her client, a regular visitor and an agreeable young man, was suffering at the hands of his old uncle. Known for years to be his uncle's heir, he had been played with, tormented beyond reason by the old man, on whom he was financially dependent. Finally the chap had informed his nephew that he was to be cut out of the will, that he (a keen theatre-goer) was leaving the entire fortune to the Garrick Club in London, to be distributed to indigent old actors. Our client spent some time outlining to Thaïs exactly what he wanted to see done to his uncle by way of retribution. His fantasy was amusing. He saw his uncle centre

stage at the Garrick Theatre, spotlit of course, knife in his heart and an orifice unmentionable in mixed company stuffed with banknotes."

"Oh, good Lord!" said Joe. "November 1923?"

Alice smiled. "I told my friend jokingly about this, and to my surprise he didn't laugh. He was intrigued. He gave way to a fantasy of his own. 'What a cracking notion! Well, why not? Tell Thaïs to whisper in the boy's ear that all his dreams can come true! Overnight he will become a very rich and very grateful client, will he not? Let's put a proposal to him. We undertake to set the stage and provide the body for a fee to be agreed. How much?'

"Thinking he was playing a game, I suggested a sum.

"'Ridiculous! Triple that. The overheads will be tremendous. People to pay off…Thaïs must be rewarded…and Vévé.'"

"Vévé?"

"Vincent Viviani, my Zouave. In the end, my friend went to London with him to smooth his path."

"Obviously a successful outing. I remember the case. No one was ever arrested. Yes, a smooth beginning. You were inspired to continue?"

"Yes. Suddenly he was talking about what 'we' would do and I realised I'd lost control. There was nothing I could do about it—I've told you, he is well connected and powerful."

"And you made a profit from these excursions into Hades?"

"Oh, yes. But it was more than that. He enjoyed what he was doing. A game, you know."

"You must have exercised a measure of control over him? In the selection of victims, Alice?"

For a moment she was puzzled, trying to guess his meaning.

"You appear, like the black widow spider, only to kill the

males of the species. I have yet to hear—apart from the unfortunate Mademoiselle Raissac, who merited punishment
as an informer—of a female victim."

Alice breathed out—with relief? "Of course! You must
have noticed our clients are men? They have aggressive fantasies about other men in their lives. Men blocking their
advancement, men deserving an act of revenge on the battlefield or in the boudoir, questions of inheritance. Sometimes
a vengeful fantasy will be triggered by a hurt done to a female in his circle: the father who requests that his impressionable daughter's young man, whom he has discovered
to be a penniless male vamp, be thrown from the Eiffel
Tower..."

"You don't jib at academics, Alice?" Joe asked, interested
in her methods. "I'm thinking of a case in 1923—must have
been towards the very start of your activities. A professor
who ended up inspecting, rather more closely than he would
have liked, the inside of a mummy case. In the Louvre? In
front of a delighted audience of fellow academics? No?"

"No. Not one of ours. I'm sure if we'd been asked...he
couldn't have resisted."

Joe was tiring of her games. "Bonnefoye, Alice here confessed to me while we were alone in the back of the taxi
that she went to the theatre that night to save the life of
Sir George who was—as we suspected—the real target." He
filled in the details, which came as no surprise to the
Frenchman.

"I'm sure Sir George will be most relieved to hear that he
survived!" He grinned. "And doubtless pleased to hear that
Miss Alice did what she could to divert the knife from his
throat onto a more deserving one. Can't wait to tell him!
But, Joe, there is one detail in this nasty piece of entrapment
that puzzles me. The tickets and the note that drew him in—
I'd like to hear her account for that."

"You'd shudder if you knew how much they cost, those tickets! But Somerton was determined to have his fun—you might almost say desperate—and offered to pay well over the odds for a good performance."

"And the note? The note that lured George to the theatre? How did you know about his relationship with his cousin at the Embassy? Did he speak of it in Simla?"

A trap.

She looked puzzled. "Why, no. I believe I must have left India before ever his cousin took up a post here...Not certain. He never mentioned a cousin at any rate."

Then she looked at him and smiled. And Joe felt the furry feet of the spider easing their way up his spine. Selecting a soft place for her fangs.

"My boss, as you call him, wrote the note himself."

"Taking a reasonable shot at the handwriting, it would appear?"

"Why would it not be an entirely reasonable shot? Not necessary to fake one's own handwriting, Commander!"

Chapter 25

"Before I say another word, Commander…Inspector… I want your reassurance that I may walk free from here when I've told you what you want to know. I came here as a witness and will leave as a witness. I'll sign any statement you care to draw up, but I must go free. I will give you an address at which I may be reached. If you require me to attend a magistrate's hearing or a trial I will, of course, do that. So long as the man I denounce is in custody."

"And if we don't agree to that?"

"Then, one morning, you'll find me dead in my cell in the women's prison. His reach is a long one. And the killings will go on. Is that the proof you will be looking for?"

"Up to you, Bonnefoye. I don't trust her."

He could see his young colleague had been fired by the chance of landing a male suspect. A foreigner, a well-to-do foreigner. Fourier would not have hesitated. Was it likely that the madam of a brothel, no matter how successful, could devise these murderous attacks? No, there must be a

male intelligence and will underpinning everything. And who was to say he was wrong? Here was Alice on the verge of trading a devastating betrayal for her freedom.

"I agree to your terms," Bonnefoye said after a long pause. "And, madame, please do not think of deceiving me. I too have a very long reach."

"John Pollock," she said simply, and held out her mug for more coffee.

Joe got to his feet, agitated, barely able to keep his hands off her. He wanted to shake her until she told the truth. A different truth. "I don't believe a word of this. Nonsense! I've met the man. A cousin of Sir George's would never…" He stopped himself from further reinforcing her jaundiced view of men. He was quite certain that she resented the easy camaraderie between them. Why should he trust John Pollock after a half hour's interview and herself not at all after five years, was her flawed reasoning.

"Pardon me, madame," said Bonnefoye, icily polite, "but to clarify: you are accusing Sir George's cousin not only of masterminding a series of improbable murders in the French capital and now we must understand in London also—but of accepting a commission from a fellow country-man to kill his own cousin? You say he did not question the projected crime but went along with it, planned it, and had it not been for your intervention, would have exe-cuted it?"

Alice considered. "Yes. That's just about it. Well done. Will you write that down or shall I?"

"I think we ought at this point to mention the word 'motive.' Why on earth would he do that?"

"Oh, come on! Can you be so unaware? What sort of de-tectives am I dealing with? Must I do all the work?"

"Be kind, Alice," warned Joe.

"Very well. George doesn't talk much of it but he's actually filthy rich, you know. Stands to reason! The man had a finger in every pie in India and many of them are full of plums. That's what India was all about, you know. John Company...exploitation...Empire...it all boils down to cash. In accounts in Switzerland in many cases. George, with his knowledge of the way things would go—and he it was who pushed them where he wanted them to go on occasions—was well placed to make the most spectacular investments. He's retired and come home to enjoy the fruits of his labours. He has no heir. For many years his cousin has been—still is—named in his will as recipient of his wealth. But John has lately become concerned about his cousin's intentions...his state of mind...Unleashed from the stifling routine of India, he seems about to plunge into a world of gaiety. Who knows? Perhaps he might even be entrapped into marriage by some girl on the make? And produce an heir of his own within the year? It happens a dozen times a season in Paris! Pity I didn't think of it myself! Much safer to accept Somerton's timely commission. After all—the responsibility lies with the client, doesn't it?"

"Jack Pollock earns a perfectly decent salary. He may well be ennobled in the near future off his own bat. He doesn't need, like Frederick Somerton, to wait around to inherit a title."

Again he was rewarded with the pitying, world-weary gaze. "Do you have any idea how much it costs to underpin the life of a titled man? The estate? The household? The ceremony? The motorcars? The city house? The upkeep of a future Lady Pollock? He is like, yet not like, George. Don't be deceived. They are opposite sides of the same coin. Made from the same metal, but the features are different. Jack is

extravagant, fast-living. Ruthless, they are both ruthless, but, unlike George, his cousin has no conscience."

"Set and Osiris," Bonnefoye murmured. "I knew that ugly creature would stick his bent nose in before long. Good God! That little scene at the Louvre must have given him the idea for all this carnage! Planted a seed!"

Alice looked from one to the other in puzzlement. They didn't bother to explain.

Half an hour later, a document had been drawn up to Alice's satisfaction and she signed it.

"My gun, Joe? May I?"

He took it from his pocket and handed it over hurriedly as though it would burn his fingers.

"Well, I think I'll be off now. Don't bother to get up. I'm sure I can find my way out. I'll mind my manners and pause to thank Moulin graciously for his hospitality and be on my way. I'll leave you to curse me when my back's turned."

"Moulin keeps his brandy in a bottle behind *The Man in the Iron Mask*," said Joe heavily. Bonnefoye poured out generous measures into the dregs of the coffee and they sipped it silently.

"Which of us is going to tell George?" asked Bonnefoye.

"I will. You must be getting pretty fed up with all this palaver. Foreigners messing about in your life, murdering each other on French soil. Jolly bad form, what!" he finished in an imitation of Wilberforce Jennings' braying voice. "And I must find time to stroll into the Embassy and slap the cuffs on Pollock."

"And we'd better watch our backs on the streets. I haven't forgotten there's a pet Zouave slinking about."

"Well, well! Who'd have thought Fantômas, stalking

the streets of Paris, would turn out to be a blue-eyed Englishman reciting the latest cricket scores!"

On their way through the morgue, Joe averted his eyes from the busy scene at three of the marble tables. He'd had enough of death for one day. But he was not to be allowed to ignore it entirely. Moulin called out to them as they appeared. He was holding something bloodstained up to the light in pincers and, carrying on with his work, said: "Somerton. Your last customer but one. The toxicology report came through. No, he wasn't poisoned but they mentioned that he had a very high level of an opiate in his system. A pain-killer. I took a further look at the body. And there it was. A cancer. Well developed. I'd say he had no more than a month at the most to live. Pity the killer didn't know that. He could have saved himself a tidy sum."

Quietly Joe absorbed the news and, going to stand at Moulin's shoulder while he worked on, murmured: "The killer did know. The killer, the instigator of the crime, was Somerton himself. He knew, then, he hadn't got long and was determined to treat himself to a variety of luxuries before he snuffed it. He wanted to see Sir George suffer and in the most dramatic way..." He filled in the story as far as it was known to them.

"Mon Dieu! But—what a lucky escape! You must take your friend out to celebrate his good fortune."

"He's not going to be much in the mood for celebrating when he learns the identity of the man we've been calling Set."

"Great heavens! You managed to get it out of her? I heard no squeaks of outrage, no rattling of irons?"

"In the end she was all cooperation. Largely, I think,

because the information she was giving us she knew was most unwelcome to our ears. Set is, in fact, the alter ego of Sir George. The obverse of the medallion—his young cousin. Very sad and disturbing. And it's not over yet. We're just off into the night to find and arrest Set. Can't say I've ever tangled with the God of Evil. Any suggestions? Ah, well..."

"Do I need to prepare a few more slabs?" said Moulin lugubriously. "For goodness' sake, take care, Sandilands. What gun are you carrying? Are you armed?"

"Not so much as a toothpick," said Joe.

"Here, take this," said Moulin, selecting a shining silver tool from his tray and rather embarrassed by his gesture. "Put it away in your pocket. It's my best scalpel. Razor sharp. Don't touch the edge! Handle with extreme care."

Chapter 26

They stepped out into the grey and gold light of a spring evening. There was a faint glimmer in the sky to the west and, across the river, dying rays were caught up and given a last flicker of life by the open windows of high attic rooms, still hot from the day. But a mist was already beginning to curl up from the Seine and Joe shivered.

"Now, I know you won't want to hear me say this," Bonnefoye began cheerfully, "because I'm quite aware you're all fired to go and stick your newly acquired weapon into the black heart of Set, but there are two people we must see first. Fourier and Sir George. Any preference?"

"As we're on the spot—Fourier. Let's start with him, shall we?"

"I'd prefer it. I have to report back on the fracas in the boulevard just now. He'll be waiting to see me. Seems to be taking more of an interest. He grudgingly gave me ten blokes to mount the raid, after all! Feel up to the stairs, then, do you?"

Police headquarters was busy. Fourier, they were told, was busy but he had asked to see them as soon as they arrived. The chief inspector appeared not to have left his desk or changed his clothes since Joe had last seen him on the morning after the murder. A closer look, however, revealed a different pattern of coffee stains on his shirt front.

Juggling papers and cards, the inspector demonstrated his busy-ness and asked them to take a seat. The enquiry, he informed them, was progressing. His sergeant dashed in with a sheet of foolscap. Fourier was instantly absorbed by what he read there and, taking out his pen, made a few alterations and additions to the text.

"The copy," he announced. "The copy, as we call it, for the press. I have it. Anything vital missing? Not having had your report yet, Bonnefoye, I'm working in the dark. What do you think?"

He began to read out the salient points. "Now then... *Brigandage in Bohemia*. Here we go. Guaranteed to get them going—a reference to brigandage... *Officers working under the direction of Commissaire Casimir Fourier... dramatic shootout... three gangsters dead... no bystanders hurt... police squad remain on the alert and ensuring public safety in this erstwhile peaceable quartier...* Well? What are you thinking?"

"Can't argue with the facts, sir," said Bonnefoye. "It will do as a preliminary account."

"Had you thought, Fourier, you might insert something on the lines of: *The peace of Mount Parnassus was shattered last night when...*"

"Good. Good." He scratched in the insertion. "Now. Next. Take a look at this line-up, will you? You requested it, I believe. Anything there you like the look of?"

He passed them a hand of six Bertillon identity cards. They shuffled ugly face after ugly face complete with cranial measurements and descriptions of distinguishing features.

Three had accompanying fingerprint records stuck along the bottom of the card. All the men were aged between twenty and forty and all had a scar on the right jaw.

They spotted him at the same moment.

"That's him!" said Joe.

"Gotcha!" said Bonnefoye.

He handed one of the cards to Fourier. "Everything we need to know about our knifeman. Vincent Viviani. You'll find, sir, he's known in his milieu as Vévé. Ex-Zouave. Scar as reported by Miss Watkins. He works for the outfit who run, or have been running until this evening, the premises in the boulevard du Montparnasse. And—icing on the cake!—some genius in the ID department bothered to take his prints when he was last a guest here, evidently. Sir, if you can get someone to check the fingerprints from the box at the theatre, you'll find a sticky one to the left of the exit. Fixed in pomade from the dead man's hair. We think it will correspond with the prints recorded here."

Fourier exchanged a glance with Joe. It trembled on the edge of enthusiasm.

"Though, of course, we need to take the man into custody in order to make a comparison," Bonnefoye said carefully.

"You're telling me you haven't got him yet? I would expect him to be standing in manacles outside the door by now," grumbled Fourier.

"We've been busy tracking down, not this underling—vicious killer though he be—but the mastermind who has set the whole organisation in operation," said Joe. "Bonnefoye, will you tell him?"

Bonnefoye's account was succinct, sure and surgically precise. It just managed not to be sarcastic.

"And now I'm to understand that, though you have an identity for the killer, he's beyond our reach? Another bloody diplomat! Buggers! Corral the lot in their embassies

and you'd reduce the crime in the city by half! I sometimes think they send their rogues and scallywags over to us to get rid of them. Now what the hell do we do? Can't touch him. He can sit in there as long as he likes, drinking tea. And when he's ready, he can jump in the back of an Embassy car, pull a rug over his head and scuttle off back where he came from on the next plane."

His eyes narrowed in cunning. "You!" he said, addressing Joe. "These are your countrymen. You can gain access. Go in there and get him out. As soon as he's out of protective custody, so to speak, he can be provoked into a rash act and you can shoot him. We'll back you up—swear it was self-defence. There'll be an almighty stink but they'll just have to accept it. And better if the whole thing is set up by one of their own. It's the only way. What do you think?"

"You're suggesting I enter the Embassy, slap his face with my glove and call him out? 'The Bois de Boulogne at dawn, Pollock! Your choice of weapon,'" Joe drawled. "Oh, very well. It's a plan, I suppose. Just leave it to me, old man."

As they made their way over the courtyard to pick up a taxi Bonnefoye spoke, concerned. "Sandilands, you're not—"

"Of course not!" said Joe. "But, all the same, I'd rather Fourier left it to me. Not that he has much of a choice. You know how slow these negotiations with embassies can be. It was crudely put but Fourier was right. There'd be representations, accusations, rebuttals, counter-accusations... oh, a mountain of work for the eager young tail-waggers they employ over there. And it would all end exactly as he forecast. Pollock would disappear in the night and the French would retaliate by blackballing the English entrant in the Gold Cup race at Longchamp. Or even worse –withdrawing the loan of their string orchestra. We've got to sort this out

ourselves. And we'll take advice from the best-placed source."

"Sir George?" said Bonnefoye. "Oh, my God! Right then. It's back to the Mouffe!"

Sir George and Amélie Bonnefoye were playing a game of pi-quet at the kitchen table and attending to what smelled like a lamb stew when the two men arrived.

After a shrewd look at their expressions, George put his cards down and said quietly: "Would this be a good time to have a drink of wine or do you have to maintain a clear head for the rest of the evening?"

"Both," said Joe. "So—one glass would be most welcome, Madame Bonnefoye."

She brought a bottle and four glasses and a dish of olives and settled down with them in the salon.

"Maman, if you don't mind...we have some disturbing things to reveal..." Bonnefoye started to say.

"I don't mind. So, go on then—disturb us."

"Sir," Joe began, "I have now met and interviewed your cousin at the Embassy. He is well and sends his warmest regards, and hopes to see you when this is all over and you come out of hiding. Though whether such a reunion will ever take place now remains to be seen..."

Sir George listened calmly to the account, occasionally shooting a question to Joe or Bonnefoye, but without exclamation or hand-wringing or hair-tearing.

"So that's why she was there, at the theatre," said Madame Bonnefoye. "Your guardian angel! She was protecting you. Fearful for *your* life, not her own. Thank God she was there!" She patted his hand comfortingly.

Confidences, it seemed to Joe, had been exchanged over culinary activities at the kitchen table.

"But where is she now? You let her go like that, un-escorted, friendless, into the night? She must be feeling very uneasy at large in the city with two men pursuing her? I'd have taken my chances with you and Jean-Philippe," Amélie Bonnefoye said loyally.

Finally George spoke up. "You're right, Amélie, so we must assume that she, in fact, is *not* in any danger. She's a calculating woman. Always comes out on top. I admire her for it. Wouldn't want to see a woman of her quality humiliated by the likes of this pair of hounds, in fact. And, to look at this positively—of whom exactly does she have to be afraid? I think she's been pulling the wool over your eyes, you fellows. Her Zouave? Saved his life, did you say? Well, there you are! Sounds like an eternal ally to me. He was probably waiting for her on the street corner. Seen this with the roughest, toughest fellows you can imagine in India—give their lives to protect the Memsahib."

Bluster, Joe thought with a stab of pity. Even Amélie looked away, uneasy.

"And her other nightmare is, as she and you would have it—my cousin. My cousin! Little Jackie. No, he's a good fellow. Opinionated, over-active, too clever by half and something of a bounder in his early years but—by God!—the man's a gentleman!" He thought intensely for a moment and added: "I think you'll probably recognise *me* in that description? And you're right. He's very like me, you know. Do you seriously believe *I* would go about taking orders for bespoke crimes?" He put on the unctuous tones of a Savile Row assistant: "'And does Sir have a style in mind? We can offer the assisted leap from the Eiffel Tower, the dagger in the ribs at the Garrick and, on special offer this week, blood-letting in the Louvre? A snip at two and six!'"

"I understand, sir, that you have met your cousin at long intervals... people change... similar men may have just one

slight distinction which sends them spinning off in different directions. You've heard of the villain Fantômas? Bonnefoye tells me his twin brother was the police inspector Juve of the Brigade Criminelle. Two men incredibly alike in their cunning, perseverance and energy. But at some point in their history, their paths diverged and their similar qualities carried them off towards opposite ends. One good, the other evil."

George considered this. "Balderdash!" he concluded. "Psychological piffle! Fiction! This is real life we're considering."

"But real death also, George," murmured Madame Bonnefoye.

"Amélie," he said. "My coat! Only one way to settle this. I'll go and find Jackie and ask him." Catching her dismay, he hesitated and then added gently, "But not, perhaps, before we've sampled the *navarin d'agneau printanier*. I've put a bottle of Gigondas to breathe. Hope that was all right?"

"Perfect! But, listen! It's a stew. It will reheat beautifully," she said comfortably. "Tomorrow, or later this evening. Just come home for it. All of you."

Chapter 27

"Sir George! At last! Welcome, sir. How good to see you out and about again ... Gentlemen ..."

Beneath Harry Quantock's bluff greeting Joe sensed a trickle of tension flowing.

"To see Pollock? Well, of course ... and yes, he is in the building at the moment. Um ... look—why don't you come along to his study and wait for him there? I'll have him paged. He's upstairs in the salon dancing attendance on the ambassador's lady. Actually," he confided, "this could be rather a bad moment. They're just about to take off for the opera. His Excellency can't abide the opera so John usually undertakes escort duties. Are you quite certain this can't wait? Oh, very well ..."

They went to wait in the study, choosing to stare at the cricket photographs rather than catch each other's eye. George was looking confident, in his element. Bonnefoye was looking uncomfortable. Joe was just looking, taking in the neatness and utter normality of everything around him.

All papers were filed in trays and left ready for the morning's work. The flowers in one corner of the desk had been re-plenished. On the mantelpiece, the photograph frame surrounding Pollock's mother's smiling Victorian features had been polished up. In the bin, a week-old copy of *The Times,* open at the crossword puzzle. Completed.

Pollock swept in a few minutes later, handsome in evening dress. He surprised Joe by heading at once for George, who had risen to his feet, and enveloping him in a hug. The two men muttered and exclaimed together for a while, holding each other at arm's length to verify that, yes, both were looking in the pink of good health and Paris was obviously agreeing with them.

He turned his attention to Joe and Bonnefoye, and George introduced the young Frenchman. Pleasantries were exchanged. Joe had the clear feeling that Pollock was trying hard not to look at his watch.

"I'm sorry to disturb your evening, Pollock . . ." Joe began.

"So you should be!" he replied with an easy grin. "I'm just off to hear René Maison singing in *Der Rosenkavalier.* A first for me—do you know it?"

"Yes, indeed. Charming entertainment. Full of disguises, deceit and skulduggery of one sort or another. The police dash in and solve all the problems in the end, I recall. I think you'll like it."

George threw him a withering glance and took up the reins. "We have a problem, Jackie. Or rather, these two Keystone Kops have a problem. Which you can solve. I want you to tell them you're not a degenerate and a multiple murderer."

"I beg your pardon? I say, George, old man . . . what *is* going on? I really do have to rush off, you know. Look—can you all come back and play tomorrow?" He looked uneasily over his shoulder, hearing a party forming up in the foyer.

"I'm afraid it's no joke, Pollock," said Joe. "A certain accusation has been made..." He abandoned the police phrasing. "Alice Conyers has shopped you. She's told us everything. Her—your—organisation has been shot to pieces, literally, while you've been sipping sherry and humming arias in Her Excellency's ear. It's over. The crew in the boulevard du Montparnasse are stretched out either in the morgue or on a hospital bed."

Pollock tugged at his starched collar and sank onto a chair. "Alice?" he murmured. "Is she all right?"

"Right as rain. Not much looking forward to seeing *you* again. But she's gone off into the night—armed."

"You know Alice, Jackie?" George was unbelieving.

"Yes. 'Fraid I do! Oh, my Lord, I knew all this would catch up with me! Never thought it would be *you*, old man, who brought the blade down on me, though. I say—is there any way of keeping this under our hats?" He looked anxiously at the door again. "I wouldn't like His Excellency to find out his aide is a bit of a bounder." He grinned sheepishly. "I'd have to kiss goodbye to my evenings at the opera and the ballet and the gallery openings. And I enjoy all that sort of thing enormously. I'm sure he'd understand if I explained it all in my own words and in my own time... I mean—we're not puritans here—we're men of the world, don't you know! The gossip would soon burn itself out... in fact, my image might even be burnished in some people's eyes..."

Bonnefoye could keep silent no longer. "Bloody English! Is this the understatement you are so proud of, Sandilands? Six deaths in three days, your own life in danger, Sir George a candidate for the guillotine and the perpetrator confesses he's a bit of a bounder! Well—rap him over the knuckles and let's be off, shall we?"

He got to his feet in disgust.

Joe joined him, shoulder to shoulder.

"No joke, Pollock," he said stiffly. "Alice has told us how you took over her business and turned it sour. Used it as a base for a very hideous assassination bureau. I don't think you were involved in any way in the Louvre murder—except as a man casually caught up by circumstances—but I do believe that you learned from that episode . . . were inspired by it . . . recognised there a service that was not supplied by anyone else. You could name your fee. No client could complain about the outcome without condemning himself. Absolute security. You became Set."

Pollock slumped in his seat, apparently stunned, lost in thought. Finally he waved them back to their chairs. "I think you'd better hear this," he said, heavily.

"I fetched up here in . . . what was it, George? . . . 1923. I liked my employment. I'm good at what I do. Round peg in round hole. Ask anyone. Only two things I missed, really." He looked shiftily at Joe. "Yes, you've guessed—the cricket. But apart from that—female companionship. I had a mistress . . . or two . . . in Egypt, my last posting, and I was lonely here in Paris. Yes—lonely. They do things differently here." He smiled. "Oh, lots of commercial opportunities, street girls, chorus girls available. Not my style. I like women, Sandilands. I mean, I really like them. I like to talk with them, laugh, swap opinions, have a nice hug as well as the more obvious things.

"I met Alice at the theatre one night. She spilled her drink on my shoes in the bar. Scrambled about on the carpet with her handkerchief, trying to make all well. One of her tricks, I was to discover later. Who can resist the sight of a beautiful, penitent woman at his feet? She took my address, saying she wanted to write a note of apology. She was swept off at that moment by a large and protective gentleman. You can imagine my astonishment when, next day, a box arrived for me. Containing a wonderful pair of shoes. My size—she'd established that much while she was down there. And much more

expensive than any I could have afforded. I was flattered, intrigued, drawn in..."

Bonnefoye stirred impatiently.

"Upshot was—I met her for tea. She told me about herself... quite openly... and the way she made a living. I was interested. I went along and approved. And then I realised what she really wanted me for."

"Go on."

"Contacts! I was to be her opening into the diplomatic world." He paused, reflecting, and then smiled his boyish smile again. "Not quite the teeming pool of skirt-chasers she had anticipated, varied lot that we are here! But I liked what she had to offer. I liked Alice! I became a regular customer. And, I had thought, until you burst in here with your hair-raising and ludicrous stories, a friend. I trusted her. I had thought we were very close. How could she? I don't understand... How could...?"

To Joe's horror, he saw the blue eyes begin to fill with tears and looked tactfully away.

"My poor chap!" said Sir George. "Many suffered similarly in India. Ask Joe! We all learn that the woman keeps no friends. She is totally self-interested. Unscrupulous." He turned angrily on Joe and Bonnefoye. "Now do you see what we've done? Jack is not one of your criminal insensitives, you know."

"You're generous to say 'we,' George. You should know, Pollock, that your cousin would hear not a word against you. He didn't believe Alice's story. And he was right. She used your relationship, the details of her close familiarity with you, to convince us that you were the guilty party behind these crimes." He gave a sharp, bitter laugh. "She traded a man's reputation and possibly his life for her freedom. And who knows where the hell she is now?"

"Out in the mists, armed, calling her Zouave to heel, plan-

ning her next murderous display?" said Bonnefoye. "What clowns we are! She's made monkeys of the lot of us! She's the one behind it all, isn't she? There is...never has been a Set."

"More of a Kali, perhaps," muttered George. "Indian Goddess of Death."

"Look, you fellows, you've already ruined my evening. Bursting in here like Ratty and Moley with old Badger brandishing his stick, come to tell me the game's up..." Jack Pollock grinned at George. "Why not come back again tomorrow and ruin my day? I've heard only a fraction of what you have to tell me but really—you will understand, George—when her Excellency calls, the aide comes running. That was her calling and here I am—running." Pollock got to his feet. "Fascinating story! No—truly fascinating! You could make an opera of it."

He went over to the desk and plucked a red rose from the vase. "Must get into the part, I suppose. Der Rosenkavalier— here he comes!" He nodded his head to the three of them, stuck the rose defiantly between his teeth and tangoed to the door.

With a sickening vision of the red roses swirling away on the current down the Seine, Joe called after him impulsively: "Pollock! If you have to go over a bridge, take care, won't you? Oh, I'm so sorry! How ridiculous! Do forgive me!"

Pollock, wondering, took the rose from his teeth and threaded it through his buttonhole. "No bridges between here and the Opéra, Ratty. It's a straight dash down the riverbank. See you all again tomorrow, then? Harry will show you out."

"Bridges?" said Bonnefoye when the door closed behind Pollock. "What was that all about?"

"Oh, a phobia of mine. Some people fear snakes, some spiders, others heights . . . me—I can't abide crossing rivers. It was the rose that triggered that display of weakness."

George wasn't listening. "Look—Jackie's got the telephone," he announced. "Why don't you use it to ring up your mother, Jean-Philippe? She'll be concerned. Tell her we're all coming home safe and well."

"But I never ring my mother—"

"Then I think you should start. Not easy being the mother of a policeman."

Bonnefoye made no move to oblige and, with a snort of exasperation, George seized the receiver and took up the earpiece. He spoke in his Governor's voice, friendly but authoritative: "Hello? This is Sir George Jardine here. I'm down below and I want you to connect me with this number. It's a city number. Got a pencil to hand, have you?"

After the usual arrangement of clicks and bangs they heard Madame Bonnefoye reply. "Hold on a minute will you, madame? I have your son on the line." He beckoned to Bonnefoye and held out the earpiece.

"Yes, it is me, Maman. Oh—well! Yes, it went well. A waste of our time, I think. False alarm. Nothing sinister to report. Look, we're all going to climb into a taxi and come back for supper. We'll need to stop off for a minute or two at the Quai to brief Fourier . . . we don't want him inadvertently to go laying siege to the British Embassy . . . and then come straight on home. Half an hour."

As their taxi moved off, a second, which had been waiting across the road and a few yards down, started up and slid into the busy traffic stream behind them.

Chapter 28

They had left George sitting in the back of the taxi in the courtyard while they trudged up the stairs to confess to Fourier that they'd been given misleading information. They emerged fifteen minutes later, silent, dismayed by the chief inspector's glee at their predicament.

Before they could cross the courtyard, they were alerted by the sound of running feet clattering down the stairs after them. Fourier's sergeant shouted their names and they waited for him to catch up with them. "Inspector! Sir! Message just came through to the Commissaire. Emergency down by the Square du Vert Galant. Roistering. There's been roistering going on. They will do it! Young folk got drunk and someone's been pushed in the river. You're nearest, sir. Can you go down and sort it out?"

"No. I'm busy," said Bonnefoye. "Do I look like a life-guard? We have a two-man detail down there from nine o'clock onwards for these eventualities. This is for uniform. They'll deal with it."

"That's the point, sir," said the sergeant, puzzled. "Can't be found. They've buzzed off somewhere. What should I do then, sir? You'd better tell me... just so as it's clear." He evidently didn't want to go back upstairs and report the inspector's refusal of an order.

Bonnefoye groaned. "I'll go and take a look. But I warn you—looking's all I intend to do. I won't get my feet wet!"

Turning to Joe: "Look—not sure I like this much, Joe. It's... irregular. I'd rather deal with it myself. I'm not so quixotic as you—you'd jump in to save a dog! You go on back with Sir George. I'll grab another taxi when I've found those two sluggards who ought to be here."

"No—I've a better idea," Joe replied. "I'm coming with you. But we'll send George home as advance warning that we really are serious about supper. George!" he shouted, opening the back door. "Slight change in arrangements. Something to check on down by the river. You carry on, will you? Jean-Philippe and I will be along in say—half an hour. Driver, take this gentleman to the address he will give you as soon as you're under way."

He banged peremptorily on the taxi roof to deny George a chance to argue and watched as the taxi made its way out of the courtyard.

They began to run along the Quai des Orfèvres towards the bow-shaped point of the city island beyond the Pont Neuf. A romantic spot, green and inviting and dotted with willow trees, it was a magnet for the youth of the city with proposals and declarations to make but also for the many drunken tramps who seemed to wash in and out with the tide. A hundred yards. Bonnefoye gave warning of their approach by tooting insistently on the police whistle he kept in his pocket. No duty officer came hurrying up to join them with tumbling apologies.

"Why *us*?" Bonnefoye spluttered. "A whole bloody build-

ing full of cops behind us and who's rushing for a dip in this open sewer? We are. Must be nuts. Where are the beat men? I'll have their badges in the morning!"

They paused to get their breath back on the Pont Neuf. The loveliest bridge, Joe thought, and certainly the oldest, it spanned the Seine in two arms, divided almost exactly by the square. Centuries ago it had been a stage as well as a thoroughfare and marketplace, a paved space free of mud where comedy troupes could perform. The Italian Pantaloon, the clown Tabarin, uselessly flourishing his wooden sword, had drawn the crowds with burlesque acts of buffoonery. In an echo of the rather sinister jollity, each rounded arch was graced with a stone-carved gargoyle at its centre, grinning out over the river. Joe and Bonnefoye added their own stony profiles to the scene as they peered over the parapet into the gloom, searching the oily surface of the fast-flowing water, the only illumination the reflections of the gas lamps along the quays and a full moon dipping flirtatiously in and out of the veils of mist rising up from the river.

"Spring surge," said Bonnefoye. "Quite a current running. If anyone's fallen in there, they'll be halfway to Le Havre by now. Hopeless. Listen! What can you hear?"

"Nothing."

"Exactly. No one here. Not even a *clochard*. At the first sign of trouble they're off. So there has been some trouble, I'm thinking. Sod it!"

A strangled scream rang out from below in the park and to the right. Male? Female? Impossible to tell.

"Here we go," groaned Bonnefoye. "I'll go down and investigate. You stay up here and be spotter. Give me a shout the moment you see something." He clattered off down the stone staircase to the lower level, still tooting hopefully.

Left alone on the bridge, Joe clung with tense fingers to

the stonework of the parapet, steadying himself. It always
hit him like an attack of vertigo. A combination of height
and the insecurity of seeing a dark body of water sliding,
snakelike and treacherous, beneath his feet. He closed his
eyes for a moment to regain control and heard Bonnefoye's
whistle cut off in mid-blast.

Joe looked anxiously to his left, aware of a slight movement along the bridge. A tall figure was approaching. He
moved nearer, coming to a halt ten yards distant, under a
lamp, deliberately showing himself. Dark-jawed, unsmiling,
chin raised defiantly to the light, right hand in pocket. The
Zouave. Waiting.

Angrily, Joe looked to his right to check his escape route
and his second nightmare hit him with the force of a bolt of
electricity. His body shook and he fought to catch his
breath. A figure, also ten yards distant. Not so tall as the
first but infinitely more terrifying. He could have been any
gentleman returning from a show, shining silk top hat on
his head, well-tailored evening dress, white waistcoat, diamond studs glittering in his cuffs. Urbane, reassuring, romantic even, until you noticed the black mask covering the
upper half of his face. In a theatrical gesture, he raised his
left hand, white-gloved, to cup his chin, looking specula-
tively at Joe. His right hand, ungloved, went up and slightly
behind his back. Slowly enough to show the gleaming zarin
it held.

Joe began to breathe fast, steadying his nerves. Two men.
He didn't fancy his chances much. He thought, on the
whole, he'd go for the toff first. The leader. Though by the
time he'd closed with him, the Zouave would have sunk his
knife into his back. Take the Zouave first and the Fantômas
figure would be ripping his throat out from behind. He remembered Dr. Moulin's hands in the morgue, clutching his

hair, demonstrating the hold, and his skin crawled. That's how it would happen.

No gun, he'd have to fight with his fists and feet. Then he remembered the doctor's parting concern and his strange gift. He felt in his pocket, encountering the cold steel of the surgical instrument. Better than nothing and they wouldn't be expecting it. These creatures only attacked the defence-less and the unready, he told himself. "It's razor sharp," the doctor had warned. But all Joe's instinct was pushing him to explore, to handle his weapon. To decide—slashing or stab-bing? Which would be the more effective? His safety—his life—depended on the quality of the steel implement. By the time he closed with his assailant, it would be too late to find out. Worth a cut thumb to be certain. And the quick flare of pain would jolt his senses fully awake. Tentatively he ran a thumb along the cutting blade. He repeated the gesture, more urgently, pressing his thumb down hard, the whole length of the cutting edge. And moaned in distress.

There was no edge. It was blunt. Not a scalpel. It was as much use to him as a fish knife. He held it in his hand any-way because he had nothing else. It would still glitter in the gaslight. It might fool them into thinking he was armed. And then, with a rush, with a flash of insight that came hours too late, he realised.

He could deceive no one. He was himself the fool. No mis-take had been made when he was handed the useless tool. It was a stage prop. He was standing here, gaslit from both sides, at the stone prow of the island, framed up for his au-dience below, a modern-day Mr. Punch. The only thing lack-ing was the cap and bells on his head and the hurdy-gurdy musical accompaniment.

Strangely, he felt a compulsion to play the part handed to him. To let them know that, however belatedly, he had

worked it out. He held up the instrument before his eyes in a parody of a scene from *Macbeth*. "Is this a scalpel which I see before me?" he mused. "Or could it be an earwax remover?"

He looked to the right again and saw the smile start in the masked eyes, the nod that acknowledged his moment of understanding. He looked to his left and the Zouave, with panther stride, began to close on him. He pushed the scalpel back into his trouser pocket, took a deep breath, put both hands on the parapet and vaulted over, leaping as far out into the void as he could manage, hoping he'd miss the built-up quayside and hit the water.

The cold of the spring surge waters knocked the breath from his body and he struggled to the surface gasping and choking. The stench of the river water was sickening. An open sewer, Bonnefoye had called it. He stared as a dead dog, bloated and disgusting, swept towards him and then bobbed away before it made contact. He struck out for the bank, glad enough to be carried by the current at an angle to the Pont Neuf, away from the two creatures on the bridge. He wasn't a strong swimmer and his jacket was heavy with the weight of water, dragging him down. He spent a few moments treading water while he struggled out of it. Noises behind him. A gunshot rang out. He ducked under the surface and allowed himself to drift a few more yards.

They could with ease plot his course downstream, he thought, with the treacherous moon now lighting up the river like a satin ribbon. One could remain on the bridge watching for him to break the surface, the other could intercept him at any point along the quay, and be there, standing waiting, while Joe struggled on the greasy cobbles that revetted the quayside. He would have to slip and slide and claw his way up over the green scum only to find a fresh and armed adversary looking down on him. Might as well drift

straight down the centre and head for—what had Bonnefoye
said—Le Havre?

And then anger took over. He'd been fooled. Completely
fooled. He raged. His aggression mounted. He kicked out for
the bank again. They could at least only take him one at a
time now. And he wasn't intending to go down easily.
Whichever man had run down to confront him there on the
quay was going to take his life at some cost. He didn't want
his body to be pulled, leaking water and bodily fluids, from
the Seine miles downstream. To fight and die up there in the
open air had, in a few short minutes, become his only goal.

A dead rat floated by, brushing his face. Retching with
horror, Joe trod water, waiting for it to pass, but then, on an
impulse, he reached out and seized it and squashed the
swollen body down inside the front of his shirt. A gassy
eructation burst from the rat and Joe gagged and spluttered.
Then he gritted his chattering teeth. "Brother Rat!" he muttered, knowing he was on the verge of hysteria. "More where
that came from? Let's hope so!" He was as prepared as he
could ever be for the confrontation. He just hoped that his
enemy would feel impelled, as most villains did, to explain
himself. To talk. To give Joe time to get his breath back and
plan his retaliation.

If he encountered the Zouave he could rely on no such reaction. His only language was Death and he would deliver it
in one unanswerable word.

Taking his time, steadying his breathing, he judged the
moment and made for the part of the quay where a set of
slippery steps had been made for the use of the river traffic.
Panting, he pulled himself together, taking the useless
scalpel in his right hand.

"Thought you'd make for this place. How are you
enjoying the show, so far, Commander?" The remembered
voice purred down at him from the top of the steps.

There was the Fantômas pose again. Eyes glittered through the holes in the mask.

Joe responded in short panting phrases, one for each step as he climbed. "Not the best evening I've spent in the theatre. Never been fond of melodrama. Overacting sets my teeth on edge. Kinder not to look, really. I've decided to bail out at the interval."

He'd got almost to the top. Near enough. This would do. Affecting a gulping cough, he put his left hand to his chest and seized the rat, grasping its slimy fur in his fingers. "I was wondering, Moulin…" he began, and a moment later had hurled the squashy and stinking corpse into the masked face. The man took an instinctive step back, with an exclamation of disgust, hitting out at the creature with his left hand. In an instant Joe had closed with him, pushing him off balance, a frozen but iron-hard left fist closing over the knife hand and squeezing with the fury of a madman. The zarin clanged onto the cobbles and the man looked down and sideways to find it.

A moment of inattention which cost him the sight of his left eye. Joe brought up the blunt scalpel and drove the point through the nearest hole in the mask.

A yell and a curse broke from him but he struggled on, strong right hand breaking free from Joe's slippery clutch. He scrambled to pick up his knife. With the scalpel still sticking out of his eye socket, he rounded on Joe, screaming, beside himself with fury, knife once again clutched in his hand. With both his feeble defences used up, Joe crouched and circled, only his fists left and his cunning. He was intending to work his way around his enemy, wrong-foot him and push him into the river.

Just as he was beginning to think he stood a chance, another shot rang out. The nightmare figure was hurled backwards away from Joe by the force of the bullet tearing into

his chest. A dark stain was already spreading over the white waistcoat before he collapsed onto the cobbles inches from the drop into the river.

Joe, shaking with cold and effort and shock, could only turn his head and mumble, "Bonnefoye? Jean-Philippe, is that you?" into the darkness.

"Er, no. It's me, my boy," said Sir George, emerging from the shadows, Luger in hand. "Thought you were up to something, sending me off like that. Nosy old bugger, as I keep reminding you. Not so easy to shake off. Had to investigate. Taxi's on the bridge, engine running. Thought we might need to make a swift exit. Who's your friend?"

He moved over to the body, pistol at the ready, Joe noticed.

"Who *was* your friend? He's dead. Police not very popular in these parts, I see. I had to take strong action to disable the other bloke on the bridge who seemed to be taking too close an interest. Vévé, I'm assuming. He's dead too, I'm afraid. But, Joe, who was this fool?"

George bent and tugged the mask off the dead face, carefully pulling it away from the scalpel which still projected.

"No fool! Madman perhaps? Moulin. The doctor. The pathologist."

"Pathologist? Is he so short of customers he has to . . . oh, sorry, Joe. It just seems very peculiar to me. So, he's the one who fancied himself as Set, is he? But why on earth is he got up like this? Was he on his way to a masked ball?"

"He didn't have time to explain. I'm just guessing this was his last commission. Someone paid to watch me die, George. But where on earth has Jean-Philippe got to? He was down in the square, whistling . . . Oh, my God! There were three of them!"

Chapter 29

Joe doubled over and vomited up a litre of river water before he was ready to run on unsteady legs back along the bank, up onto the bridge and then down again to the level of the small park, calling out Jean-Philippe's name. In his exhaustion, he found that George was well able to keep stride with him. They paused by the statue of Henry IV. The dashing young monarch, Le Vert Galant, the Green Sprig himself, peered majestically down from his horse at the panting old man and the drowned rat as they battled to get their breath and take their bearings.

"There was a third man on the loose. One of the wolves. Got away during the raid. I heard Jean-Philippe whistling down here on this side. We'll split up and search."

"No, we won't," said George firmly. "You stay by me. I'm not losing sight of you again. No telling what you'll get up to. Fancy dress balls ... midnight swimming parties ... some fellows live for pleasure alone," he muttered, checking his pistol. "Six left. Should do it. And in the dark I don't want to

put one of them into you by mistake. Eyes not what they were, you know."

Back to back, they quartered the ground, working their way out towards the pointed tip of the park.

They found them under a willow tree.

Bonnefoye had had no time to draw his revolver, his hands were empty, thrown out one on either side of his body. The handle of a zarin gleamed in the half-light, sticking out of his back.

George groaned. "Ambushed. Taken from behind." He expressed his grief and rage, cursing in a torrent of Pushtu.

Joe was on his knees, feeling for any sign of life. "George, do shut up! He's trying to speak! He's alive...just. It's all right, old man. We're here. Look, try to stay still. You've been stabbed...I expect you noticed...yes. What we'll do, if you can bear it, is leave the blade where it is—it's actually stopping the blood from flowing. We'll summon up a stretcher party and get you up to the hospital...it's only a step or two away."

He bent his ear to the chill mouth which was barely able to move, yet determined to convey something. "What's that? Oh, yes, you got him. Or *someone* got him...The wolf. He's lying here right beside you." Joe glanced down. "Shot through the back of the head. Small calibre bullet, I'd say. .22? But well placed. Not you, I take it? No? Ah, there's a puzzle...Sorry, what did you say?...Yes. I'll send George in a taxi to tell her. I'll stay by you...What day? It's Monday, old fruit...We've just had what we call in England a long weekend."

He was grateful for the soldierly presence of Sir George, still covering the pathways with his Luger. Gently, Joe removed Bonnefoye's police revolver from its holster and held it at the ready. But he knew the flourish was in vain. The wolf's killer had made off into the night and was a mile away by now.

* * *

The next three days gurgled their way down life's plughole, barely distinguishable from each other by Joe. A day of sickness and shivering, spent in Bonnefoye's room in the rue Mouffetard, being Amélie's replacement son while her own boy was in hospital, passed like a bad dream. He remembered the bowls of chicken soup, the cool hands on his forehead, George's gruff voice from the doorway: "Just back from the hospital. Thought you'd like to hear—the lad's going to be all right. Blade went in at an angle—the thought is that the attacker was disturbed before he could place his blow more accurately. No vital organs damaged but he lost a lot of blood. He's on his feet already and clamouring to come home."

The day after, which must have been a Wednesday, he spent in Fourier's office making statements, colluding in the fabrication of various pieces of subterfuge. Nodding in agreement as the commissaire outlined the dashing attack of the Brigade Criminelle officer (trained and directed by Fourier himself) who had gone in against great odds to the rescue (from an attack by a gang of apaches) of two theatregoers, one a visiting tourist, his companion a Parisian and a distinguished doctor. Sadly, the latter had succumbed to a bullet fired by one of the gang, the former was lucky to survive being hurled into the river by his assailants.

This lively scene was, as they spoke, being worked up by an artist into a cover for *Le Petit Journal*. Under Fourier's direction, of course, he reassured them. These creatures were attacking in the very heart of the city now! But thanks to the bravery of the aforementioned police officer, two had been shot dead and would trouble the peace of the city island no more. Patrols on the Square du Vert Galant had been doubled.

"Seems to be paying off, Fourier," said Joe. "Though I'd have preferred on the whole not to be summoned down to the river on a wild-goose chase on Monday night."

"Ah, yes. Clever devils! Some bugger diverted the two *agents* on duty down there. And rang directly through to my office, someone knowing my number, leaving a message so official-sounding my sergeant passed it straight on. Moulin. He knows ... knew the numbers, knew the tones that get attention. Probably expected to catch you while you were still up here sitting in front of me."

He frowned and fiddled with his pen. "I can make this sound convincing enough, Sandilands, for general consumption, I mean, on paper. But I can't make any sense of it"—he gestured to his head—"up here. What in hell did the stupid bugger think he was doing? Clever man. Reliable. Thorough. My best."

"Well placed to cover up a whole crime wave of his own creation?" Joe suggested. "You'll never know now."

"And who's going to take his place? Good Lord! He's down there on the slab as we speak! I haven't been to see him yet ... I don't suppose ... ? No?"

"Who's going to perform the pathology on the pathologist?"

Fourier burst out laughing. "*Quis medicabitur ipsum medicum?*" he said, surprisingly. He rose to his feet to show Joe to the door.

"And I'll add a second thought on similar lines," said Joe cheerfully. "Who will police the policeman? I'll tell you—I will!"

In a moment his foot had come out to trip up the commissaire and his hand simultaneously pushed him hard between the shoulder blades. Fourier's head banged against the corner of his desk as he went down and he swore in pain and confusion.

"Bad luck!" said Joe. "You really ought to have that rug tacked down, Fourier. There was a loose end there somewhere, I think."

"Poor old thing! You look jolly peaky still," said Heather Watkins, pouring out a cup of tea for Joe at Fauchon's. "But I can't understand why that woman would *do* such a thing...I mean...Well, I can just about see why she would undertake...um...the profession she undertook..." Heather blushed and hunted about for the milk jug. "But how could she have let herself be led into a life of crime by that appalling villain?"

"I think what she gave me and Bonnefoye was a true bill. Ninety per cent of it. The client who insinuated himself into her establishment probably had some strong hold over her...blackmail...contrived involvement in one of his early excursions...I think he took over her life like a cancer, eating it away. He was using her girls as agents in his schemes. Alice was left only nominally in charge and beginning to realise she was herself replaceable. Good liars tell the truth as far as they possibly can and slip in one big falsehood. She told us truthfully what happened—just gave us the wrong name. Picked an entirely innocent Englishman, knowing he would be able to talk his way out of it—and anyway, Jack Pollock was safe enough behind the walls of the Embassy. The worst thing that could have happened to him in the event of an enquiry was a rap on the knuckles from Her Excellency! And a suspension from opera escort duties. But I believe Alice was truly alarmed by the sadistic nature of the man she found herself tied to. By his complete ruthlessness. It defies explanation, Heather! A professional man, clever, sharp, kind to me when in role. And the other side of him, dark, greedy and murderous."

"But why? I know men murder others for the satisfaction, even enjoyment, it can bring them." She shuddered. "But his victims were not known to him in a personal way. Where was the satisfaction in that?"

"I think he was a bit mad. Working in that place—it would send any man off the rails. And I believe he sensed this was happening to him. He made an effort to keep the stone walls, dripping with sorrow, at bay. It didn't work. The corpses kept piling up and he kept on slicing and carving and witnessing the very worst man can do to man."

"He lost his sensitivity? Like a knife losing its edge?"

"I think so. He had been a sensitive man. He enjoyed the theatre and the opera—he had posters and programmes all over his room and, Heather, the strangest thing—I'd noticed a photograph on his desk. A pretty dark girl. Her face was vaguely familiar. I checked his room yesterday—I went to return a book he lent me . . ." Joe's turn to shudder. "I thought it might be his girlfriend. I asked the assistants if they knew who she was. They looked a bit shifty, I thought, but one of them spoke up. 'Don't you know her, sir? That's Gaby Laforêt. The music hall star. Nuts about her, he was! Went to every show. Used to joke that one day when he'd made his fortune he'd . . . Well, we all need our fantasies, working in a dump like this, don't we?'"

"But why would he want *you* dead, Joe? How did *you* figure in his fantasies?"

"He overrated my insight, I think. Thought I was nearer to putting it all together than I actually was. After all—I'd confided in him, shown him my cards, in fact. One professional to another. And if you see your opponent is holding a Royal Flush, you assume he's going to play it. He never suspected that I hadn't recognised the significance of what I had. So—I had to be eliminated. And—possibly as his grand finale—he couldn't resist stepping onstage himself for a

change. I think no one paid him for that display on the bridge. He treated himself to a private performance. He fancied himself as Louis XIV perhaps, that ardent supporter of the theatre, the Sun King, strolling on in the final scene."

"Horrid notion! All the same, it's doubly depressing to think that a man got his thrills by carrying out another fellow's fantasies! I expect the money was the more important element, you know. But, there, you survived! And so did Jean-Philippe. That's all that matters. Is he back at work again?"

"Oh, no. He's been given a week's leave. But he's back at home, firing on all cylinders, driving his mother to distraction. Claims he's fully fit and she must stop fussing over him. She's given up on him and decided to go and spend a few days with her sister in Burgundy. George went back to the Bristol to put up his feet for a bit, get his heart rate down and then start on his packing."

"Poor soul! Has he had enough of France, then?"

"Not a bit of it! He's bought a first class ticket on Friday's Blue Train to Nice. The overnight express. Paris seems to have lost its charm but he's not quite in the mood for Surrey yet. I think his cousin has cause for concern there! George is showing every sign of going off the rails as soon as he can get up the right speed. He's booked himself in at the Negresco! Best food in the world, he tells me. And I'm dug in again at the Ambassador for the next day or two. Lively scene! I say, Heather, they've got a dinner dance and jazz band on tonight if you'd be interested?"

"Oh, Joe, I have to leave on Friday—that's tomorrow!—for the Riviera myself. First game of the tournament on Sunday morning. Must be fresh for that. So, if you can guarantee you won't step too heavily on my feet and break a toe or try to get me drunk—yes, I'd love to! And then you can wave me goodbye on Friday—I'm on the same train as Sir George. Joe,

why don't you try to get a few days off and come down and watch me play? You look as though you could do with a bit of southern sun..."

The Gare de Lyon was bustling with smartly dressed travellers, porters hurrying along behind carts piled high with luggage. Trains whistled and panted and whooped. Joe and Bonnefoye struggled with Heather Watkins' hand luggage and packages, hunting for her compartment. Finally settled, she leaned out of the window to talk to them.

"Well, here we are... Oh, good grief! Joe! Jean-Philippe! Do you see who that is—down there, thirty yards off, just getting in. Crikey! Shall we pretend we haven't seen them?"

Joe looked along the train, puzzled. "George! It's George! I said goodbye to him this afternoon at the hotel... I don't need to show my grinning face again."

"The last thing he'd want to see at this moment, I think," said Heather mysteriously. "Look! He's with a woman."

Bonnefoye saw her at the same moment. With one hand she picked up the hem of her dark blue evening cape and with the other grasped the hand of Sir George standing gallantly at her side. Laughing, she stepped nimbly up into the train, turned and pulled him up after her into her arms.

"They've gone into a sleeping compartment," said Bonnefoye, astonished.

"That's what people do on the Blue Train," said Heather, giggling. "What fun! How smart! She's very pretty! And—I have to say—what a lucky lady!"

"That was no lady—that was my mother!" spluttered Bonnefoye. "What the hell! Visiting my aunt Marie, indeed. And she has the nerve to go off wearing my birthday present."

"Glad to see it got there on time," said Joe, smiling.

"It was *you*, wasn't it?" Bonnefoye rounded on Joe. "Duplicitous fiend! It arrived with a card—*Amélie, with eternal gratitude from an English Gentleman*. She thought it was from George!"

"If he'd been aware, I'm sure it *would* have been," said Joe. "I didn't quite like to disillusion her. Delphine in the rue de la Paix was very understanding when I nipped in with my cheque book and a disarmingly salacious story. Let's hope they're as understanding at Scotland Yard when I present them with my expenses! So that's what you earn in a month, Jean-Philippe? You're really doing rather well, aren't you?"

About the Author

BARBARA CLEVERLY is the author of ten novels of historical suspense, including *The Damascened Blade*, winner of the CWA Ellis Peters Historical Dagger Award, *The Last Kashmiri Rose, Ragtime in Simla, The Palace Tiger, The Bee's Kiss, Tug of War, An Old Magic, The Tomb of Zeus,* and *Bright Hair About the Bone*. She lives in Cambridge, England, where she is at work on the next Laetitia Talbot novel, *A Darker God*.